Psychoanalytic Perspectives on Puberty and Adolescence

Puberty is a time of tumultuous transition from childhood to adulthood activated by rapid physical changes, hormonal development and explosive activity of neurons. This book explores puberty through the parent-teenager relationship, as a "normal state of crisis", lasting several years and with the teenager oscillating between childlike tendencies and their desire to become an adult.

The more parents succeed in recognizing and experiencing these new challenges as an integral, ineluctable emotional transformative process, the more they can allow their children to become independent. In addition, parents who can also see this crisis as a chance for their own further development will be ultimately enriched by this painful process. They can face up to their own aging as they take leave of youth with its myriad possibilities, accepting and working through a newfound rivalry with their sexually mature children, thus experiencing a process of maturity, which in turn can set an example for their children.

This book is based on rich clinical observations from international settings, unique within the field, and there is an emphasis placed by the author on the role of the body in self-awareness, identity crises and gender construction. It will be of great interest to psychoanalysts, psychotherapists, parents and carers, as well as all those interacting with adolescents in self, family and society.

Gertraud Diem-Wille is Professor Emeritus at the University of Klagenfurt in the field of Psychoanalytic Education. She is a training analyst for children, adolescents and adults (IPA) and has pioneered and supported the training in psychoanalytic observational approaches to training in psychoanalytic and educational fields in Austria. She is the author of *The Early Years of Life* (Karnac 2011), *Young Children and Their Parents* (Karnac 2014) and *Latency: The Golden Age of Childhood* (Routledge 2014).

Psychoanalytic Perspectives on Puberty and Adolescence

The Inner Worlds of Teenagers and their Parents

Gertraud Diem-Wille

Originally published as Pubertat – Die innere Welt der Adoleszenten und ihrer Eltern. Psychoanalytische Entwicklungstheorie nach Freud, Klein und Bion by W. Kohlhammer GmbH

Translated by Benjamin Mcquade

First published as Pubertat – Die innere Welt der Adoleszenten und ihrer Eltern: Psychoanalytische Entwicklungstheorie nach Freud, Klein und Bion © 2017 W. Kohlhammer GmbH, Stuttgart.

Published 2021 by Routledge
2 Park Square, Milton Park, Abingdon, Oxon OX14 4RN

and by Routledge
52 Vanderbilt Avenue, New York, NY 10017

Routledge is an imprint of the Taylor & Francis Group, an informa business

© 2021 Gertraud Diem-Wille

Translated from German by Benjamin Mcquade.

Published with the support of Austrian Science Fund (FWF): PUB-721-Z

The right of Gertraud Diem-Wille to be identified as author of this work has been asserted by her in accordance with sections 77 and 78 of the Copyright, Designs and Patents Act 1988.

All rights reserved. No part of this book may be reprinted or reproduced or utilised in any form or by any electronic, mechanical, or other means, now known or hereafter invented, including photocopying and recording, or in any information storage or retrieval system, without permission in writing from the publishers.

Trademark notice: Product or corporate names may be trademarks or registered trademarks, and are used only for identification and explanation without intent to infringe.

British Library Cataloguing-in-Publication Data
A catalogue record for this book is available from the British Library

Library of Congress Cataloging-in-Publication Data
A catalog record for this book has been requested

ISBN: 978-0-367-36852-4 (hbk)
ISBN: 978-0-367-36850-0 (pbk)
ISBN: 978-1-003-14267-6 (ebk)

Typeset in Times New Roman
by Apex CoVantage, LLC

Contents

List of figures		vi
Acknowledgments		vii
	Introduction	1
1	The body ego	4
2	Psychosexual development in puberty	20
3	Development of feeling	85
4	Development of thinking	118
5	The search for the self – identity	129
6	Lost by the wayside – overstepping limits	145
	Epilogue	259
	Bibliography	265
	Index	273

Figures

1.1	Estrogen-progesterone waves (from Brizendine 2006)	7
1.2	Testosterone levels throughout male life (from Brizendine 2010)	14
1.3	John with his friend (16 years old)	18
2.1	Original text: beginning of the story Elfi wrote with her analyst	63
2.2	James' drawing: NIGGS (NICHTS)	73
6.1	Age and criminality of men from a) 1842 and b) 1977 (from Gottfredson and Hirschi, 1990)	151
6.2	Lifeline as drawn by B. (from Staudner-Moser 1997)	153
6.3	Violent scene by B. (from Staudner-Moser 1997)	156
6.4	Lifeline of R. (from Staudner-Moser 1997)	160
6.5	The broken heart of R. (from Staudner-Moser 1997)	167
6.6	Worldwide suicides in relation to age and income (from WHO 2014)	247

Acknowledgments

My thanks is due to all who have supported and encouraged me through the realization of this project. My understanding of the inner world of adolescents has been influenced by my analyst mentors and teachers, above all Betty Joseph, Robin Anderson and Michael Feldman. Their suggestions and comments enriched my understanding. Practices of psychoanalytic observation and attention were revealed to me through the fascinating methods of Isca Salzberger-Wittenberg and Anne Alvarez. I also learned much from conversations with the parents of the children entrusted to me in my analytic work. Children and adolescents have fascinated me with their creativity, bringing their inner conflicts in such vital and unique form to analysis and establishing intense emotional relationships to me as their analyst; this has in turn enriched my analytic work.

I thank my students Janette Erhard, Eva Pankratz and Andrea Staudner-Moser for so eagerly allowing me to use and quote passages from their Master's and PhD dissertations.

I thank my family for their intensive participation in the origins of the book. My daughters Katharina and Johanna, as well as my grandchildren Samira, Karim and Olivia, allowed me to experience their adolescent developmental phase with them; here, a grandmother's perspective affords more space for reflection than the direct involvement of a mother would.

Without the support and encouragement of my friends, the writing of this book would certainly have lasted far longer. My friend since schooldays, Christiane Siegl, was my first critical and encouraging reader, followed by further comments and enrichments from Erika Trappl and Gerti Wille. I was able to enlist Samira Hadaya as academic assistant, who carefully assembled and proofed the book's academic research, illustrations and annotations.

My editors Celestina Filbrandt and Ulrike Albrecht conceived this idea of extending developmental theory from the early years of life and latency to adolescence – an idea I was glad to take up. For providing the illustrations, I thank Lukas Dostal, Karim Hadaya, Peter Diem and Johanna Hadaya-Diem.

Introduction

Puberty is a time of tumultuous transition from childhood to adulthood. This transformative developmental spurt is activated by rapid physical changes, hormonal development and the explosive activity of neurons. My book will describe both this physical development and the typically adolescent "state of mind" – something that can remain active long after adolescence is over. When the child attains independence, this developmental step demands a difficult balancing act from parents: they must be able to release their child without cutting their ties to him. Thus, accompanying an adolescent through adolescence constitutes a difficult emotional task for parents and teachers, although this development is also a quite "normal drama". This "normal state of crisis" lasts several years, with the teenager oscillating between childlike tendencies and his desire to become an adult. The more parents succeed in recognizing and experiencing these new challenges as an integral, ineluctable emotional transformative process, the more they can allow their children to become independent. In addition, parents will ultimately be enriched when they can also see this often painful crisis as a chance for their own further development: they can face up to their own aging as they take leave of youth with its myriad possibilities, accepting and working through a newfound rivalry with their sexually mature children, thus experiencing a process of maturity, which in turn can set an example for their children. In parents' interaction with children, the quality of a marital relationship is also important. Are they truly a creative, Oedipal, loving couple, capable both of love and of taking opposing positions? Can they support one another and master this turbulent time together?

First, let us clarify the often diffuse concepts of puberty and adolescence. "Puberty" is derived from the Latin word "pubertas", meaning sexual maturity and/or capacity, and refers to the period when the child's body transforms into an adult body capable of reproduction. This process of physical change is initiated by hormonal signals from the brain transmitted to the female ovaries and male testicles. With both genders, secondary sexual characteristics also develop during this period. For girls, puberty begins with the first menstruation between the ages of nine and eleven, and is concluded between the ages of sixteen to seventeen; with boys, puberty begins with the production of fertile sperm between the ages of eleven and twelve, and is concluded between the ages of sixteen and seventeen.

2 Introduction

"Adolescence" is derived from the Latin word "adolescens", which means growing up or towards; "adolescent" denotes the individual who is growing, i.e., the adolescent female or male. It encompasses the mental and emotional reactions to physical signs of puberty, including a particular transitory outlook from the world of the child to that of the sexually mature adult. The biological capacity to conceive and give birth to a baby poses completely different questions than does the emotional readiness to embark on an intimate, responsible relationship to a partner. It is difficult to draw a clear and general distinction between puberty and adolescence. Waddell writes:

> For in essential ways they (puberty and adolescence, GDW) are inextricable – the nature of adolescence and its course are organized around responses to the upheaval of puberty. Adolescence can be described, in narrow terms, as a complex adjustment on the child's part to these major physical and emotional changes. This adjustment entails finding a new, and often hard-won, sense of oneself-in-the-world, in the wake of the disturbing latency attitudes and ways of functioning.

> (Waddell 2002, 140)

Thus, puberty is a more limited concept than adolescence and refers to physical changes and maturing. The time range of adolescence has been defined variously. In the USA, adolescence is equated with the "teenager years", from 13 through 19. In Europe, its time range is seen differently, from 16 to 24 years, with a distinction drawn between early, middle and late adolescence (Zimbardo and Gerrig 2004, 449). The World Health Organisation (WHO) defines adolescence as the period between ages ten and twenty. Cultural and societal conditions are also of major significance here, both for the onset of physical changes and for the mental and emotional tasks of finding a place in the world.

Only at the beginning of the 20th century did the term "adolescence" begin to be employed in academic or scientific discourse. G. Stanley Hall (1904) founded the sub-branch of psychological research into childhood and adolescence. He wrote:

> At no time of life is the love of excitement so strong as during the season of accelerated development of adolescence, which craves strong feelings and new sensations.

> (Hall 1904, Volume I, 368)

This understanding of the turbulent "storm and stress" (the German *Sturm und Drang*) period became the object of intense discussion, and was questioned by anthropologists such as Margaret Mead, since she could not detect this phase in other cultures (see also Arnett and Hughes 2012, 9–10).

The developmental phase of adolescence long constituted a "neglected area" (A. Freud) in psychoanalysis. Anna Freud dubbed it *Sturm und Drang* in reference to a Romantic epoch of German literature.

Today, the adolescent phase is viewed to be equally as important as the first three years of life, since in both phases essential aspects of the personality are formed, giving rise to a coherent, stable self. The difference among individual adolescents can be enormous: whereas in earlier phases development centers on more general tendencies, in adolescence individual characteristics come into relief, widening the divergence from one adolescent to another.

We will seek first to describe the emotional cathexis (emotional investment) of the body as body ego, then the development of feeling, psychosexuality and thinking. These various aspects cannot be separated from one another, but consideration of them all should sharpen our view of each, even though they are interwoven as in a musical score: only together can they yield a sonic experience, as it were – the understanding of this phase of life.

1

The body ego

There is no period – aside from the time in the womb – when the body alters as much as in puberty. Bodily changes are subject neither to a person's will nor their control, erupting and eliciting fiery emotions in the adolescent. Later, massive physical changes occur during pregnancy and aging, significantly affecting our emotional state, sense of identity and fears. Freud emphasizes that we cannot directly rule our bodies and that a person cannot experience objective biological gender identity; instead, we "libidinally cathect" our bodies from some inner source, consciously and unconsciously, linking a given drive energy to our body or some part of it. This in turn determines whether a person views his body as native or alien to him or as a mere mechanism – and whether he loves or hates his body in whole or in part. Each spurt of growth or change through growth or illness alters this emotional attitude toward the body. For instance, if a tooth or toe causes pain, a special contingent of attention and devotion is mobilized: the person then thinks only of this tooth or toe – for a given time, it constitutes the center of their emotional life.

During the relatively stable phase of latency, focus is on increasing body skills and mobility, with physical skills, sports and movement in competition with peers constituting important and pleasurable outlets. Now, without prior warning and without the child's participation, the body they have grown so familiar with undergoes a fundamental change, with no definite end in sight. This physical growth often already occurs at the end of latency, with the attendant emotional impact only following one or two years later: for instance, girls today often experience their first menstruation at the age of ten, without any mental and psychic readiness for motherhood. The great psychic task of adolescence consists of the adolescent finding his own place in the world and accomplishing the transition from his family to the greater world of adults. We will first describe the physiological changes of puberty, and then the adolescent's emotional and mental answer to them.

How massive these changes are – changes to be mastered within a short period of time – is indicated by the difference in physical appearance between 12 and 20 years of age. Some people change so drastically that they are virtually unrecognizable: out of a little girl emerges a sexually attractive young woman, or out of a little boy a tall, powerful man. Within a few years, adolescents must brace themselves for a change not only in size but also in strength. The body's new form, an adolescent's changed voice, newly developed primary and secondary sexual organs: all elicit a new sense of body, with the most essential difference consisting in the biological capacity for becoming a mother or father. As Anderson writes: "What we see clinically in adolescence is the way the body that the adolescent relates to is a container for a whole history of sexual and other primitive object relationships both dyadic and triadic" (Anderson 2009, 1). The adolescent's massive bodily growth is accompanied by an alteration in emotional balance, influencing the deepest layers of the personality. Many adolescents arriving in therapy exhibit somatic symptoms such as anorexia, drug abuse and self-harm (slashing, for example) – all indicating deep subconscious fears. Anderson feels that these often bizarre symptoms – that could otherwise point to borderline or psychotic phenomena – should instead be seen as an exaggerated form of normal alteration in the personality. Adolescents now perceive the necessity of defining themselves anew – not only as their parents' son or daughter, but taking their own place in the world, becoming a potential husband or wife and acquiring the capacity for intimacy and sexuality in a close relationship.

These tasks must be accomplished during a time when the deepest wishes and passions from early childhood are revived. Adolescents must embark on a love relationship to someone of their own age and renounce earlier desires for their parent of the opposite sex. The adolescent must reorder his inner life. Contradictory wishes exists parallel to one another.

The wish to be loved, cared for and nourished – and to possess the source of these qualities – is accompanied by the wish to become independent and attain a better, more interesting place in the world. We will examine the adolescent's emotional and mental development in later chapters. First, we turn in more detail to physical alterations – not forgetting that both the secretion of hormones and attendant physical changes will awaken and intensify emotional and mental conflicts.

In his *Three Essays on the Theory of Sexuality* (1905), Freud writes of the changes puberty brings:

> With the arrival of puberty, changes set in which are destined to give infantile sexual life its final, normal shape. The sexual instinct has hitherto been predominantly auto-erotic; it now finds a sexual object. Its activity has hitherto been derived from a number of separate instincts and erotogenic zones, which, independently of one another, have pursued a certain sort of pleasure as their sole sexual aim. Now, however, a new sexual aim appears, and all the component instincts combine to attain it, while the erotogenic zones become subordinated to the primacy of the genital zone.
>
> (Freud 1905, 206)

Particularly characteristic for this developmental phase is the setting of new priorities, where erogenous zones such as the mouth, skin and anal area – as well as pleasurable observing and gazing – are all subordinated to the goal of sexual

6 The body ego

unification. However, Freud repeatedly emphasizes that this "partial instinct" (observation, exhibitionism, oral gratification, etc.) also plays an important role in foreplay and in enhancing the sexual act.

1.1 The body as an object of observation

Changes in the female body

One peculiarly adolescent phenomenon can be seen when a girl gazes at great length into the mirror, something that can go on for several hours a day, to parents' astonishment. To the parents' great surprise (and often enough, to their irritation), adolescent girls begin to spend considerable time in front of the mirror, examining their changing bodies from all angles, trying on various clothes and posing in front of the mirror – apparently a more satisfying observer than the human eye – as if it were a camera. This mirror-gazing is often subsumed or concealed under the ostensible motives of skin and hair care, blow-drying, etc. Pimples and other blemishes are examined precisely, removed or examined yet again when they become inflamed. Groups of girls go to flea markets, buying clothes for reworking, hats and unusual accessories, which they often turn into surprisingly attractive features. They apply makeup alone or in pairs. They photograph themselves or each other in various poses and facial expressions, then posting the pictures online.

What motivations can be detected in these behaviors? The frequent complaint heard from parents, particularly fathers, is that their daughter has become vain, never tiring of her appearance. But from the psychoanalytic perspective, this accusation is too shortsighted. As discussed earlier, an adolescent's physical growth, both desired or undesired, is always accompanied by considerable feelings of insecurity. The latency child's unquestioning, carefree relationship to his well-functioning body is now disrupted. A new relationship, a new sense of the body, must now be discovered. But why do girls then observe themselves so long in the mirror?

The neuropsychiatrist Louann Brizendine traces this behavior to hormonal changes in the female brain, describing the process as follows:

> The teen girl's brain is sprouting, reorganizing and pruning neuronal circuits that drive the way she thinks, feels and acts – and obsesses over her looks. Her brain is unfolding ancient instructions on how to be a woman . . . the high-octane estrogen coursing through their brain pathways fuels their obsessions. . . . They are almost exclusively interested in their appearance . . . they spend hours in front of the mirror, inspecting pores, plucking eyebrows, wishing the butts they see would shrink, their breasts grow larger and waists get smaller, all to attract boys.
>
> (Brizendine 2006, 31ff)

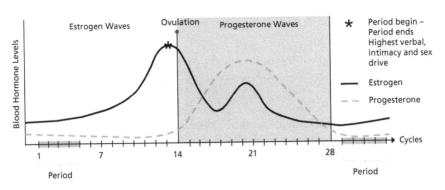

Figure 1.1 Estrogen-progesterone waves (from Brizendine 2006)

Brizendine holds chemical changes – effects of the estrogen level in the female body – responsible for this behavior (Figure 1.1).

The psychoanalytic perspective focuses on an adolescent's inner world and asks which early experiences become revived in adolescent behavior. Gazing happily into a mirror is hardly innate – it constitutes a result of learning from experience. Only when a baby or young child has had the experience of being lovingly observed by its father or mother can it internalize a positive self-image. The child experiences: "I am worth loving; I can make my mother's eyes shine". Indeed, the baby is metaphorically mirrored in its mother's eyes, which function something like a lovingly focused mirror in which the baby views itself. Winnicott asks:

> What does the baby see when he or she looks at the mother's face? I am suggesting that, ordinarily, what the baby sees is himself or herself. In other words the mother is looking at the baby and *what she looks like is related to what she sees there.*
>
> (Winnicott 1967, 110)

A mother's eyes express her feelings towards her baby: if she loves her child, she looks at it lovingly, but if she is full of agitation or depression, her gaze is stiff and seems to pass through her child. The child's gaze then cannot establish contact to its mother, just as the child cannot feel contained or accepted. André Green (1993) described how a baby might experience its depressed mother, with her empty, expressionless gaze, now devoid of her pre-depression vitality; as Green puts it, the child experiences his mother as "dead" – physically present, but looking exclusively inward, without a mother's loving gaze at her infant. Green's concept of the "dead mother" describes the baby's experience of its mother in depression, as opposed to her normal self. Inside this child, a "spiritual hole" arises where there was hitherto space for the love object (mother). The gaze and attempted contact are no longer possible; the child is left to its own devices and must hold

8 The body ego

itself emotionally, which it attempts to do through a pseudo-independence and premature maturity.

> I can make my point by going straight over to the case of the baby whose mother reflects her own mood or, worse still, the rigidity of her own defenses.
> (Winnicott 1967, 112)

Such early experiences form the roots of a child's personality. Psychoanalysts presume that the emotional reaction a baby evokes from its mother supplies it with a sense of its own "reality" – the sense that it is indeed alive. The baby internalizes this experience, which in turn serves as a basis for the fundamental feeling of self-worth. Only when we have experienced the feeling of being loved and observed, admired, can we love ourselves. Winnicott continues:

> To return to the normal progress of events, when the average girl studies her face in the mirror she is reassuring herself that the mother image is there and that the mother can see her and that the mother is *en rapport* with her.
> (Italics in original; ibid, p. 112)

Winnicott believes that girls see not only themselves but (unconsciously) also the image of their mother here. We must remember that no mother or father always looks upon their baby with love. Winnicott speaks of a "good enough mother", who encounters her baby mainly with love, while sometimes reacting in annoyance, irritation or tension. The adolescent girl now graduates (so to speak) from her mother's gaze – which is effectively replaced by her own gaze into the mirror, as well as observation by her peer group. Particularly for an adolescent, it is of vital importance to be considered attractive by friends, and to be viewed – gazed upon – affectionately and with interest.

It is a fact that some autistic children cannot look at themselves in the mirror, since – for diverse reasons – they could not embark on a relationship to their mother, instead withdrawing into their private world. Schizophrenics also avoid looking into the mirror, and indeed are more likely to shatter a mirror than to gaze into it.

In a footnote to his paper "Formulations Regarding the Two Principles in Mental Functioning" (1911), Freud pointed out the function of maternal nurturing in the infant's emotional development.

> It probably hallucinates the fulfillment of its internal needs; it betrays its unpleasure, when there is an increase in stimulus and an absence of satisfaction, by the motor discharge of screaming and beating about with its arms and legs, and it then experiences the satisfaction it has hallucinated. Later, as an older child, it learns to employ these manifestations of discharge intentionally as methods of expressing its feelings. Since the later care of children is modelled on the care of infants, the dominance of the pleasure principle can

really come to an end only when a child has achieved complete psychical detachment from its parents.

(Freud 1911, 219)

We can only speculate how many memories of her parents' loving, happy, solicitous (or also annoyed, baleful) gazes are evoked when the adolescent girl gazes into the mirror.

Another motive for adolescent mirror-gazing is the two-fold revival of Oedipal desires: the adolescent compares her body to her mother's both in a spirit of rivalry and as a model for comparison and emulation (libidinous identification – the admired person to be emulated). Lari, a 13-year-old girl, writes in her diary:

> Daniel said that I have the best figure of any of the girls at the ski course! I like that, but I haven't become conceited because of what he said. . . . I went home: at home I tried on Mom's gold evening dress, it fit me well. I'm beginning to get a womanly shape. And now I'm sitting here writing my diary.
>
> (Erhard 1998, 54, translation McQuade)

A child's fantasy of wearing the Queen/mother's golden dress can only become reality with an adult body, even when she poses secretly before the mirror. The impression from Lari's diary is that she has internalized a loving image of her mother – an admiring mother who is glad her daughter is growing up and becoming a woman. Lari seems very happy at her friend's compliment that she has the best figure, accordingly viewing herself as the victor in an imaginary contest. And yet two days later, we read in her diary how unsatisfied she is with her body.

These extreme mood fluctuations – similar to early childhood – are one characteristic of puberty we will examine more closely in Chapter 3 ("Development of Feeling"). Lari writes:

> Oh God, I'm so fat again (51 kg), and so ugly. My nose is getting bigger and bigger and my behind too, my eyes are getting smaller and smaller and wrinkly and I just look ugly as a whole.
>
> (Erhard 1998, 54)

During this period, bodily changes can constitute a threat. Body proportions alter drastically – to Lari, it almost seems her body is no longer her own. Although she wishes for it to stay the same, she is nevertheless glad when Daniel declares she has the best figure, of course including her posterior curves.

The body stands at the center of attention – both the adolescent's own body and other adolescents' bodies. Girls often sit together and rate individual body parts, discussing and evaluating their legs, shins, waists, hands, noses, mouths, eyes, eyelash length, etc. Girls derive satisfaction from this communal rating; typically, one girl will profess what she dislikes in her own body and the others vehemently disagree, attempting to convince her otherwise. The exhibition and

10   The body ego

observation – plus evaluation – of individual body parts can occupy considerable psychic space. Lari writes in her diary:

> I'm writing a list of whom I like the best right now (I feel like doing that right now);
>
> | I | Eva J. | 1. LARI P. (ha, ha) |
> |---|---|---|
> | II | Caro M. | |
> | III | Babsi R. | |
> | IV | Sabine M. | |
>
> (Erhard 1998, 59. Note: Lari's original grammar and layout are here reproduced.)

She only enters her own name later, penciling in "(ha, ha)". She is able to express her narcissistic wish to be the most beautiful ironically, assigning herself an Arabic numeral and the others Roman numerals. She evaluates her friends' appearance and also her own. The particularities of girls' friendships are discussed in more detail in Chapter 3 ("Development of Feeling").

Let us now examine an adolescent girl's self-description as she experiences changes in her body. At the time of this interview, Katharina is almost 15 years old. To the question of how she feels about the changes in her body, including menstruation, she answers as follows:

K: I am glad I don't feel anything with menstruation. Some girls in my class have pain and even have to take medication for it, like my friends. Sometimes it seems stupid that I don't feel it, I don't know when it's coming. I only see that my underwear is red; then it's dirty, not hygienic and smells, too.

I: And otherwise, with the other changes in your body?

K: I only now grew underarm hair, first I grew a bust. My doctor said either the bust is first and then armpit and pubic hair, or the other way around. I liked it that way. I got my period when I was eleven and the others when they were twelve or thirteen. They complained about their underarm hair. My waist has changed, my hips are wider now – that's when you look like a woman. I like that. I look in the mirror – my parents say it's too much. I feel so insecure. Earlier I couldn't have cared less how I look. Now I do my hair much more often and put on makeup. Right now I don't have any makeup on. When I do sports I don't care how I look.

I: Are you satisfied with your body as it is now?

K: On the whole, yes – I'm neither a top model nor am I ugly. I'm not really thin and not really fat – more or less normal. It doesn't look good when you don't have a feminine form. I'd like to be thinner, but food tastes so good. I don't want to be unhappy, what can you do?

I: What do you find NOT beautiful in your body?

K: Basically, I think my feet aren't good-looking.

Discussion

Katharina seems quite satisfied with her body's development; although she is further along than her friends, she sees this as something positive. Her friends seem to be waiting impatiently to become "womanly", and see themselves as children still. Katharina can speak of these matters with unusual freedom and without embarrassment, as natural developments that are basically pleasant for her. We can view an adolescent's situation before the mirror as a triangle. In Katharina's imagination, her mother is standing behind her, observing her approvingly and happy that her daughter is taking the step towards becoming a woman: in fact, Katharina later tells how her mother, when Katharina informed her she had menstruated for the first time, fell weeping into her arms as she welcomed her to the realm of womanhood. She and her mother enjoy buying clothes together and evaluating which clothes fit each of them; they also enjoy putting on jewelry and generally making themselves beautiful.

A mother's dismissive or indifferent reaction to her daughter's first menstruation will have a different impact on the girl. One patient, Ms. P., said:

> I was eleven when I had my first period. I was very excited and ran to my mother, expecting her to be happy with me. But she seemed to find nothing of importance in what I told her, turned around, came back with a sanitary napkin which she handed over to me without a word and then went away. For four years after this, I didn't menstruate, never spoke with my mother about this. When I then did menstruate, I obtained the necessary items for myself.

The fact that Ms. P. did not menstruate for four years indicates the traumatizing effect of this massive dismissal by her mother. It is a psychosomatic reaction to this dismissal, as if she interpreted her mother's behavior to mean that the mother did not wish her to become a woman. Instead of feeling welcomed into the woman's world, as Katharina did, Ms. P. had to find her own way. Her mother's dismissive attitude had an even greater effect since Ms. P.'s father was an exceedingly insecure personality – an alcoholic who became so drunk each Friday that he would destroy the furniture or china. We will speak later of how the adolescent selects a love object; in this case, Ms. P. chose a violent alcoholic and was unable to extricate herself for many years.

The interviewer asks Katharina:

I: And what's the situation with boys?

K: . . . something changed. When I was ten, I could walk down the street, boys came by and I didn't pay them any attention. Now, boys come along and I look at them – first their feet and shoes, and then upwards – the same thing with girls. I like to look at people first, their feet, shoes, whether I like them. Whether he's my type.

I: How exactly do you do this?

12 The body ego

K: When a boy comes my way, I glance at him quickly, then I look again and think about whether I could have something with him, whether I'd like to get to know him.

I: How does he register this?

K: Sometimes they look at me – because I look at them? Maybe so. It's a reflex – it sounds a little like I'm a girlie. I look quickly, only five seconds, and then look away. If I'm together with a girlfriend, we talk about it. It just happens, I can't help it. I'm like an animal looking for a mate. (She laughs.)

I: And how do you know when a boy likes you?

K: When he looks at me, when he stops to look at me, then I think he must like me.

Discussion

Katharina can describe her behavior with a certain self-irony – something that surprises even her. Her behavior is unplanned: it simply happens – as with a female animal hunting for a male. Although the idea of sexual union seems far away, she enjoys putting her attractiveness to the test. Her self-perception is shrewd as she gives boys a swift glance, then immediately looks away. Complex studies of girls' and boys' non-verbal behavior in a disco have come to similar conclusions as Katharina: girls were found to initiate the first eye contact much more often than boys, only to yield the initiative for beginning a conversation to the boy. Katharina's conversations with her girlfriend help to exchange criteria for what is considered attractive.

In this time of inner conflict, the adolescent's presentation of her body can be contradictory for various places and situations. One patient reported that she tended to exhibit her body provocatively at discos or at school, but shamefully hid it at home. Indeed, she described her exhibitionism in a playful, proud way, and her shame in a shameful, small voice, in fragmented phrases.

Now an excerpt from one of my analytic sessions with a 30-year-old patient I will call Fritzi. In the previous session, she had described the great tension and lack of tenderness she experienced as a child and how cruelly her older brother treated her and her younger brother. She began the session with these words:

P: Nothing fits in my body. Nothing is built right, the different parts don't fit together. Especially down there.

A: You're quite vague about this.

P: My boyfriend – I was in love with him this summer – judges every part of my body: this is good, that isn't so good, he says: your back is nice, your (incomprehensible).

A: You want to see whether I am like your boyfriend, you want to make me judge every part of your body and every sentence you say. Or whether I can see that

The body ego   13

basically something's wrong with you. You think, there's no place where you are desirable; you're convinced that there's nobody who will take you and your body as they are.

P: (in a stronger voice): With me, everything went so fast. Within two years I got breasts and hips. Everyone in my family made a comment. I was so ashamed and wanted to cover up my body. I always put a sweater over my waist when I went in the kitchen.

A: You lived together with three men (the father and two brothers) at home.

P: My mother was the one who commented most, and everyone found it so funny. One time it was really bad. I had on a pair of pants with an oil spot. My mother said: the oil is dripping out like crazy. Everyone laughed. I had gained three kilos. (Pause) When I went out with my girlfriends, it was different. We put on funny clothes and set forth: halters, shorts and high boots, you could see everything in between.

A: You liked being under the protection of your girlfriends, when you all showed off your bodies and were admired. There, it was provocative and fun. At home, you hid your body and were ashamed, in order not to provoke your jealous mother.

Discussion

Fritzi first told me in a broken voice, in disjointed sentences, of how shameful she found the changes in her body. Before the changes she had dressed like a boy – wearing her brother's clothes, with a short haircut. Then everything became different. Instead of helping her to accept her new body, her family mocked her and it. Presumably, there was rivalry with her mother, who may have found Fritzi's transformation from a "little tomboy" to an attractive young woman threatening. (The topic of mother-daughter rivalry will be examined more closely in the following chapter on psychosexual development.) Remarkably, Fritzi covers her body in loose, long dresses even at the age of 30. As an adolescent she lacked the confidence to exhibit her new curves, instead tying a sweater around her hips. Yet in her circle of friends, she embarked on campaigns to show off her body, making it an object for admiration; in order that boys could not overlook her body, she at times donned particularly extreme clothes. These two patterns of behavior were not integrated but had a parallel existence. Now, we will turn to the development of the male adolescent's body.

Changes in the male body

Changes in the male body – and the adolescent's reaction to them – manifest themselves in diverse ways. Growth of secondary sexual characteristics is activated by the secretion of the masculine hormone testosterone. The neuropsychiatrist

14 The body ego

Louann Brizendine compares the abruptly initiated change in the boy's brain with a "construction site", writing:

> Between the ages of nine and fifteen, his male brain circuitry, with its billions of neurons and trillions of connections, was "going live" as his testosterone level soared twentyfold. If testosterone were beer, a nine-year-old boy would get the equivalent of about one cup a day. But by age fifteen, it would be equal to two *gallons* a day.
>
> (Brizendine 2010, 53; italics original)

Testosterone causes enlargement of the testicles, activates growth in muscles and bones, stimulates growth in facial and pubic hair, lowers the pitch of a boy's voice and increases the length and thickness of the penis.

The scope of change due to this hormonal activity lasts eight to nine years, according to Brizendine (Figure 1.2). According to Halpern et al. (1998), puberty sees a pronounced change and increase in sexual and aggressive thoughts, with testosterone the driving force behind this heightened tendency toward aggression (see also Archer 2006). Testosterone levels also rise before competitive situations and contests.

For an adolescent boy's sense of his body, these alterations are confusing. In contrast to girls, the sign of sexual maturity – the first ejaculation – is not as (potentially) evident to the world as the first menstruation. According to Kaplan, the awakening and growth of the so-called inner sexual organs – testicles and scrotum, prostate, seminal vesicle and Cowperian gland – tend to remind boys of femininity, passivity and weakness, characteristics they were able to suppress in the years before puberty. Boys in puberty often see their testicles as feminine organs like breasts or ovaries; the German slang word "Eier" (eggs) is an indication of this view. The softness of the first pubic hair threatens to make conscious the unconscious fantasies of being transformed into a woman (Kaplan 1991, 51).

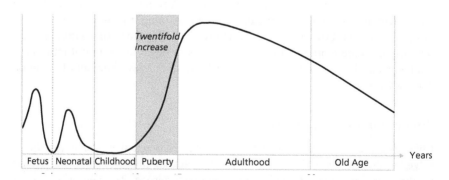

Figure 1.2 Testosterone levels throughout male life (from Brizendine 2010)

The body ego   15

How does the 15-year-old Sebastian describe the changes in his body?

I: When did you notice that your body was changing?
S: I don't know, I didn't notice at all when it began. I never really was aware of it. Earlier I was very short and then I just grew and grew. I felt better then. I'm still not a giant (author's note: Sebastian is 1 meter 75 cm), and I always wanted to be very tall.
I: What did you notice about puberty then?
S: My parents began to get on my nerves. There are things where they really piss me off. No idea. It's still that way. Going out was never a problem. No idea, when we make meals, even if I don't want to, I still have to do it.
I: How did your body change?
S: The way it does when you're in puberty. You get hair where you get it when you're in puberty. No idea. I didn't care. I was always that way – I never got too surprised when something changed, as long as it didn't change too fast.
I: Did your penis get bigger?
S: Yes, the penis does get bigger; well, that's nothing special. Of course I noticed, no idea; I don't compare it. I really couldn't care less. No idea.
I: What else changed?
S: You get more interested in girls, you get self-involved. No idea. The way you are as a person. Sports – no idea. What kind of girl do I like? No idea.
I: Did you have wet dreams?
S: Yeah, sure. No idea.
I: How did you notice?
S: Well, after the dream, like any normal guy. It was just there.
I: Was it pleasant?
S: I didn't care.
I: Did you talk about it with your friends?
S: Yes, but only much later. My body got bigger, more muscles. Sure, it was nice. My voice also got much lower. Dad showed me videos where I had a little squeaky voice. Now, it's much better. When I talk very fast and loud now, my voice still goes way up and squeaks at the very end. It changed very slowly. I noticed it when I sang, no idea, I couldn't sing the scales all the way up anymore.

Discussion

Although Sebastian is glad not to be the shortest in his class anymore, he only mentions his recent growth quite casually. It is remarkable how often he emphasizes the slow pace of his bodily changes. Only in retrospect and when he compares his squeaky voice to his current one can he praise his new, lower one. His often-employed "no idea" – current Austrian slang – is a form of defense, but it also expresses that he truly has no idea yet the uses to which he will put his new body. He plays football in a team and practices twice a week, with games on weekends. He is very talented at football and is often praised, yet does not

16　The body ego

mention this once in his self-description. He is too "cool" to notice that he has grown six centimeters over the past summer.

How has his interest in girls developed, and how does he discuss this with his friends?

I: What's the situation with looking at girls?

S: I look at them completely differently now. First I look at their faces, then how their body is. And then I imagine what they're like as people; I don't care whether it's true. That all goes quickly. Before, I would just look at them, hmm, a girl.

I: Do you talk about it with your friends?

S: Sure, but how? No idea. "I just think she's pretty." Or: "Did you see her, she has a good figure."

I: When you think about who you are, what do you think?

S: For instance, I think about my strengths in sports – no idea. Whether you're an individual competitor or – now I noticed I'm really a team player. I like to be with other people. With friends.

I: How is it going with Dad?

S: With us, family is intense, the weekends are intense, fishing. Before we did much more together, now I do things with friends on the weekends.

I: Are you better at sports than Dad?

S: I was never better, it was never a competition.

I: Do you sometimes tell him how things go?

S: It's not that I think I'm better. I just like showing him how things go. The point is to go fishing with Dad, not by myself, and he makes it possible.

Discussion

Sebastian is laconic when he describes his view of girls, without establishing undue contact to his feelings – perhaps he finds this emotional distance important to his observations.

Conspicuously, Sebastian emphasizes that he has no rivalry with his father. He only enjoys showing him how something should go. In reality, Sebastian is the best in almost all sports when his family goes windsurfing, kite-flying or fly-fishing with other families. Sebastian baits the lines and fishes so skillfully that many more fish bite his line than the others. Perhaps his numerous experiences of easily taking up sports unfamiliar to him helped develop his self-confidence. He is very independent, good at using public transportation in Vienna, traveling alone to visit a friend or to return home from a sports event. The great importance his friends hold for him becomes only indirectly evident when he mentions that he spends most of his weekends with them. Regret is implied when he speaks of his formerly "intense" family activities. He avoids a precise description of his physical changes: they are like those of any boys undergoing puberty. He finds it hard to put his own sexual excitement into words.

Female sexual organs exhibit their maturation through a sustained, ostensibly visible sign – the monthly menstruation – which can become an unconscious aspiration for male adolescents, too. The first menstruation represents a break with childhood, demonstrating a woman's power to bear human life and give birth. The procreative capability of the man is demonstrated through his first "wet dream", but this phenomenon is more private, less noticed or acknowledged in the social realm.

In conclusion, I would like to describe a phenomenon observed by Bruno Bettelheim with his emotionally deeply disturbed children in the Sonia Shankman Orthogenetic School.

In his book *Symbolic Wounds*, Bruno Bettelheim hypothesized that "one sex feels envy in regard to the sexual organs and functions of the other" (Bettelheim 1962, 19). Initiation rites can be understood as an attempt to express envy of womanhood through rituals. Self-injury is meant to result in a bleeding similar to menstruation.

In the Sonia Shankman Orthogenetic School for emotionally disturbed children at the University of Chicago, founded by Bettelheim, several professionals noticed that adolescents were damaging their genitals in order to make them bleed. These spontaneous "rites of initiation" on the part of 12- and 13-year-old girls and boys started as a secret club with the plan of cutting their genitals once a month to mix the blood together (see Bettelheim 1962, 30). The schizophrenic girls exhibited various reactions to their own menstruation: they viewed the blood as "disgusting" or "dirty", yet they spoke almost exclusively of menstruation and showed the others their sanitary napkins. All the boys under his care saw it as a "cheat" or "gyp" that they had no vagina. (Some even said: "Why can't I have a vagina?") When somebody else was crying, one boy said: "I know why he's crying – it's because he wants to have a vagina" (Bettelheim 1962, 30), "Viewing menstruation not as something debilitating but as something that confers extraordinary magic powers may make genital sexuality more acceptable. The new power again makes men seem less enviable and dangerous and sexual intercourse with them less hazardous" (Ibid, 51). Based on his analysis of various rites of initiation, Bettelheim posits the thesis that such rites can be understood as a somewhat hidden fascination centered on pregnancy and giving birth.

In all phases of puberty, the body also becomes a medium for protest, provocation and propaganda. Although manifestations thereof vary markedly in the 20th and 21st centuries, adolescents have always attempted to gain hegemony over their bodies, which in itself often constitutes a provocation for parents and teachers.

1.2 The body as a medium of protest, provocation and propaganda

The transformation of the child's body into that of an adult transforms the adolescent's sense of his body along with its structure. Attendant insecurity and shame is often turned outwards in the form of provocation, reversed into the opposite pole: instead of a transformed but concealed body, the body becomes an agent for protest – in conscious contrast to more "adult" modes of presentation.

In Figure 1.3, the two adolescent boys are presenting their attractive, mature bodies in a regressive and provocative fashion – on the one hand reminiscent of babies exhibiting their behinds, and on the other hand like a broken taboo, as they shamelessly expose their rear ends.

18 The body ego

Figure 1.3 John with his friend (16 years old)

In every successive generation, divergence from the previous one has been exhibited in a different fashion. In the German-speaking countries, an early 20th-century adolescent *Wandervogel* youth movement expressed rebellion against bourgeois constraints through clothing, propounding a free life in harmony with nature instead of narrow sartorial restraints and militarism. The nude body was meant to inspire liberation from strictures and morality. With their guitars and knapsacks, these youths wandered the woods and sang romantic songs by the campfire.

Neither these outward trappings and closeness to nature nor the protest against military drill kept the movement from being co-opted by a completely opposite, authority-oriented ideology. The youth movements between the two World Wars – such as the *Wandervogel* and the *Pfadfinder* – segued smoothly into paramilitary national movements and later into the Nazi Hitler Youth. Uniforms, boots and flags and powerful hierarchical structures took the place of the formerly freedom-loving, individualistic ethos. Wilhelm Reich made the disciplining of the body through military drill a central focus for examination.

In 1950s Germany, what was called the "swinging 50s" (as distinct from the "swinging 60s", both in Germany and elsewhere) swung the pendulum once again in the other direction: modest, tight-waisted, broad-belted petticoat dresses conquered the fashion world; girls got engaged quite young, married and quickly became pregnant. With the possible exception of Elvis Presley's hysterical fans, there were no protests. Young men dressed like their fathers and aspired to emulate their successful careers.

Only in the 1960s did a broad movement emerge from what had originally been a student counterculture – the hippies. This subculture propounded a new lifestyle: instead of success and perseverance, love and communally experienced music were the new ideals. Music festivals such as the legendary Woodstock Festival were crystallizing events. Inspired by The Beatles, male adolescents wore their hair longer, causing controversy with parents and teachers. Today, we might have difficulty imagining the eruptive force of long hair, especially since it was often not much longer than before – and yet it still elicited vehement reactions. Girls tended to wear mini- or maxi-dresses, with their hair free (Miles 2005). The previously rigorous sartorial distinction between the sexes was dissolved: inspired by Indian clothes, young people wore batik fabrics, symbolizing a break in gender roles. Tattoos, piercings and blackwork tattoos were popular. The "Jesus sandal", a healthy form of footwear, was the opposite pole to the preceding bourgeois tweed jackets, dirndls and loden look (in German-speaking countries) of youth culture. The core of the hippie period was between 1965 and 1971. In the 1980s, the hippie movement segued to alternative movements such as punks and the "no-future" movement, but before (and after) this, men and women alike often wore long hair and jewelry. "Free love" and free drug consumption became widespread, with The Beatles' song "All You Need is Love" embodying the hippies' motto. Today as well, adolescent fashions often trigger conflicts with parents, leading to denial and opprobrium.

Why is the body of such importance as a locus for provocation? Especially during this period of fundamental physical change, the body is most intimately linked to the ego. "The ego is always a body ego," writes Freud (1923, GW XIII, 253). Since all dimensions from the relatively peaceful latency period are in flux, the adolescent now finds a kind of refuge in his body – even though it is also a source of insecurities and fears as it rapidly changes. Even if the adolescent suddenly knows nothing about himself – about his values, his desires, his position within the family – at least (he believes) he can control his own body. Just as the infant derives direct reinforcement from his corporal sensations and the experience of being held, the adolescent uses his body to evoke massive reactions from his parents and other adults. Hotpants revealing everything but a girl's posterior, or bushy hair under a headband, become the object both of commentary and power struggles: the question of who should control the adolescent's body becomes a controversy between adolescent and parents, one which I describe more closely in Chapter 3. Parents, who have until now guaranteed the survival of their children through devotion and loving care, now are meant to feel a border: "I control my own body!". This constitutes a painful rejection and a new positioning of the parents vis-à-vis their adolescent children, as responsibility is transferred to the children step by step.

If physical changes were at the center of this chapter, in Chapter 2 we will examine the emotional responses to them and psychosexual effects.

2

Psychosexual development in puberty

Eating is the second most important thing in life.

—Honoré de Balzac

Psychosexual development in adolescence has a special significance, since now child sexuality develops into its conclusive form. A "re-formation" occurs, causing Freud to speak of a "double time frame of drive development". During this phase, three tasks must be mastered: 1) to once again work through infantile sexual urges, integrating tender impulses with sensual impulses; 2) to choose a love object, i.e., the person to which these impulses are directed; and 3) to develop a stable sexual identity.

Melanie Klein emphasizes the significance of the adolescent crisis for the growth of personality and development of the adolescent's character. The psychosexual reformation affects all layers of the personality, going back to the baby's early feelings of helplessness/solace and including the passionate Oedipal longings and rivalries that were put on the back burner during latency. Before we turn to psychosexual development in puberty, we will examine the extended concept of sexuality in Freud, the concept of bisexuality and the phenomenon of ambivalence.

The extension of the close concept of sexuality to *psychosexuality* can be understood as an expression of Freud's deep-lying interpretation of love, eros, tenderness and the body, which he linked to desire and passion. Here, sexual aspects of seemingly asexual behavior and phenomena are described in a systematic form (see Niztschke 1976, 362). Through this extension of the concept of sexuality, the border between pathological and "normal" sexuality becomes relativized, since "normal" and "abnormal" manifestations of sexual drives can only be understood in conjunction with each other. As Freud propounds in his "Introductory Lectures on Psycho-Analysis" (1916–17), there are only quantitative, not originally qualitative factors characterizing psychic health or illness – including in the sexual realm. Both for adolescents and for parents, it helps to be aware of this flexible border when attempting to understand adolescent behavior as a developmental phase of sexual experimentation.

When a girl dresses in a provocatively erotic way, her parents might uneasily interpret this as an indication of promiscuous or exhibitionistic behavior. This could indeed be the case, but it also could be her attempt to find favor with boys and attract attention. Homosexual experiences with both boys and girls can be a transitory episode, or also the beginning of the establishment of a homosexual identity. Clearly, during the transitory phase of adolescence, a given behavior does not constitute an unambiguous symptom. Particularly during this phase, a behavior that appears to be outlandish or pathological might be transitory. As is shown in the case of Fritzi (see Chapter 3), modest and provocative behaviors can alternate with each other, as an expression of deep insecurity.

Contrary to the seemingly simple and clear separation between the sexes into masculine and feminine with the goal of reproduction, Freud posits the differentiated version of **bisexuality**. Wilhelm Fliess and later Oskar Weininger were decisive in the shaping of this paradigm. Freud propounded the thesis that each human being comprises an inborn masculine and feminine sexual nature. The development of sexual identity depends on biographical factors.

> A certain degree of anatomical hermaphrodism occurs normally. In every normal male or female individual, traces are found of the apparatus of the opposite sex. . . . These long-familiar facts of anatomy lead us to suppose that an originally bisexual physical disposition has, in the course of evolution, become modified into a unisexual one, leaving behind only a few traces of the sex that has become atrophied.
>
> (Freud S.E. VII 141 1905, quoted in Laplanche and Pontalis 1988, 53)

New research in embryology (Sherfey 1966/1972) has shown that the human embryo is primarily "feminine" in nature. Only through the masculine hormone androgen do the male sexual organs then become differentiated from the female.

> The clitoris is from the beginning on a part of the female sexual apparatus. From the embryological point of view, the penis is therefore an extended clitoris – not the other way around, the clitoris as a stunted penis, as was previously believed.
>
> (Fleck 1977, 26, translation McQuade)

At the same time, the urge to live out both male and female components is both fascinating and unsettling to adolescents, who often try out various sexual practices in their search to discover their own preferences.

Another important phenomenon is the "ambivalence of feelings" Freud first discussed in 1912 in his "The Dynamics of Transference": the same person becomes the object of both love and hate; this person is meant both to become jealous and trusting or emotionally accessible. Such ambivalent feelings can be found in childhood – but in adolescence, they are often linked to overwhelming

22 Psychosexual development in puberty

sexual tensions striving towards fulfillment, and thus become especially confusing and threatening.

An adolescent goes through the various stages of psychosexual development once again, but this time with a new intensity. At the deepest level, psychosexual development is linked to the experience of separation from the womb in the first three months of life – and in turn, to giving up a fantasized omnipotence and control of the love object (the mother). Here, the baby must integrate the different part aspects of the mother to a whole person, thus experiencing the loved and hated parts of the mother and of the self, formerly split in its fantasy, as belonging to one person. A second level is linked to the turbulent Oedipal desires for the parent of the opposite sex until the age of six, and the third level is linked to the consolidation that takes place in latency, between the ages of seven and eleven.

In writing this chapter, I found it very difficult to describe a simple idea: that during puberty, every phase of development becomes newly agitated, and that each phase proves to be either stable or in need of modification or collapse. For weeks I tried to find various ways I could capture these thoughts. I was overwhelmed by the complexity of the task: first, to sketch all the preceding psychic and cognitive developmental phases, the two modes of experience comprised in the mature and the archaic view of the world, primary objects and of oneself. This seemed at first well-nigh impossible, since these matters must be presented simultaneously as occurring in their original stages from childhood and in their new manifestation during adolescence. Only when I realized that my feelings of being over-challenged by the unlimited scope of this basic idea corresponded to the feelings of adolescents themselves, living through this process, did I regain my confidence. The transformation from childhood to adulthood is an everyday matter – and yet constitutes a huge, emotionally challenging task: it is both simple and impossible. My description must of necessity remain an incomplete sketch, and for every step of the way, knowledge of all other aspects is a prerequisite. During the following description, the reader must always be aware that all aspects are simultaneously in play, even when they can only be described separately.

2.1 The mother-baby couple as a model for romantic love

The first loving relationship develops between mother and baby, and they constitute a love pair – an experience laying the foundation for the romantic love which will come later. A baby seeking love and protection is often abruptly overcome by its own primitive rage and hate when it cannot control its mother (or a part aspect of her) in accordance with its fantasies of omnipotence. Immediate measures taken to gratify its wishes – basically impossible to satisfy since total satisfaction is never immediately possible – must necessarily lead to frustration. Further developments depend on whether the mother is capable of noticing and appropriating these primitive sensations and becoming emotionally involved with her baby. Only when she is capable of emotionally digesting these primitive

Psychosexual development in puberty 23

elements – Bion (1962) calls them "beta elements" – can she return them to the baby in a modified form, by putting them into words. The result of this transformational process from primitive sensation (beta elements) into descriptive words is called by Bion "alpha elements". This early form of communication is termed the Model of Container and Contained, where the mother supplies a "container" for the primitive, archaic fears which the baby has projected into her. The mother's ability to intuit what her baby fears is called by Bion "reverie" – a dreamy state of intuition and empathy. In situations of hunger, thirst, sickness and fatigue, the baby feels it is surrounded and attacked by hostile powers both inside and outside its body. As long as it cannot differentiate between inside and outside, it quickly feels threatened. The child requires solace and support from its parents in order to bear these fluctuations between happiness and desperation, security and persecution, patience and frustration. Phases of desperation, rage and powerlessness exist alongside moments of peace, solace and love (Lebovici 2003). In *Young Child and Their Parents*, I wrote:

> An infant's initial experiences are somatic in character. Psychoanalysis has helped us understand that the first love between baby and mother constitutes a prerequisite for romantic love between man and woman later in life. In adult love, we recollect the psychic experience of baby-mother or baby-father love. The first love between mother and baby forms the foundation for an adult's later capacity to love; it is impossible to love without having experienced being loved. An unloved baby will find it difficult – although not impossible – to fall in love as an adult, and such a love is likely to be painful, characterized by a lack of satisfying unity between two lovers.
>
> (Diem-Wille 2014, 73)

The special, unique relationship pattern in this mother-baby dyad, together with the father who is meaningful for them both, helps set a pattern of connectedness in the baby's inner world – a pattern that constitutes the basis for later romantic love relationships.

From the pleasurable satisfaction experienced in nursing, where the baby ingests not only milk, but also love and security, the baby must proceed to the disappointment represented by weaning. The ability to ingest solid food brings increased independence from the mother and relegates the more intense oral satisfaction (according to Freud, the "first erogenous zone") through breast-feeding. Now, through the adolescent's sexual urges, these early wishes for oral satisfaction arise once again: the first kiss conveys memories of early feelings of pleasure and desire, vibrating through the adolescent's entire body. These feelings are hardly limited to the oral region, but overtake our entire bodies and evoke the stimulation and satisfaction of our time as babies. However, we are incapable of directly connecting to these early desires, since they were already converted to their opposite during the process of weaning. In place of the longing for oral gratification, the disgust of bodily contact takes an upper hand: saliva at first seems

24 Psychosexual development in puberty

revolting, and it requires the full dose of sexual desire to overcome this feeling of disgust. A 14-year-old girl, whom I will call Beate, describes her thoughts and images of kissing. She describes her first examination at the gynecologist's, and then proceeds directly to the kiss:

> At the gynecologist's, I got an ultrasound exam. He put in a huge rod. My mother was more nervous than I was – I said I'd just do it. It wasn't bad, I didn't feel anything. "That's how it is when you sleep with somebody", said my mother. I hadn't wanted to know. I want to have my first sex when I'm eighteen or nineteen. I haven't yet had a tongue kiss – with spit. For me, that's gross. But it will happen sometime. I'm only fourteen.

Beate's mother accompanied her to the gynecologist as a preparation for the time when Beate should experience sexual contact and already know the doctor: she can then pose her questions to him more comfortably. The questions regarding gynecological examinations, sexual union and the ("gross") first tongue kiss arise in close proximity to each other. Beate emphasizes that she has no desire to know about sexual intercourse, but she shows how intensely she has considered all of these questions. She is far from the idea that a kiss can be pleasurable, and she cannot access her memory of pleasurable nursing as a baby. All of these associations remain unconscious, yet have an effect on Beate – evoking both fear and longing.

The adolescent's wish to cuddle with his mother like a baby stands in crass contradiction to the parallel wish to become an adult and assume physical distance from her. A young teenager now does not wish to take leave of his mother with a kiss on the cheek in front of the rest of the class. These contrary wishes alternate with each other and cannot be predicted by the parents, since they alternate so abruptly. Here is a scene with 14-year-old Sebastian:

The evening before, Sebastian went out with his friends and only returned home at a late hour. His parents are having breakfast at 10:00 am on Saturday. Around 11:30 am, Sebastian's mother goes up to his room to wake him up. Ten minutes later, Sebastian comes downstairs sleepily, stopping midway down and remarking, with his mouth turned down at the corners, "You can't wake me up that way".

His mother, shocked, asks him in a friendly voice: "What did I do, sweetie?", then stands up and puts her arm around his shoulders.

Sebastian: You open up the door and say (imitating her militaristic tone): "Eleven thirty! Get up!" No kiss, no hug, nothing. (He is fighting back tears.)

Mother: Oh, Sebastian, I'm so sorry. (She then hugs and kisses him, which he enjoys; then he goes with her to his place they set at the table.)

The mother is visibly surprised that her son – 1 meter 72 cm and quite independent – desires this childish ritual of awakening, although the day before he energetically warded off any influence and control from his parents. He often emphasizes that he can

Psychosexual development in puberty   25

take care of himself and will manage everything on his own – he knows to get home punctually, for instance. This constellation is reminiscent of the child's first separation out of the initial amorous couple: the mother and her baby.

Discovering the body

After birth, the mother and father investigate their baby's body, stroking it lovingly, squeezing its fingers and toes, inspecting its head, eyes and ears, as they compare it with their fantasies of an imaginary baby. The English pediatrician and psychoanalyst Donald Woods Winnicott characterizes the "shine in its mother's eyes" as an essential component of "primary maternity" for a baby. Psychoanalysts assume that the parents' affectionate gaze and tender stroking convey to their baby steadiness and protection.

A lover, too, undertakes a similar voyage of discovery over the beloved's body, caressing it and holding it. This touching unconsciously evokes the same pleasant feelings from early childhood – this time, making tangible the lovers' mutual pleasure in their skin and bodies. As it passes over the partner's body, a lover's hand heightens sexual tension:

> If the excitation now spreads to another erotogenic zone – to the hand, for instance, through tactile sensations – the effect is the same: a feeling of pleasure on the one side, which is quickly intensified by pleasure arising from the preparatory changes (in the genitals), and on the other side an increase of sexual tension, which soon passes over into the most obvious unpleasure if it cannot be met by a further accession of pleasure. . . . If an erotogenic zone in a person who is not sexually excited (e.g. the skin of a woman's breast) is stimulated by touch, the contact produces a pleasurable feeling; but it is at the same time better calculated than anything to arouse a sexual excitation that demands an increase of pleasure.
>
> (Freud 1905, 209)

In her "Ensemble, c'est tout" (2004), Anna Gavalda describes the discovery of the body of the lovers:

> He consumed her from head to foot. . . . At first he fell upon her freckles, then nibbled, picked at, chewed, licked, swallowed, ate up, fed himself, bit and gnawed at her to her bones.
>
> (Gavalda 2004, 467, translation McQuade)

She then describes how the woman also gets to know her lover's body, "she too acquired the same taste, paying him back in kind."

For adolescents, these sensations are confusing in two ways: first, unconscious memories of early bodily sensations arise that were hitherto successfully repressed; second, everything in an adolescent's body aims towards increasing

26   Psychosexual development in puberty

sexual excitement, which is new to the adolescent and causes him fear; often unplanned, this excitement can overcome him against his own will. The fear of not recognizing one's own body and its reactions is mixed with desire and inflamed sexual excitement, demanding its own intensification. In phases of infatuation, lovers often find it essential to maintain virtually uninterrupted body contact – touching hands or feet under the table.

Eye contact

The body language of love is expressed through corporal proximity. A mother, too, cannot "see enough" of her baby, as she gazes upon it during diapering and nursing; baby and mother often seem to dissolve into one another. The human being is the only mammal who immediately seeks eye contact with its mother after birth. Protracted wordless gazes constitute either a sign of heightened intimacy or of aggression, as a ritual of initiation before fighting (Stern 2001, 219). A baby who continually avoids eye contact with its mother shows that their relationship is fundamentally disturbed (Norman 2004, 255ff). Autistic children who have withdrawn into their private world avoid all eye contact, since they have no hope of establishing an emotional relationship to other people. The loving eye contact between mother and child also satisfies part drives, including voyeurism and exhibitionism, which are part of normal development in the construction of an emotional relationship. Refusal to look at another person can constitute a sharp form of punishment, leading to disorientation for a small child. "I don't want to look at you" is a powerful and cruel weapon that can leave deep wounds in the child.

A baby has the natural capacity to follow its mother with its gaze as she moves about the room, which helps it to bear separation from her since their emotional bond is sustained. A sensitive mother can maintain eye/voice contact to her baby even while performing other household tasks.

Eyes are of major significance in romantic love: they are the first medium of contact – gazing, glancing or catching a gaze are often-employed methods for flirting. The excitement that makes another person attractive or beautiful is conveyed through their eyes. Freud wrote:

> The eye is perhaps the zone most remote from the sexual object, but it is the one which, in the situation of wooing an object, is liable to be the most frequently stimulated by the particular quality of excitation whose cause, when it occurs in a sexual object, we describe as beauty. (For the same reason the merits of a sexual object are described as "attractions").
>
> (Freud 105, 209)

Freud maintains that the rubric "beautiful" must be grounded in sexual excitement and have originally denoted sexual attractiveness. As the body became increasingly concealed over the course of civilization, this vitalized sexual curiosity – then sublimated in art, which manages to sustain interest in the entire body. Melzer

(1988) takes up this idea and extends it, speaking of "aesthetic experience". With this, he means the overpoweringly passionate love for the mother, a "beautiful mother", where all the child's loving, tender and happy experiences come together in an image. The image of a beautiful mother can be undermined through painful, frustrating or disappointing experiences, rendering the baby skeptical and distrustful. Isca Salzberger-Wittenberg, a pioneer of psychoanalytic baby observation in the method of Esther Bick, writes:

> Observations show how much the infant responds from moment to moment to the mother's changing emotional state: her love at one moment, her anger at another; her depression, her inner deadness, anxiety, fragility, her being preoccupied, out of touch with him – all these are sensed and arouse in him, in turn, love, admiration, fear, as well as concern.
>
> (Salzberger-Wittenberg 2013, 28)

The anxiety elicited in an adolescent from a desirous, admiring gaze is depicted by Turrini in his collection of poems, *Im Namen der Liebe (In the Name of Love)* (2005, 11) in the chapter "The Burning Heart":

> A look to you
> And I see
> Such beauty
> Such shyness
> Such temperament
> Such courage.
> What will I see
> When I risk
> A second look?
> > (Translation
> > McQuade)

Turrini is describing a twofold risk: whether the girl reciprocates his gaze and shows interest in him; and what might occur inside him as his sexual excitement rises or his knees tremble, overcome and enslaved as he is by her beauty.

The language of lovers

The language of the first mother-infant pair (a universal phenomenon across many cultures) is called "baby talk", marked by an exaggeratedly melodic cadence, high voice and pauses between sentences. Even though a baby might not comprehend the content of what is said to him, he takes in the mood, emotional message and basic syntactic structure, answering with facial gestures or noises in place of words. "An infant's searching look also is an expression of something. His joyful or fretful excitation when undressed is also information. His screaming – with

28 Psychosexual development in puberty

its modalities of summoning or suffering – is a sign that speaks directly to his mother" (Lebovici 2003, 254, translation McQuade). The infant's entire body serves as a medium of communication.

In romantic love as well, a couple will develop its own language, with particular words and gestures assuming special meanings; facial gestures are exaggerated and tailored to each other, as if the lovers were completely synchronized. Indeed, lovers also like to move in a synchronized fashion, with to-and-fro movements symbolically enacting separation and reunification (see Person 1988). Sharp noises or a loud, angry voice can frighten a baby or a lover, making the baby cry.

The inability to love – which can be traced to unsatisfying experiences or inadequate harmony between baby and mother – brings many people to therapy. Falling in love is a different matter from achieving a lasting love relationship. Behind the ostensibly irresistible Don Juan, who boasts of 2,064 conquests, lies the inability to achieve a lasting, fulfilling relationship with its attendant psychic pain, which is then concealed behind a forced drive for new sexual activity. As soon as such people have filled their urgent need for proximity, they feel panic at being locked in. A baby's initial love for the mother is both ecstatic and impossible, and can shift from love to hate. Falling in love, being in love, *tomber amoureux*, denotes various emotional states that can differ greatly. "Falling in love" implies an event outside of our control and hence a form of helplessness.

For each of us, early experiences remain active and vital for our entire lives. Erik Erikson (1950) speaks of this time as a phase of primal trust or primal mistrust. If the primitive self – Bion calls it the "psychotic self" – originally managed to experience another person in a loving relationship, then it can develop a life-affirming attitude. If the loving relationship goes unfulfilled, then the fundaments of the personality are unstable, and an adolescent can break down under his newly erupting drive development. Primal mistrust is based in unfulfilled experiences from early childhood and is manifested in various forms. One patient related that her mother often forgot her in her baby carriage: her loud cries often went unheard for a half hour, even though she occasionally cried so loudly that she lost consciousness. Her mother would also withdraw to the bathtub for hours on end, oblivious to the outer world. This diminished significance in her mother's eyes caused the patient deep long-term confusion, insecurity and doubt as to whether relationships were indeed possible: in place of trust, mistrust dominated.

At times in the inner world, two convictions may oppose each other. The subject's hope of being loved by somebody (mother or father as primary object) – having somebody who wants him to live – opposes the deep doubt as to whether the subject's life is relevant for another person, or in fact absolutely irrelevant. In one adolescent's suicide note, she wrote that "nothing matters". She had never felt wanted by her parents and had lost all hope of having any significance for another human being. Even her analyst – who attended her funeral – could not overcome her deep distrust.

For a time, this deep vulnerability can be hidden behind the arrogance of narcissistic personalities – a structure Bion dubs a "disaster" in his article "On

Arrogance" (1957b, 86). The case study of Mark (Diem-Wille 2004) depicts one adolescent's narcissistic defense against vulnerability. In most cases, arrogance in puberty represents a thin façade covering great insecurity, vulnerability and sexual fears. When the feelings behind this façade are addressed in therapy, this façade collapses and the adolescent bursts into desperate tears. From the practical standpoint, this collapse of this unstable defense is not a favorable development, since the sudden absence of his protective defense (arrogance or belligerence) delivers the adolescent up to his massive feelings, rendering him even more fearful and usually resulting in his breaking off the therapy.

The analyst then must ask herself whether her own feelings were at work, albeit unnoticed, behind her "correct interpretation" – which although correct, was perhaps not made in the right moment or with the right words. Could this "correct interpretation" be an expression of the analyst's turbulent, envious affective reaction to the adolescent's appearance or provocations? Here she must ask how she deals with her aging body and the aging process, particularly when confronted with the adolescent's fresh beauty and charming body language.

The narcissistic adolescent's insecurity as to whether his parents "wanted" him can become blown out of proportion – and concealed behind an arrogant attitude where other people are discounted, with the adolescent presented in an arrogant and distanced light. The narcissist's motto is: I don't need anybody, I am enough for myself, I can satisfy myself sexually – for then I become invulnerable and independent. Even with sick people, there exists an – often small – healthy part with which the therapist attempts to establish a working relationship. The extreme tension between dependence and vulnerability that is always part of love contrasts with arrogant independence. Can I allow proximity if it renders me vulnerable and fragile? Can I bear the psychic pain of unrequited love?

Crass reactions to insufficient bonding ("attacks on linking", as Bion termed it in 1959) provoke extreme reactions of withdrawal: in autism, a person creates his own world, a refuge promising safety from harm and frustration, without any link to the outer world (Alvarez and Reid 1999). Or the fragmented parts of the self could not be transformed to thoughts through the containment embodied in a loving relationship, and paranoid-schizoid mechanisms took the upper hand. The lack of established, stable emotional relationships can be observed in schizophrenic children, whose bizarre and dismissive behavior reveals the unconscious aspiration to re-establish the experience of social interaction through their testing borders between the senses and reality, between words and their social significance. All undesired feelings and thoughts are projected outward.

Puberty's wild explosion of desires and sexual fantasies revives Oedipal desires and early unresolved conflicts regarding separation from the mother, which appear threatening and insoluble. If the adolescent cannot meet his developmental challenges, a psychic collapse can ensue. When he experiences psychic restructuring through therapeutic help, the unconscious conflicts from early childhood can be investigated and sorted out. According to the experienced psychoanalyst Moses Laufer, who led the Brent Adolescent Center in London, this constitutes the last

30 Psychosexual development in puberty

opportunity to avoid lifelong character deformation: manifestations of adult psychotic illness in the adolescent "were showing signs of what might be considered in the adult to be psychotic but instead were signs of a temporary, although severe, break with reality rather than the presence of an established and irreversible psychotic illness" (Laufer and Laufer 1997, XII). Therapeutic help at this stage can help the adolescent to once again launch the developmental process which had collapsed due to his excessive fear.

Early experiences influencing the deepest layers of the personality are the most difficult to decipher, since they involve archaic organizational forms of the psyche. The ability to experience oneself as a person separate from the mother and to see different parts of the mother as belonging to the same person lays the basis for an integration of part aspects and a relatively secure relationship to reality. Another important developmental step is the solution of the Oedipal conflict.

2.2 Flaming up of Oedipal desires

The Oedipal situation is a particularly significant crystallizing point for child development, and how the child masters it will structure his thinking and feeling fundamentally. In its central meaning, one can compare the Oedipal situation with the Copernican revolution. The Copernican departure from a notion that the earth is the midpoint of the universe (geocentric image of the world), along with acknowledgment that the earth moves around the sun (heliocentric image of the world) entails a change in the position of the human being as observer of the world. The earth and thus the human being are no longer the midpoint of the world, but instead part of a larger system (Kuhn 1957). Similarly, the child's egocentric view of the world is altered by the increasingly powerful reality principle – that not the child, but instead his parents, a sexually active pair, embody the family's center. In his fantasy, the child experienced himself as the world's center, loved and cared for by his mother and father. In his fantasies of omnipotence, he saw himself as ruler of the world, at the center of attention: "his majesty the baby". Through his powerful cries, he has the capacity to call his parents, and through his smiles and progress in growth, he elicits their praise. Or, alternatively, he experiences himself as powerless, at the mercy of the world, furious, full of mortal fear. The baby attempts to expel these threatening feelings in order to retain his idealized view of the world. Freud calls the Oedipal complex the "nucleus of neurosis".

The child's actual experience that her omnipotent desires are partially fulfilled through love and succor, however, also constitutes an important base for the development of her personality, self-worth and thinking. Melanie Klein emphasizes the significance of real, positive environmental conditions for the child, loving care on the part of its mother and father (Klein 1940, 20). Behind the omnipotent baby's image of the ideal world, there lurks the opposite specter of utter powerlessness in an inimical world where it has no chance to survive. The swift shift from the small child's feeling of omnipotence to powerlessness constitutes a major challenge for its parents.

The relationship between his parents is only partially visible to the baby: in his fantasy, the parents can also constitute a threat as a sexual pair. The baby vacillates between two modes: either he believes that his parents are only together in order to better care for him – as Winnie the Pooh believes that bees only collect honey for him to eat it. Alongside this first belief, the child believes that his parents are only together in order to exclude him. Freud assumed that every human being had a concept of the *Urszene* (primal scene), the sexual union of her mother and father, where the child is excluded and only has the role of an observer. In his "Moses and Monotheism" (1939, SE XXIII, 3), Freud proceeds from an unconscious, archaic scenario that is solidified through early observations. This would constitute an inborn, archaic knowledge, an *Urphantasie* (primal fantasy). Melanie Klein believed that in order to not acknowledge this gradually acknowledged relationship between his parents, the child develops the Oedipal fantasy. Between the ages of three and five, he increasingly gets to know his parents as sexual beings and possible partners. In the continuation of his fantasies of omnipotence, the boy now sees himself as his mother's lover and wishes to assume the position of powerful king alongside this "queen". The mother, whom the boy has already taken up as his first love object in his imagination (although he may often have experienced her as frustrating and inadequate) is now desired by him in a more mature stage as a sexual woman. In his fantasy, he forms a couple together with her. At the same time, he senses that with his much smaller penis (than his father's) he cannot create babies – but this frustrating and simultaneously relieving thought is suppressed to the periphery.

At the same time, this diffuse knowledge lessens the boy's great fear of his father's vengeance. In his imagination, the father becomes a mighty rival whom he aspires to defeat, but who will then take vengeance for his deposition by stealing his son's penis – a notion that Freud called "castration anxiety". Since the boy also loves his father, turbulent inner conflicts arise, as well as guilt feelings and self-reproach. At times, the boy also devises a solution that spares the actors involved:

> A therapist's five-year-old son, who was affectionately attached to him, often attempted to drive him from the marital bed by saying he ought to go read Freud. One day, the son said he wanted to build a big castle for his mother and himself and rule there. The father asked his son: "Where should I go then?" The five-year-old reflected and then said: "In the garden there will be a little house for the gardener, you can live there."

This father, who was theoretically familiar with the Oedipal concept, was still surprised how clearly his son expressed this wish. He felt expelled, but was glad that his son had found a place for him (the garden house) in his inner world. In the father, turbulent feelings of exclusion from his childhood were revived. The fact that he was able to talk with his son in this way evoked painful feelings, since he could never speak with his own father about such matters and had no chance of being understood.

32   Psychosexual development in puberty

During adolescence, however, the boy now discovers that he has a powerful penis, and he is distraught and fearful over what he could do to his mother with his penis. He is fearful because he feels destructive and confused. In this turbulent phase of development, the boy fantasizes himself to a greater or lesser extent as part of another couple. He subjugates himself to a "king" and selects him as a love object. In his fantasy, his mother is rejected or killed, with only he and his father remaining, who rule the world. Freud called this configuration "negative Oedipus". Human bisexuality renders both constellations possible and lays the foundation for later same-sex love relationships or friendships.

In this developmental phase, the girl finds herself in a more complex situation. The girl also experiences her first love relationship with her mother and must alter this priority as she turns to her father as a love object of the opposite sex. "I would like to marry daddy", thinks (or says) the girl, and then plays that she will get many, many babies (with her father). These games are seldom played with her mother, but instead with an aunt or grandmother: they are more likely to grant her the "king" than her mother, who in her fantasy is jealous.

Freud assumed that the girl turns away from her mother when she discovers that her mother did not provide her with the desired penis. The wish to bear children was interpreted by Freud as an ersatz for the withheld penis. Today, psychoanalysis proceeds from the assumption that a girl is well aware of her vagina and that the wish to have children is of great significance not only for girls but also for boys. Melanie Klein (1945) speaks of "womb and vagina envy", characterizing this phase in a boy's life as a "femininity phase". Yet the girl's partial emotional distancing from the mother as primary love object gives rise to deep feelings of guilt (Chasseguet-Smirgel 1974). The wish to outdo the maternal rival can be far stronger than with boys, since the mother as original love object is now replaced. These wishes are often repressed, split and projected outwards: the mother becomes the envious person who is unable to admit the girl's triumph vis-à-vis the father, begrudging her beauty and attractiveness, persecuting the beautiful princess, even wishing to poison her like the evil Queen poisons Snow White; this fantasy is an alternative to its opposite pole, where the girl wishes to see her mother as old and needy, cranky and unattractive. In the back of the girl's mind, she realizes that with her small, breastless body, she is not truly capable of making a baby with her father, and although this realization is sad, it is also calming. However, the situation suddenly changes with the girl's first menstruation, since she now possesses the necessary biological equipment, causing not only her but her father enormous anxiety. The sudden ceasing of all physical contact between the adolescent girl and her father can be traced to this unconscious fear. Teenage pregnancy – which will be discussed later – represents a form of acting out and displacing these conflict-ridden wishes. Due to the necessity of the early break between mother and daughter, their relationship is much more conflict-ridden than the relationship between the boy and his father. The girl feels inadequate and reproaches herself for harboring these wishes against her beloved mother to whom she owes so much; this often leads to a poor self-image.

If, however, the girl chooses her mother as love object, she need not turn away from her, instead experiencing her as part of a love relationship – a feminine union – where men are rendered superfluous and excluded. The unconscious negative feelings of rivalry vis-à-vis the mother are projected onto the masculine sex, to be battled in that arena.

The resolution of the Oedipus conflict takes a similar course for both sexes, shaping impulses, fantasy, fears and defenses into a central pattern of conflict. This consists in the child's painful recognition of his parents as a sexual couple, whose relationship fundamentally differs from their relationship to the child, thus creating a definitive break between generations. Even when the girl or boy fantasize themselves as sexual partner for one of their parents, the reality of this difference becomes ever more apparent. In the best case, this painful recognition leads to the acceptance of the parents as a loving, creative sexual couple who can produce something new – the baby. Inherent in this recognition is also reconciliation and a turning away from inimical impulses against the rival parent. The child renounces its sexual desires and identifies itself with the parent of the same sex, now becoming part of a triadic relationship: father-mother-child. However, the girl or boy is still excluded from the parents' sexual relationship. Only when the child grows up will it be able to enter into a sexual partnership with another person and have a baby; at this point, the child's sexual identity – already founded at the age of 1 ½ – becomes solidly anchored. Only with the renunciation of the all-powerful Oedipal wishes does the child accept a triangular relationship, with a "triangular space" (Britton 1998) opening within the child, who can now recognize that her parents are not only occupied with one another but can also think lovingly of their child. The internalization of a positive Oedipal couple lays the foundation of a child's self-reflection and conscience: it now can take distance from its actions or feelings and reflect on itself, as his parents do on the child. The child, who was the object of its parents' reflection and concern, now acquires in a stepwise fashion the competence of reflecting on himself. The child internalizes its parents' values and forms a conscience, a mature "superego" (Freud emphasized paternal values above all, but maternal values were later recognized as equally important). If the child is unable to relinquish his or her (positive or negative) Oedipal wishes, then she remains fixed at the according developmental stage.

Melanie Klein and Hanna Segal have pointed out another consequence arising when the child overcomes his Oedipal situation. The triangular inner space now allows the child to further develop his capacity to symbolize: he can now clearly differentiate between the symbol, what the symbol symbolizes and himself as a thinking person – a mental triangular relationship. "The triadic relationship between ego, symbol and object finds its correspondence in the triangular situation where the child finds itself simultaneously linked and separated with his parents", writes Weiss (2014, translation McQuade), describing this analogy. If the child instead mounts unconscious attacks on the parental couple, disturbances in symbol formation often result (Segal 1991).

34 Psychosexual development in puberty

Michael Feldman further extends this notion of the triangular space, describing how the child deals with his own thoughts. If he can establish connections between his own thoughts just as his parents come together in sexual intercourse, then he can establish new, creative thoughts. The way in which the child has internalized the Oedipal couple – whether he sees it as creative or destructive, vital or inflexible – constitutes the model for experiencing his own thoughts and their interconnections.

> One important consequence of this view of the oedipal configurations . . . has an influence on the (patient's) basic mental functions. If the patient negotiates the Oedipus complex in a relatively healthy way, he has an internal model of an intercourse that is, on balance, a creative activity. This seems to be directly connected with the development of the patient's capacity to allow thoughts and ideas to interact in a kind of healthy intercourse. On the other hand, the phantasy that any connection forms a bizarre or predominantly destructive couple seems to result in damaged, perverse or severely inhibited forms of thinking.
>
> (Feldman 1998, 106)

In place of fantasies of omnipotence, confidence in one's own creative capacity takes the upper hand. This clear border between the parents' generation and the child's generation constitutes an important step in the child's consciousness, bringing with it clarity and differentiation in thinking.

In the latency phase, emotional turbulences lessen and are followed by a phase of consolidation and relative security. The child develops his psychic, emotional and cognitive capabilities, turning towards the outer world (Diem-Wille, 2018). He largely adopts his parents' values, which constitute a reliable inner and outer order, and does not question his membership in his family. The child between the ages of seven and eleven (latency) has achieved some kind of balance, but this balance depends on the world being relatively stable, both internally and externally. He lives in relative harmony with the inner and outer worlds of parents and school (see Anderson 1998, 3). This world then changes radically and will never be the same as it was. The crisis of adolescence extends into every area of life. Not only is the world no longer the same, but the adolescent is no longer the same person he was, with his child's feelings, wishes and fears. Nevertheless, psychoanalysis has shown that the core of a child's personality structure is preserved, determining the way he overcomes this crisis. Therein lies a tremendous source of great tension. Anderson comments that:

> part of us wants never to have to give up our early desires and the means of gratifying them and now is confronted by changes that more than ever are in conflict with this world. Sometimes directly opposing old satisfactions and at others, threatening the self because it offers the infant self the power to gratify some of its most dangerous wishes – both sexual and violent ones.
>
> (Anderson 1998, 2)

Psychosexual development in puberty   35

This all becomes altered through the adolescent's developmental burst, with pressure arising from two sides. Due to his sexual development, early Oedipal wishes are revived, and simultaneously the search for an identity demands that the adolescent poses fundamental questions of parental ideals and values. The search for a sexual partner also demands giving up the early parental love objects and replacing them with new objects of sexual desire.

This paradoxical situation consists in the adolescent desiring his parent of the opposite sex with a new intensity, and yet preparing for a thorough distancing in order to free herself for a love object of the same age. The male adolescent who wishes to make babies with his mother would be physically capable of this, which creates enormous unconscious fears. What was formerly a harmless, childish wish now becomes a threatening goal. The male adolescent's fear often leads to violent actions in order to be rid of this inner pressure. By the same token, the female adolescent's wish to have her father's baby is now a real possibility. Even though the distaste for incest will prevent this wish from being fulfilled, it can become reality in a displaced form, through teenage pregnancy.

These contradictory demands create great tension, which can be manifested in self-destructive behavior such as cutting, thoughts of suicide, psychic breakdown or retreat from reality. The threatening nature of incipient physical changes is demonstrated in Kafka's *Metamorphoses* (1915). Here, a young man named Gregor Samsa perceives how his body slowly takes on the form of a beetle, with his hope that this change is only temporary soon to be disappointed: he must accept that the change is permanent. An adolescent must also change every aspect of his relationship to himself – his views, wishes and goals – which we in fact call the process of adolescence. The balance of the latency years is lost.

> Indeed, it seems to be those young people who have the inner strength and resource to bear to continue the experience of being naturally out of balance, as well as an environment that can support this, who can achieve the best adjustment in adult life.
>
> (Anderson 1998, 3)

In a family where parents prepare themselves and their children for the stormy period of adolescence, the younger brother may ask his sister – already in puberty and fighting her parents – "When will I finally enter puberty?" He may expect the requisite changes in his body, but their intensity can hardly be imagined.

Various views prevail as to whether the Oedipus complex constitutes a common, necessary phase of development or a pathological element. Britton (2014) emphasizes that the fashion in which an adolescent overcomes this developmental phase has a particular influence on the individual pattern of the personality, contending that when the Oedipal situation is newly experienced in every new life situation over the course of one's life, then this experiencing is useful and fruitful for psychic developmental and spiritual growth. However, when every new experience of a triangular situation evokes regressive tendencies, causing the

36 Psychosexual development in puberty

subject to revert to a fixated version of the Oedipus complex, then we can infer an underlying pathological tendency (compare Britton 2014).

Adolescence demands a new ordering of Oedipal patterns from early childhood, where successful forms of mastering them can be once again employed, or unresolved conflicts can arise and be newly ordered (given favorable conditions). In the following section, we will examine particular forms of "wish revival" from early childhood.

The longing for union with the primary love object

The longing to be as close as possible to the mother's body or withdraw into the protection of the womb is not experienced consciously, but manifested in various forms – for example, the immersion in loud music. Just as the baby hears its mother's heartbeat at approximately 90 decibels, corresponding to the sound of a sports car, adolescents might experience loud music in a disco or in any closed room as if mutely immersed in a virtual trance. Percussion almost demands that we move to its rhythm, and this movement reminds us of being rocked in the womb. During slow, close dancing, there is also a sensual attraction, an unaccustomed form of body contact, that reminds us of cuddling and being stroked by our parents; in intimate proximity, the dancing couple experiences this memory, as well as fear, excitement, arousal and desire – the erotic tension that urges us towards its intensification. Dances such as the tango or the Viennese waltz also can entail the man placing his leg between the woman's legs.

In the lyrics of hit songs, fantasies are also put into words – fantasies of becoming one with the love partner, along with the unavoidable fear and pain of separation attendant upon these aspirations. One such song (written by Marks Simon and Gerald Marks) describes this longing to be one person, called: "All of Me". It says: "Why not take all of me/Can't you see I'm no good without you/Take my lips/I wanna lose them/Take my arms/I'll never use them". The song describes the pain of separation if she does not love him anymore, because she "took the part, that once was his heart".

And a similar theme has the title "Heaven, I'm in Heaven". Why is the singer in heaven and how does he experience this feeling? It says: "my heart beats so that I can hardly speak/And I seem to find the happiness I seek/When we're out together dancing cheek to cheek . . . Heaven, I'm in heaven" (lyrics by Irving Berlin). The memories of this tight dancing experience is remembered all over again. Girls and adolescent boys can sit for hours remembering the words and the experience of touching the body of the beloved person during the dance.

When a boy whispers these lines in the ear of a girl he is in love with during dancing, her entire body reacts to his passion. These arousing experiences become the subject of daydreams. The wish to give oneself up also has another side: "do with me what you will", "I want to be your slave", i.e., the pleasures of sexual dependence or addiction. This wish constitutes a portion of every infatuation. Freud (1905) characterized the first phase of being in love as something that transcends or transgresses normality. In fantasies, the reliving of an infant's total dependency on its mother can also signify the core of a masochistic or sadistic exercise of power – a common theme in masturbation fantasies.

For adolescents, music is a means for expressing their wishes and longing to dissolve the borders of the self, creating a floating feeling in the listener. Music can serve as a sanctuary when an adolescent feels lonely and lost, withdrawing and listening to loud music. Not only can the adolescent lose himself in music, but it also constitutes a background for daydreams. The nostalgic dimension of music becomes clear when teenagers listen to children's songs in the last hours of an all-night party, with grief over the passing of childhood hovering over their nostalgic enjoyment of the old songs.

2.3 Daydreams with Oedipal themes

When we say "daydreams", we mean fantasies and imaginings – in the waking state – where normal strictures of reality are excluded. The adolescent imagines erotic or ambitious desires and sees them fulfilled in the daydream. Here, attention to the outside world is cut off; all the scenes in the daydream are short, pleasurable, expectant, recurring fantasies that follow the daydreamer's imaginings. Erotic scenes are often recalled again and again, like a film or record put on "repeat".

> As people grow up, then, they cease to play . . . (build) castles in the air and create what are called daydreams. . . . The adult . . . is ashamed of his phantasies and hides them from other people. He cherishes his phantasies as his most intimate possessions, and as a rule he would rather confess his misdeeds than tell anyone his phantasies.
>
> (Freud 1908b, 144)

In the street, we can recognize a daydreamer by his absent-minded smile or her talking to herself. Satisfying "castles in the air" are constructed. A love relationship is often fantasized with celebrities, singers, actors or pop stars, where the celebrity chooses the fantasizing girl – immature as she is – to be his lover.

After seeing the movie *Gone With the Wind* (1939), one 14-year-old girl fantasized for weeks of being kissed by Rhett Butler (Clark Gable) as he kissed Scarlett O'Hara (Vivien Leigh) in an elegant recline. Later she dared to fantasize that Rhett Butler had invited her to Hollywood, taking her passionately into his arms at the airport. As he had to Scarlett, he whispered in her ear: "You should be kissed and kissed often, and by someone who knows how". She would reconcile her misunderstandings with him and have his baby, since the first child died during a riding accident. She would be a better, more understanding wife than the self-centered, vain Scarlett.

Here, the girl's Oedipal wish seems clear, since she puts herself in the mother figure's place, placing her idol in the position of her parent of the opposite sex. This idol constitutes a transitional figure between a real and a purely fantasized

38 Psychosexual development in puberty

love object (since Clark Gable, as Rhett Butler, actually existed). Paradoxically, the girl retains enough distance to have no doubt she will fall in love with him and adore him. For the "father", i.e., Rhett Butler, she is the better, more understanding wife. Her admiration for the beautiful mother is mixed with competition and jealousy. Like childhood games, daydreams constitute a "transitional space" (Winnicott 1969). They contain elements from the past, have their trigger in the present and include the future. Usually, fantasies stop at kissing; seldom is a baby fantasized.

For male adolescents, daydreams consist of dangerous situations that they master and for which they are then rewarded. Adolescents have given up their childhood games and must therefore renounce a familiar pleasure. As compensation, the male adolescent builds castles in the air for the rest of his life. At the same time, he must conceal these fantasies, since he finds them childish and is ashamed. Such daydreams are adapted to the daydreamer's life situation, interlinking elements from the past, present and future:

> we must not suppose that the products of this imaginative activity – the various phantasies, castles in the air and daydreams – are stereotyped or unalterable. . . . Mental work is linked to some current impression, some provoking occasion in the present which has been able to arouse one of the subject's major wishes. From there it harks back to a memory of an earlier experience (usually an infantile one) in which this wish was fulfilled; and it now creates a situation relating to the future which represents a fulfillment of the wish . . . and thus past present and future are strung together, as it were, on the thread of the wish that runs through them.
>
> (Freud 1908a, 147)

This psychic work is linked to some actual event, taking up childhood memories in order to fulfill future wishes. A poor student imagines the triumph of becoming the best student.

A girl imagines herself to be the most beautiful at a party, to pass her exam with honors or to be the fastest runner. Monika relates that she and her sister withdrew to an "after-lunch rest" on Sundays. They darkened their shared room, put on one of their favorite records and daydreamed in bed. Each of them sank into her own fantasy world, but they enjoyed doing this together – although they never discussed their fantasies. In Monika's daydream, there was a dangerous situation: soldiers approached her aggressively and erotically, threatening to rape her. Then, their superior appeared, saving her from their clutches and restoring her to her parents. He fell in love with her at first sight, and she returned his love. Carefully, he touched her arm and kissed her. Then Monika broke off the dream.

Monika's fear of rape presumably has its roots in the fantasized violent sexual union of her parents, although at the same time she is saved and protected by a paternal figure; the soldiers would seem to represent the sexual urges she would enjoy and nevertheless fears. She selects these (often recurring) images when she goes to bed.

As Freud writes in his book *Interpretation of Dreams* (1900), various parts of the self are relegated to various personae in a dream, then altered, compromised, transformed into their opposite or into different people. All dreams are the result of unfulfillable wishes and longings. In a daydream, the daydreamer becomes a hero or desirable woman in a kind of try-out for life.

Such daydreams are part of normal development, so long as they do not replace actual social relationships. However, when daydreaming leads to an increased social withdrawal, this indicates great fears that hinder the adolescent from forging contact with her peer group. Children with family problems or violent parents tend to flee into a fantasized ersatz world. In Japan, the phenomenon of an adolescent's total withdrawal has a name: "hikikomori" is the term for people who refuse to leave their parents' house, shut themselves in their room and reduce their contact even with their family to a minimum. The length of this phase varies. Some close themselves in for as long as 15 years (or even longer). How many hikikomoris exist is difficult to identify, since many of them conceal this condition from fear of stigmatization. Estimates range between 100,000 and 320,000 hikikomoris, above all young people. The main cause is considered to be the great pressure for achievement and conformity in school and society (Flasar 2014).

Sexual fears can also be manifested in daydreams (as well as ordinary dreams). The central unconscious fears male adolescents have are to be enclosed in a dark place, caught in a trap or to lose one's penis or mind. The fantasy of being chained by a strict mistress points to the sexualized helplessness of the infant, who is unable to escape without the help of an adult. Sex shops and advertisements of prostitutes illustrate this dimension of sexual fantasizing, where early pain is transformed through sex into pleasure, to then be lived out either in fantasy or reality.

Girls fear the possibility of being broken into – a corporally violent threat that could harm their bodies. The sexual original fear of the destructive power of sexual union originates from early childhood fantasies, when the child perceives this original scene as an aggressive act: the small child interprets cries of pleasure and groans as threatening (Klein 1928). The fact that sexual love is dangerous and does not always turn out well is the basis for Shakespeare's *Romeo and Juliet*. Already at the outset, the tone is set by feud, death and agents of separation. Here, the love story is a rebellious one, which cannot have a good end. A central question is: is there sex without death? – i.e., sexuality is something dangerous. In French, the orgasm is known as the "little death". In primitive fantasies from early childhood, sexual intercourse is seen as something fatal – a violent sexual union turned against the child. The male adolescent's attitude towards sexuality also depends upon whether feelings can be discussed in his particular family. Can they talk about love, jealousy, longing and competition, or are feelings taboo? Can the parents embody a positive example of a couple who treat each other lovingly

40 Psychosexual development in puberty

and can also speak with children about sex? If the mother has a defensive attitude towards her sexuality and if no sexual relationship exists between the parents, this constitutes a confirmation of the child's fear of the fatal union between father and mother: the father would hurt the mother, and she must protect herself. Sebastian (12) had the following dream:

> I and my girlfriend were on a boat. We were playing a chasing game. Then a huge monster came and caught us. The monster wanted her to jump in his mouth and he wanted to swallow us. We ran away. Then the monster came from the other side. We both jumped overboard over the railing. I woke up.

In association, Sebastian believed he thought in the dream: "She shouldn't die. I want to save her." Then he said he was reading a book where there was a monster with a huge mouth – not a factual book, but a storybook. In this book there was a village in the sky, a ship and a small forest, where many monsters lived. The boy, 16 years old, has never been called a man yet. He wishes to prove his strength. He travels with the ship to the forest and meets a monster. Then he kills this monster and brings it home. He is a hero and is praised as a man. He is meant to conquer other monsters – but at that point Sebastian stopped reading. In her analytic work with very young children, Melanie Klein investigated children's fantasies about monsters. They represent an image of parts of the parental body, distorted by jealousy and envy, linked together in a dangerous fashion. This "combined parental figure" (Klein 1952, 92) can arise in an idealized or threatening form, represented as a monster in children's games.

Sebastian indicates that he identifies himself with the hero of this book, but his fears of the monster are much too powerful; he cannot bring himself to read on, but must flee with his friend. He feels he is no match for such dangers and escapes to the safe harbor of childhood.

Katharina describes her mood while she daydreams at the age of 15:

> Since three weeks ago, I am constantly tired. I just sit in front of the TV or lie down in bed. Then, time passes so quickly: I doze off and try not to think of anything, try to turn off. Just float. Then I rotate, when I think of homework I ought to do! Instead, I think of love. It is just so beautiful. I feel so safe with N. We understand each other so well, we laugh a lot. He is the first one I trust enough to say everything, and the things that bother me about him. I'm not perfect – he is *really* perfect – too good for me. We have really funny discussions about sex. He is almost two years older than me: one year, one month and one day. Both of us are too young, we're not ready yet.

Katharina speaks only indirectly of her daydreams. She is tired and dozes off in bed – a state between waking and sleeping. With her exciting, beautiful thoughts, time passes so quickly. She then jumps to a description of the boy she is in love with: N. Both are too young to have sexual experiences, but they talk about it, which is "really funny". Her parents have noticed how she seems to float through life in a trance, with an absent smile. Katharina also talks about this:

> The only thing that's uncool is that I fight so often with my parents. The thing that annoys my father is that I eat so slowly . . . because I'm tired . . . because I'm happy. He doesn't understand that, and I'm fed up with this. I don't know how I can explain it to him. I do everything so slowly and smile to myself. I can't help it if I'm in a shitty mood or happy. It shifts so quickly. I'm depressed – or happy. It changes every hour! Especially when I listen to music, I get sad, even though I'm happy. I don't know myself – I'm in love – that's what my life is about now. . . . . I'd like best just to sleep the whole day.

Katharina describes eloquently how little influence she has on her mood swings. She is simultaneously happy and sad: when she daydreams she feels good, but her parents are irritated and confused at her state of mind. Her daydreams are something of a no man's land – outside of the protected family zone, but not yet part of the foreign realm of adults (Larson et al. 1982).

Erotic and sexual tensions strive for resolution, achieved by physical manipulation of sex organs and attendant masturbation fantasies.

2.4 Masturbation and masturbation fantasies

Satisfaction of sexual tension proceeds through masturbation – genital stimulation – and is accompanied by particular fantasies. The guilt feelings often attendant upon masturbation are not only confined to religious qualms or fear of sin, but also manifested in masturbation fantasies, which often have aggressive, masochistic or perverse characteristics confusing to the adolescent who finds these fantasies both alien and native to him. The pleasure of masturbation can be both intense and also alarming, with fantasies often linked to situations of fear or pressure. Motifs include beating and being beaten, torture, imprisonment – or, in the masochistic version, seeing oneself as a victim. Earlier, masturbation was considered a sin and subject for confession, and supposedly had fearful consequences – acne or brain rot. Today, Facebook offers "masturbation aids", where masturbatory practices are described and compared, but also quite unenlightened questions are discussed: can you die from masturbating? Is masturbation healthy? What do I do when my son masturbates on his pillow? In the Internet, "domination workshops" are also offered. In general, most people today believe that masturbation is a normal phenomenon, and yet parents still have trouble talking about it with their sons. (With girls, the physical traces of masturbation are not visible.) In this area, psychoanalysis has made an important contribution to lessen the taboo status from masturbation that was earlier embodied in rituals of humiliation – for instance, a mother exhibiting the sheet from a boy's "wet dream" in order to shame him.

In his book *Die Verteidigung der Kindheit* (*The Defense of Childhood*) (2015, 54), Martin Walser writes of *not* speaking openly about masturbation, with the special quality (including guilt) this affords:

> Klara was never angry or hard or even strict. She was simply there, when something bad needed to be prevented: a fall, an injury, masturbation. You understand me, I hope? Now, his mother wished to say that if he had kept his masturbation within bounds from the beginning on, then he would have better nerves now – he'd sleep better, wouldn't need his pills, and wouldn't even know what a migraine is. But from the very beginning, they had conveyed to him that masturbation was something bad. Damaging, ugly, evil. Although neither his father nor mother had ever spoken with him about it, he knew exactly how his father and mother thought about masturbation. And he would – he knew this – think until his dying day how his parents had conveyed this to him without ever talking about it. . . . With other people, one could be tolerant. Only with yourself do you experience the course things took, plus the shame installed in you. That you've failed yet again. That the payback for this would come. At least until after his exam, he wanted to control himself. . . . And when he submitted, he knew that he would never pass the exam. His nerves! Someone who masturbates so uninhibitedly is a nervous wreck.
>
> (Walser 2015, 54, translation McQuade)

Inner pressure towards self-control heightens sexual tension, and thus sexual pleasure. The inner battle between desire and self-control is steered by a cruel, intolerant superego. All the references to masturbation that were not explicit in the mother's comments create a strong impression, making for shame and self-devaluation.

However, if masturbation replaces actual social contact to other male and female adolescents, then this can indicate a psychic problem, with the masturbator then requiring help and encouragement towards forging real social contacts, however painful or confusing. Free access to pornography, especially when sadistic, can elicit confusing feelings; it is better when adolescents discuss these practices together, "coping with" their wishes through discussion.

In this phase of budding sexuality, adolescents have trouble accepting their parents' sexuality; they tend to believe their parents are already "beyond" these questions and are sometimes shocked if their mother once again becomes pregnant. Parents often underestimate their adolescent child's emotional reaction to the inevitable prospect of renouncing them as their most important love object. An important part of the child's self-image was bound to the fact of being his/her parents' son or daughter. Accordingly, dethroning the parents often entails diminished self-respect – the sensation of an empty abyss adolescents often describe. Adolescents are primarily interested in themselves during this period between childhood and adulthood, with the "self" at center stage.

Psychosexual development in puberty   43

In his essay "A Child is Being Beaten", Freud (1919) describes precisely how some of his female patients could hardly relinquish their daydreams of a child being beaten. Freud describes his interpretation of these fantasies step by step: "The child being beaten is never the one producing the phantasy, but is invariably another child, most often a brother or a sister" (Freud 1919, 184).

In the first phase of the girl's beating fantasy, the father is beating one of her siblings, exposing her secret wish: "'My father is beating the child *whom I hate*'" (Freud 1919, 185). In a later phase, the fantasized child herself is beaten, where the beating has a definitive masochistic character. "Now, therefore, the wording runs: 'I am being beaten by my father'" (Ibid, 185). These pleasurable fantasies were told to Freud by one patient who could not recall any physical punishment at her father's hands. In the third phase, another child is beaten by a different adult (such as a teacher), with these fantasies accompanied by a clearly masturbatory, orgasmic excitement. As an explanation for why these initially sadistic aspirations became a permanent libidinous facet of his female adolescent patient, Freud singled out factors from her childhood: the young girl had (presumably) done everything to inspire her father's love, thus sowing the seeds of hate and rivalry for her mother; a younger sibling provoked her jealousy, which easily explains the first phase of beating the small child: "'My father does not love this other child, *he loves only me*'" (Freud 1919, 187, italics original). The girl's wish to have a baby with her father was disappointed when the new sibling was born, with her incestuous longings causing her guilt that spoils her triumph: "So far as I know, this is always so; a sense of guilt is invariably the factor that transforms sadism into masochism. But this is certainly *not* the whole content of masochism" (Ibid, 189). The third phase of beating constitutes a concomitance of guilt and eroticism:

> *It is not only the punishment for the forbidden genital relation, but also the regressive substitute for that relation*, and from this latter source it decries the libidinal excitation which is from this time forwards attached to it, and which finds its outlet in masturbatory acts. Here for the first time we have the essence of masochism.
>
> (Freud 1919, 189)

The essence of masochism thus becomes clear: the wish for coitus is supplanted by beating – pleasure and punishment together. However, details of this common fantasy of being beaten – also often represented in pornography or played out in contact with prostitutes – can have various meanings. The search for pleasure through real or fantasized pain may be difficult to understand. Freud struggled with a conceptual definition of sadomasochism as well as the complex links between conscious and unconscious fantasies. Cultural phenomena such as S&M bars for homosexuals or the bestselling book *Fifty Shades of Grey* indicate the wide scope of this subject. Indeed, 70 million copies of this trilogy have been sold worldwide; it depicts the relationship between a female student and a businessman six years older, who motivates her to bondage and sadomasochistic practices.[1]

44 Psychosexual development in puberty

When questioned, the owner of an S&M store said 90% of his customers were heterosexual (Person 1997, XI). It is not difficult to understand that adolescents feel threatened when they experience such daydreams and masturbatory fantasies.

The connection between early (usually repressed) Oedipal desires and their consequences for adult genital sexuality creates an inner pattern that can either be temporary or become a fixation: real experiences adults have had of being beaten as punishment, now sexualized, can determine masturbatory fantasies. Human sexuality is flexible, and since it is derived from libidinous impulses not subject to will or reason, fear can also become sexualized, with dangerous or humiliating situations evoked in order to enjoy this sexual tension. In his book *Confessions* (1953), Jean-Jacques Rousseau describes how a nanny beat him on his naked bottom; only when she noticed what secret pleasure this afforded him did she abruptly stop. Rousseau remained fixated on this erotic ritual for the rest of his life, as he describes.

In Leopold Sacher-Masoch's novel *Venus in Furs* (2000, first published 1870), he describes extreme swings of emotion. The main character, Severin von Kusiemski, seeks to make the rich widow Wanda von Dunajew into his domina, who will satisfy his secret wishes for complete submission and humiliation and physically/ psychologically torment him in various forms. The tension is heightened when she at times falls out of this role, instead becoming a conventionally tender, amorous partner. Behind this fantasy, we can easily recognize the strict mother from Severin's childhood, who punishes, humiliates and excoriates the small boy. The protagonist must always give thanks for being beaten or humiliated – a common practice in child-rearing of that era. The psychiatrist Richard von Krafft-Ebing propagated the terms "sadism" and "masochism", which originated in Sacher-Masoch's book and were taken up by Freud (Ammerer 2006). Adolescents can be confused or shocked by the link between sexual pleasure and pain, and these subjects are thus kept secret or repressed. Sadomasochistic daydreams can acquire an addictive character and evoke strong guilt feelings in an adolescent. In "Beyond the Pleasure Principle" (1920), Freud attempted to understand the phenomenon of sadomasochism, which contradicted his basic assumption that the human psychic apparatus avoids displeasure. In his deliberations, he found it necessary to broaden this basic assumption, then including the death instinct alongside the life instinct in his theory of the psyche.

Han Henny Jahnn's "Self-Experiments" shows the extent to which masturbation can be burdened with guilt feelings:

> all this was an expression of what uncanny sexual fantasies were pent up in me. I was a completely exalted human being, a personality who was marked but monstrous. But in all this there lay a huge potency. What foolishness I committed then. It was the time of my first sexual experiences – the time I first masturbated. I considered it a sin and suffered terribly: much later I realized that my excesses in this direction were quite harmless. I had arrived at the thesis that this sin was "tolerable", in other words within the limits of commission.

Tolerable – if I only masturbated once every six months. I punished myself for this by inflicting a wound in myself every time I committed this sin. Today, I can count on my legs how often I masturbated for one particular year.

(Jahnn 1974, 12, translation McQuade)

At the age of 16, Jahnn conducts this – as he calls it – "life and death struggle", emerging as the winner. Over time, Jahnn wounds himself, turning his sexual tension into self-aggression in order to punish himself. But the entire time he struggles against these temptations to cut himself and suffers, he is preoccupied with fantasies of harming himself. It is difficult to say how confused this inner struggle made him, since he also writes of the "appearance of Christ on the cross on the wall", apparently exhibiting signs of religious delusions.

Nevertheless, adolescence is a time of revolt – even if we can discuss whether an adolescent's behavior is normal or exhibits signs of a present or future pathology. Every individual must experience *his* own adolescence. Moses Laufer, who with his wife Eglé Laufer established the Brent Adolescent Center in London, sums up his long experiences in the following sentence:

There is only one cure for adolescence and that is the passage of time and the passing of the adolescent into the adult state.

(Laufer 1995b, 4)

Another way to psychically work through early childhood and adolescent wishes is artistic activity such as films or novels. From a huge range of examples, I will here examine and interpret one cult film and two novels.

2.5 Working through themes from early childhood and puberty in art

In his essay "Creative Writers and Day-Dreaming" (1908a), Freud pointed to the similarities between daydreams and the creative work of a writer. Already in childhood games, the child creates a fantasy world where the child takes on various roles, also playing out and satisfying her wish to be an adult. In a similar way, the writer creates people in "plays" who interact with each other. "Actors" embody these interactions in the theater or in film. In novels and short stories, heroes are created with whom the reader can identify, living successfully through adventures and being saved in fantastical ways. In spite of great dangers, the reader retains the feeling of safety for the hero, since the novel would end with his death. "It seems to me, however, that through this revealing characteristic of invulnerability we can immediately recognize His Majesty the Ego, the hero alike of every daydream and of every story" (1908a, 149). Freud quotes the comforting "Nothing can happen to *me*!" of the Austrian playwright Anzengruber, since the hero is always saved. The difference between daydreams and poetic works

46 Psychosexual development in puberty

lies in aesthetic satisfaction. Reading an impressive literary work, we experience a working through of psychic tensions, called by Freud the "fore-pleasure" or "incentive bonus" (Freud 1908a, 152). The spectator identifies himself with the work and the inner world of the artist as represented in the work.

Hanna Segal (1952) further develops this idea when she assumes reparation to be the origin of all forms of creativity. She sees the aesthetic experience of beauty and harmony as the successful attempt to restore destroyed inner objects and link them to reality: "The artist communicates at the same time both the destruction of the internal world and the capacity to repair it" (Segal, as quoted in Quinodoz 2008, 23). In order to answer the question of how these destroyed inner objects come into being, a short detour is necessary.

We have already seen that from birth on, the baby must cope with contradictory inner forces between the life and death instincts. The inner capacity to love is balanced against dark powers. The baby fears the effects of his hatred and destructive fantasies on persons whom he both loves and hates. In his fantasy, he damages those parts of the mother that withhold instant gratification – the voice or the breast; they are attacked or destroyed. I assume, along with Melanie Klein, that these fantasized attacks on the bad part aspects of the mother are split off and ejected. As Bion has shown, an empathetic mother can take in these elements projected into her, mentally "digest" them and return them to the baby in a loving way. Bion calls this model (1962) "container-contained", since the mother takes in the baby's primitive feelings and fears like a container. The baby feels himself, along with his dark feelings, held and understood by a strong and loving mother, and this strengthens his loving aspect. In this way, split aspects can be integrated, and the feeling of a totality comes into being, also including the grief and regret the baby feels for what he has done to his mother or father in its thoughts. But if the child has very strong aggressive impulses, they are more difficult to integrate: they stand their ground, threatening the baby's emotional balance. These childlike aspects remain more or less vital in every human being, just as do the internalized, damaged maternal or paternal inner objects. Freud, Melanie Klein and Hanna Segal all believed that artists have a particularly lively access to the childlike part of their psyche, since they have preserved their childlike powers of observation and curiosity. Like a child, they can take in situations or impressions in a fresh and unprejudiced way and forge links to their inner world and inner objects. The wish to compensate for attacks the child carried out in his fantasy constitutes a powerful drive to depict these themes in symbolic and artistic fashion. In art production, it becomes evident whether the working through and integration of early fears and wishes is achieved in a primitive or mature way. Even in relatively forceful works of art, libidinous powers take the upper hand over destructive powers, since new links are created during the production of art and something new is created – as with the internalized creative sexual parental couple (Bion 1957a).

The particular reformation of an adolescent's inner world will now be discussed using one film, *Bad Taste*, and two famous youth novels – Goethe's *Sorrows of Young Werther* and Raymond Radiguet's *The Devil in the Flesh*. All three works of art were perceived in their time as provocative and were either forbidden or censored – a result no doubt intended by the rebellious young artists who created them.

The depiction of adolescent sexuality in works of art

The Sorrows of Young Werther (Goethe 2004) – first published 1774 – is considered to be the first novel centering on the stormy feelings of young people. In letter form, Goethe brings the reader into the hopeless love young Werther had for a married woman, Lotte, depicting his emotional wounds, hopes, love and desperation until the point of his suicide. The reader follows his intimate feelings as revealed to a close friend in letter form.

The great success of this novel, above all with young readers, shows that Goethe caught the mood of his epoch, often characterized as *Sturm und Drang* ("storm and stress"). This mood also corresponds to the particular emotional hue of adolescence.

Synopsis

The young law student Werther leaves his hometown in order to forget an unhappy, Platonic love and to bring his mother's inheritance into order. He enjoys his liberation from everyday duties and undertakes long walks in nature, which he also describes in images:

> A peculiar serenity has taken over my whole soul, like the sweet spring mornings that I enjoy with all my heart. I'm alone and I take joy in my life in this region, which was just made for a soul like mine. I'm so happy, dear friend, so deeply immersed in the feeling of a tranquil existence, that my art is suffering from it. . . . I've never been a greater painter than in these moments. . . . When I lie in tall grass . . . a thousand different grasses attract my attention; when I feel closer to my heart, the swarming microcosm between their blades, the innumerable, unfathomable forms of the grubs und gnats.
>
> (Goethe 2004, 7)

Through mutual friends, he becomes acquainted with Lotte, the oldest daughter of a widowed civil servant. Werther describes a particularly vivid scene when he observes Lotte taking care of her six younger siblings:

> I caught sight of the most charming scene I have ever beheld. In the vestibule six children, ages two to eleven, were swarming around a shapely girl of middle height who was wearing a simple white gown with pink bows on her arms and bosom. She was holding a loaf of black bread and was cutting slices for the children around her, each slice proportioned to their age and appetite;

48 Psychosexual development in puberty

she handed each one his slice with great warmth, and each one called out an artless "Thank you!". Each one had stretched out his little hands way up, even before the slice had been cut, and now, contented with their supper, they either dashed off or, if their nature was placid, they walked off calmly.

(Goethe 2004, 11)

At a dance they come into closer contact, but Lotte informs Werther that she is practically engaged to Albert – fulfilling a promise she made to her mother on her deathbed. Werther seeks Lotte's company, since he has found a kindred spirit in her. However, Albert's return alters the situation: although he at first tolerates Lotte's meeting with Werther, the growing attraction Werther feels for this unattainable woman leads to his increasing depression. The dichotomy between Werther, with his stormy emotions, and the reasonable, reliable Albert, becomes clear.

Werther flees, taking a job at the court, and then returns to Waldheim, where Lotte lives. But his supervisor's pedantry and the rigid conservatism of courtly etiquette conspire to defeat him, since as a bourgeois he is not considered of requisite rank. This deep insult and Werther's role as an outsider lead to his breaking off his relations with the court. When he then learns that Lotte has married Albert during his absence, he once again visits her and sees that he is still in love with her. However, this love can no longer be lived, since she is married. In a moving conclusion, he says farewell to his love for Lotte, his life and nature's beauty, then shooting himself.

Discussion

The stormy feelings Werther discovers within himself and describes in the letters to his only close friend, Wilhelm, are similar to the diary entries of adolescents. In an access of enthusiasm, he enjoys nature's beauties, feels himself as the center of the world as a great painter – even though he can only observe and not yet paint. His love for Lotte is hopeless, since she is already engaged. Here, we can see the basic structure of the Oedipal situation – when parents exclude the child from their sexual relationship. Werther thinks he is closer to Lotte (representing his mother) than to his rival (standing for his father). This passionate courting of the already married woman becomes the novel's focus, conquering the reader. Through Lotte's words, Goethe makes it clear that she interests Werther because she belongs to another man – that he is attracted by the triangular situation where he might deprive Albert of Lotte:

She was holding his hand. "Just one moment of calm thinking, Werther!" she said. "Don't you sense that you're deceiving yourself, voluntarily destroying yourself? And why me, Werther? Why me, when I belong to another man? This, and nothing else? I fear, I fear that it's only the impossibility of possessing me which makes that desire so alluring to you".

(Goethe 2004, 27)

Lotte is addressing the paradigm of Oedipal competition: the point is not the woman, but taking her away from the other man (father figure). However, on an emotional level, this wish to possess the mother constitutes a necessary step in the son's independence.

This rebellion is directed against societal constraints, the rigid rules of politics and society against which Werther rebels. Goethe contrasts these rigid strictures with the value of passionate feelings, Werther's genius, his originality as well as his love and submission to nature. Instead of valuing only reason, intuition, feeling and passion are here elevated to a quasi-religious attitude that links the human being to his divine creator. The dissatisfaction of the adolescent with oppressive rules is also addressed.

In his autobiographical book *From my Life. Poetry and Truth* (1811–13), Goethe emphasizes that he conceived Werther upon an autobiographical foundation: his own unhappy love and the death of his good friend Jerusalem, since he perceived his own similarity to him. He then withdrew from the world, writing his *Werther* in four weeks (Goethe 2003, 344). In his article "A Childhood Recollection from *Dichtung und Wahrheit*" (1917–19), Freud addresses Goethe's relationship with his mother, citing a scene Goethe describes where he throws bowls, pots and a heavy pitcher out the window. As the neighbors applaud and encourage him, he throws more and more plates out the window and enjoys seeing them break. Freud interprets this act of throwing as an expression of the unconscious, jealous wish to defenestrate his own siblings. "This 'out!' seems to be an essential part of the magic action and to arise directly from its hidden meaning. The new baby must be got rid of – through the window . . ." (Freud 1917–19, 151). The heavy pitcher, for its part, indicates a mother laden by pregnancy; when he throws it out the window, he symbolically defenestrates her too, as he is embittered and angry over the incipient rival in her womb (Ibid, 151). Goethe was the oldest of six siblings, of whom only he and his sister Cornelia survived: the four other siblings died at the age of six (Hermann), one (Katharina), two (Johanna) and eight months (Georg). In *Werther*, Goethe describes with particular tenderness the scene where Lotte takes care of her six younger siblings – as if Goethe were reawakening his dead siblings to life. A psychoanalyst might presume that the young jealous Johann Wolfgang had mixed feelings when his murderous wishes became reality and the siblings were actually buried. "*Goethe, too, as a little boy saw a younger brother die without regret*" (as Hitschmann writes, quoted by Freud; italics original, Freud 1917–19, 151.) In a corollary, the psychoanalyst might assume that in the creative act of writing, the fantasized guilt for the siblings' death is redeemed. Lotte's six siblings could stand for the dead and living children – six altogether: in Goethe's fantasy, they are all alive and eating a meal together. The potential usurper then commits suicide. At his birth, Goethe was difficult to bring to life – at first, he seemed lifeless. He might have felt himself to be a "lucky child", an uncontested mother's favorite, as Freud emphasizes. Yet he might also have felt himself guilty for death wishes towards his siblings – wishes that came true in a magical way, but now could be assuaged through Werther.

50 Psychosexual development in puberty

Now we turn to a work written 150 years after *Werther*, one that describes the unhappy love of a young man for a married woman.

At the age of 17, Raymond Radiguet wrote the novel *The Devil in the Flesh* (1968, first published 1923), considered by critics at the time to be a tasteless act of provocation. Three years later, the author died of typhoid fever.

Synopsis

Radiguet tells the story of a 16-year-old adolescent, Francois, who is in love with the 18-year-old married woman Marthe, whose husband is a soldier fighting in World War I. Francois is in the middle of his adolescence, whereas Marthe is already an adult, but very lonely. This story of adultery is vividly described from the perspective of the young lover, who goes practically mad from love, in the process subjecting both his and Marthe's emotions to a kind of experimentation. The evil, seductive woman can be said to have "the devil in the flesh". Francois reflects on his behavior: "something is driving me", he believes. His rival Jacques is a soldier on the front and defending his country, whereas Francois, a spoiled boy, neither attends school nor has a job. His concerns are love, his lust, his budding bad conscience and his cruelty towards Marthe, whom he observes and describes closely.

Radiguet depicts two souls in their upward soar, their common dreams and the physical rapture of their night together. In spite of subterfuges and lies, they cannot keep their affair a secret for long. Marthe becomes pregnant, although it is unclear whether by her husband or Francois. She then dies giving birth, but only after naming the child Francois.

Discussion

Radiguet perceptively describes Francois' inner contradictions, fueled by his youthful passion, as he experiments with his and Marthe's feelings: "Happiness makes you egoistic" (Radiguet 1968, 27). Every detail of their mutual seduction is described, but Radiguet also describes this young man's own contradictory nature and fear:

> "It's not because I'm afraid," I repeated to myself. "It's only her parents and my father that are stopping me from leaning over and kissing her."
>
> But deep inside me another boy was only too pleased that such a barrier existed.
>
> "What a good thing I'm not alone with her," he thought. "For I'd be just as afraid to kiss her and would have no excuse for not doing so."
>
> Which is how the timorous deceive themselves.
>
> (Radiguet 1968, 23)

Francois acutely observes how his longing draws him to Marthe – he breaks his resolution not to visit her earlier than they had agreed; although he finds an excuse, he calls this his "weakness". He resolves not to think of her, "which naturally causes me to think of her all the more" (Ibid, 29). The fantasy level is just as important as reality – for instance, when Francois helps Marthe pick out furniture for her marital bedroom; he is certain that she will think of him, not her husband, during her wedding night.

> Like the first taste of a strange fruit, my first kiss had been something of a disappointment. We derive our greatest pleasure not from novelty but from familiarity. A few minutes later I had not only grown accustomed to Marthe's mouth – I could not do without it. And then she spoke of depriving me of it for ever.
>
> (Radiguet 1968, 41)

Although Marthe is only two years older than Francois, she is described as an "older woman". She belongs to another man. Francois' life is determined by his budding sexuality. Since he has dropped out of school, he can completely concentrate on his mood swings and inner ambivalence, examining his own thoughts, fantasies and behavior. With great candor, Radiguet presents the reflections of a 16-year-old who seeks to weave his lover into a net of passion, meanwhile realizing that he is caught in this same net. Here, there is no regulation from a peer group or parents concerned with their son's development: both parents tolerate or overlook the dangers involved, leaving the two adolescents to their own devices.

The book's tragic end corresponds to the dramatic synopsis of many daydreams. The swift switch between happiness and desperation, proximity and loneliness, greed and renunciation also encapsulates the adolescent's search for identity. The dream of losing oneself in an amorous relationship becomes a nightmare. Without the support or aid of understanding parents, without outer limits and structure, Francois and Marthe come to grief with their difficulties. The Oedipal pattern once again manifests itself at the novel's conclusion, with Francois wishing that he, not Jacques, is the father of Marthe's child. In the novel, Radiguet lets her die, the "faithless mother", symbolizing the Oedipal mother who has a sexual relationship with the father and neglects her son's wishes. Here, murderous hate against the mother becomes evident, who prefers the father and shuts out the small son. In bitter triumph, he learns that Marthe has named the child after Francois.

According to Raymond Radiguet, he based the novel on his own experiences: he also dropped out of school at 15 and fell in love with an older woman. This painful experience of separation – the theme of his novel – caused him to move to Paris and form a close relationship with Jean Cocteau.

As a third example of an artistic treatment of adolescents taking distance from their families, I will now discuss the film *Bad Taste*, a "splatter film".

Bad Taste (1987), the first film of New Zealand director Peter Jackson, is an excellent illustration of primitive modes of experience, concrete processes of splitting and fantasies of forced entry into the mother's body – in this case, fantasies come true. Since this film, Peter Jackson has become famous through his trilogy *Lord of the Rings*, also winning several Oscars.

Synopsis

A group of aliens from another star has landed in the (fictional) New Zealand coastal city of Kaihoro. Their goal is to kill everyone there and bring parts of the corpses back to their star for their intergalactic fast-food franchise. They proceed to murder all the inhabitants – brutally and with great satisfaction, slashing their bodies, bludgeoning their heads with a large hammer and pushing the brains spilling out back into the skulls.

Four agents from the New Zealand government are assigned the task of stopping these aliens. In wild orgies of violence, the aliens are mowed down with knives, tanks and automatic weapons. Through this massive use of violence, the government agents finally vanquish them.

Discussion

The special quality of this film's ironical slapstick-cruelty gave it cult status – a new genre, so to speak, since it constituted a parody of gory splatter-films. (A "splatter-film" can be described as a horror film where excessive violence and blood are the main focus, with the plot relegated to a subordinate role.) For its fans, the film attained cult status not only through its many bloody effects but also through its offbeat humor.

Peter Jackson himself plays a double role in the film – a mad scientist and an extra-terrestrial. For the film's production, masks were formed out of salted dough and baked in his mother's oven, and the weapons used were cheap toys. The film was shot with Jackson's friends on weekends between 1983 and 1987.

But how does the film connect to the working through of early emotional conflicts in adolescence? The main mechanism here consists of depicting threatening and repulsive inner images so that the viewer can experience the requisite disgust and repulsion. In this way, impulses incapable of being processed are instead projected outwards onto another person – a psychic mechanism Melanie Klein called projective identification: in this case, the protagonist's disgust is now experienced by the audience. We can assume that the objects of fear or disgust are primitive, archaic processes; when in Jackson's film victims' stomachs are slashed open and their innards spill out, he renders concrete the young child's wish to penetrate into its mother's body in order to destroy new babies there or find the father's penis it fantasizes inside her body. Since the wish to clear out the mother's body is so great, only men's bodies are shown in the film – there is not one woman. This serves to conceal the hidden aggression against the mother's body. The idea of acquiring the father's (or mother's) strength through cannibalism is realized through eating the victims' brains. The "aliens" represent that split portion of the adolescent's self which is indeed alien to him. At the same time, the adolescent can distance himself from his fears through macabre humor, reveling in the horror and terror he sees adults experiencing: he is superior to them. The fear of brain damage through masturbation is represented in the film when the inhabitants'

Psychosexual development in puberty   53

brains become diseased or broken: Giles, a collector for charities, discovers his brain is leaking out the back of his head, so he stuffs it back in and uses a hat to hold it in place. Indeed, virtually every punishment imagined in a nightmare is actively depicted in this film.

These macabre scenes are similar to the "bizarre objects" Wilfred Bion described from the fantasies of psychotic patients – objects the patients view not as products of their fantasies but as truly existing and truly persecuting them. Bion describes the difference between psychotic and non-psychotic personalities as such: 1) the preponderance of the destructive impulses are so strong that even loving impulses are affected and become sadistic; 2) hatred of reality as extended to all aspects of the psyche; 3) derived from these two points, the psychotic has an unremitting dread of imminent annihilation and fear of direct destruction; and 4) only a thin, immature relationship to other people can be established, since the psychotic's entire energy is focused on the conflicts between destructivity and sadism, incapable of final resolution (Bion 1956, 36).

In the film *Bad Taste*, all of these dimensions of the psychotic personality are embodied by the aliens, whereas the government agents represent the non-psychotic parts of the personality. The film's leitmotif is the wish to kill and annihilate all human beings, spiced with cannibalistic desires: as in Freud's book *Totem and Taboo* (1912–13), the human beings' strength accrues to the aliens when they eat their brains. There is no reality, and the alien dominates the village. Between the aliens, there is no emotional connection; the plot swerves between destruction and sadism, with the aliens finally annihilated.

In puberty, all early and primitive feelings become reawakened and accordingly threaten the ability to think. Through creative artistic depiction, they can be tamed and integrated, often with the help of the viewer's emotional processes.

In the following section, I describe two therapies with adolescents where it was possible to work through Elfi's early denial of sexuality and James' violent fantasies, opening psychic space for the development of their sexual wishes. In this sense, we can consider adolescence to be a second chance.

2.6 Adolescents in therapy

Particularities of adolescent therapy

Therapeutic work with adolescents demands a special understanding of this psychic transitional phase. The clinical setting is simple and stable; the therapy sessions always take place in the same room at a pre-arranged time. Some of the same formal elements from child therapy are also offered: paper and magic markers for drawing, perhaps also a pair of scissors, glue and a ruler. However, focus is on the spoken word.

In child analysis, the initial consultation is usually with the parents (without the child); with adolescents, this depends on the individual case. Sometimes, adolescents have contacted the therapist or a clinic, in which case they are present at the

54 Psychosexual development in puberty

initial consultation. The adolescent is asked whether meetings with the parents should be regularly held or confined to minimal exchanges of information. If the adolescent explicitly wishes no contact between therapist and parent, the therapist attempts to discuss his or her reasons for this, aiming to establish at least a written communication with the parents with the adolescent's consent.

The particular situation of adolescents – their emotional step away from the parents – often makes it difficult for them to establish a truly reliable relationship to the therapist. The urge for independence is often manifested in the adolescent skipping sessions. A wavering or damaged self-image can lead to a contrary reaction on the part of the patient, in turn demanding a careful and respectful approach. Melanie Klein speaks of the particular inhibitions and difficulties of patients in puberty (Klein, Inhibitions and Difficulties in Puberty, 1922, 54ff), since the strongly ambivalent feelings towards the father are transferred to the teacher, and the teacher becomes the object of extravagant love and admiration – but also the object of unconscious hostility and aggression. This applies to interaction not only with teachers but also with psychotherapists. The adolescent patients' skipping or tardiness from scheduled sessions raises a vexing problem for therapists, since the analyst weighs the privacy of the analytic process with the parents' help in ensuring the patient shows up. In some cases, this failure to show up or showing up too late constitutes a kind of communication. It is difficult to generalize, but I understand a patient's tardiness – even to the point of 20, 30 or 40 minutes – as a message, and then try to interpret it as such. However, it is most important to wait for the patient, even if the session ends up only lasting five or ten minutes. Important insights or developments can often emerge during this short time. If the adolescent does not show up for the entire hour without any explanation, I also wait for them at the next scheduled session, paying especially close attention to indications from the analysis as to why they were absent. If they do not show up for two sessions in a row, I contact them by text message or letter, casually mentioning their absence and asserting that I expect them at their next scheduled session. I always inform the patient from the outset that if he misses three sessions, I must inform his parents. One boy with Asperger's syndrome, who in the five-year course of his analysis often appeared exceedingly late or not at all, was able to receive my written notifications without his parents learning of them. He seemed to need my written "invitation" to his next session.

The therapist's goal – helping the adolescent to reflect on his inner conflicts and fears in a manner previously unfamiliar to him – is sometimes contradicted by the adolescent's impulse to act instead of think. Waddell describes this situation in the following way:

> Inner conflicts and anxieties are aroused, which many seek to avoid . . . some seem to stop thinking independently altogether and submerge themselves either in the shared mentality of group life, and/or in activities that can be literally mindless or self-destructive – drugs, alcohol, substance abuse, or the

often quite addictive worlds of social media . . . some may try to rely on cleverness and cognitive acquisitiveness as a mode of defence against facing and thinking about new, turbulent, and often contradictory feelings – as a way of avoiding intimacy and evading engagement.

(Waddell 2018, 115–116)

Only when this defensive system fails does an adolescent (or his parents) turn to a therapist for help. I consider it very important that the adolescent himself contacts a therapist, even if he is only doing so "because my parents want it" – in fact, even if the parents are standing next to him at the telephone. In this way, the message is conveyed that his opinion and wishes count. Even after a crisis such as attempted suicide, panic attack, self-mutilation, or disorders in eating, work and relationships, the adolescent's own insight that he wants help is central. During an assessment (usually up to four sessions), it is necessary to explore the extent of the patient's own motivation in seeking help: will he endure the requisite self-examination under the analyst's guidance and the resulting discoveries or changes this entails? Can he bear the possible discovery of his fears and ambivalence in reflection together with the analyst? Bion said that "pain is easier to bear if it can be thought" – a process of "detoxification".

The therapist must pay special attention to the feelings the young patient evokes in him (i.e., countertransference). Anderson points out that

When adolescents are assessed, professionals often find themselves in a parental type of role, in receipt of these projections. This is uncomfortable, and at times unnerving, but it also very informative, and enables them to get a feel of what is going on.

(Anderson 2000, 12)

When adolescents threaten to harm themselves, and it is difficult to avert this risk, a considerable emotional burden devolves onto the analyst. Adolescents may try to provoke or involve their therapists (as they do their parents) in their self-destructive behavior.

The patient might also perceive his attempt at self-reflection as a regression into childlike dependency.

It is particularly difficult when they are put in touch with their infantile and childhood longings. They can feel as if they have lost their often fragile grip on adulthood and collapsed back into a child world from which they will never escape. For this reason, we attach great importance to how we open a dialogue with our young patients. We try to show them that we respect their fragile sense of separation from their parents, often by asking them to contact us themselves even after they have been referred by a parent or professional.

(Anderson and Dartington 1998, 4)

56 Psychosexual development in puberty

The emphasis here is on the patients' own interest in their inner worlds and their taking responsibility for their own lives. The goal is to encourage them in discovering their own capacity for mastering life's difficulties – the privilege and burden of adolescence – rather than remaining passive victims of this phase of development and of their environment.

Freud contended that every psychological disorder finds its correspondence in the patient's psychosexuality. In analytic work with children, such psychosexual disorders are often hidden behind acute problems. Using two case studies, I will show how the various levels of the inner world can be rendered transparent and can be worked through.

Case study: Elfi

Elfi was eight years old when she came to me for analysis due to her severe emotional and learning problems. At first it was not clear whether her learning problems were caused by her emotional problems or whether she had a subnormal intelligence. She attended private school where she was the worst student, and she was initially mocked and teased as an outsider. She could not read, inventing simple stories and words instead of reading the actual letters. She was also unable to speak in complete sentences, often confused the words for he, she and it, seldom spoke and was very fearful.

Family background

Elfi was the youngest child in her family and had two older brothers; she lived with her father, a successful businessman, and her mother, who employed an au-pair girl in a large house with a garden. Behind the façade of a well-rounded family, the marriage had collapsed already several years before. The mother had emotionally withdrawn from the father, and became pregnant with Elfi due to an unplanned sexual intercourse – after this, they never had sex again; they merely lived in the same house together. However, the mother kept up this façade; the two sons took turns sleeping with their father in the marital bed, with the mother sleeping either in that son's bed, or in Elfi's room on a floor mattress. The father was very attentive to all three of his children. The mother emphasized to me that he was an excellent father. When the father had met the mother, she had been a fearful aristocratic 18-year-old who had hardly come to terms with real life. Her own mother had died when she was 10, and she had a tense relationship with her stepmother. She and her brother were attended to by various nannies. Elfi's father had taken a quasi-paternal interest in his wife before they had children, and encouraged her from the very beginning.

I will here summarize Elfi's development in analysis up until adolescence; her analysis took place three times a week.[2]

Elfi was very fearful, not confident enough at first to even touch the toys I had offered her – she always wanted me to tell her what to do (which I did not).

Her impulses and curiosity were at first totally inhibited. She kept asking which game she should play; she not only gave the impression she was unwanted and compelled to do whatever she must merely in order to be tolerated, but she also was obviously attempting to guess in advance what I expected from her. At home, she was a support for her mother, and they did everything together. Like a clown, Elfi was able to cheer her depressed mother up by telling funny stories and performing gymnastics. Concealed behind this, however, was Elfi's desperation and loneliness. She was a friendly, patient, pretty little doll, who allowed her mother to take care of her. She had no real wish to go to school, but would have preferred to remain a child in kindergarten. Nobody realized just how desperate she was.

During my periodic meetings with the parents, the mother's situation gradually became clearer. She was surprised, rather than pleased, by her third pregnancy (with Elfi). Because of her deep religious beliefs, she would not even consider the idea of an abortion, and yet on the unconscious level she rejected this unwanted child. She was a depressive personality, unhappy in her marriage and yet unwilling to change it, instead propping up the façade of a "good" family, and was barely aware of her own ambivalent feelings towards Elfi. For her part, Elfi felt responsible for her parents' bad relationship: she was profoundly convinced that her parents could get along better without her existence. Elfi's mother sees her as a cheerful, carefree child who can make her laugh. Presumably, she has never had access to her daughter's depressed, desperate feelings, so that Elfi feels rejected and misunderstood by her own mother. Elfi shares with her mother a rejection of all men: at the beginning of analysis, she didn't want to do anything together with her father. The father (who also was in psychoanalysis, unbeknownst to his wife) was attempting to reflect on Elfi in his analysis.

At the beginning, Elfi scorned all sexual thoughts and impulses. When I used words to describe her body in my interpretations, she would not listen. She considered terms such as "baby", legs and my descriptions of physical contact to be dirty. She was afraid of her own vitality. The only living being she felt close to was her beloved dog Baxi, whom she often drew pictures of and cuddled with in order to feel less lonely. Only Baxi was allowed to be vital. Nobody was meant to hear how hard her life was. She was afraid of life, of her feelings and of her sexuality. She rejected her own body, demonstrating this by casting herself as the grunting, disgusting pig when she played.

Slowly, Elfi began to trust me and revealed her situation to me through play. In role playing, I was cast as the stupid, incompetent pupil. As the little pink wooden figure, she was able to fly through the air, execute acrobatic feats and tell me what a failure my little blue figure was. I was meant to cry since I was so unhappy, whereupon she consoled me generously. Alternatively, she wanted to seduce and imprison my blue figure. I was meant to feel the fear and helplessness that she felt when she was excluded and laughed at, when nobody came to her with help. When we played, she was the strong one, with everyone listening to her words. She either accepted my interpretations of her behavior or corrected them, e.g., when she told me I should cry more and show more fear.

At other times, she made me into a doll who can only take small steps and has no ideas of her own. Then, she fed me and told me how good I was. Later, she threatened to give me away to a stranger. She showed me she felt herself an unwanted child and could accept my interpretation of this. Behind the façade of a stupid, cheerful little girl emerged her rage and hope that I could accompany her in her loneliness and desperation. She wanted to see if I would recognize the truth and discuss it with her.

In countertransference, I was often overwhelmed with the feelings Elfi projected onto me because she could not feel them: I was plagued with doubts as to whether I could truly help her, sometimes feeling I had completely failed as an analyst and had no right to ask for money to play games with a small child. Only when I wrote down my feelings of incompetence and doubt did it become clear to me that these were an exact description of Elfi's own feelings. It is as if Elfi were forbidden to use her mind. She was intelligent enough to know she was different from other children, and this knowledge made her feel angry and helpless.

She quickly exhibited considerable changes. She began to speak in complete sentences and stand up to her older brothers and wild children in her class. She stopped refusing to learn and tried to read and write as well as she could. After a year of analysis, she could convince her mother that she should come to our sessions alone after school, and was very proud of this: coming alone to me via public transportation gave her self-confidence.

Only in her second year of analysis did it become dramatically evident that Elfi did not only have great emotional problems but also a subnormal intelligence. For her parents – but also for me – it was painful to recognize that I would not be able to bring Elfi to a satisfactory academic level by working through her fears, as I had with other children in analysis. I had wished not to see my handicap – not to recognize the limits in my patients and myself. I had to dismiss my ambitions of extraordinary results in my work as an analyst, and instead work with Elfi in a realistic framework. Would I be able to help her develop her modest capacities? Elfi often surprised me with her realistic assessment of her limitations. She was the only one in her family who could call problems by their name. She once asked her father whether he still loved her mother, completely surprising him, since the two older sons did not trust themselves to pose this question.

Elfi's analysis during adolescence

Very slowly and tentatively, signs of erotic and libidinous desires began to reveal themselves in Elfi. She viewed her bodily alterations such as breast and figure development positively, but viewed her first menstruation negatively. Her mother had treated it as a sickness, taking her to the doctor. In analysis, Elfi described it vaguely; she categorically denied my attempts to put her feelings about menstruation into words. In the parental discussions, Elfi's father was able to explore this issue, but the mother did not wish to talk about it.

She began to buy her own clothes and not wear the childish things her mother had bought for her. She came to one of our sessions wearing a funny t-shirt with an owl on it, with the eyes at the precise point of her nipples, which was impossible to overlook. She wanted this attention, but also complained about boys looking closely at her breasts.

In transference, Elfi's sexual curiosity became evident. She was very interested in finding out something about my husband and family, and commented on any bodily changes she saw in me – a new haircut, a new ring that she fantasized my husband had given me. She began to see herself as my rival – an important positive sign of adolescent development. Elfi saw me as a robust maternal object who could withstand her rivalry.

Against her mother's will, but with her father's support, she bought youth magazines such as *Bravo*, *Xpress*, *Yam!* and *Hey!* with her allowance from her father. In our sessions she read me various articles and commented on them. (At the start of her analysis, she could not read.) Later, she read me personal ads for pen pals. She was only interested in girls her exact age: if they were even one or two years younger or older, she would not consider them. However, she never dared to actually write a letter.

In school, Elfi now had two good female friends she did things with together – much to her mother's chagrin, who had seen Elfi as her own girlfriend and now suffered from her absence. Although in our parent meetings the father often raised the question of whether Elfi's mother should engage in some social or charity work, this solution to her loneliness did not come to pass.

Adulation of pop stars

Elfi developed an intense adulation for pop stars such as Justin Bieber and Madonna. In her daydreams, she saw herself as Justin Bieber's girlfriend; she downloaded hundreds of photos of him from the internet and showed them to me during the session. In adolescence, the father becomes more important for the girl, and this love is deflected onto a remote star. Elfi's father was able to understand and tolerate this; he managed to assert himself against her mother. I was also an analytic mother for her, who told her: "You can have a loving relationship with a man (in fantasy, with Justin Bieber) as I do with my husband, and I allow you to be in love with your father." Elfi's father then began to go to the museum with her. During the trip there, they could sometimes talk together. He admired her appearance and was proud of what a pretty girl she had become. Elfi's mother found it difficult to further this development, tending to burden her daughter with her negative attitude towards all men and the world.

I would like to show an example of how Elfi, at the age of 14 ½, developed hope in a satisfying relationship through a long story we wrote together. It was important to let her lead me into her fantasy world. My countertransference consisted in encouraging her to develop her fantasies without taking the lead. I was glad that she was thinking about a healthy sexuality, and I helped her to discuss her sexual

60 Psychosexual development in puberty

fantasies with me – a space I offered her that she was able to use. At the beginning of one session, Elfi suggested that we write a story together, where we alternated sentence for sentence. Elfi wrote the heading, then I wrote the first sentence.

My summer holidays (story)

Analyst: This summer I went with my parents to Egypt.

Elfi: I took my pal and was glad he came. I never thought he would do it. It will be fun and nice and I hope we'll have fun.

Analyst: The first evening, there was a beach party.

Elfi: It was cool, we were silly and danced funny. It looked so strange, because we couldn't dance right and just did it somehow or other, stumbling, cool. We danced hip-hop too, since he and I go to a hip-hop dance school.

Analyst: We got very hot and we wanted to go swimming in the sea, but unfortunately we didn't have any bathing suits.

Elfi: Then we went to bed to sleep, each in his own room. I had room 3045 and he had 3047. He had a room all to himself, how unfair. We had a friendship hug and said goodnight.

To be
Continued
Tuesday
The
Bla-bla-bla
Of
Bla-bla-bla

Discussion

In this sequence from our analytic sessions, I was attempting to keep my contributions openly enough formulated to give Elfi the opportunity for expressing her wishes, hopes and fears more clearly and completely. It was important that I not bring my own ideas into the story, even if they were well-meant, and instead explore Elfi's inner world. She confided thoughts to me that she hardly dared to formulate alone. Presumably, it was easier to formulate her hope of a boy's taking interest in her in her analyst's presence, whom she fantasized being in a happy relationship. Elfi, who has problems with grammar due to her intellectual inadequacy, and thus never wanted to write (she was also reluctant to read), now wrote complete descriptive sentences for several hours – often in a fantasy grammar, but clearly comprehensible.

She could express her fantasy of bringing a "pal", showing that she finds boys and girls good for each other. She can imagine a good, happy coexistence, a healthy sexuality, and she knows that her analyst can accept this without envying her. She is interested in the budding relationship between her and the "pal", which is a good sign for her awakening vital energy, previously so inhibited.

Psychosexual development in puberty   61

With her last lines, Elfi shows her wish to continue the story in our next session. At this point she still needs her analyst at her side to think these thoughts and feel these feelings. The next day (she was coming to me three times a week) she started continuing the story. Since she had written the concluding sentence in the previous session, she requested me now to write the first sentence.

Analyst: We went to sleep exhausted, sank completely into our memories of the dancing, and I had a dream:

Elfi: . . . that our friendship would last forever, and that it would be more than a friendship. (Smiley)

Analyst: I was very excited and woke up with my heart beating: What would happen today?

Elfi: I got up sleepily, it was exactly 7:00. I ran out of my hotel room and crept into my pal's hotel room, because he had forgotten to lock his door.

Analyst: My pal was still in bed, fast asleep. His brown arms and legs were all stretched out.

Elfi: And his face was so sweet, he lay there so cute. I didn't even want to wake him up, but I couldn't help it, I was too excited what was going to happen today.

Analyst: How should I wake him up? Should I whisper something in his ear? Tickle him? Call his name? I thought about it for a long time and looked at him closely.

Elfi: Yes, exactly, I shook him first, then I tickled him – he's very ticklish, and he began squirming and giggling.

Analyst: I tickled him and began to laugh myself when I saw him squirming.

Elfi: He said: "Let me sleep." I said: "No, aren't you excited about what we're going to do today?" When he heard that, he jumped up and was embarrassed, since he only had a pair of long underwear on that was very sweet. It said on the long underwear: I love you, and I love you too and lots of faces and hearts and I laughed.

Analyst: He blushed when I looked at him so lovingly. Then he looked at his long underwear and didn't know what he should do. He ran quickly into the bathroom.

Elfi: He took his clothes and locked the door and got dressed. Then he came out and was still blushing. He said to me: "Sorry, that you saw me that way." I said: "Doesn't matter, it was a sweet long underwear. Besides, I see my brothers walking around in their underwear."

To be

Continued

Tomorrow

At 3.

Sure enough. (Smiley)

Discussion

In the second session we write together, Elfi exhibits far more confidence. She had been looking forward to continuing the story and immediately went to take the pad of paper out of the drawer it was in.

Elfi projects her feelings of embarrassment onto the boy in the story: he is ashamed of his "cute" long underwear, and she is the one on top of things, who has seen her brothers in their long underwear. She is interested in the boy's body, she touches and tickles him, and this gives her a good feeling – but she finds it easier when I am participating in the story. I attempt not to intrude any substantive points into the plot, but to investigate her feelings and encourage her to express them. She shows very clearly that she enjoys expressing this fantasy of being together with a "pal", which gives hope for her development. Clearly, I should not disturb this fantasy through offering interpretations, lest she break off her fantasizing.

In countertransference, I am glad for Elfi's story, and afraid that she will break off if I interpret it. Elfi and her story manage to retain their lively quality without becoming too "heavy". This entails a delicate balance between exploring sexual fantasies further and not being intrusive. I had the impression of allowing Elfi, like a shy animal, to leave her psychic retreat and to investigate the free world of fantasy, thus exposing herself to the world. It was possible to let her experience together with her analyst what it is like to playfully sketch out an erotic experience with a boy. This playful experience gives hope for Elfi's later imagining a loving relationship to a boy.

In the next session, Elfi immediately proceeds to her drawer and takes out the pad of paper. She first reads the story out loud, correcting some mistakes she notices, and then hands me the pad. We are meant to alternate sentences as before, continuing the story. She begins, saying: "It's your turn."

Analyst: He says: "What should we do now? Do you want to have breakfast or just go to the beach?"

Elfi: Let's have a big breakfast. He says: "OK, let's go eat something and see who gets there first".

Analyst: Both of them start off . . .

Elfi: Later after breakfast, Felix discovers a path. He discovers eight water slides, and they're supercool and dangerous. Beside that was a beach with banana boats, surfboards and water-skiers.

Analyst: He shows her everything you can do on a beach. She says: "This is a REAL water paradise; I didn't see that yesterday. Where should we begin?"

Elfi: He says: "Let's start with the slides, they are super. Oh God, you're right, the slides with a U-shape are super". They slide together and had a lot of fun. They both had a strange feeling while they were sliding. Felix said:

Analyst: "Super. While I slide I have such an exciting feeling in my body. Let's slide again".

Elfi: "I also have such a funny feeling but kind of unpleasant but also fun. Let's slide three times more and then go on to another slide".

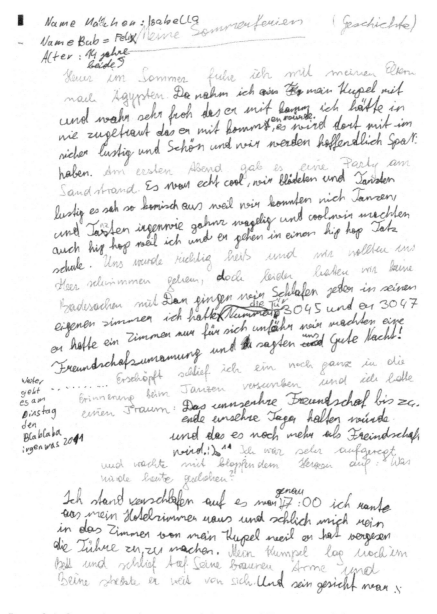

Figure 2.1 Original text: beginning of the story Elfi wrote with her analyst

Discussion

Elfi is concerned with the question of whether she will be able to find a partner who will care for her lovingly. In her story, Felix wants to do the same things she does. When the analyst describes the connections, Elfi is willing to develop the

64 Psychosexual development in puberty

story further. Her sexual fantasy finds a locus in the story's water slides. Sliding or falling in water signify sexual excitement and touching, something both adolescents in the story are enjoying. Her analyst develops this story together with her, thus helping Elfi to describe her healthy sexuality and wishes: she examines what she and Felix can do together, and enjoys experiencing something together with a boy, a cause for hope. The analyst grants her the freedom to express and explore her unconscious wishes. She is cautious and I am too – to not over-interpret, so that she will not interrupt her train of fantasy thought. Elfi's involvement in the story is palpable. At the end of the story, Felix and the girl go into the deep water and the girl hurts her foot, perhaps bitten by an animal – but for a few short moments, Elfi's image of a satisfying, happy sexual relationship became manifest.

Elfi's normal, healthy idea of taking center stage sexually, relegating her parents to the periphery, also causes her unease. The question of "who will take care of my mother?" arises, causing her to feel guilty. Her father will not take care of her mother, since he no longer loves her. Is Elfi allowed to be happy? Apparently, Elfi finds it a relief to think I have a husband and family: I will be able to let go of her, not clinging to her as her mother does.

This development of her sexual fantasy is all the more remarkable since for years, Elfi immediately put her hands over her ears every time I used "sexual" words: even the word "baby" she scorned, and she only hinted shamefully at her first menstruation. She often implied certain things, which I then put into more concrete language for her, but she still refused to discuss them. In her story, she is the one who introduced and developed the erotic level. Elfi can imagine developing like her older brothers, who both have a sexual relationship. Sex could be as fun as her beloved water slides. Can she be allowed happiness when her mother leads such a limited life without sex? It is as if I am empowering her to develop her adolescent longings like a flower that is slowly opening. She is now also able to clothe her body so that it is attractive – an expression of her new physical positive self-consciousness. This example of analytic containment is meant to show how important it is for children to compensate in analysis for lack of containment by their parents.

But Elfi also has a critical "Greek chorus" that seeks to discourage her, keeping her small and dependent. On her holidays, when her mother does not allow her to visit her friends, she stays in her pajamas all day, either in bed or with her mother.

In the following session, I would like to show what kind of feelings arise during transference and countertransference.

A session in May:

Elfi: is already waiting for me in front of the door. She enters, walking slowly to the couch, and is silent.
Analyst: What did you bring me? (I take my chair and sit by her next to the couch.)
Elfi: It's the same thing. I don't understand anything. (Long pause)
Analyst: Was it especially difficult today?

Psychosexual development in puberty 65

Elfi: (gazes sorrowfully in front of her)

Analyst: Can you give me an example?

Elfi: (is silent. She seems to bear an infinite burden. She begins to speak, then stops.) No.

Analyst: Maybe you can give an example of something you didn't understand?

Elfi: I won't say hardly anything, because I have nothing to say. I'm just tired. (She lies down.)

Analyst: It is really terrible when you think all your thoughts are wrong.

Elfi: (is silent)

Analyst: You can't talk at all, because everything is so awful.

Elfi: It's getting worse and worse. There's no hope for me. (She sits up again.)

Analyst: (I also have tears in my eyes and would like to weep with her or take her in my arms. She seems so lonely and lost, she has such a hopeless, desperate facial expression.) It is difficult to be alone with these thoughts. You must have never told anyone about them, but instead tried to act cheerful.

Elfi: Yes. (is silent)

Analyst: It feels very good when you share them with me. Do you think I take you seriously and understand you?

Elfi: Yes. In gym class I couldn't hold onto the rings. We were supposed to put our legs in the rings. I couldn't do that and I was stuck there, it hurt.

Analyst: It's hard for you to hold on and feel your strength. You don't know whether your strength is blocked or if it's not enough. Do you have hope sometimes?

Elfi: There's no way out for me.

Analyst: Then it's especially sad that you have no session this Friday since I cancelled.

Elfi: It's always the same. I don't feel anything. (in a very quiet voice)

Analyst: You think it's painful for me too when I see how much you are hurt and how sad you are. You think Daddy and Mommy don't want to hear anything about your desperation. For a long time you couldn't talk about it, since you were convinced I didn't want to hear about it either.

Elfi: Yes. (Pause) It hurts so much. (She looks deeply into my eyes.)

End of session

Discussion

Elfi feels emotionally finished, almost dead inside. But when she recognizes – with her analyst's help – that she is going through a difficult phase, she finds respite. She is able to bring her desperation to me in the session and experience that I really listen to her and want to know how she feels. I am someone who can tolerate her when she feels so terrible. She assumes I do not believe that she is finished and hopeless, but that she is capable of development – and this is indeed the case. She has developed into a very pretty, lively young girl who is curious

66 Psychosexual development in puberty

and interested in music, stars and films. She is intelligent enough to know that she is at the lower end of achievement among her classmates. She knows she is not like the other children – which she sometimes takes to mean she is nothing, and then hates herself. The abilities she does have do not seem to count for her, and this means she robs herself of the possibilities she actually would have. This constitutes a form of secondary deprivation – a terrible feeling. When Elfi observes her mother, she sees her as just as unhappy and finished. Is the image of her analyst one of a woman full of life, who lives out her sexuality, and also has the hope and trust that Elfi will be able to embark on a loving relationship to a man? The melancholy session described previously suggests grieving: if Elfi is able to grieve for what she cannot have, this shows that she has inner powers. Her permanent fatigue indicates a depressed state; she identifies with her mother. If she can remain in inner contact to me as someone who feels good about her, who trusts her to accomplish something, this makes her feel better. But this belief in her potency and power exists only during analysis. Can she internalize the image of her analyst? Can she develop these qualities in herself?

In countertransference, it is important that the analyst not follow the impulse to avoid this psychic pain and desperation – not to console Elfi instead of accompanying her on her painful path of self-knowledge, but at the same time not to give up hope in the analytic work. When the analyst allows herself to be emotionally touched by Elfi's desperation, take it up and put Elfi's feelings into words, this is a bigger burden on the analyst than merely crying with her or consoling her.

How important this shared experience was is demonstrated by developments in the following weeks. Elfi is in a good mood, has a crush on a boy and arranges things so that he calls her up on her cell phone during one of our sessions. However, when he does this, she is so afraid that she immediately hangs up and hides her phone. In the following sessions, Elfi takes the initiative in cheerfully sharing her exhaustive knowledge of stars and singers. She shows me 100 photos of Justin Bieber in many poses she has downloaded from the internet. She begins cautiously to speak of her budding longing and interest in boys.

In the following session, Elfi let me see behind her façade of the cheerful, stupid girl, allowing me to accompany her in her loneliness and deep desperation. She wanted to see if I would see the truth or – like her mother – console her away from her feelings and pacify her. In truth, this was a painful session, one moving to me too: it was not easy to retain my analytic attitude.

(This session took place on a Friday.)

Elfi: enters, inspecting me attentively, notices my red fingernails and my fresh hairdo. She asks me appreciatively: "How are you?" After a pause, she says, "As usual, you won't answer that."

Analyst: You look at me closely and think things you don't want to share with me.

Elfi: (She takes the pad of paper out of her drawer and sits down at the table. For a long time, she inspects the name of the film she wrote there in larger letters:

Psychosexual development in puberty   67

BREATHLESS. In the previous session, she told me about it in detail. The film is about a boy who sees the picture of a kidnapped two-year-old boy in the internet, and also sees another picture which shows how that boy would look today. This picture looks like a portrait of him. He finds out that he was in fact kidnapped from his parents as a boy, and when he tries to find them he learns that they are dead. In the following sessions, she was able to talk about her fantasy of being the child of other parents – parents who were cheerful and do things with one another.) After a bit, I say that she is looking at the title of the film for a long time and is remembering our discussion. Pensively, she asks how it would be if she lived somewhere else.

Analyst: Perhaps you sometimes wonder what it would be like if you lived with me and my husband to see how we are with each other, what that would feel like.

Elfi: Then I would be much older. (This refers to our age difference.) As she speaks, she writes the following words: "I don't want to come here all my life." After she stops speaking, she writes other words I am unable to read. When I ask what she is writing, she turns the pad to me so that I can read it: "For a long time, I haven't wanted to come here – thank God I have my friends. NOTHING HELPS."

Analyst: (I read this aloud and she comments that it is written in "killer-letters". I experience a strong countertransferential reaction, feel excluded, rejected, become irritated and sad.) When you give me that to read, you want to show me how it is to be unwanted. You don't want to come to therapy but instead to my house, to see how I live.

Elfi slowly writes on: I don't want to have to come. Why? It doesn't help and is a waste of time and money. If I don't want to come, why do I have to? My friends don't want me to come here.

Analyst: You want me to understand how it is to feel unloved and a nuisance. Maybe you sometimes think how it is when a child feels unwanted by its parents.

Elfi: (strong reaction, looks at me in surprise) How can you read my most secret thoughts? (Then she shakes her head.)

After a short pause I continue: You are showing me how surprised you are that I recognize your most secret thoughts and understand you are asking yourself if you are an unwanted child.

She nods musingly.

Analyst: And then you are afraid how it would be when you wouldn't come any-more and nobody would recognize that, and you ask yourself how you would survive without our sessions.

In large letters, she writes: YOUR BIG CHANCE and asks me to spell it.

Analyst: (I tell her she is expressing that our sessions are a big chance for her to understand more about herself, express her feelings and be understood.) You want to see whether I have hope for you that you can develop further and are capable of thinking.

Elfi: My development has nothing to do with here, it's just my development. (She says this without conviction.)

Analyst: You are torn between your father's opinion that analysis helps you and your mother's opinion that it doesn't.

Elfi (very clearly): Yes, that's true!

Analyst: You are glad that your sessions here are not yet over. Even when it is painful, we can look the painful truth together in the face.

When Elfi leaves, she looks at me thankfully.

Discussion

In this session, it was very moving to gain insight into two central topics in place of the denial and defense I so often encountered. One topic is her secret thought – her knowledge – that she is deeply rejected by her mother, who only decided to have Elfi because of religious scruples. This rejection is particularly burdensome for the child, since it was never clearly formulated and nevertheless determines her life. Any child can stand a painful truth when it is possible to talk about it; trying to prettify it doubles the emotional burden. The second topic is experiencing together the desperation that is projected onto the analyst. When suppressed or secret aggressions can be revived and interpreted in transference, there is a basis for hope. In transference, the analyst must be able to psychically bear the feeling of rejection, to "emotionally digest" it and then put it into words. In this way, the patient experiences how a projection of psychic pain can be transformed into understanding, which then can be reintrojected into the child as his own feeling. Through this process of transformation, grief can be felt together. Emphatic rejection and the state of being unwanted are projected onto me – I feel the massive rejection under which she suffers her whole life and which oppresses her. Being able to bear this painful feeling and reflecting on it made it possible to detoxify it and return it as a thought, so that she can also reflect on it. The point is to show Elfi – through her experience with me – that it is possible to feel rejected at the moment. She can then take her projections back and see them as belonging to her. She is surprised and shocked that I can speak about her problems and her secret wishes. Then her fear becomes evident – the fear that she (like her mother) can never go out and lead her own life. She longs for love and for a real boy. Will I allow her to have a boyfriend? Does she have the confidence for one?

I suggest that she switch from the child therapy room to the room for adults. Elfi agrees immediately and can hardly wait. She wishes to bring only a few of her materials – only the pad of paper and colored pens. She examines the new room. When I interpret that she wants to leave her childhood behind and become an adult, she says, the best thing is being an adolescent:

Elfi: It's boring being a child, when you're grownup you have to work and slave away and take care of kids. A teenager can go to parties. (Pause) When you earn money yourself, you can get your wishes. I want to buy a dog.

Psychosexual development in puberty 69

Elfi begins to trust herself enough to have a crush on a real boy, as can be seen in this excerpt from a session:

Elfi takes her pad and draws: I (heart) him.

Analyst: You want to make me curious who "he" is.

Elfi: His name is Marcel, his parents are from France. I've had a crush on him for six months already. But I spoke to him once in the streetcar. He sat next to me when everyone got out. From outside, he drew a heart and wrote my name. I was so excited that I wanted to get up and leave.

Analyst: You are very happy that you can speak to me about him and know everything will be kept in confidence here. What do you like about him?

Elfi: He is beautiful inside and outside. Five people already know. . . . I knocked down a boy who called me fat. I'm really proud of that.

Analyst: You are happy you can defend yourself.

Elfi is afraid of her feelings, but now has the confidence to resist her impulse to run away. She has enough trust in her analyst to speak about this. At the same time, she expresses her wish to stop analysis. She thinks that ending analysis means growing up. At the same time, she is overwhelmed by strong feelings of being in love: she feels dizzy and stays home for two days. She can relate her experience with Marcel, but not yet reflect what it means to her, how glad and fearful she is. She talks as if she is lovesick. She rejects my interpretation; she would rather be physically ill, since the mother is constantly speaking of physical illness. Elfi is actually sick from longing; Marcel says he likes her, but nothing has happened yet. She is skeptical as to whether her mother will allow her to be loved. Marcel is affectionate and attentive, just as she finds her analyst to be. She links her adolescent transition to the question of whether I will allow her to leave me. Do I trust her to master her life without analysis? Her wish to end analysis also has a manic quality – as if she could relinquish all the powers that hold her back, leaving them with me.

Her adolescent development in the direction of independence expresses itself in missing sessions. She begins to dress better and also looks better; she has a positive self-image of her body and is able to move in a relaxed way. She has a well-developed sense of reality and can accurately assess her own (intellectually very modest) achievement. For me it is also important to recognize and accept the real limit posed by her handicapped intelligence, even given the progress she has made. With great effort and daily tutoring, she manages to graduate from the non-academic high school. In analysis sessions, however, she is hardly obtuse; she can empathize very well with other people, observe fashion models and identify their differences to her own body. Unlike her mother, she no longer allows herself to fall into depression. Through her identification with her analyst, she is able to develop a positive self-image and formulate her wishes (she wants to work with animals or plants). Nevertheless, there remains an inner voice that seeks to oppress her wishes. Her relationship to her father – whom she earlier rejected

70 Psychosexual development in puberty

entirely – is improving, and they go to museums together. The father finds it difficult to speak with her on a simple level. The mother, who was massively against Elfi's analysis, is able to say to me at the end: "It did help, thank you!"

Case study: James Frost

I will describe this second case study of an adolescent in psychic crisis not from the therapist's perspective but from his teacher's, who played an essential role in James' recovery. This demonstrates how important a psychoanalytically trained teacher can be – as a supplement to therapeutic help – in accompanying the troubled adolescent. But first, a digression to explain this concept of the "psychoanalytically trained" teacher.

The teacher H. took a Master's degree in the "Psychoanalytic Observational Studies" offered at the University of Klagenfurt, which was developed according to the Tavistock model in London. The goal of this course was to acquire a psychoanalytic attitude and understanding, characterized by an openness in observation, reflection on the interactions between pupils and teachers. Here, emphasis is not on conscious but rather on unconscious motives, wishes and fears of students and teachers. Since unconscious processes are not accessible to direct observation or conscious control, they require special methods to be investigated: the course trains its participants in sensitivity to the detection of unconscious processes in the observer and in other persons in the pedagogical field. The goal is to understand which feelings from earlier relationships a child unconsciously projects onto his teacher ("transference") or other persons, and which feelings are evoked in the teacher ("countertransference"). I will now briefly describe these methods, which are discussed in more detail in Bick (1964), Bion (1962), Miller et al. (1989) and Diem-Wille and Turner (2012).

This course of studies is based in three modes of teaching experience-oriented learning (Bion 1962): the method of psychoanalytic observation (in three different fields), the reflection on the teacher's own way of teaching in "Work Discussion Groups" and the study of psychoanalytic theory. Students practice Esther Bick's mode of psychoanalytic observation in their first semester in a kindergarten, whereas in semesters two through four a particular baby is closely observed one hour per week in the context of its family, and in the fifth semester interactions and unconscious fears are closely observed in an educational institution one hour per week. These unstructured observations of interactions, as well as the feelings evoked in the observer, are then recorded in detail in written form. In a seminar held by a psychotherapist, hypotheses are formed concerning the conscious and unconscious psychic processes of the persons observed. Using further observations, the hypotheses can be modified or further developed, so that the forming of the baby's personality until its first birthday is thoroughly observed. This simple but brilliant method enables understanding of early, archaic feelings, dependence, longing for protection and love as well as the child's fears of losing its way. The group collects, describes and reflects on various experiences of a baby's early interactions in her family, the child in kindergarten and teachers with each other.

In Work Discussion Seminars, the participants attempt to describe and reflect on concrete scenes from their pedagogical practice. This reflection enables the participants to detect deeper layers in the personality and ameliorate their negative effects, while exploiting their productive and creative potential. The situation of James Frost (as dubbed by his teacher H.) was discussed both in the Work Discussion Groups and later in an individual supervision (Rustin and Bradley 2008).

I have already described in detail teacher H.'s pedagogical experience with James in his first two years in my book *Latency* (2018). Here, I will summarize this experience in order to continue on to James' psychosexual inner conflicts and their treatment. In conclusion, I describe teacher H.'s continuing help for James during his puberty years. I would like to particularly focus on the psychoanalytic attitude informing H.'s pedagogical practice, while retaining a clear distinction to therapy. In her dealings with James' parents and grandmother, H. could make a clear case for private therapeutic help, so that James then also entered psychotherapy.

James' family and school background

James' parents separated when he was three. We know nothing of his early contact with his father, but by the time James entered school, there was no more contact. He had a very close relationship to his mother; she essentially clung to him, allowing James to sleep in the marital bed until she (when James was seven) entered into a new relationship. James was very jealous of his new stepfather and tried to provoke him. When his mother told him that she was expecting a new baby, he flew into a rage, taking a kitchen knife and trying to attack his mother. His stepfather, however, was able to take the knife away from James and protect his wife. James' maternal grandmother then offered to take James to live with her and the grandfather.

At the age of ten, James graduated from grade school to the (non-academic) secondary school. After half a year, he had a violent outburst. After a quarrel, he attacked a fellow student and tried to strangle him. When a teacher intervened, James attacked him as well. The police were called and James was sent to a psychiatric ward, where he remained for five months, a dreadful experience for him: he threatened suicide if he were ever put into a psychiatric ward again. At that time, he could accept psychotherapy for a while. However, he soon broke it off and refused to see a psychiatrist.

Due to his emotional and social problems, he was deemed to require "special pedagogical support"; for such children, a supplementary educational teacher is assigned to the class. In James' class, H. filled this role for five children in James' situation.

Discussion

This initial information on James' early years of life indicates that the roots of his psychic problems may lie in those very years. He seems not to have experienced himself as a person separate from his mother. Presumably he was convinced that his omnipotent fantasies of completely possessing his mother had come to pass, since he was the only man in the family and he slept in the same bed with her. In a ordinary family, these child wishes fail to become reality since the mother and father are seen as a sexual pair, and consequentially a healthy separation from the children comes to pass. When James' mother took up a new relationship, he was seven. Suddenly and without his participation, he was cruelly driven from the marital bed. We are not familiar with the details of his inner world, since we have no data from his therapeutic or psychiatric diagnosis. His inability to experience himself as his own person led to a psychotic episode, causing his violent outbreak and his admission to a psychiatric ward.

The solution of moving to his grandmother's was on the one hand helpful, since he was removed from the new family situation that had so infuriated him, but on the other hand, his rage and desperation seem to have only increased: now, he was not only a fatherless child, but also a son who had suddenly – and, as he perhaps felt, definitively – lost his fantasized position by his mother. From his perspective, he was truly "abandoned".

When the seminar group reflected on whether H. should commit herself to helping James, it became clear that this would only be possible if James' massive psychic problems could be treated through psychotherapy.

Summary of psychoanalytic-pedagogical aid for James until puberty

The point of departure in the Work Discussion Group[3] here for discussing James was his refusal to attend school, which H. had also discussed with James' grandmother. Since H. was the only person James would talk to, she visited him at home with his grandparents. She was surprised that he was willing to speak with her, established eye contact and told her many things about himself. Shortly after her visit, another escalation occurred: James attacked his grandmother with a knife. Since he refused to go to a psychiatric hospital and also threatened suicide, his mother and stepfather decided to take him back. The close contact between the mother and H., who called her daily to report James' failure to attend school, constituted an important support (containment) for the mother. In the Work Discussion Group, participants reflected on possibilities for affording access to school for James. His teacher H. suggested to the mother that James could send in his three assignments via email, and James not only accepted but sent in the assignments three days later. They all received As, and this enabled him to graduate that year. He was allowed to choose the subjects of these assignments, and they demonstrated the turbulence of his inner world. His biology paper was about sharks, his history paper was about Pompeii and his geography paper was about volcanos. To everyone's surprise, James appeared at school for the graduation ceremony.

In the following school year, James attended class and did well academically. He was often ill, with strong headaches, bladder infections and colds. Whenever he felt he could not stand being in class, he was allowed to leave. He was often emotionally incapable of fulfilling the assignments, instead laying down his head on the desk. H. managed – often through unconventional means – to motivate him to do his schoolwork: for instance, in drawing class, where he professed to do "nothing", she encouraged him to draw the work "nothing" (Figure 2.2). The drawing was then given an A and hung up for viewing (Diem-Wille 2018, 104). H. was always available for a talk with James and maintained close contact to his mother. The stepfather took a close interest in James; they did sports together, and the stepfather even went with the class when they went hiking and climbing, making it easier for James to participate.

James as an adolescent

James' condition is much improved, yet he experiences mood swings and depressed feelings. Just as with disturbed young children, James finds physical contact threatening; he can hardly maintain eye contact, not only with his parents but also with H., who often feels she must be careful not to come too close to him. He avoids physical proximity and shrinks back when someone approaches him too closely.

Figure 2.2 James' drawing: NIGGS (NICHTS)

74   Psychosexual development in puberty

When overwhelmed by intense feelings, he cannot concentrate on his task and often must leave the room. Since James has already tried once to strangle another student, it is important to give him the chance to physically remove himself from the class. One of H.'s important tasks is to make her fellow teachers understand that James' withdrawn behavior is neither a sign of disinterest nor a rejection of the teacher, but instead expresses his desperation and unhappiness. His resistance to learning is linked to an inner pressure that floods him with images or affects. There are other times when James can work well for hours; he is actually a very fine student.

Now an excerpt from a Work Discussion paper:

> Today, James is working in shop/crafts class in an exemplary fashion. He accepts suggestions, asking what to do with the piece he is making. He can bear my physical closeness. He looks in my eyes as I approach him and I think he shows interest. He does not shrink away when my fingers touch his as we must hold the piece tightly. He listens attentively when I give him instructions about how to use the tool, and then tries to follow my instructions. James seeks my gaze and seems to expect my confirming nod. There is no friction between the boys, they are well-motivated and are pleased with how the work is proceeding. . . . We compare the pieces the boys have made and I praise various aspects of them. . . . The two hours go by quickly, and James works without being made to do so.

Discussion

H. seems surprised that James now works independently, without being pressured to do so. He makes contact on his own initiative by looking at her. Although he ordinarily avoids body contact, he can now tolerate the teacher's fingers touching him. This constitutes a huge step in development, yet it is often astonishing how casually such a development manifests itself after a long period of struggle. Letting himself be touched symbolically expresses that he feels emotionally touched by H. and has developed trust. His rock-solid conviction that he is unwanted, has been abandoned by his father and removed from his family has been supplanted by a cautious confidence. It is of great significance that James once again is living at home with his mother, stepfather and brother, and feels accepted by his family.

James has altered greatly in his outward appearance. Instead of black clothes, he now has a light grey pair of pants on with a black-blue-white sweater. In the last two years, he has grown 13 cm and looks well – athletic and energetic of gait. James' development is nevertheless not as straightforward as it might seem from reading these examples. In spite of all the positive developments, dangerous affects are lurking in the background, with their peaks and valleys. In the Work Discussion Group, the participants hypothesize what massive aggressions James must be fighting against when he refuses to cooperate or lays his head on the desk. The group suggests encouraging James to work on the assignments that correspond to his feelings, without grading them. In German class, the students are asked to describe the feelings of a person depicted in a picture they are shown. James at first refuses to participate until H. asks him to simply write whatever occurs to him, which he does hesitantly. H. is shocked by the result. James describes the pictures of two persons whose feelings are meant to be identified by the students.

The first picture is a young man in rage.

The first question is: what is this person feeling?

James writes the following answer: I would say she is furious, but since I couldn't care less about this whole fucking feeling soup, I just say SMD! (author: suck my dick!)

The second question is: What has happened to make this person feel that way?

James: SMD

Third question: What is this person saying?

James: SMD

The second picture:

Fourth question: What can we do to make this person feel better?

James: Kick her in the ass, wipe out her whole generation, spray sulphuric acid in her eyes, rub shit in her hair! And then we drown her in her own blood! Because I can shit!!

The third assignment is to write an "Inner Monologue".

James writes:

A small kitten . . .

Meow! I've been waiting a half an hour for my mother! And then she comes to me with the excuse that she's hungry too! Oh! Finally she brings me a bowl of food. Meow! That tasted good. Oh! Wasn't that a dragonfly out there? Maybe I can catch it! A delicious dessert wouldn't hurt me. Hm – it got away! Oh well, I'll climb up the tree there, I will find some insects up there. Mhm! There are indeed! A fly, a spider and a beetle! Oh my God! My mom is coming. Why is she always worried when I climb up a tree? No thanks, I'm full and don't want to get down yet! Puh, she's going back down . . . but maybe too soon the all clear? Now she's coming back with the ladder . . . one level higher, and I'm already out of reach! Haha! . . . Well, it is higher than I thought, but finally I am on top. She has an extension for the ladder?! Super! Why do I have to get down now? Probably she doesn't want me to stay outdoors when it's getting dark. But never mind, I'll lie down in front of the fireplace.

Discussion

Here, we see a split between James' murderous aggression, murderous "shit" and thoughts of blood and death on the one hand, and his longing on the other hand. In his essay, he is the kitten whose mother is looking after him. H.

76 Psychosexual development in puberty

promised James she would keep his assignment private so that he could freely write what he felt, untrammelled and uncensored. It was quite disturbing for her to read what he wrote, and by implication the emotional baggage he constantly carried with him. An accompanying therapy is essential for enabling James to speak about his threatening aggressive fantasies, to act them out in play and work through them. H. did not speak about James' assignment with him, since she was neither willing nor able to assume any therapeutic position. However, she managed to understand what James was struggling with behind his passivity.

In the same lesson, James was the little kitten fed by his mother and brave enough to climb up the high tree. The kitten had a caring mother who wanted him in the house by dark. Later we learn that James has two cats at home. When the teacher asks if he has photos of his cats, he answers: "I have hundreds! The whole wall is full of cat photos."

At school, James managed to improve his capacity for showing his friendly side, and we can assume that the therapist has succeeded in working through and newly ordering his dark and threatening feelings in therapy. Now, another excerpt from a subsequent Work Discussion transcript:

> For the first time, James has had no absences – on the contrary: he actively participates in class, takes up social contact to his fellow students, and does not draw attention to himself in any untoward way as far as I can see.
>
> His clothing is currently mostly dark or black, but his behavior seems to be anything but dark: he laughs, moves around in an unfettered way (at least that's my impression) and with youthful grace. In the breaks . . . he jokes with G., I., St. and occasionally also with another boy. He pays no attention to girls yet.
>
> He even seems to like gym class, which he had formerly avoided. Although the games could make him aggressive due to their competitive character and the boys' roughhousing, James does not fall out of the picture when he is in the middle of it. He also accepts the referee's decisions without reacting particularly.
>
> For the last two weeks, he shows up at school extremely punctually. Before, you could set your watch from James: exactly 8:00 when he walked in the door, and without a hint of hurry . . . he would leisurely take his shoes and jacket off. Often he was right behind the teacher herself. But the last two weeks, he came 15 minutes before class began. In his homeroom, he takes his seat and participates in conversations with friends. I can't escape the impression that James has grown into the community . . . he accomplishes assignments swiftly and without dawdling, without distracting himself through chattering. Until recently, he was easily distracted.
>
> In the last two drawing classes, the students were asked to collect ideas for a bizarre object. James doesn't seem able to concentrate on one bizarre object – he pasted five different little montages together on his paper. In my opinion, they do not reflect a peaceful inner world: one picture shows Gulliver

with the dwarves, attacked by a chainsaw . . . but laughing, absurdly. Underneath this there is a wooden stamp with the large black letters DEPORT. At the lower right, there is a cartoon figure who is being shot down by a machine gun. The combination of images chilled me, I don't get a good feeling looking at them. They are in diametrical opposition to James' behavior and the aura I feel around him. They make me think twice, and make me anxious.

Discussion

At first it is obvious how happy H. is over James' progress. She is almost proud that he can appear punctually for class, has friends and has integrated himself well into the class. His academic achievement was always good, and therefore does not get special attention here. However, H. is disturbed when James' creative work reveals dark, aggressive and destructive feelings. And yet we can interpret this positively: James now has the confidence to show his destructive fantasies in his work, especially appropriate to a collage. Melanie Klein (1944) and Hanna Segal (1952, 1991) further developed Freud's thought that artistic depiction constitutes a liberation from tensions in our psyche (Freud 1908a, 223). In a satisfying artistic expression, the artist is able to deal with his inner destructive and harmful objects and seek an artistic solution that constitutes a reparation for the damaged object. The conscious and unconscious confrontation with psychic pain, ugliness and death in the artist's inner world leads to a reparation and thus to aesthetic experience. Important burdensome themes for the artist, which often cannot be expressed in words, are expressed artistically. I would also understand and interpret James' collage piece as a form of artistic expression.

Revealing feelings creatively in drawing class is very helpful for James, even if it disturbs his teacher. The image of a young man tied to the ground by dwarves and threatened by a large chainsaw is supplemented by a picture pasted over this, showing three soldiers with a machine gun. The title "Born to be Wild" presumably expressed an aspect of James' feeling for life: he has long missed his protecting family and become "wild". The stamp with "DEPORT" can be an indication of his "deportation" to his grandparents, as well as his own father's outcast status. We see that James can now express his feelings in quite a normal fashion; he no longer employs explosive psychotic part objects centering around murder and feces, but instead uses socially acceptable modes of representation.

The teacher accepts James' collage. How do his fellow classmates react? Are they as disturbed as H.? As can be seen in the transcript:

> At the beginning of drawing class, the "bizarre objects" are hung on the wall. At first, the "audience" members try to interpret them. After this, each artist explains. The students find James' dark, bloodthirsty picture witty; they laugh at the soldiers, one of whom is in his underwear. They pay no attention to the title "Born to be Wild". Homer – the cartoon character – can't be shot down anyway, as they astutely observe. All in all, James' work is received with mirth.

78 Psychosexual development in puberty

When I question him, James says he was not thinking of anything in particular when he chose the photos and combined them for his collage. I don't let him off the hook and ask who is holding the chainsaw. Could it be an instrument of liberation? Or is one of the dwarves using it? James says no to all my suggestions. When the class is completely still, since they are all waiting for the answer, he says laughingly: "It's just sticking in his neck!" It seems to me the boys in the class are laughing at this, too. "What does the stamp mean? Is it a stamp for the man?" I ask. "I found it, and since I couldn't think of anything else, I pasted it on," says James. "Is it supposed to do something to the person?" I insist. James reflects, hanging his head to the side. "No, I couldn't think of anything." I do not wish to attribute too much importance to James' work, and thus enter an A into my book and turn the class' attention to another work.

Discussion

The students cope with the unconscious content of violence and threat by laughing. With their laughing, they defend themselves from the threatening aggression and destruction that they sometimes also experience themselves. We can also speculate what James is expressing with the phallic aggression of soldiers shooting and fighting, which interests all male adolescents to a lesser or greater extent. For the first time in school, James can answer his teacher's questions – before, he would just shrug his shoulders mutely and avoid eye contact. Rather naively, H. expected him to be able to articulate the unconsciously arranged topics of deportation and annihilation. But he immediately is seized by inhibitions: when James says the images have no meaning, this means these feelings are blocked on the conscious level. Yet he says the chainsaw is sticking in the man's neck. We can recall that James tried to choke a fellow student and afterwards was committed to a psychiatric hospital. By saying "I couldn't think of anything", he is trying to distance himself from this meaning, which is nevertheless clearly visible in the work and thus serves as an outlet for these painful feelings. All in all, we can understand this form of handling unconscious conflicts as an important aid for James to creatively depict (and also talk about) aspects of his dark side. His fellow students deal with him empathetically, although the girls are neutral.

In child analysis, symptoms and difficulties in school or within the family often disappear quickly, which still does not mean that the adolescent's inner world is now ordered and stable. Therapy is still necessary to open space for the child where she can express her conflicts through play.

In small episodes, James managed to talk of his dark threatening memories and thoughts with H. With a social worker, James visited a special education facility, and H. talks with him about it:

"How did it look?" I asked. "There are rooms with two beds, they look new." "Did you also see the classes?" I ask. "Yes, a little bit. They look like here," he answers. "Can you go outside there?" I ask, returning to my original thoughts; "What did you think when you saw the classes?" He widens his eyes, pulls up his shoulders a bit, leaving them in this position, and says slowly: "I don't know." A pause arises, he looks in the classroom, which I interpret as a sign he wants to break off the conversation. "Maybe you found it to be ok and thought 'everything great', or you thought 'Get me out of here!'" He turns his head quickly back in my direction and says "Right! Get me out of here!" His attention is once more completely on our conversation. "I know even less about a psychiatric facility, and that's why I'd like to ask you how it was in the clinic. Were you allowed to go out there?" James shakes his head. "No. In the first week I was in the green section, that's the closed section. There's also a red one, an orange one and a yellow one. But I don't know the differences between them. After a week, they put me in the red section." "It's good you're past that," I say, looking in his eyes. He grins crookedly and nods . . . "You can be sure that I won't say any of this to anyone. Unless of course I was worried that your health was at risk." James nods, murmurs "MHHHM!" and continues munching on his roll.

Discussion

At first glance, it is amazing that James visited the education facility with the social worker. He seems to be completely convinced that he will not be made to stay there. He knows his mother and his stepfather will not send him there against his will. Still, James has surely been under great stress. H. helps him to talk about and order his upsetting experiences. She can at first accept his defenses, expressed in "I don't know", allowing him a short pause. She then supplies him with two alternatives – either he found it ok, or he wanted to get out. His spontaneous answer shows that she guessed correctly: he wanted to get out. H. can empathize with his agitated state and the danger that he will once again be committed to an institution. However, she does not press him further, also not interpreting his answer but instead expressing her wish to learn more about the clinic. James can fulfill her wish, and he begins to speak with her about this subject for the first time. H. is able to express for James how glad he is to be past this episode. He feels understood and supported (contained). James' mother also reported that James can now speak with her about his horrible experiences in the psychiatric ward. Since we have no information about his psychotherapy, which is proceeding simultaneously as this period at school, we can only presume that the therapist has succeeded in working through these traumatic experiences with James. The teacher learns from James' mother that she visited him daily in the clinic, but that he did not wish to see her – not once. He rejected her as he felt rejected by her. At the same time, it was presumably very important to experience how much he meant to his mother, since she refused to give up and kept visiting him daily.

80   Psychosexual development in puberty

Often, however, desperation and thoughts of suicide break through, as in the following incident. James had just left the classroom:

> James sat alone on the steps, looking completely defeated. I made a sign for him to follow me and we both sat down. He looked first at me and then at the ground. "How are you, James?" I asked. He shrugged his shoulders and said "Not good . . ." "Why do you feel bad?" I said gently. "Nothing means anything. I want everything to end. I don't want to be here anymore. Then everything would end." He shook his head. After a short pause, during which I considered how I should react, I asked: "Are you sure? How do you know whether it would be better over there, that everything's at an end?" I tried to keep my voice calm. "Maybe it's worse over there." James looked at me, unconvinced. "As long as you are here, you can change things and control them. Maybe only a little. We don't know anything about how it is over there. But we know what we can expect here."

> In this moment, the door opened and a teacher entered, asking something about the skiing course.

Discussion

H. has often heard from James' mother that he threatened to kill himself if he were placed in a psychiatric ward again. Yet hearing his desperation face to face conveys a different level of urgency. In supervision, we had already spoken of how important it is not to gloss over talk of suicide but to take it seriously. It is important to vehemently counter the common idealization of death as a calm, peaceful locus of redemption. There is nothing after death – not even the observation of how sad the survivors will be and what they will say about the suicide candidate: everything is truly over. But as long as an adolescent is alive, he can change himself along with some aspects of the world around him. In fact, James looks unconvinced when H. does not share his view that suicide can compensate for everything. Her confident attitude shows James how important it is for H. (as well as for his mother and stepfather) that he lives. She wants him to continue trying in this world even if it is wearying and strenuous for everyone concerned. Perhaps a side factor here is that James believes he is a burden to everyone, and that they would be glad if he were no longer there. Although H. sounds so calm and tries to keep her voice gentle yet determined, the encounter deeply disturbs her, and she worries whether it will be indeed possible to keep James from his suicidal aspirations.

James' development can be compared to a rising vector – albeit with dips and setbacks. When James feels overwhelmed by inner images, he takes his earphones and listens to music – something only he is allowed to do in class. When James exhibits the behavior of a typical adolescent – rebellious and provocative – a psychoanalyst would observe this as significant progress: he is showing that he is stable enough inside to test the teacher's authority. But for his teachers, who have afforded James a special position through the last three years, exercised great patience and challenged him academically (James has always

Psychosexual development in puberty   81

been an excellent student), this change is almost unbearable. Escalation follows swiftly. Here is an example of how H. manages to find an empathetic, transactional approach between the emotions of her colleagues and James' emotional situation.

From a Work Discussion transcript:

> When I enter the conference room at 12:45, they seem to have been waiting for me. My hand is still on the doorknob when one colleague who does not teach my students comes up to me and asks angrily: "Guess what Frost said to me today when I said he should take his feet off the table?" (Free hour during religion class.) "What did he say?" I ask, as expected of me. "He just said: What will you do if I don't take them off? So I discussed it with him for five minutes until he finally took them off the table."
>
> "He thinks he can do whatever he likes," agrees a second teacher, "we haven't had a student like that for a long time!" "Was James alone?" I ask K. "No, a whole group of your students was sitting around the table and laughed stupidly! Why should I have to talk about something so banal? What should we do really, when he won't do what he's told?" Her voice sounded irritated, her eyes were blazing as she addressed me. E. chimed in: "We aren't a nuthouse! Students like that shouldn't be in our school." I can feel irritation rising in me; I feel on the defensive. Taking time, I choose my words carefully and try to gain distance from my emotions. I realize that I am taking up my colleagues' anger, which thus is not truly my anger. I exhale slowly . . . if they spoke to James in the same tone of voice, I'm hardly surprised at his (or the class') behavior, I note to myself.
>
> "Obviously, James is in the middle of puberty and like many others exhibits obnoxious behavior. I will contact his mother right away and talk about his behavior . . . by the way, it is easier to withstand student behavior when you don't take it personally. Adolescents in puberty are trying to test their limits, and they feel particularly strong in the group. If I remember correctly, it was just the same in our generation . . . but apart from these connections, I will call up Mrs. Frost right away." I believe I see satisfied faces on both colleagues and the school director.

(H. then arranges a conversation for the following day with James' mother.)

> Meantime, the outrage seems to have subsided somewhat, and since I can expect more consideration now, I say: "If we compare James' behavior from a year ago and today, we can see quite a bit of progress: he attends class regularly, hasn't missed any homework at all, and in his science subjects he can be judged without any difficulty. Besides this, he maintains regular contact to his fellow students, which was not the case a year ago. All in all, he has improved his standing; tomorrow I will discuss his provocative behavior with his mother." Both the school director and one of my colleagues nod their heads at this statement.

82 Psychosexual development in puberty

During the conversation with James' mother, H. emphasizes the progress he has made, but also makes clear that he must stick to the rules – otherwise, the teachers reach their limit. James' mother says that she has been very busy with building onto their house and had not seen to it that James attended therapy regularly, but now she would.

Discussion

H. often has to achieve a difficult balance: she must show James his limits and require him to follow the school rules, but at the same time promote understanding for his special situation in the other teachers. The way she has chosen is a wise double strategy: calling James' mother up is an indirect demonstration that the school and James' home are in cooperation (which is indeed the case, to a large extent). Her pointing out James' great progress also constitutes an indirect praise of her colleagues, who have enabled James in this very progress. Her message is that their special efforts for James have not been in vain. Reminding them of their own adolescence might well have helped to create some distance and evoke memories of that turbulent time for them as well.

Indeed, H. was able to make clear to James' mother that he must respect limits, which he then proved able to do. When we observe his social situation, he moved from his outsider status in the back row to an integrated student confident enough to be impudent. This means his aggressions are no longer suppressed and threatening, but can be expressed in a milder form.

He is also now able to engage in conflicts with his fellow students without becoming violent or timidly withdrawing. At 15, James begins to get interested in a girl, who visits him at home to study, since he is so good at explaining math.

At the end of this last year of school (before he goes on to a technical high school), a climbing excursion is planned. At first, James does not wish to participate. His stepfather Ch. then volunteers to accompany the class. This exchange was described by H.:

"I would like to thank you for your help, Ch. You were indispensable. I'm not sure if I could have done it alone," I said. He thanked me, with a shy smile. "What were your impressions from the climbing excursion?" I asked. Ch. took some time before he answered, and then said: "It was a completely new experience for me. Besides that, I was surprised at how the boys kept getting more and more into it. At first they hesitated – they didn't hesitate to say they were spooked by the whole thing – and then within minutes they collected so much experience on how to move that they seemed like old hands at it. I was really surprised. It was a great experience for me." "I'm glad," I answered. "What was it like for you, James?" I asked him. His voice lively, he answered: "It was great! I was totally surprised that the time passed so quickly, I would have liked to take another round!" "Unfortunately, there wasn't enough time. The five of you had a real expert in climbing with you. The others weren't confident to make it up all the way," I remarked.

Through his stepfather's participation, James was one of the five especially capable climbers, and was proud of his accomplishment. He was the son of this good climber – no longer a fatherless son, but instead a boy wishing to become like his (step)father.

James wanted to take the entrance exam for a demanding technical school. After he passed, H. and James' math teacher suggest he study more demanding material than the others, in order to have better chances during his first year there. James takes up this suggestion and fulfills his extra assignments with distinction.

Concluding remarks

In this case study, we can only make conclusions as to James' inner world and inner conflicts in hindsight, since we have no access to data from his therapy sessions. We are interested here in the importance of his teacher H. and her clear position with regard to his situation at school. H.'s special capacity to empathize with James and be moved by his psychic pain, mentally digest it and then speak with him about it constituted a decisive help for him. Perhaps for the first time in his life, he felt understood and held, while simultaneously experiencing the expectation that he must fulfill his assignments and keep to the rules. H. succeeded in constructing a support system for herself: in the Work Discussion and individual supervision, she could speak of her feelings, fears and hopes, so that she felt less alone. She also succeeded in gaining the full support from the school director and informed her on each individual step she took. It proved especially difficult to obtain the requisite collaboration from fellow teachers.

It is unclear to what extent the decision to keep James at school also gave his mother courage to take him in again. The close contact between James' mother and H. – when he refused to attend school, their contact was daily – was presumably helpful to both sides and enabled a close cooperation, preventing many potential escalations.

Case studies often describe dramatic developments with unhappy ends, where an adolescent falls lower and lower, gets into trouble with the law, becomes violent or is committed to a psychiatric clinic. Positive developments are no less dramatic and moving, but are often manifested in small or even minute incidents and sequences. Important decisions can be made in short conversations during a break, and discussions of life and suicide may occur between other events. Small encouragements can vitiate feelings of loneliness and desperation, when the adolescent's psychic pain succeeds in moving his teacher. In retrospect, such difficult but often life-determining acts of help may seem completely simple and casual.

In conclusion, I quote an appreciation of H.'s psychoanalytic-pedagogic work from James' parents. After many critical assessments of Austrian and German teachers, this report demonstrates that H.'s enthusiasm helped James to find his way back to school and the classroom. H. writes:

> As I already mentioned, James' mother and I had made an appointment to meet. James was in Krakow with his class from the technical school, and Mrs. Frost was accompanied by Timon, James' younger brother, and his stepfather

Christian. At first we chatted about general matters, then Mrs. Frost reported happily about James' development: his success at the technical school was very satisfying, and he was organizing his life on his own for the most part. He didn't go out much, did not have many friends, sat for hours at the computer – but he was very amiable with his family and had no "incidents" anymore.

I was glad to hear this, and then reported how I had experienced James in my class.

I then related the episode when I showed James a cartoon of Simon's Cat, in connection with an assignment he had: we both giggled and James became so enthusiastic that he forgot to go home, which he previously said he needed to since he had a headache. Mrs. Frost now eagerly told me how James had downloaded these cartoons at home and asked her to watch the little film together with him. In an emotional tone of voice, she said this was the beginning of a new kind of relationship between them. From then on, there was step-by-step progress in their family life. With a laugh, she also remembered the time James suggested drawing "nothing" in drawing class. He had never really liked drawing, but this idea appealed to him so much that from then on he started drawing "conflated letters" – as she called them – and never again complained about drawing class at school. Instead, from that point on he began to tell more about what happened at school, and actively sought communication with his mother.

In a short pause, Christian interjected that they had all had great luck that James had by chance fallen into my "hands". It seemed to me that his eyes got moist. I was very glad for these appreciative words and answered that "we – James and I – as far as school is concerned and as far as I can tell – achieved an enormous learning process. Just as I told him in my farewell letter to him at the end of the fourth class." (At that time, I wrote every student in my class a personally encouraging farewell letter, where I also thanked them for the chance at a commonly shared learning process.)

With a little smile, Mrs. Frost told me that James had immediately read this letter aloud – even before receiving his diploma – and then had kept it in a safe place. This makes me glad, too. . . .

I hope this description has elucidated the path of James' continued development.

Notes

1 The author cannot here describe specific contingencies of masochistic wishes. The masochistic person gives his/her partner a "contract" for designing their painful interactions in order to provide pleasure. The masochist and sadist can assume control by turns: often it is unclear who is fulfilling whose wish, since the "compulsion" to assign this contract is part of the arrangement.

2 In my book *Latency – the Golden Age of Childhood* (2018), I describe in detail Elfi's analysis between the years of eight and eleven (132–40).

3 The form of Work Discussion developed by Martha Harris is intended to make psychoanalytic thought useful in work situations (Rustin and Bradley 2008).

3

Development of feeling

> I would there were no age between sixteen and
> three-and-twenty, or that youth would sleep out the
> rest; for there is nothing in the between but
> getting wenches with child, wronging the ancientry, stealing, fighting . . .
> —Shakespeare, *A Winter's Tale*, Act III

This quote from Shakespeare resonates with those parents who ask why the period of adolescence is so troublesome, and why they must feel they can do nothing right. It is difficult for parents to realize that solutions to the problems of adolescence require time. Particularly in this phase of life, adolescents have an urgent need to be emotionally accompanied by their parents.

Parents and pedagogues know that children entering puberty often exhibit quite extreme changes in character and psychic difficulties. Children who earlier were cheerful and trusting may become stubborn and withdrawn adolescents, rebelling against their parents. Instead of admiring their parents, they criticize and denigrate their lifestyle: a child previously ambitious and eager to learn may now reject school, while others are possessed by pathological ambition and desire to learn. Both behaviors – at least in their extreme form – point to a wavering or damaged self-image. Neither permissiveness nor strictness on the parents' part can make these changes disappear. It is helpful for teachers and parents to understand which psychic dynamics lie behind these changes. Many parents up the ante where they should actually hold back, not trusting their child's capabilities when he most needs encouragement. When the child brings home good grades, they may assume too readily that everything is in order. Concentration on academic success distracts from the much more important dimension of what problems lie behind the academic ones. Adolescents usually do not know why they are now behaving differently from before. Melanie Klein (1922) points out that it is very helpful when parents understand the unconscious tendencies of development revealed through psychoanalysis.

Changes in the adolescent's body occasion changes in his psychic balance. Stabilizing tactics that functioned beforehand are no match for this new attack of

86 Development of feeling

physical changes. It is important to recall that "the difference between 'normal' and 'abnormal' is one of quantity and not of structure, and empirical finding constantly confirmed our own work" (Melanie Klein 1922, 55). She explains: "Hence children who had felt or appeared quite healthy, or at most a little nervous, can suffer quite serious breakdowns as a result of even moderate extra strains" (Ibid, 55). The causes of such pathologies are derived from early impressions and developments that laid the foundations of character formation.

Psychoanalysis sees these massive personality changes in puberty in the context of the deepest – i.e., earliest – layers of the personality. The child's early longing is to be loved, cared for and fed, as well as to totally possess or control the source of love and food, or become that source. Giving up this strong desire is difficult, and the desire is often secretly retained, for instance through the child's becoming sick in order to be cared for. In normal development, these wishes are countered by the opposite urge – to become an adult, to move away from the mother towards other interesting loci. In the years preceding puberty, a balance has usually been developed between the two opposing impulses. But now, hormonal and other physical changes effect an unconscious intensification of this conflict. The relatively stable self-image from latency – also found in children who later have major problems in adolescence – then may appear in retrospect to have been a delicate truce between two opposing wishes and priorities, which only held because the tension between them was not yet so great.

This compromise does not consist of a single identity; the girl wishes to be like her mother, yet different, or the boy wishes to become like his father and yet a completely different man. We are speaking here of a "collection of identities" (Anderson 2009, 3). Bion (1957b), influenced here by Melanie Klein, called the more primitive of the two inner functional parts of the psyche the "psychotic", and the mature one the "non-psychotic" part – for anyone and everyone. Out of these two mechanisms, the personality is formed. How the personality is structured depends on the particular balance between these two functions – sometimes dominated by integrating forces that enable an inner order oriented towards unity, but also enable the person to see other persons as complete objects who can cooperate with each other as parents do. Bion then speaks of a movement in the direction of the "depressive position". Alternatively, a primitive, disintegrative pressure towards splitting and expulsion may dominate in an attempt to resolve conflicts. Bion speaks of a movement in the direction of the "paranoid-schizoid position". With healthy development, a disturbance in the previously existing balance is manifested by an adolescent's major mood swings and restless behavior – yet still dominated by the integrative part of the personality. The changes in puberty can increase an adolescent's fears to such an extent that his inner balance also becomes disturbed and the psychotic part of the personality becomes dominant.

Due to physical changes, adolescents are confronted with their increased strength, which can elicit euphoric or disquieting feelings of power: for males, the sense of physical beauty and strength afforded by an erection, with the capacity

Development of feeling 87

to procreate; for females, the power to have a baby, to have breasts that produce milk, to have an attractive body that draws attention. These new possibilities may fascinate, but they are also linked to the baby's early feeling of omnipotence in order to counter its feeling of helplessness. For a child, the primitive wish to possess and control the object was only a fantasy; an adolescent would now be able to actually fulfill these fantasies. Thus, it becomes necessary to newly order and work through early forms of identity and development.

> The very physicality of the changes, their concreteness (the fact of male potency, the reality of real pregnancy and a real baby) is a reassurance to the more normal (neurotic) part of the personality, but for the more primitive parts of the self, these changes are the means of realizing primitive and often destructive phantasies. Intercourse is not a longed-for act of procreation (and pleasure), but the means of getting inside the other: at the benign end of the spectrum, to become totally cared for; and at the negative end, to overpower and destroy, all in the service of very infantile wishes. It is these concrete desires which cause disturbance in those who cannot contain them, and great anxiety about the fate of the object and the self in those adolescents who are coping but fear that they won't.
>
> (Anderson 2009, 4)

Anderson is describing a psychic organization in the adolescent where early defense mechanisms such as splitting and projective identification now (re)appear. The adolescent's changes threaten to reactivate his early, primitive bonds to the primary object – bonds that were subsequently repressed and split off; these contingencies now strive towards the surface, into adolescent consciousness. To the adolescent, these unintegrated, powerful primitive wishes represent a threat. Their potential fulfillment would flood thought itself with arousal and aggression, a consequence which the adolescent perceives as a catastrophe. Powerful defense mechanisms come into play to keep these impulses unconscious – such as self-mutilation, drugs, anorexia, teenage pregnancy, etc. I will now provide two short examples, with a more detailed treatment following later. The psychoanalytic view helps us understand that such troubling behaviors serve to protect adolescents from even more threatening inner wishes.

Dorothy, 15

Some time after her first relationship with a boy had ended, Dorothy began to cut herself severely. Since there was no immediate dramatic impetus for this, her parents were very worried.

In therapy, Dorothy spoke of her early childhood, when her father had an affair with another woman, subsequently abandoning Dorothy and her mother. However, he then put an end to this relationship, reconciled with his wife and returned to the family. Recently, Dorothy discovered and read her mother's diary. In the

88 Development of feeling

period where Dorothy was a small child, her mother had been very unhappy and unable to find joy in her new baby.

I understand Dorothy's breakdown after being left by her boyfriend as a revival of her early traumatic experiences. Not only did she feel abandoned by her father, but she identified with her abandoned mother – although she had more or less neglected Dorothy during this difficult time.

If we wish to understand why Dorothy selected self-mutilation (cutting) as a form for expressing her inner conflicts, we must reflect further. In her imagination, her father was strong and powerful, whereas she and her mother were helpless and subject to his arbitrary wishes. She unconsciously identified with her strong and cruel father, who caused her pain – just as she caused herself pain with a knife (=father). At the same time, she was her helpless mother, who also was caused pain. Thus, she was an active agent cutting her own body, nevertheless feeling relief, strength and potency, mixed with guilt. In her fantasy, she embodies her parents' union – she is both the giver and the taker, with her body as arena. On the conscious level, she only felt her inner tension dissolve after cutting herself.

Self-destructive behavior can have various causes; for each adolescent, the links from his life history must be investigated and analyzed, although we can assume that the true causes cannot be found without therapy. The pain from cutting can also counter the adolescent's feeling of numbness, since feeling pain is an authentic sensory experience – proof to the self-mutilating adolescent that he exists.

Rosalin's story is completely different from Dorothy's.

Rosalin, 15 ½

Rosalin is 15 ½ when her older sister, with whom she has an especially close relationship, marries. She has three older sisters, and her parents have a harmonic relationship. When her older sister enters a steady relationship after graduating from school, Rosalin reacts with outbreaks of tears and depression. She begins to make friends with girls in her class who dislike school, and through these girls she becomes acquainted with three boys who refuse to go to school. She is drawn more and more strongly into this gang, who also deal in drugs. Her parents try to talk with Rosalin, but she denies all their help, accusing them of being conservative, middle class and contemptuous of people beneath their social class.

Discussion

Martha Harris (2007) describes the background behind this crisis which caused the parents to seek a therapist's help. Rosalin perceived her older sister's academic success and romantic relationship as a terrible loss. Her reaction was to break out of her dependency on the family and forge her own path, thus denying her family's values of academic achievement. She criticizes her parents. Behind

Development of feeling   89

this reaction, however, lies the insecurity and panic of failure and abandonment often felt by teenagers.

Rosalin is the youngest of four children, and the other three are considerably older than she. She had the role of the spoiled baby, who received attention due to her pretty appearance and friendly manner. Psychically, she lived more through her sister with whom she identified, in this way avoiding getting in touch with her feelings of jealousy, envy and frustration. By now choosing a circle of friends whose values were diametrically opposed to her family's, she demonstrated her contempt and dismissal of her family's values. Rosalin had played a parasitic role as spoiled baby. However, within her peer group of these down-and-out adolescents, she also played a special role: she was from a solidly middle-class background and had a large allowance: thus, she was a giver.

It is important that Rosalin's parents set clear limits to her contact with this gang. They must expect heated arguments. If they help Rosalin to address these conflicts openly, she can then show her anger and nastiness without losing her parents' basic acceptance. If her parents are capable of hearing out her (often unfair) accusations without feeling hurt, they will recognize that Rosalin is attempting to convince herself and them that they mistreat her, as well as distracting herself from the real issue of her perceived abandonment and loneliness. For Rosalin's sense of self-worth, it is important that she resume studying in order to pass her exam, which would enable her to learn a profession. Can her parents convey their confidence to Rosalin, believing in her capability of finding her own way? It would be most unfavorable if parents break off contact to their son or daughter due to a deep feeling of hurt. This would drive the adolescent further into drop-out society, making a return to normal society more difficult.

3.1 Problems for parents of children growing into puberty

> He's happy he's young.
> I was young too once
> Maybe younger than him.
> —Karl Valentin

Karl Valentin's aphorism shows how difficult it is to see one's children become adults: it refers to the type of father who is not only superior and more competent, but even wants to be younger than his son. Even though Valentin extends this rubric *ad absurdum*, he perceptively captures the parents' basic attitude. Initiated by the younger generation and tolerated by the parents, a radical, mostly unintended and often painful reversal or new orientation occurs during adolescence. The same parents whom the child previously admired and wished to emulate now are criticized, provoked and devalued – not as a planned strategy but as something that seems to happen by itself. The paradox is that this emotionally fraught

90   Development of feeling

process of separation from the parents can seem desirable in theory, but is felt as something emotionally painful.

In the maturing process of puberty, the adolescent is faced with the task of parting from his parents as primary love objects in order to find inner space for seeking a partner among his peers. At the same time, opposing currents are activated: at times, the early Oedipal desires to win the parent of the opposite sex as a lover are revived. This is something like a car accelerating inexorably but with the driver's foot also on the brake now and again. This situation reminds me of an experience I had in a bus in Havana, Cuba. The bus driver always accelerated before a red light, before sharply braking. The passengers, mostly standing, were thrown amongst each other, held onto each other, their bodies thrown into contact, laughing and apologizing simultaneously. Nobody seemed surprised or irritated. Thus did a routine experience of stopping for a red light become an intense group experience. Adolescents and their parents are also thrown towards and away from one another. These forces of nature become comprehensible when we understand that while massive changes are occurring not only in the adolescent's inner world, deep layers of the parents' personalities and inner worlds are also stirred up. Parents must deal with real changes in living with their growing children: sexual maturity and physical changes demonstrate their daughter's or son's awakening sexuality and remind them of their own aging process. One generation will take over for the previous one, i.e., the younger generation pushes to center stage and attempts to push back the older generation. The sexual maturity of the parents' children often coincides with a wane in sexual potency and the end of child-bearing in menopause. The adolescents have something that the parents can envy. Winnicott (1984, 203) writes of adolescents' inexhaustible but precious potential as eliciting adult envy. On a deeper, often unconscious level, fears, hopes and experiences from the parents' own adolescence arise, as well as the basic patterns of their own experiences of separation. All experiential patterns of separation, beginning with birth, weaning, loss of Oedipal illusions (the boy as mother's lover, the girl as father's princess), become virulent. It is very difficult to deal with all of these unexpected feelings now emerging, to perceive them, reflect on them and accept them as a part of oneself. It is easier to not perceive them in oneself but instead criticize them in one's son or daughter. This tendency to find the problems in others and not in oneself can also be found among adolescents.

An important characteristic of adolescence is the tendency to not reflect but instead project one's feelings onto others, acting instead of reflecting. Adolescents unconsciously want to elicit in their parents the feelings they prefer not to see in themselves. Admiration for the parents turns to its opposite, with the parents described in unflattering terms and rendered ridiculous. Adolescents often blatantly display their sexual attractiveness in order to provoke their parents' envy. This means that the parents must bear a double burden: as they are bombarded by their adolescent child's projections, they simultaneously must deal with their own unconscious envy. Bion compared the image of bearing projections with the soldier's experience at the front in World War I: remaining capable of thinking "under fire". Bion's remark (2005) that "the intelligence one has must be available for use 'under fire'" applies not only to psychoanalysts but also to the parents of children in puberty.

Katharina, 15

A 15-year-old girl whose body development is already clearly visible returns to the kitchen from her bath scantily clothed, with only a towel around her hair. Her father, who was preparing dinner together with her mother, looks in the other direction. Her mother looks at her and tells her she should put something on. The daughter ignores this comment, helping to set the table with dance-like movements. After some time, the father does look at her appreciatively, which elicits a satisfied smile on her part. Then he says bluntly: "Katharina, put something on already!" Having achieved the effect she intended, she leaves the room to do so.

In this example we can discover various aspects: the daughter's wish to exhibit her body and see her father's reaction and appreciation. She wishes to attract her father's gaze, something he actually resists because of her age. Katharina's mother seems to be comparing her own body with her daughter's budding body, partially glad to identify with her, but also feeling sadness at her own passing youth. Then, the father bluntly defends himself from his daughter's attractiveness and shows her how she is to comport herself in the shared rooms of the apartment: clothed, but she can see his admiration in his eyes.

Betty, 14

The 14-year-old Betty, whose mother has entered into a loving relationship with a man for the last two years, runs naked through the dining room to her bedroom after a bath. Her mother's partner looks up from his book and an admiring smile crosses his face. "Ludwig!" says the girl, indignantly. "You're looking!" "Yes," he answers, "when such a pretty girl runs by, I look."

Once again we observe childish exhibitionism of a beautiful female body and the wish to be admired by the (step)father, followed by playful indignation that he actually looks at her. It is not hard to see parallels to a scantily clad three-year-old girl delightedly dancing before her parents in order to elicit their attraction.

The same situation can have a completely different meaning, when the parents react differently and the basic setting is different. In the following example, similar behavior led to the threat of the girl being thrown out of her home.

Christine, 15

Christine came to therapy in the Tavistock Clinic because she was stealing from her mother and grandmother. Her mother's new boyfriend had recently moved in; previously, the single mother had lived with Christine, whose father had left the family when Christine was a baby. Shortly after Paul moved in, Christine began

92 Development of feeling

to steal. Paul was particularly enraged when Christine ran through the apartment with little clothing on. She reported that he told her: "We will have to throw you out if you go on this way."

In conversation with the therapist, Christine contended that she had no problems, but that the mother was jealous of her attractive body; she didn't understand why the two of them were so upset (Waddell 2002, 155). Christine and her mother had had a very close relationship, and Christine felt she was driven out of this relationship by Paul. Her stealing – a common occurrence in puberty – shortly after Paul moved in presumably signified that she could take back something that had been taken from her. She stole her mother's wedding ring and grandmother's jewelry. Instead of envying her mother, she projected her envy onto her. Paul let himself be provoked by Christine; perhaps he was also excited by her body, needed to block this feeling and became irritated. He threatened to throw his stepdaughter out of the apartment.

How can the same situation – making in one case for an amusing scene, resolved through humor – constitute a threat to the family? As opposed to Christine and her mother, who were abandoned by the father at an early stage, Betty had spent ten years in a "good enough" family with an affectionate father and a mother who allowed this closeness between father and daughter. Her rivalry to her mother was ameliorated by their loving relationship. Betty at first also looked askance at her mother's new partner, but gradually he was able to win over Betty and her sister through friendly attention. Soon, the whole family saw him as a enrichment. Betty's new stepfather also had three grown children of his own and did not feel threatened by Betty's "seduction", but instead rather flattered.

Parents – but also teachers and other pedagogues – have difficulty admitting their envious feelings, linked to grief at the passing of youth and their youthful bodies. This emotional burden often leads to action on the parents' part, for instance, when a father gets a new lover (often his daughter's age) in order to prove that he is still attractive and potent. Or the mother can launch into a passionate relationship with a youthful lover. Or parents (self-)consciously behave as youthfully in their language and clothing as their children do.

Parents then might become ashamed of these impulses or repress them behind vehement attacks and moral judgments – children are criticized for their inappropriate clothing, extravagant haircuts or provocative behavior. To an extent, such criticisms can be justified – and to an extent they originate from unconscious envious reactions. It is helpful when parents can talk together about their ambivalent feelings, understand each other and support one another. Sometimes, parents manage to undertake activities together in the phase where the children are exiting the family – activities they previously could not find time for during child-rearing: dancing, mountain climbing, travelling to foreign countries and sports.

3.2 Adolescent perspectives

Let us first illuminate the complex relationship between parents and children from the adolescent perspective.

When Sebastian was asked, "When did you first notice you were in puberty?" he answered as if shot from a pistol: "Your parents begin to get on your nerves!"

He does not consider himself difficult; instead, his parents get on his nerves with their demands that he fulfill his household chores. As in early childhood, the adolescent sees himself as the center of the world: the small child's egocentricity celebrates a comeback. The revived Oedipal desires – just as in the first three months of life – are experienced in an abrupt shift from feelings of solitude to solace and protection. Sebastian is unable to reflect on his actions; he perceives his parents' reaction to his rebellious behavior as unjust and irritating.

He goes on to describe his unwilling participation in those household chores where his parents insist he does his share.

Sebastian speaks of his father with great respect, and he is glad they used to do so many activities together with the rest of the family. At the same time, he describes how much has changed in the last two years:

> I'm more interested in girls now, I look at them. . . . I meet up more with my friends, we meet in the evening and go to the movies, for instance. There are four or five of them I know from school or from sports camp. Some of them have ideas and there are others who come along. We don't fight often.

Although Sebastian realizes that he spends a lot of time going out with his friends, he still regrets that the family so seldom does things together anymore.

In order to understand this reaction, it is important to take into consideration that the child or patient always experiences (from the childlike perspective) separation from the father or mother – or, in analysis, cancellation of a session – as abandonment by the adult. Even when the adolescent (or patient) knows on an adult level that he was out with his friends (or that a patient cancelled his session), he emotionally holds the adult responsible and feels snubbed. Many parents hear from their adolescent children: "You are never here!" or "You never have time for me!". Parents often find themselves in the position of comparing such complaints with the reality that although they wanted to do things with their child, he neither made time nor showed interest.

As soon as the adolescent has distanced himself from his parents, a psychic space opens where the first feelings and experiences of love occur.

Sebastian (13) reports on his first "real" love, Iris:

Interviewer: What's the first "real" love like?

Sebastian: A feeling that I can't describe too well, because it's connected to different things. I can't move, my heart and my pulse beat 1000 . . .

I: What was the first kiss like?

S: She took me to the movies, *Bridesmaids*, and both our friends came, too. There were four of us. During the film she wrote me a text message: "Are you still in love with me?" She showed it to me. I answered on my phone: "Yes!" She wrote: "Maybe I'm also still in love with you!" I wrote: "You should have waited with ending it." She read it and wrote: "I never should have ended it."

A few minutes later she wrote: "And what now?" I wrote: "This here!" and I kissed her on the mouth. She was surprised and happy.

Both adolescents are torn between their surging feelings and fear of the unknown. As soon as they meet, Iris wants to break up again – not because she dislikes him, but because she likes him *so much*. But her intense feelings give her no peace – she needs to know whether he is still in love with her. He explains how he feels and surprises not only her but probably himself with a passionate kiss on her mouth. The distancing achieved through communication via cell phone seems to diminish their fear. Although they are sitting next to each other, they use the cover of darkness for their first kiss.

The longing and fear of being torn between new and unfamiliar impulses are shown in their further communications. At midnight the next day, Iris writes Sebastian:

> Do you know how it is when the most important person isn't there? You know, it's as if a part of me isn't there. The way you held my hand, I felt sooo good, your kiss made an eternal wish of mine come true and I love you more than anything (smiley). I want to never lose you (heart). When you smiled at me, I knew – you're the one, I want to be with you forever.
>
> (heart with two sad smileys, two stars as kisses)

It is difficult for adults to comprehend the surge and intensity of these hitherto unknown feelings (although they may be recollections of the surging, intense feeling of the first love pair: mother and baby). The deeply suppressed "emotional recollections" from the first years of life now come to the surface. The first kiss evokes the blessed, pleasurable memory of oral satisfaction at the mother's breast – suppressed, but operative. After the painful separation of weaning, this romantic love in adolescence is perceived as eternal. Adolescent lovers experience the total body sensation of pleasure and solace as a union of two souls: for Iris, a part of her is missing when Sebastian is absent.

In the first phase of being in love for 13- to 15-year-olds, a third person often plays a role – a rival, another girl or the previous boyfriend. In Sebastian's case, the previous boyfriend writes on Facebook:

> "Treat her well, she's something special."
> Sebastian answers: "She's not only something special, but the best in the world."

It is not difficult to recognize here the early pattern of the "paranoid-schizoid position" (as Melanie Klein terms it), the archaic form of splitting into good, idealized and bad worlds. Just as the mother – or her satisfying breast – was the best mother in the world, Iris is also ideal. This babylike quality is also evident in everyday life: when Sebastian finds nothing to interest him after breakfast on vacation, he simply goes back to bed, sleeping or watching TV.

Development of feeling 95

Bed is a safe place for dreaming and daydreaming. During the daytime, Sebastian looks at cartoons, films or soap operas on TV or documentary programs such as *In the Realm of Black Gold* or *Deep Sea – Tree Trouts in the Amazon*. When he comes home, he leaves his clothes on the floor after he takes them off. After a few days, his mother advises him of the need to keep order. Reluctantly, he brings his dirty clothes to be washed.

His love for Iris comes to a swift end. Since she lives in a small city and not in Vienna, she writes him a farewell text message after his first visit: the geographical distance between them is too great, so she feels she should let him free. The unhappy Sebastian accepts this.

It is important to understand that the dissolution of bonds with the parents and the approach of a relationship to another adolescent (an "emotional cathexis", as Freud calls it) are connected with each other. When the adolescent boy's admiration for his father – the great king, noble master and threatening rival – wanes, then more psychic space is freed for a new relationship. The beloved and admired father now becomes devalued in the adolescent's eyes and becomes a target for mockery; if the father can bear this and "play along", then their loving relationship can continue.

The relationship between adolescents and parents is complicated by the fact that the adolescent does not consciously decide to behave childishly or be the rebellious teenager, but instead something in him – beyond his control, a biological trigger – causes him to behave that way. He is often himself surprised, feels guilty and overwhelmed.

In adolescence, previously dependable patterns of how parents care for their children are no longer a given. Instead of gladly accepting the parents' loving behavior, adolescents may treat them with denial or indifference, which can be very painful for the parents. Here is one example:

> The family of a 13-year-old son and 15-year-old daughter arrives home together at 21:00, after the parents have just picked up their children from sports camp. The mother makes cheese dumplings, and the father suggests making scrambled eggs, too. He gets the eggs, cuts tomatoes; the grandmother cuts fresh parsley from the garden. The father puts in six eggs and remarks that his son Sebastian loves this dish since he came back from his trip to the USA. The daughter sets the table – dressed in a tight t-shirt, long earrings, a mini-dress and an amusingly styled head scarf. The mother serves the cheese dumplings, and the daughter sits down, takes two pieces and begins eating. The mother sits down too and calls her son, who is presently listening to music on his earphones and playing with a big flashlight. Sebastian comes in, keeps his cap on and looks at them. The mother gives him a stern gaze, whereupon he takes his earphones off and hangs them around his neck. After a minute, the mother says:

>> "Sebastian, you know you have to take your cap and headphones off at the table." Slowly and leisurely, his face expressionless, he takes off his cap

and puts the headphones by his side, ignoring his mother's outstretched arm. His sister asks him whether he wants cheese dumplings – something he usually doesn't eat.

Today, he answers: "Yes, two pieces, please."

His father is still standing at the stove, cooking the scrambled eggs. He takes a cheese dumpling for himself and some of the scrambled eggs, too. The mother and daughter also take some and praise them. Then the father asks his son whether he also wants some eggs. Sebastian looks at him skeptically. The sister lets him taste one bite of hers. He grimaces with his mouth and turns up his nose, since he doesn't like how they taste.

The father reacts angrily: "You shouldn't grimace that way if you don't like the way it tastes. You can make yourself something to eat."

Sebastian: "I didn't say anything. I kept myself from saying something negative."
The father is insulted.
Sebastian: "Is there any cheese?"
Father: "You can make yourself some bread and butter."
Sebastian gets up, cuts himself a piece of bread and spreads it with butter.
Father: "There are still eggs, you can make yourself scrambled eggs," which Sebastian proceeds to do, eating them with pleasure.

Instead of enjoying being lovingly looked after by his father, Sebastian rejects the dish that was cooked especially for him. Only with reluctance does he follow his parents' rules that he take off his cap and headphones at the table. He wants to make his own rules; what the others find tasty, he doesn't. His reaction is unexpected and unpredictable. Instead of an affectionate celebration of the children's return from sports camp, tension gains the upper hand. The subject of Sebastian's cap continues:

The grandmother asks whether they are allowed to keep their caps on at school. Sebastian says "no".
Grandmother asks: "Why do you wear them?"
Granddaughter: "They're supercool."
The father says he also always enjoyed wearing a cap.
In an ironic tone of voice, the daughter says: "But you wore them completely differently."
Sebastian also says there is no comparison. He demonstrates how his father wore his caps – like a country boy, with the cap drawn over his eyes – and imitates a mentally retarded man. Everyone laughs. Then Sebastian puts his on again, but with his bangs free and the ears covered. He turns to his sister, and when she turns away, her bare belly is revealed, whereupon he gives an exaggeratedly surprised look and imitates a sexually interested man who would like to take a closer glance at her. The sister laughs and pulls her t-shirt down, which then renders her breasts and bra visible. Everyone laughs. Sebastian continues teasing her, and they both laugh; she pulls the t-shirt up and down once again. Then they both decide to

Development of feeling 97

shoot photos with their iPhones outside. They stay outside quite a while, laughing audibly, then returning and inspecting the photos with pleasure.

In a melancholy tone of voice, the mother says that she is beginning a new phase of life at 45. Following her burst of freedom after passing her high school final exam, her time at university, her babies and building her career, she has attained everything. The father says that something new is constantly coming.

In this example from Sebastian's family, we see a mild form of mockery directed towards the father, in the context of this family's norms. The parents make an effort to provide their children with a balance between limits and tolerance. But it is clearly painful for them to do something for their son only to have him reject it. This mute rejection, accompanied by a facial expression of revulsion, shatters the father's expectations after he prepares one of Sebastian's favorite foods. Parents require a high threshold of frustration for them to constantly accept such rejections. Adolescents tend to dismiss any and every comparison made between parents and the younger generation: whatever the parents did earlier is "uncool" and unworthy of comparison to new styles in clothing, etc.

This criticism of parents and adults is founded upon an idealization and overvaluation of the adolescents' own possibilities. This prioritizes innovation: everything can be rethought, and nothing should be taken for granted. A new perspective is born where everything is questioned. The long path to adulthood consists in notching back an all-or-nothing orientation, recognizing true limitations and making compromises. As one patient expressed it: "It is much more difficult to be king yourself" – and, accordingly, to take responsibility for a family and a "kingdom".

Less than an hour later, the parents are watching a report on TV about the tropical storm "Irma" in New York. Sebastian pushes himself between the parents, cuddling up to his mother, who has stretched out on a chaise lounge. When the parents want to change channels, Sebastian is allowed to use the remote control. This scene occurred ten years ago already, when he was only five – big enough to use the remote. All three enjoy reminiscing on their early closeness and harmony.

Sebastian sits at the breakfast table. He has taken his mother's iPhone and attempts to open various programs. His mother doesn't want him to be constantly playing with her iPhone and changing things. She demands it back from him, but he pulls it away since he wants to exit the program he is in. Sebastian tries to do this in various ways, but he can't manage it. His mother now becomes irritated. "Now you've changed it again and I won't be able to get out of it. Don't do it, I've told you so often, Sebastian."

Sebastian: "I can do it, I can do it." (He tries various buttons, but it doesn't work.)
       His father enters the situation and says: "Give it to me!"
Sebastian: "No, I can do it." (He attempts once again to press various buttons.)
Father (holding out his hand): "Sebastian, give it to me!"

Reluctantly, he hands his father the phone. While the father tries to get out of the program, Sebastian thinks of the solution: "Press on the off switch and the home button for a few seconds." The father tries this three or four times, then he

98 Development of feeling

hands the phone back to Sebastian. Sebastian tries it and achieves success. Satisfied, he says: "You see, I can do it!"

Sebastian is convinced that everything belongs to him; he knows better than his parents how these new devices function. In truth, a playful attitude of trial and error is an excellent way to investigate these new programs. At the same time, however, Sebastian wishes to demonstrate that "we are the new generation – the world belongs to us!" Sebastian wishes to show that he can work the phone better than both his mother and father.

From the grandparents' perspective, there hovers a melancholy recollection of the time when their children engaged in the same kind of struggles with them. Now the parents experience what it is like from the other side – what it feels like to be pushed out of the central position.

According to psychoanalytic theory, the situation of the adolescent girl distancing herself from the parents is more difficult than that of the adolescent boy: in her Oedipal phase, she needed to give up her first love object, the mother, and turn towards her father. Thus, girls and women experience more guilt feelings due to this previous "betrayal" of the mother, as Chasseguet-Smirgel (1974, 139) describes. In adolescence, she must then renounce the paternal love object she more or less won in her fantasy. In a mature development, the girl has accepted the other, sexual relationship between mother and father and identified with the mother. The girl consoles herself with the thought that she will later become an attractive woman who chooses a husband and has children with him. In her inner world, this new solution constitutes a turbulent time. On the one hand, the girl wishes to be seen by the most important man in her life, her father, as attractive and a sexual goal, but on the other hand she wants to distance herself from him and attain recognition from boys her age. These contradictory feelings make this phase of development very difficult for everyone involved. A father's often-observed jealousy of his daughter's admirers is not only because he must give her up, but also because of her unconscious projections onto him: she does not truly wish to leave him to her mother. In every new phase of life, the Oedipal situation must be newly worked through and modified in order to integrate new elements (Britton 2014, 71). The special kind of Oedipal situation with attendant wishes, fantasies, fears and anger at exclusion is unique for every individual and shapes the basic pattern of the personality. When an Oedipal fixation develops (based on traumatic childhood events or defense mechanisms), it can lead to a regressive withdrawal from reality (Britton 2014, 77). In normal development, the current situation is enriched by the revival of earlier Oedipal situations, whereas in the case of a fixation it is instead replaced with a kind of stereotypic replay – repeated instead of modified.

Adolescents also must cope with the psychic pain, confusion and conscious/unconscious conflicts caused by changes in the body. Many behaviors serve towards dealing with inner problems, defending or protecting the self from feelings that are extremely confusing and deracinating. The motto is: better act than think, better to belong to groups or gangs than to risk independent thinking, better

Development of feeling 99

to become physically ill than feel psychic pain (somatization), better to see the world, oneself and others in an extreme light (splitting into good and bad), better to take drugs, alcohol or other addictive substances in order to cloud the intellect. Another, less recognizable form of defense is "pseudo-adulthood", where adult behaviors are exhibited but not integrated into the personality. Intellectualization constitutes another form of defense, described by Anna Freud (1992, 123), where inert knowledge is collected in order to avoid learning from experience. This reaction is often manifested in sublime but also sublimating philosophical discussions, or translation of love poems, in order for the adolescent not to have to reflect on her own feelings.

What is the perspective of 14-year-old Lucy? When asked when she was in love for the first time, she answers:

> I was twelve. I was together with a boy, kiss, kiss and hugs. Actually I had never had a real boyfriend yet. (While she speaks, she drops the wool she had into her hand into her tea, which spurts out of the glass.)
>
> There are boys in my class I text with, otherwise I have a telephone phobia. Doesn't matter if I call up a hairdresser or a boy. I'm afraid I'll say the wrong thing. Text messages are easier – or Facebook. I'm not a girl every boy would accept. I can't say I'm in love with someone from seeing him once. I like guys with a sense of humor.
>
> It was nice with Jonathan. We got along great. We were both in love. He gave me compliments: "You're the prettiest girl in school" – he's ten days older than I am. Most boys ask girls: "You want to go with me?" For me that's unnatural. Either it happens or it doesn't. I didn't know what I should do. He was my best girlfriend's best friend. His friends wanted me to go with him. They told me: "You're suited to Jonathan." They think I'm supercool.
>
> It was very sad then. I didn't say anything for a week. For a half a year, we didn't talk to each other. He had heard it from another side and was insulted. I didn't want to lose my best girlfriend. Only now did we explain to each other, we met just the two of us and went out to eat. We want to stay friends – I like him.

Two weeks later:

> Now I've told my girlfriends I met with him. They were really angry at me, because I had almost decided to be his girlfriend. Were they jealous? Elisabeth said: "Then he won't want to even talk with me on the telephone". Even though Jonathan and Elisabeth weren't a couple, they broke up! He didn't want her to influence me. I didn't know what to do. I talked to my mother about it – just a short talk, not like this. What should I do when he's so angry and disappointed?
>
> When we parted after the conversation we almost kissed – hugged – really, kissed hard – I could hear his heart beating.

100 Development of feeling

In January, my heart was beating really fast. He changed schools. He wants to be a policeman. He is 5'10", has a cool figure, looks like a blond Justin Bieber. That was it.

I wanted to change schools. They're so childish and act like children. The boys are fighting a lot. If I change schools, I won't have any friends anymore. I'm not so good at finding friends, because I'm so shy.

Discussion

On the surface, nothing seems to have happened. Jonathan would like to go out with Lucy, she likes him too, but out of loyalty, she doesn't want to risk ending her friendship with her girlfriend. All these questions and reflections have taken possession of Lucy – her thoughts repeatedly revolve around these questions. Unconsciously, her early rivalry with her mother is revived. "Who is the prettiest in the whole land?" asks the wicked stepmother in Snow White. But here it is Snow White – Lucy – who is happy to hear that she is the prettiest in the entire school. Perhaps it is not only joy but also a triumph over the other girls and, covertly, over her mother. Her dream that she would actually be a better wife to her father, would understand him and treat him better than her old mother, is also in play here. In this episode, Lucy renounces handsome Jonathan as she renounced her father. All the other girls are jealous of her – their envy is clearly visible. It is not enough that Lucy renounced Jonathan; even the fact that she considered not doing so is too much for them. But in truth, they cannot forgive Lucy the fact that he chose her and not them. When Lucy shares this dilemma with her mother, a psychoanalyst would understand this as a sign of trust, but it is also a way of telling her mother of her triumph.

Presumably, Lucy's discretion is not due only to loyalty, but also to her fear of becoming involved with a boy. From her further descriptions, it becomes clear how strongly she oscillates between happiness and desperation:

When I lie in bed, I just sob. When my brother (two years younger) calls me names, then I cry out my heart. I need time to myself alone.

It's all too much for me. What can I do with my problems, fights with my girlfriends, people who aren't perfect. I want to be alone then, I don't want to spend the night with my girlfriend. I want time for myself alone.

Once a month I cry, I cry, because I don't want to die.

Death makes me afraid. What happens after? Do you think about death too? Now for the last three months I haven't cried. There's almost something that bothers me. I try to always be cheerful. It's good when you've had a cry. Life is here for death – it's depressing. I don't want to die. I'm afraid of it. Does it make sense to live? There are good arguments, you fall in love, have a happy feeling. If I die, then somebody else is born instead of me. I probably have 80 years to live – this thought makes me cheerful again. It makes a click and I know I have to enjoy my life.

Everyone has these thoughts about death. Everyone is afraid of dying. What happens afterwards? A light comes – a white light. I ask everyone if they're afraid of death. When you're born, it's a movement forward towards death.

Discussion

Thoughts of death, the fear or longing for death are common in adolescence. Psychoanalysis understands this fascination with death as the expression of unconscious destructive and murderous wishes linked to fears of separation, as well as the fear of being excluded and abandoned. When one adolescent comes close to another, they experience a wide spectrum of attraction, exclusion, limitation and the wish for closeness and security. The group often assumes the containing function of maternal or paternal protection. Therefore, it is very threatening to be excluded by the peer group. Withdrawal or refusal to engage in close relationships constitutes a form of self-protection.

Withdrawal and solitude serve the inner need to turn inwards. Larson and Richards (1994; Larson et al. 1982 in: Arnett and Hughes 2012, 116) found that 25% of adolescents say they need more time alone, preferably in their room with the door closed; after feeling weak, lonely and sad, their mood actually improves in solitude. Larson and Richards call this self-reflection and "mood management". Adolescents listen to music, look at themselves in the mirror, brood and fantasize. When their dejection is over, they feel relieved and ready to master the joys and sufferings of everyday life. Adolescents who have this capacity to reorder themselves in solitude and develop confidence also have access to a good inner maternal object. This means they have internalized a loving mother or caring parents and can think of themselves the way they believe parents think of them. This is also how Lucy describes her withdrawal into the solitude of her room. Winnicott (1963) understood the "capacity to be alone" as an important step in development, one which becomes possible when the child perceives herself as a person separate from her mother, and yet still affectionately bound to her.

"I am alone" is a development from "I am". Dependent on the infant's awareness of the continued existence of a reliable other whose reliability makes it possible for the infant to be alone and to enjoy being alone, for a limited period. In this way I am trying to justify the paradox that the capacity to be alone is based on the experience of being alone in the presence of someone, and that without a sufficiency of this experience the capacity to be alone cannot develop.

(Winnicott 1963, 32)

This is opposed to the feeling of loneliness, which is associated with an inner conviction that one does not belong – and can sometimes be particularly pronounced while the adolescent is among his peers.

102 Development of feeling

A few months later – Lucy has now turned 15 – she relates:

L: I don't understand – I'm in love – it's the point of my life. When I'm with him, I'm in another world. Everything that's bad – it sounds like a movie – is gone. "When you're here, I'm in another world – shut up, that's so corny". But it's really that way – looking at him, he's so beautiful . . .

I: You're getting to know yourself really for the first time?

L: Yes, I've been confused recently, not in the negative sense, since on the one hand I forget so much. Some things that aren't so important, for instance, Facebook. My parents want me to do my homework. Sometimes I don't feel like it. Sometimes I have phases where I want to clean up my room. Why can't it always be that way? I tell my mother when she's criticizing me: "Mom, I also have no idea why it's this way!"

Dreams? Sometimes I think the day after that that was a cool dream or a nightmare. Sometimes I can remember them with a key word, sometimes I dream in another language. Sex fantasies? Hello, I'm 15 years old – in my dreams, I imagine what I would do – sometimes disgusting and scary.

My world is turning around right now – before it was so peaceful and now it's so turbulent. My parents can't keep up with it, I'm getting used to that. Sometimes I'm mega-fresh to them.

Nico, the one I'm in love with – he could have his pick. I ask myself why he wants to be with me? Am I attractive? I must be, a little bit, otherwise Nico wouldn't want to be with me. Sometimes I think, what are you doing here?

He likes me, I think. Otherwise he wouldn't say he doesn't want to hurt me – in case we break up, which we both don't want. It's so nice right now. Last week, we actually saw each other every other day. This week not anymore. His parents are mega-cool. We already talked about sex. He wants it to come to us. I have to get to know him well enough to be able to trust him. I've known him for six months, but we can only talk openly since about four weeks ago. My life is cool now – everything has changed. I'm getting to know new people, his friends, they see us as a couple. My friends think he's attractive and funny.

Everything's incredibly exciting, for instance, we saw each other the first on Sunday and went out to eat. That was the first time we kissed. We talked about what it should be like in school. The next day, we kissed at school – everyone saw it. Everyone converged on us – since when are you a couple? Nobody noticed that we were already in love for so long. Somebody found a wallet, brought it back to the bakery. 600 Euros reward – that's the same kind of luck I have with Nico. I don't want to tell my friends, but keep it for myself – it's my luck. During the daytime I also dream of him, of the beautiful moments we've experienced.

My phone bill is 100 Euros, I've written so many text messages. My father was mega-upset. Because I was afraid of saying the wrong thing I couldn't call him up. Text messages are easier. Now, we talk and talk on the phone.

Eight days later, she says:

> On Wednesday, Nico broke up with me. He came to my house and said he wants to end the relationship. He doesn't have so much time, he wants to put his energy into sports. I was very sad and cried a lot. I asked him whether we can stay friends, but he said no. That was very sad . . .

Lucy's spontaneous narrative conveys better than any theoretical description the longing and vicissitudes of early relationships. So many things are simultaneously at stake: testing one's own attractiveness, answering the worried question: will a boy ever love me, can I like anyone so much? How can I harmonize fear and desire? Lucy and Nico seem to have similar fears and longings, which has led them to a careful intimacy. They send so many text messages because this replaces personal (if cautious) meetings. Perception of the partner's attractiveness is strongly dependent upon the peer group. A true kind of intimacy is only created when Lucy decides not to share details of the relationship with her friends, instead keeping them to herself. But quickly – within ten days – fears seem to have gained the upper hand, and Nico decides to dedicate himself to sports and Lucy to her academic studies. The psychic pain of abandonment is often not so easy to perceive. The day after they break up, Lucy goes shopping with her friend to distract herself, and the day after that with her family to the musical *Singing in the Rain*, where she seems cheerful. However, we should not mistakenly believe her pain and offense are superficial: earlier painful experiences of separation are activated here.

It is important that Lucy's parents allow her to make mistakes, affording her the possibility to try out relationships and make her own experiences. Lucy must investigate her own mixed feelings – she herself does not know why she experiences such mood swings. Her "best friend", who comes up often in Lucy's narrative, is understood by the psychoanalytic view as standing for her mother, someone of her own age she can turn to. Discussing experiences is akin to extending them – and vicariously satisfying the wish to try things out through discussing one another's experiences. Parents need great tolerance in order to allow their children to make mistakes. A sentence children often use as a kind of battle cry with parents is: "Let me make my own mistakes!"

Letting a son or daughter learn from experience often means looking on as he or she gathers painful experiences. Sometimes, parents suffer more than the adolescent, and it constitutes a major achievement for them to allow their child to learn from the consequences of their actions, without punishment or reproach. Here is one example from Lucy's story. Her parents wish to discourage alcohol consumption, and they give their children only alcohol-free drinks. As follows, Lucy tells of her first big school dance.

My first dance – a catastrophe

"Actually, I didn't want it, I just wanted to try it out. Actually everything went so fast that I didn't notice anything. I got drunk so quickly. It was only twice

104 Development of feeling

before that I drank alcohol and that's why I can't hold it at all. In retrospect I feel pretty embarrassed that I can't remember anything. Everyone is talking about it at school, because I did such stupid things. I acted up, was making out with two boys – my boyfriend Sven and also his best friend.

"At first, Sven's friend kissed me and I thought it was Sven. Only when a friend of mine advised me I ought to stop and when Sven yelled at me did I notice that it wasn't Sven. When Sven got angry and said he never wanted to see me again, I slapped him. But he found that sexy, and told me so. I yelled at him that he shouldn't be so jealous and furious with me. He's not in love and we're only friends. I said: 'Do you want something from me?' He said 'No'. She slapped him. He kissed her for five minutes and we made up."

Lucy accepted the invitation to two cocktails that she didn't really like, but drank out of politeness. Then, giving herself up to the experience of alcohol, she danced wildly, laughed and became ecstatic. Everything became jumbled together – the music, the closeness of the dancers, her ecstatic mood: she can hardly remember now. Although this scene embarrasses her, she also finds it brilliant. Lucy expresses this syntactically by narrating the "climax" of jealousy in the third person ("she slapped him"). But the other spectators also observed the scene and talked about her shocking behavior for days afterwards.

Lucy's parents show understanding for her inexperience of alcohol. Accordingly, they change strategies and allow her to drink a half a glass of sparkling wine at parties. Neither her father nor her mother criticizes her, since she has learned her lesson from the party anyway. Through an experience like this, Lucy can take the step away from parental authority to self-discipline, but her parents' strict prohibition of alcohol was also important for her development.

Mark Twain perspicaciously describes the son's altered relationship to his parents after the hyper-critical phase of adolescence:

> When I was a boy of fourteen, my father was so ignorant I could hardly stand to have the old man around. But when I got to be twenty-one I was astonished by how much he had learned in the past seven years!
>
> (Twain 2015)

Mark Twain's remark is so perceptive because of the projective factor: not he, but his father has learned so much; Twain lives with massive projections, but can laugh at them with self-irony.

The examples mentioned earlier are from parent-child relationships that Winnicott would call "good enough". On the solid ground of a loving relationship, adolescents go to painful lengths in order to distance themselves from their parents because they know that their parents do love them and that they love and trust their parents. To the question of what adolescents do when they encounter a major problem, 19% said they always spoke with their parents, 42% said they often did, 33% said sometimes and 6% said never (Albert et al. 2010). Speaking with a friend was only slightly preferred. For the most part, parents are also considered to be confidants.

When relationships to parents are seriously fraught with neglect, mistrust, abuse, physical violence and humiliation, the situation is different. Paradoxically, freeing oneself from love-hate relationships can prove more difficult, because parents and children are intertwined in a tortured, confining pattern. The child's bitterness over lack of attention, the desire for revenge over inflicted humiliation or physical violence from parents who cannot be taken as an example leads him to reject them along with their way of life – but to unconsciously repeat the same pattern. Examples are legion from problem adolescents, including violence, teenage pregnancy, self-mutilation, drug use and contemplated suicide. A good demonstration of this basic destructive attitude attendant upon a break with parents is the Nine Bohemian Commandments in Hans Jaeger's *Fra Kristiania-Bohemen* (1885):

1   Thou shalt write thy own life.
2   Thou shalt sever thy family roots.
3   One cannot treat one's parents badly enough.
4   Thou shalt not beat thy neighbors for fewer than five crowns.
5   Thou shalt hate and despise all peasants.
6   Thou shalt never wear cufflinks of celluloid.
7   Forget not to make a scandal at the theater.
8   Thou shalt never have regrets.
9   Thou shalt take thy life.

These nine commandments derive from adolescent provocation, desperation and hopelessness packaged into the life of a bohemian – conceived against bourgeois society, the society of parents. Jaeger founded the Fra-Kristiania-Bohemian Society together with Edvard Munch. The accompanying book was banned and its author condemned to 60 days in prison. This became the object of stormy discussion among intellectuals, liberals, proponents of free expression and press, and representatives of the bourgeois parties, who saw in Jaeger's pronouncements a blasphemy and offense against public morals. The struggle between youth and parents took place on the political level. In his autobiography, Jaeger describes his extremely strict and bigoted father, who sought not to understand his son but instead to break his will. Great loneliness in childhood, physical violence and terror were the basis of this desperate, anarchistic revolt.

Let me now give an example of adolescents' turbulent quest for a partner, recognition from the opposite sex and the attendant competition with friends. In her work *The Adolescent Diary and its Function in the Mastering of Typical Adolescent Problems*, Janette Erhard (1998) quotes from adolescent diary entries. By chance, both Jan's and Lari's diary entries are included for the same evening – a party where they kissed. In his diary, Jan (16 years and 4 months old) has already

106 Development of feeling

twice mentioned his attraction to Lari, who is in his class at school. Here are some excerpts:

Then December 18th!

No Saturday is like another. A party with close friends always has a certain beguiling aftertaste. The supply of mulled wine was generous, and the consequences were predictable. Inhibitions are put aside. A new conversation. I don't know what urged me to it. Probably it was the attempt in spite of everything to change something or finally get a clear answer. The entryway is dark and uninviting. We sit down on the steps and begin to talk. The attraction is tangible. A feeling of trust and affinity. Then the "why"? someone else, one of your best friends – ALEX. How can somebody love someone they don't know? They simply can't.

Suddenly, unexpected guilt feelings towards me. She's terribly sorry. She tries to console me. Then it happens. First, we embrace each other in our desperation, then our noses rub gently and then, as in a dream, we open our lips and give the rein to our greedy tongues. The feeling of another person inside you is overwhelming. I can't get enough of it. She keeps making me go along with it. In her soul, deep inside her heart she does love me. I have to give her time. Two hours full of tenderness, then the awakening.

In front of the others, we act as if nothing has happened. Everything's in the past, but the feeling of being so close to another person remains anchored in your memory. The ancient human instinct that already made other people feel this same feeling millions of years ago. Is it really so great? There is nothing more beautiful than the love between a man and a woman. Even when it's not a happy love, there's still the adventure, the challenge and the attempt to try it out and the certainty that next time it will be more than a small, insignificant dream set to burst like a soap bubble. One has to not lose hope, believe in oneself and remain the person one is.

(Jan, as quoted in Erhard 1998, 87ff. Translation McQuade)

Jan documents his (perhaps first) kiss – at first from a distance, describing a party he was at. There is alcohol there, which reduces inhibitions, including his. As if by chance, he encounters Lari in the dark entryway. From the beginning it is clear that his love is hopeless. And it is his friend, of all people, who has attracted Lari's interest, although she does not know him closely yet. This makes Jan sad, and Lari attempts to console him. Perhaps the end of this uninitiated relationship between her and Alex supplies the catalyst for their two-hour-long kiss. Both know their encounter won't continue, and perhaps this helps them overcome their anxiety. Jan does not know what made him do it; the newfangled erotic tensions and urgent hormones are surprising and unknown. He writes "then it happened", which expresses that it was not a conscious act, but rather something in him led him to act, as in a dream, which we also cannot determine ourselves. He describes their physical and psychic attraction to one another as well as the overwhelming feeling of intimacy. From the psychoanalytic view, we understand this as a strong recollection of the first amorous pair – Jan as baby and his mother. It is love, arousal and greed – the deep wish to completely possess the object of desire – so old and yet so new and unfamiliar to the adolescent. It is not clear to Jan whether Lari is also inspired by erotic arousal, intimacy and protection, or whether her kiss is an expression of attraction to him. It is doubly difficult to understand, since the adolescent does not yet understand him/herself, let alone the other person. And immediately, hope arises: maybe she will love me later; maybe I only have to give her time.

In the last section of his diary entry, Jan tries to work through his experiences emotionally. It is surprising that other people do not notice when someone has just had a sensual experience. Jan philosophizes about basic human instincts and concludes with the insight that there is nothing more beautiful than love between man and woman. We can thus presume that Jan has gained a deep inner confidence through his parents' love – confidence that he is lovable, that they are glad he exists. He can accept his disappointment, has no regrets, but instead sees the experience as an adventure, a new experience and a challenge. He hopes that next time is more than a soap bubble. Hoping that next time Lari will love him, he encourages himself to be brave as a loving mother or father would encourage their child, convincing them that they are OK as they are.

In this special case, we have the opportunity to read how Lari describes the same scene from her perspective. During this period she has been writing almost daily in her diary. Many of her entries center on Alex, Jan's friend. She fantasizes what it would be like to be together with him, dreaming of him and describing her intense feelings she has developed for him from afar. She writes about Jan's attempt to get closer to her, something she experienced as an imposition – and yet she grows fonder of him each day. She has also heard through the grapevine that Jan is in love with her. She has told Jan she doesn't want that kind of relationship with him, but in the end writes: "I don't know what I should do."

December 18

Dear Diary!

Yesterday it was really fun in the evening, but actually it was the shittiest (sorry) day of my life. In the beginning we were in Caffecino (punch!), that was fun (everyone was a little "wasted"). Later Jan and Leo came, without Alex. Toni, Tim and Jan started putting moves on me. I thought that was fun, but Jan was sad, and especially jealous. I began to talk to him about myself etc. Everything got so stupid again, I told him that Alex is "the one". (Jan had already guessed this.) Afterwards he wanted to leave. But I followed him into the entryway and talked with him some more there. Then the hardest blow came for me. Jan told me: "Alex said he doesn't like you all because you're

108 Development of feeling

so loud etc." and if he were in my shoes he would give Alex up. Then we were both sad. I was truly so dejected, because so far I've always been rejected but the ones who did it at least liked me, just not "in that way". But Alex hates me. At first he just put his hand around me in the entryway, but later . . .

It was so disgusting for me because he was so wild, he was so happy to do what he always wanted to and he drooled on me from top to bottom. I couldn't say no. Jan kept saying that it was so beautiful although he can't kiss at all, really disgusting! But what to do? I can kiss my Alex good-bye. I don't understand it all. I did imagine Alex reacting this way, but I never thought it would actually happen. Jan wants to tell him about it too. I couldn't care less, since I can't become more insulted and sad than I am already. Why does Alex hate me so? I didn't do anything to him – on the contrary, I love him sooo much in spite of everything. I was somehow convinced that this time something will come of it, since Alex never rejected me in public. I would like so much to talk to someone about it, but it would be so embarrassing. I think I'll stop now because everything is for nothing, I'll just stay alone, but what to do? I'll just take care of Mama my whole life. I hate myself!!! I can't stand it in this world, I think I won't stay here much longer, I'm here in vain.

Someone else can take the job of filling the intermissions or being the class clown. I can't stand this shitful world much longer, that's for sure. Either I'll leave this country, or I'll go to Grandpa and James Dean forever. I don't want to live anymore. I'm fed up with only filling the intermissions. The one and only nice piece of news. – The whole experience was very beautiful.

(Lari, 16 years old, as quoted in Erhard 1998, 93ff)

At the beginning and end of Lari's diary entry, she describes how fun and beautiful the experience was. But in between, a desperate, dark mood prevails. The reader recognizes how much Lari contributes to her disappointments. She seems to conceal her true feelings behind the façade of a class clown. Presumably, nobody guesses how sad and dejected she is: apparently, she has nobody to talk with, be it friend, sister, mother or father. She also fails to see that Jan is jealous of Alex, and that his descriptions are necessarily colored by this jealousy: he has an interest in preventing Alex and Lari from coming together.

Interestingly, Lari writes dismissively of their kissing, which she terms "disgusting" and "drooling" – yet she remained for two full hours with Jan in the entryway, meaning that her negative assessments probably came only in hindsight. She is also certain that Alex "hates" her. Here, a strong tendency towards splitting is evident – Alex is either the adored, idealized fantasy lover or he rejects her entirely, in which case she wants only to die. She has no will to live. Interestingly, however, she has the idea of taking care of her mother her whole life long. Is this an indication of unconscious guilt feelings? Perhaps she would like to atone

Development of feeling   109

for her fantasized attacks on her mother by taking care of her. Lari writes of the boys' "putting moves" on her, but characterizes this as "fun". Does she find it difficult to admit her own erotic desires and pleasure? She is the one who follows Jan when he leaves the party. Her fantasized rejection by Alex may help her to carry out this "dangerous" relationship with Jan, which is also why she must denigrate his "drooling" over her.

The "separation" or rejection by Alex only occurs in her fantasy – she loved him in her dreams, but apparently was hardly together with him in reality. In her fantasy, her adored one can completely belong to her, whereas reality stipulates only a terrible rejection. The conviction of being able to totally control the adored love object can lead to exorbitant jealousy when that person turns his attention to a real person. But for Lari, daydream and reality are in osmosis. Lari experiences her rage at Alex's rejection – not as a murderous fantasy against the adored object, but against herself: she wishes to die, to join her idol James Dean in eternity, where she will presumably fulfill her secret wish to completely possess James Dean.

Although she dramatizes her feelings in writing, she is able to confide her pain, unhappiness and death fantasies to her diary, putting them into words and thus attaining relief. The diary functions as a substitute for a friend and an incipient form of self-reflection.

Taken together, the two diary entries do contradict each other considerably, although they describe similarly the basic party situation with its freely consumed alcohol. Lari and Jan diverge particularly in how they describe the long kiss – for Jan a supremely beautiful, shared experience, and for Lari something repellent that merely happened to her.

A week later, Lari writes:

> By now, I'm very happy again. Jan gave me a Christmas present I loved: a photo of him and me. I look at the photo the whole time. (Right now it's in front of me.)
>
> (Erhard 1998, 99)

At home, Lari is the baby of the family, who likes to be funny, dance and do sports. From other diary entries, we see that often, it is more difficult for the youngest child to grow up.

The fear of sexual union is strongly linked to unresolved childhood fantasies and desires that are experienced as real threats. Penetrating the vagina is then perceived through the fear of getting stuck or being destroyed in it, whereas the girl fears being damaged through penetration. Here an example from an autobiography, followed by a case study where therapy revealed unconscious connections.

Sexual fear is often not conscious but is revealed in the shunning of close, intimate relationships. In his autobiography, John Cleese (the British actor from *Monty Python* and *Fawlty Towers*) writes of how he was so occupied with other

110 Development of feeling

activities until the age of 25 that he had no relationship with a young woman. He describes the first time he fell in love, at the age of 23:

> I went a little bit mad. And the cause of this madness, which began to disrupt my work, my sleep, my Footlights life, indeed every corner of my daily routine, was this: I fell in love.
>
> When I say I fell in love, I didn't actually have much to do with it. I simply became engulfed in a storm of emotions, so unfamiliar, bewildering and overwhelming, that I basically came apart. Inside, anyway . . . I had no idea what this "falling in love" business might actually feel like . . . to one of the women who attended the law lectures. . . . I was developing obsessional romantic thoughts, even though she had an attractive boyfriend with whom she was obviously very involved. . . . I did not attempt to make them known, but you have to remember that the middle-class culture I inhabited found any public suggestions of romantic attraction problematic. And as for hints of anything more physical, these would have been viewed as a vulgar lapse. In the society in which I had grown up, the most trivial remark or moment of bodily contact could be construed as embarrassingly sexual: touching became foreplay, and a cheeky remark an invitation to risk pregnancy, while everyone sensed that the words "I love you" landed you at the altar. . . . I found myself actually unwilling to put my foot, however gently, on the first step of the romantic process; I was fearful that I would embarrass the object of my affection. . . . This . . . concern not to offend or distress was, I'm sure, the camouflage that my unconscious employed to hide from myself my deep fear of rejection.
>
> (Cleese 2014, 162ff)

Cleese supplies a number of details concerning his extremely difficult relationship to his mother, who was unable to connect to him emotionally because she was occupied solely with herself and her feelings of depression. Cleese's desperate attempt to defend himself against her fantasies and death wishes has been discussed in his autobiography. It is thus not surprising that he felt deeply rejected and unworthy of love. In his book, he asserts that no reasonable human being would want to come close to him. Certainly, the puritan sexual ideas of the English middle class play an important role here, but I would like to emphasize the intra-psychic dimension. Achieving emotional independence from a mother with whom a loving, secure relationship existed is far easier than doing so from one with whom the relationship was fraught with conflict. In the first case, the original needs of the small and older child have already been satisfied, so to speak, and the turning to a romantic relationship is thus possible. If the first love relationship is basically unsatisfying or conflict-ridden, the child is trapped in a love-hate relationship out of which he can free himself only with difficulty. Children who have been neglected or beaten are peculiarly dependent upon their parents. This is true of Cleese, who was in love but unable to give his adored fellow student a sign that he would like to become closer to her.

Some years later, during Cleese's sojourn in New Zealand, a loving woman affords him the possibility of having his first sexual experiences. He writes:

> And a few weeks later I was presented with the surprising offer of a chance to lose my virginity. . . . I met a girl – we'll call her Ann – with whom I felt really relaxed and who thought me hilarious. She found my impersonation of a mouse the funniest thing she had ever seen. We enjoyed a couple of evenings of entirely lust-free meetings. . . . I received a phone call from Ann . . . she would be staying with me at the hotel.
>
> Ann and I had a few drinks, went upstairs, and she made it easy for me, bless her. I had no idea how to please her, but she seemed perfectly happy, and there was affection, and she only asked me to do my mouse impersonation twice.
>
> This took place in the Station Hotel, Auckland, midwinter, 1964 and I was nearly twenty-five years old. When I was in New Zealand in 2006, I met Ann again, and I was pleased and proud that such a lovely and kind woman had been my first love. Thank you Ann.
>
> (Cleese 2014, 166)

Cleese's imitation of the mouse seems to not only have been a funny scene, but presumably also an expression of his self-worth. It seems that Ann managed to ameliorate (in a maternal way) his great fear and afford him this good experience.

Anderson describes one of his patients:

> For example, a young male patient told me that when he began to notice pubic hair on himself at puberty he was disgusted and horrified. For him, the presence of a sexual body confronted him with very disturbing phantasies of his parents, especially his father, arising out of his Oedipal relation to his parents, which had remained split-off and projected into his father's sexuality. Puberty meant for him an enforced intrusion, a bodily invasion of his father's body into his – a very concrete version of the more benign phantasy of becoming like his father. In his world there could be no such peaceful order: he was either a non-sexual little boy, or he had his parents' hated sexuality forced into him in the form of his father's sexual body.
>
> (Anderson 2009, 4)

The threat he feels emanating from his sexual body in rooted in his early fantasies, of which he is unconscious. He hated his father's sexual body, which took his beloved mother from him. Only when he later experienced a psychic breakdown as a boy were these deep unconscious layers revealed and worked through.

3.3 Impact on the parental psyche

Their children's adolescence also has strong effects on parents' psyches, either furthering their emotional growth or causing them to "act out" in order to avoid psychic pain.

112   Development of feeling

Parents feel their hopes and life plans mirrored as their children seek their place in the world. They compare what they have so far achieved in life to what they planned and envy their children – for whom the world is still relatively open – for their chances. The children's growing up constitutes a precursor to their leaving the family, which in turn constitutes a major separation for the parents. In particular, mothers who have given up their careers for their children now fear becoming "unemployed". A special effort is required to direct attention to the mother's own wishes and capabilities. Here is one example from a patient in therapy:

> In London, a 13-year-old boy, Ian, was brought to me for a preliminary discussion. He claimed he did not have "the problem", but instead his mother did. In the parental conference, it became clear that the mother's fears of her son's growing up were indeed considerable. In fact, she gratefully took up my offer of psychotherapy. With the help of therapy, she was able to get a job at the age of 40 and fulfill her wish of obtaining a driver's license. Only in this phase did it become clear that she had not yet become emotionally independent from her own (single) mother, who had helped her greatly but also determined much of her life. After she passed the road test, I asked her how she planned to celebrate – for her, an unfamiliar concept. Astonished, she told me in the next session that her son (whom she had considered particularly difficult) had shown great appreciation for her accomplishment. His academic performance had steadily improved since she had gone back to work. Household tasks were shared among the whole family, and she was able to assume family authority herself.

Discussion

I was able to accept the son's point of view that not he but his mother had a problem with his growing up, and we worked through this in her therapy. Unconsciously, the mother could and would not give up her son, since she had not yet cut the emotional umbilical cord to her own mother. Envy was only present in a mild form, since it was countered by love for her son. The central focus of her therapy was whether she could now fulfill her secret wishes and longings at the age of 40. Would she be able to develop and use her talents through professional training? The question in countertransference was whether I, as her "analytic mother", would allow her a professional and emotional development. As soon as we could work through the mother's pressure and projections on Ian in analysis, he felt free to study on his own account. The mother was completely surprised by how positively her son reacted when she was also learning: she then became a role model for him, instead of criticizing and devaluing him as before. Working through the mother's earlier conflicts with her own mother (and with me, through transference) made it possible for her to transform her mild envy into self-ambition – to change her own life as opposed to hindering her son in his development. In her essay "Envy in Everyday Life" (1986b), Betty Joseph writes of envy as a potentially constructive power. "Envy – involves to a greater or less extent a spoiling quality or at least hostility towards to good abilities or the other person, though this may not be recognized" (Joseph 1986b, 182). Envy leads to humiliation and insult through observing the advantages and successes of another person. The usual reaction is the unconscious wish to belittle and destroy these accomplishments. However, if there also exist loving feelings towards this envied person along with the hope of accomplishing something similar to what he has, hate can be ameliorated and the envied activities may be imitated. Adolescents are experts at provoking envy in others by teasing and mocking the adult until he loses his countenance. The same adolescent who has such difficulty controlling himself in this phase can now successfully (and triumphantly) elicit this behavior in adults. Instead of showing gratitude, the adolescent often chooses to provoke – in order not to envy the adult. Envy makes it difficult to recognize another person's achievements. When the adolescent metes out praise, it is often accompanied by a qualification: "it was good, but . . .". It is equally difficult for the envious person to accept something of value from another person; in analysis, we term this a "negative therapeutic reaction" when the patient, after an improvement in his life, engineers a relapse since he is unwilling to admit his analyst has helped him. As in Ian's case, it can constitute a major burden for an adolescent to feel responsible for his mother's depression. Ian could study independently only when his mother was able to positively change her own life.

Parents of adolescents are forced to observe themselves more precisely and come to some kind of reckoning. At first, physical growth – where the son might be taller than the father, or the daughter compares the length of her legs with those of her mother – can reminder a parent of her own aging process. Parents may notice painfully that their children no longer want to spend as much time with them: this period seems gone forever, and they must ask themselves whether they used this time of early childhood and childhood adequately. Parents automatically compare their own adolescence – their former dreams, ideas and fears – with their children's. This comparison can elicit painful thoughts if parents did not exploit their talents and possibilities adequately back then. If parents are able to admit these painful thoughts, then they can support their son or daughter even when the child embarks on a better education than they could in their own adolescence. If such reflection is not possible, there is a danger that parents will unconsciously envy their children, thus failing to support them in their endeavors.

The Irish poet William Butler Yeats communicates this issue vividly in his poem "Sailing to Byzantium" (1989, first published 1933):

> That is no country for old men. The young
> In one another's arms, birds in the trees
> – Those dying generations – at their song,
> (. . .)
> An aged man is but a paltry thing
> A tattered coat upon a stick, unless

114 Development of feeling

> Soul clap its hands and sing, and louder sing
> For every tatter in its mortal dress.
> (. . .)

Although Yeats wrote this poem at the age of 51, he conveys the clash between youthful energy with its lusty songs and his self-image of the pitiable old man. Grief over unattainable youth and physical decay is juxtaposed with the poet's narcissism, although youth share the fate of death with their elders. Can parents appreciate their capabilities and successes, their mastery of life, and grant their children their newly discovered love and pleasure?

Another important question is whether parents are satisfied with their children's development: does it follow their ideas, or are they disappointed that the children do not achieve what they want from them? Do undesirable traits in the children mirror things the parents wish not to see in themselves? Might the parents think their own inadequacies have led to this disappointing result? Has the child unconsciously been assigned the task of fulfilling unrealized wishes and hopes of his parents? If he instead turns to other activities, his parents might be deeply disappointed. It is difficult to admit the bitter thought: what did I do that one of my children does something like that?

Adolescents may not only criticize their parents' marriage but actually test it, while closely observing their reactions, seeking to find out whether this form of marital relationship should be a model for them. Do they wish to have the kind of relationship or marriage their parents do? Can their parents use their newly found space for activities together or does each of them go their own way? How much autonomy do the parents grant one another? Are they interested in one another and in their thoughts? Although in many marriages, love is affectionate and tender, with calm, trusting sexuality, many marriages are dominated implicitly or explicitly by the failure and frustration of sexual disinterest, often perceived as rejection.

Psychoanalytic theories can be understood as simplistic, for instance, when we speak of the "decline of the Oedipus complex" or the achievement of independence from the parents. It is important to recall how complex and unique each biography and pattern of the inner world is. Even when emotional independence from the mother has been adequately achieved, so that a relationship can be forged to another woman, the love between mother and son can be so strong that the father becomes jealous of the son. In this case, the adolescent state of mind is characterized by a specific constellation of jealousy and competition, later activated to a greater or lesser extent: the father might be filled with a powerful sensation of competition and exclusion when his wife shows great warmth and praise for their successful son, especially when he has long since lacked such attention from her. Here is an illustration from the autobiography of the famous American philosopher Stanley Cavell:

> Arriving unexpectedly to visit my parents in Sacramento some months after
> I entered university in Berkeley, I said to my mother (she alone doing the

driving) that I wanted to use their car to see friends the next morning, and she agreed. My father intervened to say that she had promised our neighbor to use the car at that time. My mother replied: "But then I hadn't known that Stanley would be here." I believe I can still reasonably approximate the rhetoric of his responding moral satire: "Oh, I see, Stanley is here. Therefore all obligations, all friendships, all right and wrong are to be suspended for the duration. Stanley is here. If only the reasonable request had been for any other time than just this time, then you would keep your promise. Too bad for the world and its needs. Yet the world must understand that Stanley is here! But if I am alive tomorrow morning that promise will be kept".

(Cavell 2010)

The fact that Cavell (over 70 at the time he wrote this) can quote his father almost verbatim in a scene from 50 years ago demonstrates its enormous significance to him. Although Cavell is writing of his father's anger at him, we might detect the author's triumph at managing to provoke his father via preferential treatment by his mother. He had just graduated with honors from Harvard, whereas his father had not been able to attend college. In the autobiography, Cavell describes his advantaged position with a mix of satisfaction and shame – as well as sorrow at his tense relationship with his father.

In any case, it is painful for parents to be demoted from the position of their child's premier love object. Instead of the father being his daughter's most important man, the new boyfriend is praised effusively. Fathers tend to be jealous and critical of their daughters' boyfriends – no boyfriend is good enough; or they set overly strict rules, in unconscious envy of the daughter's budding sexuality. That being said, it is very difficult to negotiate a curfew system (when the child is required to be home) that is both adequately structured and adequately flexible. If a father is not aware of his contradictory feelings, he might start behaving like an adolescent himself, embarking on an amorous relationship to a younger woman – perhaps one his daughter's age. In general, fathers are better advised to tolerate their often stormy arguments with their daughters. Lucy reports that she often has loud quarrels with her father and storms out of the room, but then she returns and apologizes, whereupon her father says everything is okay; it is good that she trusts him enough to voice her opinion and contradict him. With her friends, Lucy says, she is on the submissive side and does what they want of her.

Adolescents are striking out on new paths, an undertaking often accompanied by insecurity and fear. This is why their behavior is often so erratic. They take dogmatic positions not because they are sure of themselves but because they wish to test their opinions against their parents' resistance. Parents often do not notice that their adolescent child is covertly paying close attention to their arguments even while vehemently (and sometimes unfairly) protesting them: he might dismiss a parental warning in the heat of an altercation, only to later observe it without further commentary.

116 Development of feeling

Mothers closely bound to their sons tend to warn them of "dangerous" girls, thus increasing their fears. Only when the son has lived at home too long and takes no initiative towards starting a relationship does the mother realize how she has stood in his way.

Parents are often advised:

> to help adolescents be patient with their bodies that are altering so extremely, with the attendant drives and wishes that they cannot yet accept and deal with realistically – so that those drives explode either in the form of violence or out of a feeling of helplessness compared to what adolescents would like to do in fantasy but cannot yet achieve in reality.
>
> (Dolto and Dolto-Tolitch 1992, 158, translation McQuade)

This sounds simple enough, but the opposite is true. The transformation of their child's body into an adolescent one robs parents of their intimacy with the familiar childish body that used to cuddle with theirs – with the child often taking the initiative. Suddenly this body becomes unfamiliar, it smells different, its proportions and muscle structure are altered, evoking other associations. Whether consciously or unconsciously, it is remarkable how often parents comment negatively on the changes in their adolescent children's bodies, bodies which formerly seemed to virtually "belong" to the parents.

A patient I will call Fritzi told me that her father looked at her face and then opined: "Soon your nose will grow into your chin." Although they both laughed, she was deeply insulted. When she and her brother cannot carry heavy construction materials at home as easily as their father, he mocks them as "weaklings". The mother comments on a grease spot on Fritzi's pants, covering her newly curvaceous legs: "Your fat is already dripping out" (although she actually was on the slim side).

How can we understand what makes these parents mock their daughter so cruelly and dismissively? In fact, this father is very strongly in favor of all three children graduating from the academic high school; Fritzi is the only one to study at university, and he supports this. The father had a difficult and limiting childhood, not only financially but also emotionally. Nobody seemed to care how he was doing. On the one hand, he wishes to make a better life possible for his daughter, but on the other hand he passes down to her what he has experienced – envy, denigration and pure scorn. Seemingly, he can only praise other people's children, while denigrating his own. In parents of adolescents, unconscious conflicts with their own parents are reactivated.

Achieving independence from single mothers or fathers is particularly difficult, as well as from parents living in a marriage devoid of sexual or emotional closeness, where one parent is completely dependent emotionally on their child. In patchwork families, it is particularly difficult for adolescents to deal with parents and stepparents alike, since loyalty – often conflicted – exists to both parties. Elfi, whose peer group and analyst encouraged her to defend herself against her mother, who wanted to make her into a comic, vapid doll, began to pick out her own clothes; at pop concerts or Madonna films, her mother did not go with her, but instead waited for her outside, because Elfi wanted to sit next to her friends, not next to her mother. At home, Elfi moved out of her room, where her mother had been sleeping next to her on a mattress – and moved into her brother's empty room (he had married). As a result, the mother suffered: instead of making some change herself, she remained in her daughter's bedroom, while Elfi repainted her new room and decorated it with posters.

If the parents manage to understand their adolescent children's ambivalence and criticism as part of a developmental process – one requiring ample time – they will not take the children's pronouncements and attacks so personally. When parents remain calmer, a descriptive remark will have more influence with adolescents than a judgmental one (see Flammer and Alsaker 2011, 109). They know that their child is wavering between the opposing poles of coming into their own and the security net. Parents are faced with the difficult task of taking their adolescent children seriously and understanding them. It is important for the parents to support one another, adopt a clear position and clearly describe the contradictions and mistakes in their own life. Then they can set an example for their children in dealing with their own shortcomings.

Whether the separation from parents is more or less successful, the "inner father" or "inner mother" remains alive in each of us. The internalized image of the parents can be made conscious and then modified.

> The father lives, a life in me
> As long as I breathe, his memory lives as well
>> (Grillparzer, Libussa 1847,
>> translation McQuade)

4

Development of thinking

Adolescents think about themselves in a very different way than do children in latency. Their new self-image is shaped by the cognitive capability to think abstractly: hypotheses are no longer developed in the sense of concrete operations, but in an abstract fashion, where conclusions can be drawn. Adolescents also possess a greater capacity for memory and attention. They can understand complex relations and mutual relationships, also applying themselves to moral questions. As seen in Chapter 3, an adolescent must integrate precisely opposing tendencies. The capacity for thinking abstractly – including abstracting from one's own drives and behavior – is opposed by the adolescent seeing himself as the center of the world. The capability of posing and testing hypotheses clashes with the adolescent's grandiosity and overestimation of his own abilities, revived from early childhood. The capability to test the consequences of assumptions is opposed by the impulse to act instead of reflecting on oneself and one's motives. The capability to have creative thoughts and do new things without being limited by tradition and customs is opposed by the capability to carefully test the consequences of a hypothesis.

The development of thinking and the ability to learn is based on each individual's prior experiences. Instead of taking in mostly prepared knowledge, the adolescent is now able to independently obtain information and discuss it with his peers. Particularly in the age of the Internet, access to a wide range of information is practically unlimited; here, adolescents have a flexible, even playful approach that is especially helpful with this medium. These new cognitive capabilities can be compared to the baby's ingesting of solid food, another developmental step. With the transition to solid food, the baby is no longer dependent on the maternal breast; it could be fed by other persons or eat by itself. Many adolescents now discover new activities, pursuing their interests, trying out their new capabilities and developing a new independence from school and family.

Bion used the abbreviation K to distinguish two forms of knowledge from one another. He speaks of learning from experience as K to describe a learning from experience that becomes integrated in the personality, thus leading to enrichment and growth. Opposed to this is a purely formal, "dead" knowledge that Bion considers a collection of dead content, which he terms -K (Bion 1962, 89ff).

Adolescents typically harbor both a great desire and aversion towards self-exploration, with its turmoil and contradictions. New cognitive capabilities can be employed either to block painful insights about oneself, the family and parents, or towards self-recognition and tolerance of one's negative aspects. Bion formulates this dilemma in these words:

> The individual has to live in his own body, and his body has to put up with having a mind living in it. . . . I think it is fundamental that the person concerned should be able to be in good contact with himself – good contact in the sense of tolerant contact, but also in the sense of knowing just how horrible he thinks he is, or his feelings are, or what sort of person he is. There has to be some kind of tolerance between the two views that live together in the same body.
>
> (Bion 2005, 10)

Thus, Bion would not put pressure on somebody to embody his own ideal of a good person, but instead to recognize his positive and negative components.

The psyche can closely fluctuate between euphoria and joy to a depressed, reflective lassitude. Robert Musil describes this overheated state of mind:

> It expresses a simple spiritual fact: that the imagination works only in twilight. . . . And there is a kind of thinking that makes us happy. It gets into you so impatiently that your knees shake; it piles up insights before you in flight and storm, believing in which will absorb the life of your soul for years to come, and – you will never know if they are true. Let's be honest: you are suddenly transported up a mountain from which you can see your inner future with blissful breadth and certainty, like – let's be honest, like a periodic madman, a manic-depressive in the early stages of mania. You don't cry out or do anything foolish, but your thinking is unencumbered and gigantic as if with clouds, while the healthy mind fits thoughts together snugly like bricks and has the overriding need to test every single step again and again against the facts.
>
> (Musil 1990, 31ff)

Musil contends that this intuitive way of thinking makes us happy. This form of imagination functions "only at twilight". Imagination also bears fruit for rational thought, which Musil compares to a sewing machine that sews stitch for stitch. Writers often express more flexibly what psychoanalysis attempts to describe. Freud speaks of the significance of daydreaming in adolescence as a search for the ideal self – and/or the feared self. This search for the adolescent's self-image in the adult world entails a process of grieving for an idealized world now lost to him.

Adolescence encompasses all aspects of mental and psycho-physiological development. A sudden storm of intensive drive development also requires new

120 Development of thinking

forms of defense, which are connected to processes where an activity is (unconsciously) linked to something it suppresses and keeps affect at bay. The capacity for abstract thinking, the improved ability to remember and the broadened horizons of adolescent interest enable a kind of knowledge that serves as a defense mechanism – without the adolescent's intention or knowledge. Urgent wishes are hidden behind theoretical themes, which we call "intellectualization in puberty". This denotes a "process whereby the subject, in order to master his conflicts and emotions, attempts to couch them in a discursive form" (Laplanche and Pontalis 1988, 224). The adolescent becomes interested in psychology or philosophy, but formulates his problems in such an abstract way that they would seem to have nothing to do with him, in order to not reflect on his urgent affects and fantasies, despite an obvious jump in intellectual mastery. If boys during latency have been mostly occupied with adventures, animals and objects – real, concrete things, not products of fantasy – this might now give way to serious group discussions centering on questions of principle, relationships and love, ideas about career and life, travels and professions in faraway countries, questions of worldview and religion, friendship and autonomy. Although such discussions may well be based on a thorough examination of such themes, often a discrepancy becomes evident between these principles and how they actually influence adolescent behavior. Lofty concepts of love and fairness hardly impede adolescents from inconsiderate behavior towards one another, including infidelity and emotional insensitivity. Anna Freud wrote that the adolescent's various interests do not deter him from concentrating on the single focus of his own personality (A. Freud 1992, 125). Adolescent intellectual discussions have something of the character of daydreams in latency, without any attempt to solve real problems and tasks. Engagement with the meaning of life, revolution and death express the turbulent, warring impulses of hope and destructivity in the adolescent's inner world. A burning plea for patriotism and war can be actually governed by sadistic impulses, demonstrated by the adolescent's actual behavior. Nevertheless, this form of defense mechanism against threatening affects can be helpful as a kind of distancing. Investigation of these themes can be continued in later years (although this does not always occur), if interest does not flag.

Psychoanalytic observation carries with it the danger of according more interest to the problematic and pathological side of development and neglecting the positive aspects. The quickly growing cognitive capacity of formal thinking, the ability to abstract, deductive logic, the development of memory fill adolescents with the desire to think – which is as much a function as is mobility. To have solved a mathematical problem elegantly, to write an essay that is both original and satisfying, to make cogent arguments in a discussion – these are experiences of success, even in turbulent times. When the adolescent manages to forget his emotional turbulences and concentrate on a given task, then his self-confidence can rise. Although psychoanalysis terms the ignoring of feelings "isolation" (namely, the isolation of thoughts or behavior so that their links with other thoughts or with the person's life are broken), this can occur to different degrees, ranging from a massive blocking of the person's involvement to a mild form of distancing that will later afford him the capacity for self-reflection as well as for integrating acquired insights.

I will now describe the concept of intellectual development in adolescence as seen by Piaget.

4.1 The capacity for abstract thinking according to Piaget

Undoubtedly, the most elaborate theory of cognitive development was developed by the Swiss psychologist Jean Piaget (1896–1980). Already as a teenager, he wrote articles on the development of the natural world; after receiving his doctoral degree at 21 years old, he shifted his interest to human development. In his research into the intelligence of small children, he was less interested in their correct answers than in their incorrect answers, wherein he sought to find the key to how young children think. Piaget found that the unique quality of child thinking was manifested in the similar structure of "incorrect" answers given by a variety of children. Piaget recognized that although a child's knowledge determined his answers, there exists a biological process of maturation that makes it easy for him to understand the world – no special teaching is required. The same pattern encompasses various thought processes within a given phase of development: when a child can recognize that 15 objects remain identical although exhibited in different spatial patterns, then he can also recognize that there could be the same amount of water in a short wide glass as in a tall thin one – i.e., he already has the capability to recognize constancy and conservation.

The impetus for these changes in thinking, according to Piaget, lies in the maturation process, which in turn is dependent on a "reasonable" environment to develop properly. Yet the effect of the environment on maturation is limited: a 13-year-old child will master the thought operations typical for his age without particular instruction. Piaget understands maturation as an active process, in which children seek out information and stimulation in their environment as matching their particular developmental stage. Maturation, according to Piaget, is not comparable to genetically determined neurophysiological programming of instincts, since biology merely paves the way for how the individual deals with them (Piaget 1970, 69). Piaget assumes that the active construction of reality occurs through using "schemes" – i.e., particular structures of organizing and interpreting information. With the young child, these schemes are based in sensory and motoric information acquired through sucking and grasping, but after infancy, schemes become symbolic and represented through words, ideas and concepts (see Arnett and Hughes 2012, 83).

Piaget distinguishes between two schemes: "assimilation" and "accommodation" (Piaget 1970, 53ff). The biological conditions for his theory are founded on the following basic assumptions:

1   An organism adapts to its environment during the course of its development and in conjunction with the interactions and self-regulation characterizing its

122 Development of thinking

"epigenetic system" (in the embryological sense, epigenesis is always determined both internally and externally).

2　In its structure and development, intelligence adapts to the coordination of inner and outer information.

3　Cognitive or (generally) epistemological relations come into being that are neither a simple imitation of external objects nor an evolution of the subject's inherent structures, but instead constitute a totality of structures that arise through constant interaction between the subject and the external world (Piaget 1970, 41).

Piaget's concepts led to seeing a child not as a blank slate, but as possessing qualitative faculties for acquiring information from the outside world. The child's cognitive faculties develop according to his age, as can be seen through his play, fantasy and emotions. Because of this, Piaget considered it fruitless to pressure a child to enter his next phase prematurely; rather, the according stage of development should be supported, and the child afforded time to develop his corresponding capabilities.

Piaget identified the following stages of cognitive development:

1　Sensomotoric stage (ages 0 to 2)
2　Concrete-operational stage, including pre-operational stage, ages 2 to 7 (2a) and concrete-operational stage, ages 7 to 11 (2b)
3　Stage of formal operations (ages 11 to 15–20 years)[1]

In the sensomotoric stage, the baby/young child employs its tactile and oral faculties to investigate the world: thus, a contribution from the outside is necessary in order to develop inner structures. The subject's first priority is his own body, followed by the development of practical intelligence.

In the pre-operational stage, the child becomes capable of imagining inner symbolic representations with the help of language.

In the stage of concrete operations (to be more precisely described later), the child can already employ mental operations, but only in a concrete experience; he cannot yet think hypothetically.

According to Piaget, these stages follow one another in one immutable order. For his data, he employed three different methods: child observation, experimentation and questioning children.

For adolescence, the third stage of development is relevant. In his essay "Intellectual Evolution from Adolescence to Adulthood" (1972b), Piaget points out that adolescents exhibit major differences within this age group, depending on their social environment and career interests. In addition, he contends that we know very little concerning the transition from adolescence to adulthood (Ibid).

Between the ages of 12 to 15, the adolescent attains a capacity for formal operations (as distinguished from concrete operations), thus vastly improving his ability to think, his sense of space, his ability to differentiate and his speed of observation.

The aspects I will now describe are: formal operations, abstract thinking and deductive reasoning, and complex thinking (metaphor and sarcasm).

Formal operations

The major qualitative change in thinking occurs between latency (ages 6 through 11), where the child thinks in concrete operations, to the formal operations of the adolescent. With concrete operations, the child can solve simple tasks according to logic and systematic rules, but only in adolescence can he identify the reasons for systematic operations, as well as their results. Inhelder and Piaget (1974) demonstrate this using the well-known example of the "pendulum problem":

> Children or adolescents are shown a pendulum consisting of a weight hanging from a string and set into motion. They are then posed the question: upon what does the speed of the pendulum depend – is it the heaviness of the weight, the length of the string, the height from which the weight is set in motion or the force with which it is pushed? The children are given various weights and strings of various lengths to use in their deliberations, and the ways latency children and adolescents solve this problem can be compared.

In concrete operations, latency children tend to approach the problem with random attempts – often changing more than one variable at a time. For instance, they may try the heaviest weight on the longest string, dropped from an intermediate height with medium force. Then they might take a medium weight on the shortest string and swing it with medium strength. When the pendulum's speed is altered, latency children have no way to say what caused the change, since they altered more than one variable at the same time. Even when they find the right answer (the length of the string), they still cannot explain why this is. Indeed, Piaget devised his experiment in order to distinguish between the correct result and the explanation for it.

An adolescent – who can use formal operations – employs a form of hypothetical thinking to solve this problem, as in an scientific experiment. The thought process involved could be described as follows: "Let us first examine weight. I will try out various weights and keep all the other variables constant (length of string and height)." (The adolescent would do this and then see that there is no difference.) "Now, I will try out different lengths of string, leaving the other variables constant. Yes, now I see a difference – the pendulum swings faster with a shorter string: thus, the length of string does make a difference. But let me try height, too: no change; then force: no change either." (Piaget speaks here of the capacity to exhaust all combinations.) "But I will still try out a different height, and also a different strength of pushing the weight at the outset. No, I see no difference as a result. This means that the speed is solely dependent on the length of the string."

Through this process, the formally operational thinker arrives at an answer that is not only correct but can also be explained and defended. This is why Piaget

124 Development of thinking

calls this form of thinking "hypothetical-deductive reasoning" (Piaget 1972a) – the core of formal operations.

Abstract thinking

Abstract thinking does not merely describe concrete objects or events but constitutes a derivation thereof. It is a purely mental activity, in that it is not based in direct sense experience. Mental activities exist only in ideas such as time, faith, friendship, freedom, justice or culture. Latency children in concrete operation, however:

> can apply logic only in things they can experience directly, concretely, whereas the capacity for formal operations includes the ability to think abstractly and apply logic to mental operations as well. . . . Adolescents become capable of engaging in discussions about politics, morality and religion in ways they could not when they were younger because with adolescence they gain the capacity to understand and use the abstract ideas involved in such discussions. . . . It may be useful at this point to 'bear in mind' that recent research on brain development suggests that the capacity for abstract thinking is based on a growth spurt in the brain in late adolescence and emerging adulthood which strengthens the connection s between the frontal cortex and the other parts of the brain.
>
> (Arnett and Hughes 2012, 86)

Nevertheless, the precondition for this is that the adolescent can abstract, which the latency child cannot. In my book *Latency. The Golden Period of Childhood*, I described several of Piaget's experiments in detail, which show that a latency child cannot yet abstract (Diem-Wille 2018, 113ff). For instance, Piaget asked Paul, who had a brother named Stephan, whether he (Paul) has a brother. Paul answered yes, but when asked whether Stephan has a brother, Paul said, "No, there are only two of us in the family". Thus, he cannot abstract from his *own* position, i.e., he thinks "I am here with Stephan, and since Stephan has only me as his brother and no other brother, he *has no brother*."

Recognizing general natural laws also requires the faculty of abstracting from the egocentric worldview of a child – the worldview demonstrated, for example, when a child believes the moon is following *him* no matter where he goes; when the child stands still, he believes the moon is also standing still. The latency child slowly recognizes this contradiction and that laws of nature operate outside of his existence.

In games, an adolescent can also accept general rules without inventing extra rules for himself – and when he does this, he realizes that they contradict the general rules.

Piaget notes many logical operations an adolescent can carry out *without* identifying concrete objects for the abstract concepts of "A" or "B". One example is the transitive property: when A = B and B = C, then it is easy to see that A = C. This Piaget calls a milestone in cognitive development:

> The principle novelty of this period is the capacity to reason in terms of verbally stated hypotheses and no longer merely in terms of concrete objects and their manipulation. This is a decisive turning point, because to reason hypothetically and to deduce the consequences that the hypotheses necessarily imply (independent of the intrinsic truth or falseness of the premises) is a formal reasoning process.
>
> (Piaget 1972b, 3)

Simple logical operations are possible in the pre-adolescent stage as long as they remain concrete: the latency child can distinguish among classes, relations, numbers etc., but not in the form of hypotheses posited beforehand. Reversibility is not yet developed, as Piaget showed in a famous experiment involving two differently formed containers, one higher but narrower and the other wider but lower. When water is poured from one container into the other, a child of seven believes the quantity of water to be different since its level is higher in the narrower container. Here, the child is considering only the parameters, not the transformation involved.

> In contrast, hypothetical reasoning implies the subordination of the real to the realm of the possible, and consequently the linking of all possibilities to one another by necessary implications that encompass the real, but at the same time go beyond it.
>
> (Piaget 1972b, 3)

Such operations involving possibilities, particularly when posited under ideal conditions, are what enable mathematical thought – for instance, the knowledge of the perfect circle or an absolutely constant ballistic curve and a point without extension. Adolescents are fond of utopias and visions for the future, particularly as linked to their own ambitions (the dream of being an astronaut or movie star, for instance). Thinking in possibilities opens new, creative areas. As Goethe wrote: "One must be young in order to do great things" (Goethe's letter to Eckermann, 1811–14).

This turning point in cognitive development also leads to a new quality of discussion and entails the ability to reflect on one's own thought, a level of meta-reflection that is not yet accessible to children.

In a fruitful, constructive discussion, adolescents can address the other participants' viewpoints in the sense of a hypothesis (when they do not agree with the standpoint) and then accordingly draw conclusions. After evaluating these consequences, they can then evaluate the argument.

Through his or her ability to think hypothetically, a person can develop interest in problems extending beyond his or her own field of experience.

126   Development of thinking

Thus, adolescents can understand and develop theories and participate in societal questions and ideologies of adults. This is often motivated by the wish to change – or, hypothetically, to destroy – society in order to create a better one.

Complex thinking

Thinking in formal operations is more complex than in concrete operations. Thinking in concrete operations tends to focus on one aspect of a thing – usually, the most obvious one – whereas formally operational thinkers are more likely to see a variety of aspects of an idea or situation. Complex thinking is necessary to understand a metaphor or sarcasm. Metaphors are complex because they have more than one meaning. Poems and novels are replete with metaphors – so to speak, they have a second, less obvious meaning. One example from T.S. Eliot's poem "A Dedication to My Wife" (1957a):

> No peevish winter wind shall chill
> No sullen tropic sun shall wither
> The roses in the rose garden which is ours and ours only.

Here, the concrete level is embodied in the hard conditions of the rose garden in winter, but this image has a second meaning as well: the poet's optimism that the love between him and his second wife will survive life's vicissitudes – as the roses do. In this case, it was a "May-December romance", since Eliot's second wife Valerie, his secretary at Faber & Faber, was 38 years younger than he was. Eliot thought that with Valerie he could be happy for the first time in his life.

Adolescents can comprehend such complex meanings. Children have no clue. When children and adolescents are questioned regarding a metaphor, their divergence in understanding becomes clear. The saying "One bad apple spoils the barrel" was presented for interpretation to both children and adolescents. An 11-year-old wrote, "There is a big barrel of apples, and a woman picks up one bad one out that is rotten, and there are worms in it, and the worms go to all the other apples". An adolescent wrote, "One bad comment can spoil the entire conversation" (Duthie et al. 2008, quoted in Arnett and Hughes 2012, 87).

Pre-adolescents also have similar difficulties in understanding sarcastic remarks such as "That's a nice dress" or "Your new haircut looks great". Is this only meant literally as a compliment, or does it mean its opposite? Adolescents love TV shows that are ironic and sarcastic, such as *The Simpsons*, or magazines such as *MAD*. Their conversations are often marked by irony and sarcasm, such as when text messages imitate the formal language of adults, including salutations and "Yours truly" – even though they find these funny.

To sum up, we can say that adolescent logic constitutes a complex but coherent system that is relatively distinct from child logic. Adolescent logic "constitutes the essence of the logic of cultured adults and even provides the basis of elementary forms of scientific thought" (Piaget 1972b, 6). The transition from adolescent to adult cognitive development has not yet been adequately researched. Piaget writes: "We know as yet very little about the period which separates adolescence from adulthood" (Ibid, 1).

Addressing the question of whether every individual in this stage will attain the requisite formal thought operations, Piaget points out that a favorable environment is necessary; when such operations are carried out in common, accompanied by mutual criticism or support, discussion and identification of problems on the basis of information, then the individual's curiosity can be sparked through cultural influences from his social group.

> Briefly, our first interpretation would mean that in principle all normal individuals are capable of reaching the level of formal structure on the condition that the social environment ad acquired experience provide the subject with the cognitive nourishment and intellectual stimulation necessary for such a construction.
>
> (Piaget 1972b, 8)

Therefore, Piaget propounds an active form of instruction where adolescents can raise questions and solve problems independently. Group instruction encourages coordinated activities – an important precondition for developing reversible operations. In a group, children and adolescents can discuss their experiences, evaluate them, and draw conclusions from them (see Piaget 1972a).

After a certain level of cognitive development, individual aptitudes diverge with increasing age, with individual interests increasingly taking the upper hand over general tendencies of development. One good example is the evolution of drawing skills: up to the point when a child becomes capable of drawing in perspective, we observe a very general common progress for the test task of "drawing a man". At the ages of 11 to 13, surprisingly, great differences can be seen, and even greater differences at 19 and 20 years old. Here, the quality of the drawing has no longer anything to do with the level of intelligence. This constitutes an important example of one pattern of behavior being subordinated to general evolution at a particular stage – even though from adolescence on, this behavioral pattern has more to do with individual talent and interest. Adolescents discover their talent for mathematics; here, two different types can be distinguished, those with "geometric intuition", who tend to think more concretely, and the "algebraists" or "analysts", who think in a more abstract manner. A difference can also be distinguished in any field: between adolescents who show talent for physics or for solving logical problems, as opposed to those showing an aptitude for logic or mathematics. The same distinctions could be drawn within linguistics, literature

128 Development of thinking

or philosophy. It thus can be said that adolescents between 15 and 20 years attain this stage of formal operations in various areas, according to their interests or (future) professional specialization.

Note

1 "Stage" is also translated as "period". The number of stages varies, since some texts describe the sub-stages as their own independent stages (thus comprising four separate stages).

5

The search for the
self – identity

> One must be young in order to do great things.
>
> —Goethe to Eckermann, 11.03.1828

The central focus in adolescence is to find one's place in the world, to discover who one is, which profession one will undertake and how one will live. As Ernst Bloch describes, "youth believes that it has wings and that all the right things are waiting for its sweeping entry" (*Die Zeit*, April 1 2015, 30).

It is the time of departure, radical change, separation from the parents and a new beginning. The grandiosity of youth indicated by Bloch and Goethe is based on the grandiosity of early childhood, and it plays here just as crucial a role as the feeling of powerlessness and vulnerability. As Musil writes in his essay "Political Confessions of a Young Man", youth is the time of possibilities, rebellion and creativity. It is an important time where character is shaped, acquiring a coherent, stable form – so to speak, a restructuring of the personality.

The adolescent simultaneously both wishes and fears to become an adult. Instead of embarking on a voyage of discovery, a quest for identity, as the heroes of adolescent literature do, Peter Pan remains in "never-never-land" as an eternal child. Many adolescents conceive a longing for their lost childhoods.

The salient features of this challenging time are often only recognized in retrospect. In her memoirs, Coudenhove-Kalergi writes:

> It is a kind of awakening that I experience as a twelve-year-old in that spring, a recognition of the world's beauty, the possibilities it offers, the mission of adulthood. Is it a presentiment of what will come? . . . Something this beautiful, I tell myself, you will never, never see again. . . . To get to know Prague and gallivant through its streets is the dream of my childhood. Only in the last year before we were exiled did it become reality. . . . After school or in the afternoon, I walk through my favorite parts, with a friend or preferably alone. Through the seminary garden up to the Strahov monastery. The lilacs are blooming there in their luxurious umbellifer, and their fragrance accompanies

130 The search for the self – identity

me the entire way. On top of the Laurenz hill. Over the big staircase to the Hradschin.

(Coudenhove-Kalergi, translation McQuade 2013, 32ff)

Coudenhove-Kalergi seems to see the world and herself for the first time. Like the lilacs, her adolescent soul and body are awakening, in a mood fraught both with innovation and melancholy ("something like this, I tell myself, you will never, never see again"). She feels a sense of possibilities, not yet limited by disappointments, setbacks, guilt feelings and self-doubts. This makes for a major awakening on all levels – physical, emotional, spiritual and moral.

Puberty is a time of breakout and of loss – sometimes both simultaneously. The process of integrating divergent tendencies is always turbulent, especially when they break apart and the adolescent suffers a psychic breakdown or chooses self-destructive, anomalous behavior.

Flasar describes puberty as a crisis or collapse leading to a total withdrawal:

I believe that growing up constitutes a loss. We think we are winning something. In truth, we lose ourselves. I grieved for the child that I had been and that I – in rare moments – still heard beating wildly inside my heart. At the age of thirteen, it was already too late. At fourteen. At fifteen. I hated my face in the mirror, its sproutings and execrecenses. The scars on my hand all come from the attempt to make things right again. Countless shattered mirrors. I didn't want to be a man who believed he was winning. Not to grow into any suit. Not to be any father who would say to his son: "We all have to function". . . . This sentence was my guiding principle – a motto inscribed upon me.

(Flasar 2014, 23ff, translation McQuade)

Here, the process of becoming an adult is experienced only as threat and loss. When the adolescent observes his altered body in the mirror, it causes such pain that he turns away from or shatters the mirror – an expression of deepest desperation, rage and powerlessness leading to violence. Envy of his successful father leads this adolescent into a state of refusal. Instead of going out into the world, he opts for total withdrawal. This person becomes a "hikikomori", the Japanese word for people who refuse to leave their parents' house, shut themselves up in their rooms and reduce their contact to the family to a minimum. Some of them spend up to 15 years or even longer locked into this condition: in Japan, the number is estimated at 100,000 to 320,000 (Flasar 2014, 139).

The title of this chapter may be misleading, since the concept of "self-seeking" implies a conscious search, a thought process. This is not the case. The question "who am I?" results from the loss of the unquestioned belonging to a family that the adolescent renounces in the process of becoming an adult. Accordingly, the adolescent prefers to avoid experiencing all the painful feelings associated with this loss. Instead of thinking, the adolescent tries out various modes of behavior, presentations of the body, membership in groups. The motto could be acting instead of thinking. Earlier feelings and modes of behavior are stirred up. Like the child who has just learned how to walk and walks away from its mother briefly to investigate the world before returning to his secure maternal home base, the adolescent dares to investigate an adventurous new realm before returning to the lap of the family. The search for identity tends to occur at this age in an experimental fashion, more through action than through reflection. The focus is on investigating an unknown future. For children who grow up in difficult family situations, this time can constitute a liberation. The girl who was seen as lazy and uninterested, awkward and difficult, can bloom through the admiration of her peers, seeing herself as an ugly duckling who is finally recognized as a swan. We therefore speak of adolescence as a "second chance" for attaining a different social position in a new context, thus affording an inner restructuring of self-esteem; this is why new systems of contact such as peer groups have a central significance as a field for experimentation – "experimentation" that, fraught with irritation, shame, guilt feelings and stress, lies partly within the realm of the normal and partly outside. Adolescents often do not know why they do something, do not know why they feel as they do and then feel still worse since they do not know "why". To the question of "What got into you for you to do that?", they then often answer: "I don't know, I just had to do it."

Bion appraises the adolescent situation by describing the phenomenon of emotional turbulence as a part of "growth". He writes: "Turbulence is what is manifested when an apparently co-operative, quiet, docile and admirable child becomes noisy, difficult and rebellious" (Bion in Bleandonu 1990, 242). Adolescence is a stage where turbulence is normal and can be expected. As in the analytic process, adolescents evolve in spirals. As Bion writes about the analytic process: "We repeatedly return to the same point, but on different levels of the spiral" (Bion 1979, 85).

5.1 The development of character

Psychoanalysis deals with adolescent character development in this turbulent time via several concepts, since it touches almost every area of the psyche and environment. But we all recognize that an adolescent ending puberty will have developed a clear mode of dealing with his own life questions. His behavior, his attitudes, interests and relationships have become more predictable, exhibit greater stability and tend to remain consistent under pressure. The basic patterns of the personality (as explained earlier) were already set in the early years of life and are still relevant. Basic experiences of being lovingly held, emotional accessibility of parents, their capacity for taking in the child's projections and digesting them emotionally (containing), form a secure basis for the child's inner world with good inner objects.

If the child did not adequately experience these foundations of trust and security, then his basis becomes shaky and it becomes difficult or impossible for him to integrate contradictory claims between his inner world and the environment.

132 The search for the self – identity

In place of this integration and forming of a more or less constant character, he experiences an inner schism and feeling of being lost or lack of emotional connection. Without having an emotional homeland, it is impossible to become liberated from this state.

5.2 The search for identity

The adolescent questions of "Who am I? Who do I want to be or become" are necessary precursors to reorganizing the inner world. In his *Three Essays on the Theory of Sexuality* (1905), Freud speaks of the double-sided nature of psychosexual development. There is a strong impetus to redefine oneself, looking for new ways of being, believing and belonging.

The questions of "Who am I? Why am I alive?" constitute a discussion of real challenges on the conscious level, but on the unconscious level, the attendant feelings can express unconscious guilt for sexual desires, then eliciting an unconscious wish to be punished (see Anderson 2009).

The same adolescent harbors contradictory desires – between the deepest desires and passions present from infancy and the "almost adult man", who is relinquishing essential infantile wishes. There can often be a confusion between infantile feelings and adolescent sexuality, which can lead to disturbance and breakdown. Many fathers cannot emotionally "afford" to support their growing sons, thus becoming either frustrated or sinking into a deep depression. In a certain sense, adolescence constitutes a kind of weaning, since an adolescent must give up fantasies of possessing the mother completely, just as moving out of the parental household signifies a loss of comfort and convenience. The unconscious bitterness of this loss is often reformulated into a reproach against the older generation, who are allegedly delivering the son up to a bad world where the environment is endangered and pensions are no longer secure because they have not taken enough interest. The younger generation then describes itself as disadvantaged, seeing its adult self like a neglected infant expelled from the marital bed. From the psychoanalytic perspective, these criticisms originate from the adolescent's critical superego, attempting to avoid grief and the knowledge of all they are losing. The loss is then not experienced as individual grief, but projected onto the world. Only when it is possible to also see the good aspects of the adult world is an integration possible – an attitude that Melanie Klein (1944) calls the depressive position. There are also good things in the adult world, things the adolescent can aspire to, but a struggle is always involved. Every generation has problems, the generation of the grandfathers and grandmothers had to master two world wars, the parents the post-war reconstruction. The complex world contains both: opponents and friends, loneliness and friendship; the human being is not alone. It is always a painful process to grow up and become an adult. Adolescents blame the older generation because that is easier than to grieve and bear the requisite psychic pain. Attaining a realistic view of a world that is both good and evil, a self that is both good and evil – the depressive position – is a painful process. Only when the adolescent recognizes his own shortcomings, his own good and evil sides, can he accept the imperfect world of his parents.

As Bion contends, inside every person there are two contradictory forces – one that strives for knowledge (K) and wishes to recognize reality, and another that wishes to hinder this process. Bion calls this force the "inner enemy". We feel compelled to escape from this unpleasant world with our bodies or thoughts. Escape is a fundamental human answer. Even a young child does not want to know about his or her distress, either denying or idealizing it.

> According to Bion, existence is not enough; our existence must have a certain quality of aliveness. . . . Bion emphasizes the difference between knowing and knowing about. Idealization must give way to a realization through which one can perceive the shortcomings of the idealized image.
>
> (Bleandonu 1990, 246)

Instead of realistic insights into his own relative insignificance, the adolescent can defend himself through arrogance, projecting his own bad qualities onto others and ultimately achieving a position where he is disliked. Vulnerability and sensitivity can be concealed behind megalomania, a necessary transitory phase of the adolescent state of mind that can persist many years afterward – even for an entire life. Only reluctantly does the adolescent see the real world and accept the attendant disillusionment. Behind his envy of adults who have already achieved success hides the insecurity of whether the adolescent will achieve success, find a profession and establish a family.

As we have seen, Freudian psychoanalysis proceeds from the hypothesis that the superego is the heir of Oedipal conflict, an internalization of parental, societal values and norms occurs that we term the superego. The superego is a punishing judge in the image of a feared authority figure. In the adolescent phase, not only the real outer parents are questioned, but also the adolescent's own "inner" parents – i.e., the values and attitudes she has internalized in order to develop a relatively stable life and character. However, equally important is the idea of what the adolescent wants to be – which we term her "ego ideal". As opposed to the superego, the ego ideal is formed in the image of the love object. Nunberg describes these two agents in the following way: "Whereas the ego bows to the superego out of fear of punishment, it bows to the ego ideal out of love" (1932, 173).

The adolescent's self-image, along with his cognitive development, becomes more complex and abstract. He develops a capacity to reflect on himself and distinguish between his current self and two kinds of possible selves – the ideal self and the feared self, i.e., he can see his own dark sides. The adolescent is also increasingly able to recognize various "identities" or aspects of his identity in connection to various persons and situations – for instance, at school and at home, with friends and strangers. This also includes the knowledge of when one is more "authentic" or adapts to the ideas of others in the sense of a "false self" (Winnicott 1960).

5.3 The superego and its early forms

In his book *New Introductory Lectures on Psycho-Analysis* (1932), Freud describes the superego as a transactional structure with three functions:

> self-observation, conscience and formation of the ideals . . . (the superego has) the functions of self-observation, of conscience and of (maintaining) the ideal. . . . The super-ego is the representative for us of every moral restriction, the advocate of a striving towards perfection – it is, in short, as much as we have been able to grasp psychologically of what is described as the higher side of human life. . . . Thus a child's super-ego is in fact constructed on the model not of its parents but of its parents' super-ego; the contents which fill it are the same and it becomes the vehicle of tradition and of all the time-resisting judgements of value which have propagated themselves in this manner from generation to generation.
>
> (Freud 1932–33, 65ff)

Feelings of inferiority and guilt arise from the tensions between the ego and the superego, where guilt feelings correspond to the conscience and the feeling of inferiority corresponds to the ego ideal.

When someone writes a diary, she is satisfying her need for "self-explanation" (Seiffge-Krenke 1985, 134). Experiences, feelings, moods and hopes are confided uncensored to the diary. Alongside the relieving, cathartic function, a diary offers the possibility to master feelings and integrate moods that are often contradictory. Earlier observations are brought into perspective with later ones and modified. Since diary entries capture the momentary emotional state, they are also well suited to illustrate psychic development. Now, we will accompany Lari in her development past her previous diary, where she told of her first amorous experiences and disappointments.

An outer event changes Lari's world. She begins a new diary and writes on January 18, 1986, as a 13-year-old:

Saturday

> Today we came back . . . from the skiing course. I was so looking forward to seeing Mama, Jutta and Timmy (their pet dog). But I fought with her again, or, to put it more accurately, she started it. Mama is so sad. She has so many worries and wants us not to fight on top of that. She wants to file for divorce on Monday. I'm so sad! All my friends have a family, only I don't have one. I'm embarrassed to tell them that my parents are getting a divorce. I don't have the confidence to tell them. I feel like an outsider. Maybe my friends won't like me anymore. I hope it won't be that way. Right now I'm listening to "West Side Story". That comforts me a little. I hope everything will be good again. I was so looking forward to St Christophen. But Mama won't let me go there with Papa. Phillipp is here right now. He has it so good. He

The search for the self – identity   135

doesn't have any worries. I know I'm writing a little stupidly, but when I'm sad I write in this overblown way. Oh well. Now I gave Phillipp a few Playmobile Maxerls to play with. Now I feel quite well again. Anyway, I don't have to cry anymore. I'll write again tomorrow . . .!

Oh yeah, the skiing course was amazingly fun. I like Daniel . . . I mean, I think he's nice. He said I have the most beautiful figure in the whole skiing course! I like that, but it hasn't made me conceited. I also wanted to say: I passed math! I'm going to get a 2 or 3 on the assignment. Super! So: goodnight, goodnight, sleep well!

Lari T., 13 years old
(Lari, quoted in Erhard 1998, 51ff; translation McQuade)

5.4 Discussion

The parents' divorce often coincides with a son or daughter's puberty. I have already described how parents come into unconscious competition with their children and thus sometimes select a new partner (often the daughter's age). Not only is the adolescent searching for a partner, but the parents – in unconscious competition – may find a new partner more quickly than their children do.

For the adolescent, their parents' separation constitutes an additional burden. Unconsciously, every child – even at the age of 13 or 14 – feels he is at fault for the separation, that he has been too naughty, too difficult, too much of a burden. In fantasy, he thinks his Oedipal desires toward the parent of the opposite sex has driven them away. Paradoxically, it becomes more difficult for an adolescent to distance himself from his parents when he lives alone with one of them, but also when a new partner appears on the scene.

From Lari's diary entry, one can feel how disconsolate her mother is. As she remarks, when her parents get a divorce, she will have no family anymore. She is ashamed to talk about it with her friends, but she can confide her feelings to her patient and absolutely trustworthy diary. She is afraid to become an outsider. Lari can comfort herself by listening to "West Side Story", which features adolescent groups and early love. Afterwards she remembers that she is not allowed to go away with her father. In self-reflection, she calls her writing "overblown" – and then manages to stop crying. Also comforting is her memory of Daniel's compliment, and her success at math serves to further stabilize her emotionally. Her diary is a loving friend, one she can confide her problems and feelings to. She wishes her diary good night and a good sleep. She also identifies with her diary as her own conversational partner. Her ability to cope with her problems and reflect on them indicates a relatively stable inner world with good inner parental images.

Several years later, at the age of 17, Lari recounts her successes at school, but then her scholastic achievement falls back drastically – presumably due to her parents' divorce. She tells her diary how lonely she feels:

And now I'm bored, since there is nobody who wants to do something with me, I have neither a friend nor a boyfriend, like in "old times". Why don't I

136 The search for the self – identity

have a boyfriend . . . it would be so nice with Tim now, the sun is shining, we could go for a walk or play tennis or tetherball. Oh, I miss him so much, dear God will you finally help me? I feel so abandoned, really lonely. The only thing to provide some variety is my diary. When I write, I feel better. But I can't keep writing my diary until the end of life. Why does my young life have to be so meaningless and sad? . . .

(Lari, quoted in Erhard 1998, 110)

The diary is her closest friend; she can tell it anything. Her mood changes and she begins to feel more adult and independent:

I don't know why, but I feel so excessively happy, even though there was nothing out of the ordinary either yesterday or today to make me feel so much better. Oh well, I'm glad anyway that I feel good after such a long time . . . and I notice that I'm gradually becoming an adult. That might sound stupid, but it's true somehow. I'm beginning to develop my own personality, the one I always had inside, but never showed. I was always dependent on everyone else, and I'm trying (and even succeeding) to change that.

(Lari, quoted in Erhard 1998, 111)

Lari sounds much more optimistic than in the last 20 entries; here, she is once again beginning a new volume – like the beginning of a new life. She notices her own change and is proud of it. She sees that she is gradually becoming more adult. Bernfeld speaks of the "narcissistic love towards the own ego" as a basis for self-respect. Lari is also becoming more confident in her ability to meet academic challenges and pass her final exams. In the next entries, she notices that she is becoming "slowly more mature". Three months later, she describes her longing to be alone:

Oh God, I'm in a strange phase again: I want more than anything to be alone, without anyone at all. That has nothing at all to do with other people, but only with me; I don't need anyone, right now I want to go alone through the world like in earlier times and ignore everyone no matter whether I know them or not. I'd be incredibly interested what the reason for all this is. I thought of one explanation today: I was always a "papa-child" and I miss him unconsciously a lot, since he was always my papa and role model. You could say that I always really idolized him, and of course this feeling is still there. As terrible as it might sound, Peter is really a "substitute" for my daddy. I noticed this yesterday when I held Peter so tightly. In my thoughts it was papa I was holding so tightly so that he wouldn't go away again – even when I tell Peter how much I like him, it isn't really so . . . But I don't let anyone notice and "spoil" Peter just as always, although I actually don't want to. As I mentioned, I'd most like to be alone; go for walks alone; go shopping alone; eat alone; watch TV alone; listen to music alone; enjoy life alone. What's going on with me?

The search for the self – identity   137

And what should I do so that my fellow human beings won't later begrudge me this behavior????

(Lari, quoted by Erhard 1998, 120)

It is surprising how clearly the 17-year-old Lari can express her worries and how she tries to figure out her inner situation and gain clarity. She can admit that she is thinking of her beloved father – disappeared into the divorce – when embracing Peter. At the exact point in time she should distance herself from her close relationship to her father, he is absent due to the parents' separation, no longer daily present in a common dwelling. She can characterize herself as a "papa-child". She is even able to describe in words her need to be held as displaced from her father to Peter – presumably without ever having read any psychoanalytic theory. She can describe her own feelings and moods excellently, including the ambivalent ones. This capacity points to stable good inner objects that remain active in spite of such turbulence. Lari can reflect on herself, confide her thoughts to her diary and thus order them. As already seen with Katharina, Lari is able to make use of being alone in order to emerge from her dejection. A less internally stable adolescent might not be able to master this new situation, possibly exhibiting the kind of massive problems Elfi worked through in her psychoanalysis. Lari also is able to select idols with whose loneliness she identifies and who become role models.

Lari has idols from the world of film and musicals:

Oh God, I love Jimmy (James Dean). After I watched "East of Eden" yesterday, I rediscovered my love. I watched it alone. I watched my James – Mama and Jutta in the living room were watching something else. I can really identify with him, as stupid as that sounds. I have the same problems: I am lonely, misunderstood and searching for independence, freedom and love. Normally I'm not easily moved, but yesterday I saw myself on the screen. I sat there sobbing and kept seeing myself in the place of Carl, for instance when Aaron was with his girlfriend in the ice house and they were getting it on while Carl sat above them and was sad because nobody loved him. It's the same thing with me. But I can't do anything about it. Maybe I'll die young without ever having known love? Who knows? Today I already talked to James. I opened my heart to him and he said I shouldn't give up. I should go on my path like he did, he said. Of course I spoke in English with James. Tomorrow I'll talk to him again. I'll use my 1000 schillings to buy a James Dean calendar and many pictures of him.

(Lari, quoted in Erhard 1998, 81)

With Lari, we can observe the healing power of play, daydreams and diary writing. She withdraws to her room to watch TV. She has completely identified with her idol Jimmy in the role of Carl (for her, the actor is presumably interchangeable with his role). She too feels lonely and lost. The competitive situation between Carl and his brother Aaron – reminiscent of Cain and Abel – where Aaron is so

138   The search for the self – identity

preferred by girls and their mother, makes Lari sob for Carl and for herself. Some of her friends already have a boyfriend and she does not, making her feel excluded. Her tears also have a liberating, purifying quality. Seeking to free herself from her intense love she has for her father, she tries to convince herself that she has never been loved. Her longing for death is manifested when she remarks that she might have to die at a young age; then, her idol becomes her spiritual consoler and imaginary friend. Lari speaks with Jimmy like a lonely young child with an imaginary play comrade meant to console and encourage her. We can understand this as an inner dialogue, a part of Lari that is constructive and optimistic, encouraging and consoling herself. Lari is in the middle of a process of self-discovery and wishes to seek her own path in life. She shifts seamlessly from the imaginary to the real world. She wants to buy a calendar with pictures of James Dean, to possess him. The fact that James Dean is doubly unattainable – far away in the USA and dead in a motorcycle accident – makes it easier for her to adore him.

5.5 Homoerotic attraction

Women can see their best female friend as an emotional substitute for the mother; separation from the mother is thus made easier. Lari writes in her diary:

> Last week I was with Petra in Mittersill!! It was great. Petra told about Ireland. I like Petra soooo much. She is not only incredibly pretty, but also funny, sweet and understanding. I hope she likes me just as much . . .

Lari admires, idealizes and respects her best friend Petra – in her description, there is a similarity to boys she has a crush on. Several days later, she writes:

> Too bad Petra didn't come with us, but when we left she was still at the hairdresser's. She has a perm now (new) and looks great. She is getting prettier and prettier. I feel like the prince in "Beauty and the Beast".
>
> (Lari as quoted by Erhard 1998, 84)

Lari realizes the erotic tenor of this idealization: she compares herself to the Prince in "Beauty and the Beast", who is a changeling. Helene Deutsch contended that the strong "bisexual" phase shortly before adolescence is less suppressed in girls than in boys (because boys are ashamed of their "femininity", as she believed) (Deutsch quoted in Blos 1962, 99).

Two months later, Lari has distanced herself emotionally from Petra, as she writes:

> I like the company of the other kids at boarding school much, much better than Petra's. I'm from another kind of family and grew up with athletes: I don't belong to her kind (that sounds stupid, but it's true!). Sometimes Petra seems so affected and so on, I don't suit her really . . .
>
> (Lari quoted in Erhard)

The search for the self – identity   139

Lari's idealization has dissolved; she is looking for flaws in Petra and for the difference between them. She now begins to describe real contacts with boys her age. These two phases can often be seen during the search for sexual identity.

When homosexual fantasies are forbidden and adolescents perceive them as threatening, this can cause deviant behavior or social withdrawal in order to avoid situations where a boy could be aroused by the sight of other boys during undressing or sports. The erotic attraction need not always be conscious; it can also be diffused into the background. At Abercrombie & Fitch in Paris, the male salespeople, selected for their sexy appearance, are topless, with their photos on the shopping bags like models. At the entrance, the shopper is greeted by hosts as at a party; there is loud music and the salesmen dance rhythmically to create a mood. The store has dark wallpaper and perfume is sprayed into the air. The shop is decorated with ancient Roman and Greek sculptures; surfaces are constantly being cleaned so that no dust will be visible on the furniture. Only photogenic male models are hired to be entertainers; they represent the idol that the buyer is meant to idolize. They have to speak perfect English in order to serve international customers. When the customer enters the five-story building, s/he is photographed with one of the models. The trick is that there is no publicity for the store, in fact not even the name is easily seen on the exterior; one has to "be in the know" in order to enter, so to speak. If a passerby or tourist wants to know where the store is, s/he must ask someone carrying the bag from it. The wish to belong to a special group – although not necessarily homosexual – is thus subtly stimulated.

Moses Laufer supplies an example of an adolescent who breaks off going to school due to his fear of his homoerotic desires:

> A young man of 19 came to discuss a worry, which he described as follows: he felt attracted to other boys, and this was now affecting his work . . . at the age of 15, he had begun to feel attracted to other boys. Although he was terrified of his homosexual feelings, he nevertheless could not stop himself from thinking about some of the boys. He spent all his free time in the school library, because he felt that he could be near boys more safely and inconspicuously there. There came a point when he began to be very frightened of his own feelings, fearing that he might actually try to touch some of the boys. He began to stay away from school. This finally resulted in his decision to leave school. He then took a job as a clerk, and he was in this job when he came to the Centre for help.
>
> (Laufer 1995b, 8)

Laufer describes how the adolescent boy's worries and fear of his homosexual feelings towards other students led to his leaving school. With this decision, he jeopardized his education, profession and thus his entire path in life. It is important to offer the adolescent professional help in time or to be sensitive to the dimensions of this problem. When a student with good grades (as in this example) begins to withdraw and stay away from school, this must be understood as a cry for help. Such behavior is often misunderstood to be a lack of interest,

140   The search for the self – identity

and deeper-lying causes are not investigated. Teachers and counselors must then take up this communication and speak with the adolescent. The adolescent's true problems are with his sexual orientation and are latent. Therefore, an important consideration is how much autonomy an adolescent can be allowed and to what extent adults should and must help him in such important decisions.

5.6 Significance of the group

In the adolescent's insecurity, loosening of family relations, confusing feelings regarding the self, parents and the world, his peer group constitutes an important reference point. The adolescent's group of friends becomes his new homeland, where he feels he belong and shares the same interests. Every member of the group is more or less in the same situation regarding their changing bodies and new attitudes toward the world. The group fulfills various functions and tasks, representing a more or less secure place where adolescents can live out parts of their personality or project aspects of their personality onto other group members. Usually, this involves behavior that the adolescent cannot yet integrate, instead trying it out while observing others. Discussing other group members (and other groups) is a favorite topic.

Even when adolescents reject parental authority, they are simultaneously subjecting themselves to the dictatorship of their peer group with regard to clothes, taste in music, communication and leisure activities. Recognition and status within the group becomes a central issue, with treachery and loyalty also important. The need to belong and retain status within the group can lead to great pressure: some member usually feels excluded.

In this phase, adolescents often denigrate not only their parents but their teachers as well. One young teacher described his experiences:

> From regarding me as "God" in the first year, to thinking the "world" of me in the second, in the third *everything* I did was wrong and despicable. It was not until the fourth year that I became accepted again as a friend and teacher for whom they seemed to have some respect.
>
> (Waddell 1994, 48)

The teacher's surprise at his new, demoted image among his adolescent students is evident. From his brief description, we can feel how difficult and painful it is to endure this fall from a (presumably) earlier idealized state; here, his reaction is similar to a parent's.

Only slowly does the adolescent begin to distance and liberate himself from the group, when a close relationship to one other person gives him the requisite feeling of security. Lari describes this process at the age of 17:

> Yesterday, we started at Klaus' house. Max, Sabine, Manfred, Tom and I went over to the pizzeria after 1:00 a.m. The rest of them went to Vienna; I didn't

feel like it. After a pizza, I got home at 3:45 – a big surprise for mama, since I told her I wouldn't be sleeping at home. At Klaus', my whole life up to then (i.e., the part of it since I've been going out with Max and so forth) seemed to be playing like a film in front of my eyes – I was completely absent. And then I noticed that I'm gradually becoming adult. That might sound stupid, but somehow it's true. I'm beginning to develop my own personality, the one I always had inside but never showed. I was always dependent on everybody else, and I'm trying (actually succeeding!) to change that. Earlier I never wanted to know anybody not in our group, but now I really don't care. In fact, it's the opposite: I really want to get to know people from different circles and spend time with them, something I would have considered impossible before. For instance, I never wanted to go around with Eva, because I was afraid I'd miss out on something with my own group . . . now I've gotten to the point where I'm very happy to do something with her and also get to know new people. Sure, it's somehow nice to belong to a certain group, but on the other hand that doesn't mean you have to constantly spend time with them. Yesterday I had a new experience, and I'm "proud" of that. I feel so free and independent, a great feeling . . . I hope my good mood will last.

(Lari, quoted in Erhard 1998, 111)

This diary entry is from a new volume – evidence of a new phase in life, a turning point in Lari's life. In retrospect, Lari recognizes the limitations of belonging to a group and how afraid she was of losing her membership status – like a safe harbor – and becoming excluded. She is now strong enough to not always go out with the group, instead returning home alone. For her parents, this development is new and surprising. Lari's self-confidence is now stabilized, and she no longer requires the protection the group afforded her – indeed, she is interested in getting to know new people. She is capable of spending a pleasant time with a girl who does not belong to the group. She is proud of this step towards self-determination and autonomy.

This dissolution from the group does not occur in a straight line but in various steps, both forwards and backwards. As described in earlier chapters, the adolescent transfers Oedipal desires and conflicts of loyalty and rivalry from his parents to the peer group. A girl's best female friend often becomes especially attractive to her boyfriend, and sometimes a girl will "renounce" a potential boyfriend because he is currently together with her best female friend. But the manner she plays out this "renunciation", she makes it clear that she is in fact the more attractive of the two of them. The best compliment is to be "the most beautiful, attractive" girl in the class, at a dance, etc. – i.e., to be superior to everyone else, in order to calm fears of the opposite extreme of being unattractive and without a boyfriend. The "herd", as Lari dubs her group, represents both sides of an equation: home and safety, but also limitation and conformity. At the same time, various members of the group serve as projective screens for aspects of the adolescent she normally does not admit, attributing these qualities or wishes to others, or watching them

142 The search for the self – identity

do the things for which she lacks the confidence. Discussing this with other group members is just as important as observing them.

Lari reflects and writes with striking clarity about the painful process of distancing herself from the group. Here is an entry from January 1:

> This week, nothing special happened. That would be hard, since I'm only allowed to go out on weekends. After my feeling of happiness on Sunday, there was – as could be expected – a relapse, although it was only a small one. I suddenly feel lonely and abandoned again, friendless. I learned something again today: the time really must have come to become "more grown up": it occurred to me that even though I have a lot of "friends", almost none of them are truly friends. By that I mean that there are only a few (if any) who would stick to me in bad times as well as good times and who show this . . . for me, a friendship consist not only of somebody telling you he likes you. Right now, I'm reading a really impressive book by Erich Fromm: "The Art of Loving". Let me quote something out of it that inspired me to think about my own situation: . . . "Everyone thinks they are in safety when they stay as close as possible to the 'herd' and does not diverge from them in thought, feeling and action. But in this attempt to be as close as possible to the others, the individual actually remains completely alone and has a deep feeling of insecurity, fear and guilt, just as always when we are incapable of mastering our inherent separation from others . . . " This is all true, and it applies to me – or rather, did.
>
> Today it's Saturday, and instead of being glad to finally be able to go out, I don't want to see any of my "friends", but stay at home instead. I know this all sounds like self-pity, and if I'm honest, I do feel a little sorry for myself, but I have reason enough.

> (Lari, quoted in Erhard 1998, 113)

Several times, Lari speaks of new experiences connected with "becoming adult". She talks of friendship, but describes it in terms of pledges from Anglo-Saxon wedding ceremonies – "in bad as in good times" – familiar from the movies. The question Lari poses (in reference to the Erich Fromm quote) is: to what extent does she require the group in order to find protection, and how much autonomy does she require in order to think and live independently? These important topics will accompany her for her entire life – and which come up for the first time during adolescence.

In the group, the adolescent meets others who are in the same situation. The group is like a microcosm, with intense new relationships, jealousy, rivalry, admiration, competition, injuries and reconciliation, cooperation, caring and friendship. Loyalty to other members is important in order to define the group's outer border. Collective undesired characteristics are often projected onto other groups. Competition then arises between groups. The limits of the law are sometimes tested collectively, particularly with male groups. "Tests of courage", where legal

The search for the self – identity   143

limits are transgressed or where the adolescent's life can be endangered, often become rituals of membership. In this case, we speak of gangs.

5.7 Gangs

We speak of gangs or criminal groups when good aspects of a group are not at the forefront but instead tyranny and submission, rebellion and criminality. An unconscious motive for joining a gang is to express the destructive aspects of the personality, something that leads its members into deeper difficulties. Enormous pressure arises to do things that the individual member has not yet done on his own. There is also a basic climate of fear, with the leaders projecting their fearfulness and insecurity onto the members they oppress. They were often treated brutally as children, humiliated and dominated, and now take on the opposite role of power. It is difficult for an individual to break away from this kind of constellation, since the gang also supplies a strong feeling of membership and family. The members often come from problem families where nobody cared for the children or where exceedingly strict rules applied, and they were not recognized as persons. Gangs often represent societal sub-groups. Loners and lonely youths are invited to participate. Jack tells of his first contact to a gang:

> "I couldn't count on friends for anything but trouble," said Jack, looking back to how he was "seduced" into his thirteen-year-old gang. "I started hanging around with this group . . . one of them had come up to me and said, 'You're cool, we like your looks' and I just felt good for the first time and appreciated and wanted to be friends. But they started doing things I didn't really want to do – like bunking off school and skipping homework and I found myself going along with it even though I felt it wasn't me."
>
> (Waddell 1994, 50)

When invited to join the gang, Jack clearly did not have a good feeling about it – he was shy and had low self-esteem. The leader's "tough" character traits impressed him, and he felt part of the group, perceiving them as a home. He could then identify with the strong leader and tyrannize others, or become a victim within the group.

For parents, it is important to pay attention to their child's development and inquire who their friends are in their peer group. It is helpful when parents contact other parents of group members and exchange impressions and experiences. When examining their children's problems, parents feel powerful emotions such as anger, shame, disappointment and guilt. It is often surprising how long parents overlook unambiguous signs of drug consumption, violence and anguish in their children so as not to be confronted with such painful feelings. Although the gang massively influences individual behavior, it is important to recognize what is communicated through criminal acts or unusual behavior and to understand the adolescent's situation. "Understanding" need not signify tolerance of a given

144   The search for the self – identity

behavior – quite the opposite. In the grey area between legality and illegality, adolescents experience clear limits set by their parents as helpful, even when they may protest them.

In the popular musical *West Side Story*, with music by Leonard Bernstein, the leaders of two rival gangs battle against each other – a modern version of *Romeo and Juliet*. Two gangs fight in a New York slum for the upper hand: the white "Jets" and the Puerto Rican "Sharks". Tony, who has left the Jets and found work, lets himself be persuaded by his friend Riff, the leader of the Jets, to attend a dance where the Sharks are also expected. There he meets Maria, the sister of the Sharks boss Bernardo. Maria has just come from Puerto Rico and is meant to marry Bernardo's friend Chino. Tony and Maria fall in love at first sight.

They meet secretly, and Tony promises Maria to make sure that the impending rumble between the two gangs will be limited to a fair fistfight. But Bernardo stabs Riff, and Tony reflexively grabs the knife and kills Bernardo. Chino brings Maria the news. She believes that Tony did not consciously kill her brother and asks her friend Anita to protect him from those seeking revenge. But when Anita is sexually assaulted by the Jets, she claims that Bernardo's friend Chino has killed Maria. Tony hears of this. He runs into the street screaming. Suddenly he sees Maria. In this moment, Chino shoots him and Tony dies in Maria's arms. An unconventional balletic choreography made this musical a great success in the theater and on the screen. It impressively demonstrates how quickly the life of gang members goes out of control.

6

Lost by the wayside – overstepping limits

The testing of limits, the measuring of one's own and others' possibilities, is a normal part of adolescent behavior. Psychoanalysis understands this behavior as one facet of self-investigation and experimentation towards answering the question "Who am I?" However, such exploration becomes problematic when the border to antisocial and self-destructive behavior is crossed. Adolescents often are not aware where to delineate the border to extreme and abusive behavior (Aichhorn 1925), whether in the form of violence, alcohol and drugs, promiscuity, food or computer games.

We must emphasize that psychoanalysis seeks to understand each individual in her particular life situation and biography. Only when we attempt to understand each unique inner world can an adolescent be helped to find his way back to normality (with its full spectrum). Adolescent behavior must always be understood as unconscious communication – even when the adolescent has no idea what lies behind his alarmingly spontaneous actions. The failure to understand one's own drives threatens and confuses both adolescent and parent. Indeed, when apprehended shoplifting or involved in a fight, the adolescent might well say, "I don't know what made me do it". The major difficulty with this kind of "acting out", when it crosses significant borders, is that it expresses an inner pain that is inextricably bound up with outer contingencies. This is also complicated by the fact that adolescents often wish both to be understood and misunderstood; at the same time, parents often have the impression that the help they offer is ineffective or inappropriate – whatever they try is wrong.

It is not always easy to establish where and when the limits of parental (or societal tolerance) have been reached. A situation becomes problematic when massive antisocial and self-destructive behavior gets out of control, and adolescents cannot adequately discern where they already have overstepped limits regarding violence, alcohol and drugs, sexuality, food or computer games, often making light of their own behavior. For parents and teachers, one appropriate response to transgressive behavior is the twofold strategy of taking the behavior seriously but not over-dramatizing it (but by no means ignoring it). Certain behaviors could be the first step in a delinquent "career", or simply be a communication meant to stimulate the parents' help and care. If the parents respond by taking the behavior seriously, it might remain an isolated incident.

Adolescents have always played pranks in order to demonstrate strength, masculinity, intelligence or bravery. In his book *Symbolic Wounds*, Bruno Bettelheim pointed out that the unconscious root of many masculine rituals lies in imitating female menstruation (1962). For male adolescents, these rituals of transition to adult status can include hunting and mastering threatening situations alone or in the peer group. Only when the male adolescent proves himself at mastering these tasks is entry to the world of masculine adulthood granted.

In Western society, groups of male adolescents may voluntarily undergo exceedingly dangerous tests of bravery, some of them ending in death. These voluntary con/tests are not set or defined by the society at large but developed by the adolescent groups themselves, more or less in opposition to societal norms – for instance, climbing over train tracks or on top of train wagons in the vicinity of an electrical tower. In the famous cult film *Rebel Without a Cause* (1955), Jim (James Dean) is required to pass such a test of courage by the leader of his group, Buzz. In the so-called chicken run, Buzz and Jim race towards the edge of a cliff in their cars: the first one to jump out of his car is the "chicken". Jim jumps out shortly before the cliff, but Buzz gets the arm of his jacket stuck on the doorknob and goes over the cliff with his car.

One of the film's themes is "affluent neglect". Jim comes from a wealthy family where, however, neither mother nor father has really taken care of their lonely, lost son. This film has convincingly shown a large public the adolescent loneliness and anguish behind such dangerous deeds and tests of courage – a psychological perspective in place of the usual blame.

From literature and life, we know that earlier tolerance for "pranks" was much higher. In a lecture, the president of the Viennese Juvenile Court explained how many deeds now deemed criminal were earlier considered mere pranks and even admired. In his autobiography *My Doctor's Novel. A Report from Life*, Werner Vogt, a founding member of the political-professional group Critical Medicine in Austria and a doctor active in social causes, describes the common syndrome of "passing the time by playing a prank on someone" (Vogt 2013, 31). This was also a widespread phenomenon among adult men: hiding a neighbor's bicycle, hanging up part of a fishing rod on the laundry line or building a barricade behind a curve in the street – in Vogt's description, the butcher's car could hardly brake in time and landed in a field, with his boxes flying through the air. Another prank consisted in applying two buckets of liquid soap to the tracks of the Arlberg railway, so that the train could not move forward on steep sections. The conductor had to carefully go in reverse and then pass with greater speed and momentum over the soaped tracks. Foreigners were also the victim of such pranks – for instance, South Tyroleans, who were at that time considered "Tschuschen" (Austrian derogatory slang for foreigners from southern European countries). Luigi's room was shoveled full of snow through an open window. Peasants convinced a mentally retarded boy, Franzi, that he could jump from the roof of the mill using two umbrellas as a parachute; he landed in the hospital with two broken legs. Such stories elicited admiration – even a priest laughed at Franzi's accident. Only 40 years later did the author wonder at such socially accepted forms of cruelty and delinquency. In each of us there is a "delinquent self", expressing itself in direct form through tax evasion, stealing newspapers or books, and indirectly through schadenfreude and rubbernecking.

The exercise of violence elicits contradictory reactions. The violent adolescent seems powerful, ruling over others and spreading fear, a fascinating figure for identification and emulation. The opposite pole is helplessness and fear in the face of violence – a regression to the early experience of the helpless baby, dependent on others for its survival. When others are the victims of violence, we feel either empathy or schadenfreude, which is the enjoyment of others' misfortune, expressed either covertly or openly in mockery or (more subtly) in irony and sarcasm.

In his macabre, grotesque picture books such as *Max and Maurice* (1865), Wilhelm Busch depicted such pranks to elicit schadenfreude in the reader. Max and Moritz strangle Widow Bolte's chickens with a cord and proceed to fish them out of her frying pan. With taunts, they lure the tailor Bock over a wooden bridge they have previously sawn in two, over a brook into which he falls and almost drowns. They fill the village teacher Lämpel's pipe with gunpowder, thus causing an explosion leading to severe burns. In his introduction, Busch (in the original German version) explicitly offers readers a chance to laugh at the boys' pranks comfortably – since we will not be their victim (Busch 1865, 190).

Busch then explicitly invites the reader to giggle with schadenfreude in enjoyment of these often sadistic and life-threatening pranks. The victim of the fourth prank is the good, reasonable teacher Lämpel, who plays the church organ on Sundays. Just as he gratefully lights his pipe in satisfaction, it explodes:

> "Ah!" he says, "no joy is found
> Like contentment on earth's round!"
> (Busch 1902, 30)

Wilhelm Busch cleverly prepares the reader for this bad deed by first milking their bitter attitude towards teachers. Then, he depicts the teacher as priggishly self-satisfied – an object for the boys' envy, since adolescents envy adults for seemingly having everything, including a place in the world, a relationship, a profession, settled views on life's important questions: all the things that for an adolescent are still inchoate. The boys take pleasure in unloading their envy in an explosion, their murderous fantasy fed by their own dissatisfaction and impotence:

> Fizz! Whiz! Bum! The pipe is burst,
> Almost shattered into dust.
> Coffee-pot and water-jug,
> Snuff-box, ink-stained, tumbler, mug,

Table, stove, and easy-chair,
All are flying through the air
In a lightning-powder-flash,
With a most tremendous crash.
When the smoke-loud lifts and clears,
Lämpel on his back appears;
God be praised! Still breathing there,
Only somewhat worse for wear.
Nose, hands, eyebrows (once like yours),
Now are black as any Moor's;
Burned the last thin spear of hair,
And his pate is wholly bare . . .
Now that his old pipe is out,
Shattered smashed, *gone up the spout?*

(Ibid, 32)

It is not difficult to see in this explosion the rapturous image of an anal explosion, as formulated in child humor during the anal phase. A five-year-old girl wrote:

Oma and Opa
Sat on the sofa.
Opa shat
The sofa went splat.

(Titze 1995, 45,
translation
McQuade)

Melanie Klein pointed out that children lend their bodily excrement enormous positive or negative powers. They can be fantasized as gifts to the parents or as destructive weapons.

With Busch and his readers, the murderous impulse is ameliorated – the teacher survives (although his pipe does not). Archaic, early fantasies of bodily omnipotence are actualized. In the end, the death of the two boys is occasion for rejoicing by all their early victims.

In puberty, the adolescent body undergoes a fundamental transformation that can be confusing: on the one hand, it is clearly advantageous to have an adult body, stronger and capable of creating life, sexually attractive; on the other hand, the child's trusted body has altered without the adolescent's control: there is no choice but to accept this transformation. Under this pressure, adolescents tend less to reflection than to action, to spontaneous unloading of tension.

It is not easy for parents to decide when adolescent behavior constitutes a step towards independence, something they should support – or is antisocial, self--endangering or criminal, something the adolescent should be protected from. There is a fine line between sensible controls and helpful encouragement. If parents can trust their child to discern the border himself, then this can enormously strengthen the child's self-respect; however, if parents overlook signs of a troubling development, they are withholding significant help from their child. A fearful mother seeking to bind her youngest son to her (although he is 15 ½) might impede his plan to visit a friend in Germany by continually wondering out loud whether the parents will take good care of him; when he then gives up his plan and instead sits in front of the computer every day of his vacation, she might regret her behavior. In families where the parents find it difficult to control their own impulses – or vacillate between uncontrolled behavior and stricter limits – children usually also have difficulties with self-control. Stiffly authoritarian parents often observe things in a polarizing fashion as either good or bad; although they believe they are setting clear limits, they fail to notice that they are only encouraging their children into extreme behavior.

Now, we will investigate central problem areas in adolescence: violence and criminality, teenage pregnancy, psychic breakdown and suicidal thoughts.

6.1 Violent adolescents: violence as fascination and denial

The phenomenon of increasing violence after the onset of adolescence is widespread after traumatic experiences in early childhood. Psychoanalysis attempts to understand the inner pattern of the personality leading to the outbreak of (typically unpremeditated, spontaneous) violence. What kind of dynamic rules the inner world of the (usually male) adolescents that pushes them to such aggressive behavior directed against other persons or objects? Psychoanalysis focuses on understanding the secret, usually unconscious motives that such violent acts block or deny.

An adolescent who entered therapy due to his aggressive behavior towards other students characterized himself in the first therapy sessions as a helpless little bunny who needed protection.[1] It was not surprising to hear that Malcolm's father physically abused him already when he was a baby on numerous occasions, then serving prison time for serious injury. Malcolm also often witnessed his father abusing his mother; indeed, he would start crying when his father approached. Already in our first sessions, Malcolm's intergenerational deprivation and trauma became evident. Malcolm's mother was abandoned early on by her own mother, growing up with her father and her unloved stepmother. She then chose a violent husband who was already in jail for serious injury before Malcolm was born. The father was regularly abused by his parents, whose ancestors had been slaves. In spite of all this, the mother took her baby to the father's home in the Caribbean. When she picked up the crying Malcolm to calm him, the father said she was spoiling him. Only when Malcolm turned two years old did his mother return with him to Austria – and only after he exhibited massive psychosomatic problems, including difficulties swallowing and waking up at night in a panic.

In my three-year work with Malcolm (at first twice a week, and then after one year three times a week), the deep depression and desperation behind his violent behavior quickly became evident. In a parent conference after four months, his

150 Lost by the wayside – overstepping limits

mother said he was no longer aggressive but instead sad and depressed, asking her: "Why did you bring me into this world anyway?" In our transferential relationship, his massive aggression and destructive rage demand that I set particularly clear borders. He established an intense positive transferential relationship, so that weekends and holiday interruptions in our therapy became a painful threat, and he therefore often had outbreaks of rage at Friday sessions, where he would destroy toys. And yet he was able to construct beautiful, highly creative necklaces, various kinds of spiderwebs and complex cable cars for me out of string in the therapy room. Anna Freud called the psychic mechanism of unconsciously inflicting on other persons what one has suffered oneself "identification with the aggressor" (A. Freud 1992, 85ff). Malcolm alternated between trying to get my attention and appreciation and rage at being abandoned on the weekends and holidays.

Meanings of aggression

In psychoanalysis, there are two contradictory assumptions concerning the meaning of aggression in the psychic apparatus. The later Sigmund Freud, Melanie Klein and Wilfried Bion proceed from a notion of the human being marked by Eros (life instinct) and Thanatos (death instinct), with a continuum between destructivity and aggression existing in a mild form in every essential form of relationship – as a component of sexual activity and penetration, as oral, ingestive energy in the intake of food, in the creative force. Melanie Klein called aggression as mixed with the thirst for knowledge "knowledge desire" – the wish to get inside and take control of a person, a body or a thing. Freud emphasized that in sexual union – involving penetration and taking possession of the sexual partner – an aggressive component is necessary. When aggression is inhibited, curiosity – the wish to take something in – is also inhibited. Bion defines psychic categories with L (Love), H (Hate) and K (Knowledge). Karl Kraus referred to the aspect of hate necessary to creativity when he wrote "Hate must be productive, otherwise we might as well love" (Presse, 4. Juni 1926, S1 Spectrum, translation McQuade).

In opposition to this view, a concept of aggression as a reaction to insufficient love and care has been propagated above all by Erich Fromm, ego psychology and Anna Freud.

Sociological data

Approximately 150 years of research on delinquency and crime has shown that male adolescents and young adult males consistently commit the greatest share of crimes (see Figure 6.1).

Male adolescents between 12 and 25 years of age are not only the most frequent groups at risk for acts of delinquency, but they are also often its victims (Eisner 2002). In Western cultures, this finding has been remarkably consistent over a period of more than 150 years. In gangs, criminality and violence are encouraged and admired, even seen as a status symbol, with pressure on all group members to participate.

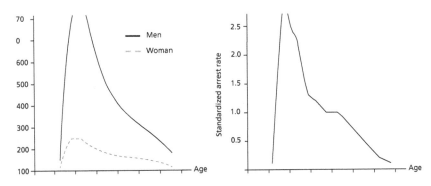

Figure 6.1 Age and criminality of men from a) 1842 and b) 1977 (from Gottfredson and Hirschi, 1990)

A distinction is made between adolescent delinquency and lifelong delinquency (Moffitt 2007, 2003). Three-quarters of all adolescents in the United States between ages 13 and 20 commit petty criminal acts such as shoplifting, vandalism and traffic violations. In the Dunedin study – a longitudinal study for New Zealand, where the subjects were investigated from childhood up to the age of 30 – both types were represented: the first group (ALDs – adolescence-limited delinquents) only came into conflict with the law once and have a period of occasional criminal activity, breaking the law with behavior such as vandalism, theft and use of illegal drugs; and those whose delinquency was long-term (LCPDs – life-course-persistent delinquents). This second group, with a "career as violent criminals", already had problems in childhood (learning problems, often ASD – autism spectrum disorder) and grew up in a difficult family environment.

Let us now turn to two case studies of adolescents who came into conflict with the law and were put in jail. In her thesis, *Social Pedagogy in Prison* (1997), Andrea Staudner-Most describes the Viennese model of "anti-aggression training" for adolescents in prison. The following two case studies are from her thesis. The data were obtained and analyzed in a one-hour narrative interview as well as participatory observation during the 24 sessions of the anti-aggression training.

> "Anti-aggressivity training", also "anti-aggression training" or "anti-violence training" are terms for training courses consisting of numerous theoretical, practical and physical exercises for a larger group of adolescents, with the goal of preventing or reducing aggressive behavior in everyday life. The oldest course, AAT, is now standardized and validated in Austria, but there are numerous other courses, with various approaches and techniques, that psychologists, pedagogues and social workers have designed for various needs and clients.

152 Lost by the wayside – overstepping limits

Any "anti-aggression training" serves the goal of preventing or reducing aggressive behavior so that it will not occur in daily life, or occur less often. To this end, cognitive and emotional factors are observed and analyzed. In addition, participants are confronted with aggressive behavior – both their own and that of their fellow participants. They should learn to renounce violence even if they have the physical strength to prevail – or avoid violence when faced with it. The courses seek to depict use of force as weak, i.e., an attacker is not strong enough to find better methods of resolving conflicts.

Training units simulate controlled situations where aggressive behavior can arise. When "trained" in non-aggressive, alternative behavioral patterns, participants learn to find better solutions. The following two case studies are of adolescents in custody.

Case study: adolescent B.

B. was born in 1980 as the oldest of three siblings; his mother is deaf. Officially, he lives with her, but he mostly stays with friends, since – as he says – "life at home is unbearable because of my mother's partner".

The mother is an alcoholic, with several unsuccessful withdrawal programs behind her. For this reason, B. was already placed in a children's home at the age of ten. He later was in other homes, although his mother always opposed this. Only for the last year has he lived officially with his mother again. Now and again, there are incidents of assault between the mother and her partner due to alcohol, where – for instance – B. attempts to protect his mother. In his first ten years, B. was very often left alone, since his mother would descend into an alcoholized condition for days and weeks at a time, leaving her children to fend for themselves.

Due to poor performance in the regular school, B. was sent to an institute for special education. He only lasted there until completing his minimum compulsory school attendance at the age of 15 – the second class of the non-academic secondary school. This lack of education also makes it difficult for B. to get a job.

B. seems older than his years. He is 180 cm tall and of muscular build. His head is shaven and he has tattoos such as HASS (hate) and SKIN on his arms and hands, although he vehemently rejects and denies membership in any radical right-wing group. He is a heavy smoker. Through his forbidding appearance and aggressive behavior, he has trouble appealing to people who come into conversation with him, and he often has physical fights with his peers, especially when he is drunk. The last time he got in a fight he injured someone, and was sentenced to five months in prison.

B. voluntarily attended the anti-aggression training.

In the seventh session, the participants are asked to draw a lifeline, with the highlights and low points of their life plotted in its vertical curves. The paper already has the periods of grammar school, high school and post-15-year-old period graphed for the purposes of orientation.

B. quickly drew his lifeline (Figure 6.2).

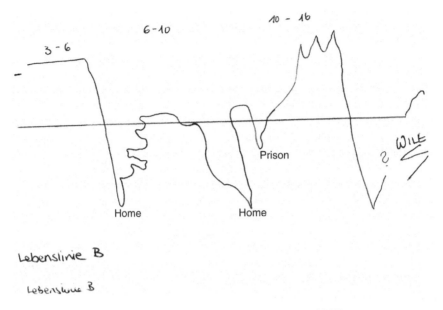

Figure 6.2 Lifeline as drawn by B. (from Staudner-Moser 1997)

Discussion

A synopsis of B.'s first six years with a mother who left her children alone for days would seem to contrast with his positive assessment of this period on his lifeline. However, we can imagine how many challenges, desperation and fear he had to endure as the oldest of three children. We do not know how many siblings there were at this time and how old they were when he had to look after them, since this data was not collected. Perhaps B. is idealizing this time. Every time he was put in the children's home is depicted as a low point on the lifeline. His rates his first period in prison as higher than his periods in the homes (possibly, there is less arbitrary violence in prison). The second prison sentence, something he spoke of quite casually in his interview, constitutes the lowest point on his lifeline. He says he misses his freedom, adding that it is now up to him to decide the quality of his future – perhaps the beginning of a new insight.

B. traces the first years of his life in the positive area, which he only reaches again (sporadically) between the ages of 10 and 16. B. also spoke about the lifeline and the picture he drew. When his mother's partner moved in, his lifeline descends. During a fight between the mother and partner, B. defended his mother and called the police.

The apparent contradiction between the objective fact of B's massive neglect during his first ten years of life and his positive depiction on his lifeline demonstrates a common phenomenon: badly abused (including sexually abused), neglected children have a particularly close, ambivalent and dependent relationship to their

154 Lost by the wayside – overstepping limits

parents. Typically, such parents treat the children in an extremely contradictory fashion, vacillating between spoiling and rejecting them. Under the influence of drugs or alcohol, a parent might completely forget her child (as did B.'s mother) or become violent (as did her new partner). When sober, they suffer guilt feelings and wish to right the wrongs they have committed, attempting to compensate for their bad behavior by giving exaggerated attention to their children. Affects are regulated only on a primitive level, in the either/or mode, with no shades of grey and no reflection on their own behavior. In the interview, B. demonstrated the common defense mechanism of splitting into good and evil as well as avoiding getting in touch with his feelings and painful experiences.

Save for a few exceptions, B.'s lifeline falls within the negative region: kindergarten, grade school, high school – each of these institutions evokes negative associations. B. says he never liked going to school, was always annoying his teachers and thus always ran into difficulties.

When asked what school he went to, B. answered as follows:

B: Elementary school and junior high school. I was also in the academic high school, but not for long, maybe half a year.

Interviewer: Did you like school?

B: In the beginning, yes, but then I was always cutting school since I didn't feel like going. It was more interesting to go around with my friends.

I: Did you have nice teachers?

B: No, none of them liked me, because I was always acting up. . . . I was never allowed to go along for the skiing course.

I: Why not?

B: Because I was always acting up. They wouldn't let me come on the hiking days either.

B. had a crucial experience at the age of 11: a firecracker exploded in his pants pocket, seriously injuring him. He had to spend three and a half months in the hospital.

B: Shortly before the operation, my mother stayed a few nights in the hospital with me.

I: Were you in a very bad way at that time?

B: Yes.

I: What were your fears? Were you afraid of illness, the doctors, of being left alone?

B: I just was afraid then, I didn't exactly know of what.

I: Were you afraid of what might happen?

B: I didn't feel much. But then it was unpleasant because my skin was transplanted off my right thigh. I didn't have stitches, but iron clips instead– about 54 of them. Then I was afraid of them being taken out. That was very unpleasant. Now I still have scars, but that doesn't matter.

(Staudner-Moser 1997, 77)

Presumably, the exploding firecracker in his pocket represents an unconscious self-destructive action. The separation from his mother and siblings, which he never mentions, his homesickness and loneliness in the home must have created a great inner tension – and in fact, the firecracker exploded. Although he was already in the home, his mother came to visit him at the hospital; we know little of these visits. B. has learned to conceal his feelings from himself and others. He was moved from home to home, since he became hard to handle. His second imprisonment constitutes a low point in his life; however, now his lifeline is proceeding upwards, possibly also because of his anti-aggression training, where he has begun to reflect on himself and his situation in images and words and learn of other participants' difficult situations. On his lifeline, he has written the word "Wile" (presumably the German word "Wille", in English "will"): he has the will to remain in the positive area, even if he does not yet know quite how.

Thoughts on the dynamics of his inner world

Since we have little data on B.'s early childhood, we must depend on the few remarks he made to Frau Staudner-Moser in their interview if we wish to form hypotheses on his inner world.

In the interview, B. described his sentencing as follows:

> It was a joke, the judgment . . . all in all, the verdict was right. Five months for two hammers (editor's note: slang for blows with the fist). He only had one boil from it. But I wasn't really violent, otherwise he would have looked different.

B. attempts to be superior to the judge when he calls his judgment a "joke". He attempts ironically to link the verdict of five months in prison with the two blows with the fist: he need not take the punishment seriously or feel his impotence. He would prefer to be the powerful one.

In one session, the participants are asked to find an animal with which they feel similar. B. chooses the lion: "Of course, I like to lie around, and whoever tries to mess with me better watch out." Presumably, with "lie around" he is referring to his unemployed state – he is not in contact with his feelings, but instead reinterprets them. When B. consumes alcohol, he becomes very aggressive: "You'd better not eat cherries with me." He hides his weakness, his exclusion from the working world behind the majestic calm of the lion, the king of beasts. In this way he transforms his helplessness into strength – he wants to be as strong as the lion, not the child who was abandoned early and also had to take care of his two younger siblings.

In another exercise, he is asked to find one word for each letter in his name. Here, he shows his other, vulnerable side. He writes "brav" (good or obedient), "ehrlich" (honest), "normal" (normal) and "Ich bin ich" (I am myself). All these words express either his positive character traits or those he aspires to. "They can say what they want about me, but I am honest," he says. "I think I'm normal", he explains. And: "I am myself", with an embarrassed smile. While writing, B. needed some time to find these words. Perhaps he is afraid to reveal something about himself through invoking the words. Questioned by a fellow participant as to whether he wants to be "good", he answered brusquely, "No – why?" (Staudner-Moser 1997, 83). When he was a child, nobody seems to have recognized his achievement of stepping in for his absent mother and taking care of his younger siblings – he was more than "good" and "honest". His deep-lying resentment and rage towards his mother are suppressed, thus protecting her from his negative feelings, which break through at the smallest perceived provocation and are directed towards other boys. Perhaps he envies his peers who were able to grow up with their families instead of being sent to a home.

When the group is formulating rules, B. writes "no smoking", although he is a heavy smoker. As is to be expected, other participants attack him for this, but he sticks to his opinion, sitting back with crossed arms expressing his superiority (Staudner-Moser's impression was that he was satisfied by the inherent contradiction). Thus does he split off his desire to smoke, projecting it onto the other smoking participants. The trainer then takes up his suggestion and in fact prohibits smoking.

Later in the exercise where the participants are told to recall an experience when they were victims of violence, B. has great difficulty drawing anything, expressing his insecurity by constantly asking the trainer whether his drawing is correct. His own drawing of his face expresses major inner tensions.

B. uses the whole paper for his drawing. He uses very strong lines, drawing relatively crude faceless figures with precisely delineated bodies – some of them

Figure 6.3 Violent scene drawn by B. (from Staudner-Moser 1997)

Lost by the wayside – overstepping limits   157

only stick figures. The scene illustrates the situation after a soccer game in the Prater Stadium, which he describes as follows:

> There was a big fight and I was in the middle of it, which I wanted, of course, and I got quite a bit of punishment, and went down. That's just how it was. The next day, someone else got the brunt of it, or in the next fight I was faster. I'm not upset about it. It comes with the territory. Usually it's me anyway who gets back up, not the other guy. Don't worry!
>
> (Staudner-Moser 1997, 89)

B. has difficulty drawing this scene and even more difficulty feeling the attendant emotions. His drawing clearly expresses the threatening situation of lying on the floor. The victor's triumph is underlined by the foot he places on B.'s back – in the pose of a game hunter placing his foot on the prize (perhaps a lion). B. finds it necessary to immediately inform the group that he usually wins the fight. When other participants ask him whether he can remember the various blows meted out within his family, he shakes his head and contends that he was never beaten. On the contrary, he has beaten up his mother's partner (as described in the police report). Presumably, he does not wish to remember the time when he was weaker than his mother's partner.

From this moment on, the group exercises start to appeal to B. – for instance, one observational game with two participants sitting opposite one another; one of them must observe and remember the posture and facial expression of the other. This "observer" then turns around while the other alters something about his position or expression. Next, the "observer" must look back, detect this change and describe it. After this, the two participants switch roles. B. enthusiastically engages in this exercise and wants to do it with other partners as well. His apathy and disinterest are gone – he seems curious and involved after he has felt understood by the group and trainer.

After 12 sessions, B. is abruptly released from prison. As we learn from letters he wrote to his social worker, he does not manage to make a constructive life for himself, drifting into the drug scene and participating in numerous fights and violent crimes. The social worker who conducted this study remains a significant link. Many years after his release, he writes her moving letters:

> When did I see you last? I think it was the time with the taxi, where I wasn't doing too well. I don't know how far you're informed as to what I've been doing the last few years. I don't exactly know myself, since I was a drug addict, as you know. When I wasn't chasing the next fix, I was either in the hospital or in jail.
>
> The last 1 ½ years brought only bad luck for me, it began with a fight where I had 5 ribs broken and two of them stuck in my lungs. Only after 8 hours did my two friends find me, and they called the ambulance. I landed in intensive care and now I have a 30 cm long scar on the side of my back . . . and 4 steel

plates inside. Shortly after I was released from the hospital, I had a lung attack (lung embolism) and was put back in the hospital. A week after I left the hospital again, the same thing happened. Then I was in the lung clinic for 6 weeks. About 2 months ago, I had a fight with the police and hit my fist through a piece of glass, cutting all five tendons to the fingers and both arteries and nerves. The doctor said it's a miracle that they could halfway save my hand, since it was almost out cold. I'm surprised I can write so well (it was my right hand).

Now I'm not addicted anymore and I'm not taking methadone either here in Unit 1. I was in withdrawal: Baumgärtnerhöhe – Breitenfurterstrasse – Baumgärtnerhöhe, then therapy in Ybbs for almost three months. I did have a relapse, but I went right back to Ybbs. On May 13 I was admitted, but I was in the SMZ Ost with blood poisoning. . . . Now I'm in custody because of reckless endangerment and bodily injury and other stuff, nothing too crude. . . . The last time I was in prison . . . 12 months altogether for breaking and entering . . . in between that I was always a few months out of prison. When I was in, I got methadone, now I don't need it anymore.

But I just can't find my way out (of prison) here, because if you want to keep in business, you have to deal and I can't and won't do that. I want to stay clean. Recently I was just running around without a goal and couldn't find a footing and it was only a question of time whether I die or get arrested. I sort of provoked my own arrest, because it couldn't go on that way. Now I have the peace to think about how it might go on instead.

(Staudner-Moser 1997, 129ff)

This letter summarizes how B. wanders around without a home – actually, prison constitutes a kind of home for him. It is in prison that he is able to get off drugs, and its closed environment helps him to orient himself, as opposed to the "outside", which is far more challenging. In his autobiography *From the Orphanage to the Prison* (1972), Wolfgang Werner describes a similar life story. Out of 27 years, he only spent four "in freedom", and he describes his loneliness, rage, hate, aggression and hopelessness eloquently in this "social report".

Actually, B. is more often victim than perpetrator when he is involved in violent incidents. After the letter just quoted, he once again drifted into the drug scene, alternating between prison and hospital. In 2015, he died in prison while serving a long sentence for manslaughter. He remained in contact with the social worker until his death; he described his relation to her was the closest attachment he ever had.

B.'s letter affords insight into his vulnerable, self-destructive side. The lion image he chose affords him a kind of pseudo-strength; in life, he remains both perpetrator and victim, entangled in an orgy of violence and flight into drugs. Often cruelly beaten and punished as a child, he now perpetrates the same role by provoking fights and violent acts.

Only after the social worker has accompanied B. for a considerable length of time does his trauma from his stays in various homes become evident: beatings, confinement, humiliation and sexual assault were everyday occurrences – and with nobody provided to confide in. As Winnicott (1984) writes, psychoanalysts usually consider this kind of violence and aggression as founded in long deprivation, humiliation and lack of love. Paradoxically, when an adolescent becomes aggressive, this constitutes a sign of hope as an alternative to deep depression, apathy or suicide. The psychoanalytic explanation for this vicious circle of hate, fear and destruction directed against the self or others is *not* a weak superego (conscience), but in fact a cruel, merciless superego from early childhood, never ameliorated by loving, empathetic parents and a secure relationship.

> If then fear of the super-ego, either for external or internal psychic reasons, oversteps certain bounds, the individual may be compelled to destroy people and this compulsion may for the basis for the development either of a criminal type of behavior or of a psychosis. . . . Hate is often used as the most effective cover for love.
>
> (Klein 1934, 260)

Children's fears are nurtured not only through their fantasy but also through unloving parents. An especially grave impetus is the real experience of being rejected or given away by the parents. Some "criminals" may seem to be lacking in feelings of love, but such feelings might be only repressed due to a kind of betrayal from the mother or father, who seemed not to return the love from their child; consequently, he now hates them – even forgetting he ever loved them. For some criminals, the world consists only of enemies, and the individual must survive alone.

> Love is not absent in the criminal, but it is hidden and buried in such a way that nothing but analysis can bring it to light. Since the hated persecuting object was originally to the tiny baby the object of all its love and libido, the criminal is now in the position of hating and persecuting his own loved object.
>
> (Klein, ibid)

B. depicted his periods at homes, replete with physical and sexual abuse, as low points in the lifeline he drew. We may infer from his letter to the social worker how great his longing is for someone on whom he can rely: possibly, the social worker is the only person who is concerned about him up to the end of his life. Prison has become a substitute home for B., who dies there under hospice care.

Case study: adolescent R.

At the time of the study, R. – a Serbian citizen – is 18. He is relatively short, carefully dressed, friendly in conversation and polite. However, Staudner-Moser had the impression that R. was somehow trying to pull her leg with his friendly remarks (1997, 80ff). Born in Vienna, R. returned there after his parents' divorce (when he was eight) after a short stay in Serbia with his father and stepmother; since then, he has lived together with his mother and younger sister.

R. always has had difficulties at school; he was left back one year in primary school, even though he speaks fluent, idiomatic German. He attended the school in a children's home for delinquents as a day student, without graduating. Since 14 years old he is unemployed; his mother provides him with generous financial support.

Since the age of 14 he has been brought to court many times for aggressive acts. His gang has often fought physically in various parks. His most recent crimes – this time leading to imprisonment – were several robberies.

Queried as to his motives for participating in the anti-aggression training, he replies:

> My behavior should change. I don't want to go on this way.... Here, we can discuss why I'm so aggressive and flip out so easily.

R. draws his lifeline (Figure 6.4).

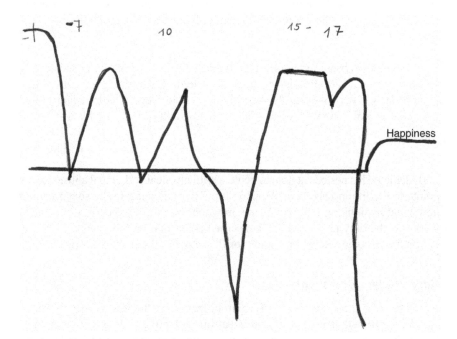

Figure 6.4 Lifeline of R. (from Staudner-Moser 1997)

The lowest point in his life story is also the cause of his being put in a home. In the interview, he relates:

R: My stepfather hit me and I had a head wound. My mother didn't want to call the ambulance, so she only put a bandage on the wound. Next day at school, the teacher asked me about it. I said I fell down. Then, I had to go to the principal. I told him the truth and then the school reported my stepfather. Then I went into the home.

I: You had to go away from your parents?

R: Only because I agreed. They asked me if I wanted to stay with my parents or go to a children's home. I said no, I don't want to go home.

I: Did you do better there?

R: Yes.

I: Better at the home than at your family's home?

R: Not at the home itself, but I felt better anyway. I always said to myself, my stepfather can't do anything to me anymore. I thought everything was simpler.

I: Is your stepfather still alive?

R: No, he died two years ago, unfortunately.

I: Why do you say "unfortunately"?

R: Because towards the end, I got along with him very well. It's all so long ago. When I went to the home because of him, I was twelve and now I'm eighteen.

(Staudner-Moser 1997, 93)

His being put into the home marks a low point on the lifeline he drew, equaled only by his time in prison. It is not known how R. did at the home. Might this low point in his lifeline also be an indication of suicidal thoughts? Unfortunately, we have no data or explanations for the two smaller low points preceding this – or the subsequent upward progression. The upward-directed line could coincide with the end of R.'s schooling. The "abuse" mentioned in his file could be traced to regular violence by his stepfather. Through his mother's "generous" financial support – which might indicate her bad conscience at not having shielded him from her husband's violence – he need not suffer consequences from being unemployed. Instead of beginning vocational training, R. tries to get money through robbery; unfortunately, data regarding these crimes are imprecise.

Alarmingly, R.'s lifeline ends at its absolute lowest point, without any upward turn – a sign of his hopelessness: instead, he extends the horizontal zero line graphed on the paper, making it rise and writing "happiness" on top. Perhaps he feels he has no real influence on his lifeline and instead longs for a *deus ex machina*, some outside force. Possibly in this case we should understand "happiness" as in fact the opposite – a form of bad luck. Only during the last two years has R. developed a better relationship with his stepfather. He had no positive male role model in his family to emulate. Now under the influence of the two empathetic anti-aggression trainers, R. very slowly develops new, non-aggressive modes of behavior for difficult life situations.

162   Lost by the wayside – overstepping limits

R's inner world becomes visible in the following exercises from anti-aggression training. In the third session, R. chooses the rabbit from the four animals meant to show how he feels at the moment. R. goes to the "rabbit corner", where the participants have cast trainers as "rabbit mothers". He sees himself as a rabbit, "since I'm good at running away", and simply "I feel good" – without explaining what he has to run from.

When asked to draw a situation in which he is a victim of violence, R. depicts a scene from his family where his stepfather is hitting him. Since Staudner-Moser does not reproduce the actual drawing, it is unclear whether R.'s mother was not involved or he simply omits her. Verbally, he describes the scene with almost the same words he used to describe how his stepfather injured him on the head (when his mother would not call an ambulance); only after he was called up to the principal at school was the abuse reported to the youth agency. R. took his drawing back to his prison cell, as if this representation carried great significance for him; perhaps this was the first time anyone had taken his feelings about the violence seriously, the first time he could speak about them and feel understood.

During the exercise in observing described earlier (in case study B.), R. is not able to detect any change in his partner's facial expression or posture; frustrated, he thinks he has failed, addressing this in the concluding discussion, whereupon the other participants console and support him.

Describing his self-image (as did B.), R. is the unprotected bunny, who only finds safety in flight. It would seem that he has no contact to his violent, criminal side, as if it were completely split off from his mind. His relationship to his mother and stepfather is also unclear.

His longing for closeness and maternal protection becomes evident in the twelfth session, when he chooses the seat next to the trainer.

In exercises where the focus is on inclusion and exclusion, R. becomes a critic, deriding a "kindergarten game" like musical chairs – and the other participants support him in this. Since their arguments against it are reasoned, the trainer retracts her suggestion. However, concealed behind this derision are massive emotional problems. R. was shut out of his family – he had no place there. His mother could neither protect him nor break with her violent partner. The idea of experiencing such a situation as a game is so painful that R. manages to gain the group's support for his refusal. In the concluding discussion, R. says he is feeling good. He gained the group's support and both trainers responded to his arguments, taking them seriously.

In the thirteenth session, the group discusses the question of why a child becomes a criminal and whether his family is responsible for this behavior.

Now the adolescents begin to tell of their difficult families – parents who beat them, abandonment, stays in homes. They talk about the difficulties that second--generation immigrant children experience between two cultures and religions. Their dejection and anguish become evident. R. relates:

> I was abandoned by my father. Papa left me in the lurch. He told me I'm his boy – but he also said he doesn't need one. He disappointed me terribly. I was

Lost by the wayside – overstepping limits   163

afraid back then that people would ask me what my father does, how he's doing, where do you live, so that I'd have to say: my father isn't interested in me. I only have my mother. I was afraid someone would laugh at me.

(Staudner-Moser 1997, 98)

Subsequently, R. talks about the situation with his stepfather and his time at the home, explaining that his stepfather died two years ago.

Somehow I miss him, but somehow I don't. It's a peculiar feeling I can't describe. My real father I don't miss at all. He knows I'm here (in prison) and knows all the rest too, but he tells my mother he doesn't care. He doesn't have a son. Why should I need him, then? He's just as dead to me as my stepfather, in fact. He simply doesn't exist anymore.

(Staudner-Moser 1997, 99)

The most important basis for self-confidence and confidence in life is parental love and acknowledgment. Winnicott (1963) speaks of the "shine in the mother's eyes" as she looks at her baby – we can extend this to a father's pride in his son. R. has experienced just the opposite: his father, although he retains contact to the mother and knows how R. is doing, still emphasizes his lack of interest in R. Most likely R. harbors mixed emotions, including longing for his father's love and rage or unwillingness to see him. In further sessions, R.'s great inner resistance against seeing himself as a victim becomes evident. From the psychoanalytic point of view, this does not indicate a dearth of emotion, but rather the opposite – in fact, R. is a greatly vulnerable victim of circumstances. To recognize himself as a victim would be so painful that he drops the whole subject, deriding it as laughable and childish. He was never given the fundamental basis of parental love to which every child has a right; now he is the robber who is taking things from others. Group discussion of various painful experiences of being abused, beaten, abandoned and mocked makes for an intensive, emotionalized atmosphere. Both trainers and participants are able to show understanding and empathy, so that each speaker feels protected and understood. Towards the end of the session, the participants question the trainers on their relationships with their own children and how they have brought them up, as if curious about a more affectionate style of parent-child relationship: evidently, some participants have an unspoken wish for different kinds of parents.

The fifteenth session centers on recognizing familiar violent patterns of behavior and trying out alternative methods. Using role-playing, situations are staged where the participants would normally react with violence, but this time they are asked to consider alternative plans and try them out, with subsequent group discussion. Here is a description (Ibid, 100–102):

With a partner, R. is meant to act out a situation at a bar: he enters his favorite bar, but his usual place is occupied by a stranger, (played by S.) . . .

The bar is simulated with furniture: a table, chairs, a few empty cups; smoking is allowed for the purposes of authenticity.

164　Lost by the wayside – overstepping limits

The other player sits comfortably at R.'s usual place, drinking a beer and talking to the waitress. R. enters. He looks around, noticing the new situation, which noticeably irritates him. He comes up to S. with his arms crossed and says in a threatening tone: "Do you know you're sitting at my place?" S. doesn't listen to him, but instead continues talking.

R. casts a pleading look at the trainers. He hadn't reckoned with this kind of reaction. He doesn't know what to do next.

Then, he rolls up the sleeves of his sweater, leans on the table and asks again – this time with more emphasis. Now, S. hears him. He gives R. a friendly smile, saying that he hasn't seen R.'s name anywhere on the chair, lifting it up to demonstrate that it isn't written on there. R.'s facial expression darkens; he calls the waitress and tries to get her to say this is *his* place in the bar, and he won't relinquish it to anyone else. But the waitress demurs, unwilling to enter the conflict, and simply takes their orders.

S. is friendly, but will not give in, ordering a beer as the tension rises. R.'s posture expresses his tension and lack of tolerance for the situation – but suddenly his face changes and he calls out to the waitress: "For me a beer too. Both drinks on me!" He takes another stool and drinks a beer next to S.

(Staudner-Moser 1997, 100ff)

During these two young men's role-playing, a conspicuous escalation of their controversy is suddenly and surprisingly dissolved. R. is first startled to find S. sitting in his place at the bar, which annoys him. With his arms crossed – a confrontational signal – R. steps before S. and addresses him in a threatening voice, laying claim to "his" bar stool. S. ignores him, which causes R. to cast an imploring look at the trainers, who do not intervene. Now R. rolls up his sleeves as if preparing for a fistfight, and asks S. once again to vacate his place, this time with more emphasis, demanding his usual seat. Mocking R., S. takes his claim to a fixed "place" literally, lifting up the bar stool and thus ridiculing R. in front of the other customers, since clearly R.'s name cannot be written on the stool. With a glowering expression, R. now turns to the authority of the waitress. When the waitress refuses to intervene and S. orders a beer, the situation is on the brink of explosion. Suddenly, R. realizes he could reinterpret the scene: he is now the host, who treats S. to a beer and thus can "invite" S. to sit at his bar stool. R. has newly defined the relationship and found a path from helplessness towards a shaping of the social situation.

In the discussion afterwards, R. says that at the beginning he had not believed the situation could end so well. He became very quickly annoyed at first – S. was looking for that reaction – and felt like an idiot. It particularly infuriated him when S. lifted up the bar stool (here, the group confirmed that R.'s posture was threatening), and it took him quite a while to consider what to do next. He also took S.'s ordering of the beer as a provocation, since he seemed to be demonstrating his claim to R.'s place.

Lost by the wayside – overstepping limits **165**

However, then R. realized he could take the wind out of S.'s sails if he also ordered a beer, assuming control over the situation. When he treated S. to a beer, he redefined the situation.

R. is relieved he could take this step, but also notes that there is no guarantee he would behave this way "outside" in a similar situation. . . .

After achieving all this, R. is satisfied with himself, smiling but also exhausted, and cannot concentrate during the other role-playing.

(Staudner-Moser 1997, 102)

R.'s exhaustion shows what an emotional strain this learning process is for him. It is important that he has found his own solution and that this solution is on a higher social level than a fistfight. R. has now mastered not only the situation but also his usurper by treating him to a beer – presumably a completely new problem-solving strategy for him. Much bravery, self-confidence and support from the group was required for R. to find his saving idea. Presumably, R. has hardly any role models for defusing a potential conflict using this kind of detached, sovereign attitude. His smile shows how satisfied he is with the solution. R. realizes that although he could find this solution in this particular protected space, there is no guarantee this will prove possible on the "outside".

In that same session, another exercise proves extremely difficult for R. The topic is closeness and distance. Two of the boys are asked to walk towards each other from a distance of four meters, slowly and without speaking, maintaining eye contact, and subsequently talk about their feelings.

R. approaches another inmate from Gerasdorf (a juvenile prison in Austria), coming relatively close to him and explains this with the words: "I know him well, it's not a problem for me. With him, for instance (he points to an inmate who is also a Serbian, but an outsider in the group), I wouldn't even be able to walk towards him." R. is asked to nevertheless try it with this other Serbian. However, he categorically refuses. He also quickly begins to question the sense of the exercise.

(Staudner-Moser 1997, 103)

R. has enormous problems with closeness and distance. He can come close to a familiar person whom he trusts. But he does not even start walking towards the other Serbian, refusing the entire exercise. What reason can we find behind this refusal?

Presumably the partner in this role-playing reminds him of his own father, who is so disinterested in him. It is unclear whether the father has ever paid alimony for his son. We can assume that the physical proximity to this other prisoner activates his repressed hatred for his father, a hatred he prefers not to acknowledge.

R's regular, constructive participation in anti-aggression training seems to have enabled a change in his self-image. At the outset he saw himself as a "bunny",

166 Lost by the wayside – overstepping limits

who can swiftly escape to security when threatened. In the 21st session, depictions of four different types of vehicles were hung up in the four corners of the room: a Porsche, an SUV, a Volkswagen and a bicycle.

> R. goes over to the station wagon. His written self-description is: "I am like an SUV . . . I am small but flexible. With the large tires, I get over lots of obstacles and come through rough terrain. I have lots of strength and endurance."
>
> (Staudner-Moser 1997, 105)

This self-description gives a good picture of his attitude during the sessions, where he attempted to find new solutions and possibilities and reflect on himself. The others now are asked to guess who wrote each self-description:

> R. is immediately recognized due to two salient qualities. He used the word "romantic"; he also longs for a loving relationship. R. only learned during the course of the sessions to see himself as tender and lovable. He characterizes himself as a romantic type who needs lots of love but would also be able to give it. In the exercises, love and relationships are often mentioned. Several hours previously, there was one exercise where the boys were asked to put their footprints on a piece of poster paper and then write what they "stehen auf" (in German, what they like). R. wrote "love".
>
> R.'s negative side is the "tricking" of others. This quality has led to his long periods in prison, but also helped him towards a quite high standard of living once there.
>
> R. considers another of his bad characteristics to be his frank and tactless way of telling others what he thinks of them – followed often by a butt to the head, which can also lead to physical fights.
>
> (Staudner-Moser 1997, 105)

It constitutes enormous progress that R. dares to confess his longing for love and speak openly in the group. The entire group seems to have undergone a remarkable evolution, since nobody laughs at R.'s remark.

A further illustration of his emotional state is supplied by the second assignment in this 21st session, where participants are instructed to draw and describe a symbol in which they recognize themselves.

> R. drew a picture of a broken heart (Figure 6.5).
>
> On the smiling side, the heart is red, with the opposite, melancholy side black. The heart is not really broken: neither side stands alone or must fend for itself – they are connected with a thick red line. Love is intimately bound to pain and unfulfilled longing. Everything has two sides . . .
>
> The drawing reminds a Turkish adolescent of a Turkish saying: "Seugin in basi yangindir, sansu ise ölümdür – at the beginning of love there is a crackling fire, at the end of love is death."

Lost by the wayside – overstepping limits   167

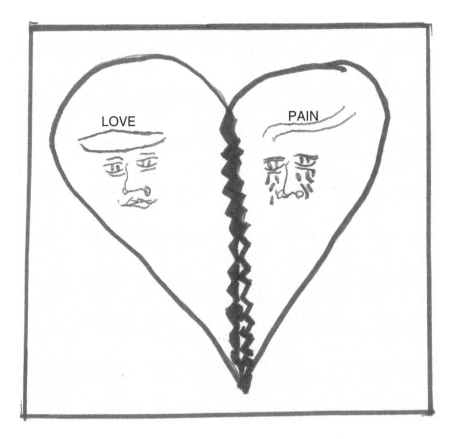

Figure 6.5 The broken heart of R. (from Staudner-Moser 1997)

R. said his drawing would sound like tender, romantic music – there are beautiful, sad songs too – would smell like the skin of a beloved person, and would taste of salt, either the salt on your skin or in tears that are shed.
(Staudner-Moser 1997, 107)

The drawing expresses R.'s ambivalence: not only pain and tears but also love are shown in a male face. Is there a possibility to integrate these two areas, or must they remain merely separate? His associations point to a sensual experience; perhaps his early experiences with his mother were beautiful and tender ones? R. can talk about his feelings impressively, and he feels accepted both by the group and the three trainers. He seems to be at the beginning of a learning process, which helps him be accepted by others with all his ambivalent feelings and vulnerability.

R. cannot participate in the other exercises. The group is asked to write a letter to a victim, which makes them uneasy. R. demurs, asking the trainer if she is

168 Lost by the wayside – overstepping limits

seriously giving him this "homework assignment". He listens to her explanation, but again expresses his unwillingness and leaves the room brusquely. The group is meant to talk about the subject of victimhood through role-playing in a TV discussion.

> R. is assigned the role of a member of an ethnic minority. . . . Nobody says a word. The adolescents slide around on their chairs, stand up, and walk around the group room together. R. shakes his head a few times, places his elbows on his knees and withdraws increasingly. He demonstrates this physically. He becomes nauseated, has to go to the open window and breathe deeply. After some time, this exercise is interrupted and they discuss how difficult it is to carry them out.
>
> (Staudner-Moser 1997, 110)

The goal of this exercise was to show the adolescents that their general rage at the "world" or life leads them to harm real people – and disregard how these real people feel. R. does not even manage to speak. Thinking about the victims of his violent acts is most unpleasant for him. The exercise fails because the group collectively resists carrying it out – whether because of the difficulty of taking responsibility for violent deeds or because of deep layers of victimhood in childhood and the attendant pain of feeling and discussing them, remains unclear.

In place of this "victimhood" discussion, the trainers offer another exercise: a "balloon trip" from the Remscheider group of games (C3). The task is defined as follows: a hot-air balloon hovers over the open sea, on the brink of falling due to excessive weight. Through convincing arguments, each passenger must make the others believe how important s/he is for the world. Each of them of course wishes to survive, but the least convincing of them must jump overboard.

R. assumes the role of navigator. Self-confidently, he claims he is important because only he knows the goal and can steer the balloon. Here, he considers himself important and has taken a meaningful task into his own hands, regardless of how his friends see him. He argues that he alone can take them safely to their destination. Thus, R. has undertaken to dispose over life and death – but in a constructive way, and not a destructive way as in his physical fights. He likes the task, and he feels wonderful "flying there", as he describes it. One group member is willing to jump overboard, and R. tells him when he can jump out at a safe place. Shortly before they reach their goal – R. already knows the balloon will land safely only if he also jumps out – he gives up his place to another passenger, who in this role-playing has a wife and two children. He then jumps out himself, but at the same safe place. Accordingly, R. is a social being to the point of sacrificing his dominant role as navigator (see Staudner-Moser 1997, 109ff).

R. is able to convince others in his role as navigator. He does not use his position to force others to jump out, but steers them to a safe place. At the end, he is able to recognize the responsibilities of another passenger – the father of a family – and hands over to him the important task of navigation. Instead of letting everyone crash with the balloon, he finds constructive solutions. During the feedback afterwards, R. is quite overwhelmed by the praise and appreciation he receives from the other participants and the trainers. He was able to undertake positive tasks for the group and thus showed a new, positive self-image. During the time between October and June of the following year, R. participated in all the sessions and made good use of the various exercises and discussions.

In the final session, the participants worked with an array of puzzle pieces with words on them describing how the individual perceived the group. The participants were then asked to choose the two pieces whose descriptions represented their feelings.

R. selected the two puzzle pieces "solidarity" and "protection". For him, the group has come to embody these characteristics. He felt well-treated by them – even when they often criticized what he said.

As a farewell, the trainers write each participant a letter. In R.'s letter, they recommend that he should trust and believe in himself more. During the sessions, he has encountered his positive sides, and he must use these experiences as a point of departure. R. takes his letter, reads it twice, and then puts it back in its envelope (Staudner-Moser 1997, 114).

R. leaves the group room and this last session as all the others do: relaxed, cool, with a cigarette in his hand and a general group goodbye (Staudner-Moser 1997, 115).

In these nine months, R. has had an opportunity to reflect on himself and his life.

Using his lifeline drawing, he was able to verbalize his experiences and give words to his loneliness and abandonment. Protected and accepted by the group, he was able to speak about his experiences of loss. Remarkably, he could demonstrate new, non-violent solutions in conflict-fraught scenes when he was supported by the group. He often became the mouthpiece for group resistance and refusal, where his arguments found considerable support. He also often managed to convince the trainers to change their program.

Both case studies demonstrate how differently the two adolescents B. and R. worked through their early experiences of neglect. Even though they were sentenced for similar crimes, they developed differing psychic mechanisms for coping. Their emotional development shows how important it is to utilize the time in prison in order to let them experience what it means to reflect on motivations and acts of violence, instead of the prisoner's inner embitterment and belligerent reactions.

From the psychoanalytic standpoint, how can we understand the apparent contradiction of violent adolescents depicting themselves as helpless little animals (e.g., a bunny)?

These adolescents are traumatized from their experiences of deprivation and violence in early childhood. In particular, protracted humiliation, neglect, intimidation and a lack of empathy or consideration for the child hinders him from creating a stable inner world with positive, loving inner objects (internalized images of the parent) – one that would afford him an inner space for good relationships and establishing the balance between love and destruction. Only when a baby has regularly had another person "contain" its unbearably aggressive/destructive impulses, envy and fears of death and dissolution – someone who takes these impulses up, allows herself to be emotionally moved, "digests" them emotionally and then reflects on them – can the baby internalize the transformation of raw impulses into verbalized feelings. Bion speaks of the "reverie", and Winnicott of the "primary maternity" that affords a child protection, acceptance and understanding. Indeed, Bion calls the fulfillment of this need for understanding of the child's loving and destructive impulses "nutrition" for the psyche. Internalizing this transformation of raw emotional elements into thoughts and feelings also constitutes the basis for self-reflection and understanding one's own psychic conflicts. If this experience seldom or never occurs, the baby is flooded with nameless fear (Bion). Bürgin (2004) writes that this destructive impulse "requires a passage through the inner world of a significant other" (Bürgin 2004, 243). Otherwise, a child cannot integrate the two split experiential worlds of an idealized and bad, persecuting mother; the mother – and, by extension, the child's view of the world – remains split into good and evil. The child (and later, the adolescent) cannot integrate her own loving and destructive qualities or observe the world in a mixture of frustrating and fulfilling aspects. The lack of such experiences of acceptance and being wanted can later damage the adolescent's sense of orientation and meaning of life.

This lack of synthesis often leads to lesser or greater learning problems: concentration is hindered by a constant sense of such deep inner threats. Emotional conflicts, hate and rage, loneliness and lack of orientation hinder a student's ability to take in knowledge – in effect a secondary handicap, evident in both case studies previously described. Instead of dialogue with parents who provide warmth, security and appreciation, these problem families offer unreliability and unpredictability. Instead of the strength embodied in internalized images of loving parents, deep despair and loneliness reigns in the adolescent's inner world: when a mother refused to bring her wounded son to the hospital in order to protect her violent partner, only the teacher and school principal attended to the son's wounds, and he consequently preferred going into a home than back to this disappointing family. His parents also failed to help him with his homework – perhaps they did not even notice if he attended school. The child understands their failure to pay attention as a lack of interest, with the message imparted that it doesn't matter whether he studies.

Such adolescents protect themselves from their painful feelings of not being accepted and understood, of burdening the mother or being denied and rejected by the father, by blocking emotional proximity. "If trauma has permanently overwhelmed the feeling of the self as an active agent, grave pathological effects result," writes Bohleber (2004, 236, translation McQuade). The adolescent never feels completely involved in his actions, with some part of his self assigned the role of uninvolved observer in order to avoid disappointment, leading to an emotional flatness and insignificance in his relationships. Such children who are neither in harmony with themselves nor the world often become outsiders, teased or tormented by stronger children at school, leading to a vicious cycle of violence and frustration.

Such adolescents have not developed adequate psychic space for reflection, and they often do not recognize their own feelings, instead reacting in affect –they are often surprised by their own reactions (as Malcolm describes it, "I flip out"). Due to their insufficiently robust emotional control and inability to reflect on themselves and others, the most trivial occasions can activate early traumatic experiences, rendering them extremely vulnerable. In order to protect themselves, they move within their bodies as if they were armored, often able to feel parts of their bodies only with difficulty and not even able to describe their feelings in words. The ego of such adolescents has become fragile through hurt, lack of respect and traumatic experiences. The intense effort to cope with some traumatic stimulus can lead to emotional numbness and a strategy of cognitive and affective avoidance. Within the peer group, other members also try to provoke the individual to lose his control – "flip out" – so that they can feel stronger than him. Alcohol, abuse of pills or self-injury can serve to numb the adolescent, helping him escape the awareness of his inner emptiness and desperation.

Freud (1920) discussed the unconscious mechanism of repetitive compulsion, which he understood as a significant manifestation of the death instinct. The victim repeats his trauma, abuse or violent experience by evoking those same sadistic feelings in another person, in turn eliciting similar (i.e., sadistic) behavior in this other person. A two-and-a-half-year-old child was able to provoke his father into a rage by his sluggish, unreactive behavior, until the father lost control, yelling at him or hitting him (Diem-Wille 2003/2009). In this kind of sadomasochistic relationship, the actors are closely interconnected – but mostly the victim is more active. Seen psychodynamically, the reversal from the role of victim to that of perpetrator, often observed in violent adolescents, constitutes a flip of the same coin. The perpetrator projects her own feelings of helplessness and fear onto the victim, then observing her immature feelings in him, seemingly in triumph – while remaining trapped in the same pattern of behavior. The passively experienced victim position is now reversed into that of the perpetrator, which Denzin (quoted in Sutterlüty 2001, 129) calls a "turning point experience". The argument that the first act of violence "immediately concludes one's own history of victimhood", as Sutterlüty (2001, 130) characterizes it, cannot be confirmed through the psychoanalytic view, since the dynamic between perpetrator and victim remains the same. In the case study of R., he nevertheless manages to attain a new stage of resolution: instead of allowing himself to be provoked by the protagonist or resorting to violence, he finds a solution through thinking. R. ultimately assumes the role of host, treating the provocateur to a beer and thus mastering the situation. The emotional liberation is considerable, since he could opt out of the sadomasochistic "game".

In anti-aggression training, an adolescent realizes that other people – not only the trainers, but also the other participants – are interested in him and his experiences. Participants discuss together their key experiences of victimhood, which helps them to develop empathy. The adolescents see how hard other participants' lives were, too. Instead of being laughed at, they develop together space for thinking and self-reflection. R.'s self-portrait and commentary, showing his inner ambivalence, helps him to find access to understanding and accepting his own feelings.

When R. refuses to approach a rival in one exercise, we can recognize his underlying fragility and difficulty with emotional closeness.

Violence as a direct path to paradise – the fascination of the jihad

Since 2015, we can observe a new radicalization of adolescents in Austria and other European countries, where some adolescents follow the promise of finding a direct path to paradise through the "holy war against infidels". Seen psychologically, this potential for radicalization is a symptom of inner ambivalence and the search for an identity. After being ostracized in European schools and feeling inadequate to scholastic or professional demands, these adolescents become heroes by deciding to become warriors of the jihad. Not only will they be rewarded with 21 willing virgins in paradise, but already on earth in the Califat when girls and young women are offered to them for "sexual enjoyment" (in effect, rape). Through the decision to join the jihad, they attain a collective identity by ostracizing infidels and joining an elite group of warriors for Islamizing the world. The requirement of following strict Islamic rules seems to overcome every other ethnic and cultural difference.

What kind of inner world do these young people have, willing as they are to renounce the security and democracy offered by European civilization in order to risk their lives in this struggle? Benslama Fethi, a French psychoanalyst born in Algeria, has investigated this phenomenon and characterized the inner attitude of the "Super-Muslim" (2016). He uses this term as a prototype for the young man who "cannot be Muslim enough" – a torturing feeling that can blaze into flaming belief. Jihadists declare themselves "dead from love" (2016, 11; Benslama translations by McQuade) and wish to avenge the insult to Islam ideals, converting all "infidels" to the true faith or killing them. This radicalization entails an alteration of values, with murder and suicide becoming a medium of communication. Killing human beings becomes a spectacle and means of propaganda, as opposed to earlier times where murder tended to be concealed and denied. "Terror wishes to be a horribly destructive power, which can be abused at whim" (Ibid, 20). Jihadists feel themselves completely innocent of human justice, since God himself is behaving through them. The cry of "Allah akbar" – originally an expression of humble subservience to God, reminding the subject of his lowly status in the face of God – is turned into its opposite, a kind of battle cry into holy war granting the power to do anything in the name of holy law, exempting the jihadist from human law. This is similar to the modification of the word "Muslim", originally meaning "the humble one", but now characterizing Islamic pride. Through the internet, the character of the jihad has been transformed, becoming a global movement, a leaderless, decentralized network that opens the gates to individual terrorism. They are searching for identity, a place in society and also a relationship, which includes the sexual sphere.

Their voluntary taking up arms points to various motives:

- Protest against their position at the outskirts of society
- Latent violence directed against other or self (suicidal thoughts)
- The longing for a new identity and belonging to a group
- Lack of one or more loving relationships to adults (parents)
- Aggression, subsumed in heroism and victim status

The political scientist and socio-cultural anthropologist Schmidinger helped found the NGO Netzwerke Sozialer Zusammenhalt (NSZ; Networks of Social Solidarity), which offers counseling to young people (and their families or friends) who are at risk of joining an extremist political movement. In its first year (2014), the NSZ counseled 70 adolescents who either wished to journey to Syria, already were there or stood at the outset of radicalization. Concerned family members of these adolescents could turn to the NSZ, which offered preventive workshops for parents, teachers, police officers and municipal staff. The book *Jihadismus* (Schmidinger 2015) summarizes Austrian experiences and field research concerning volunteer fighters from Europe in Syria and Iraq.

The radicalization process, with its attendant fantasizing, can occur at various speeds; there is no one simple explanation for it, and a whole range of motivations as well as biographical roots can be discerned in case studies.

With male adolescents, the strongest factor is the boy's preoccupation with his own masculinity – something already operative for any male adolescent. "With many boys, it is noticeable that they often come from families where there was either no father or a dysfunctional father figure," writes Schmidinger (2015, 80) – i.e., one of the causes of radicalization. Typically, the boy's father has abandoned the family, and he cannot develop a loving relationship to his mother's new partner or husband, instead viewing him with jealousy or dismissal. Unconsciously, they are searching for a masculine role model, which is then fulfilled in jihad preachers or older "brothers".

With both sexes, sexuality plays a major role – something handled quite restrictively in Islam, where arranged marriages and strict celibacy prevail. Groups such as the Islamic State (IS) promise an alternative to this not only in heaven, but already here on earth. Islamic marriages can already be arranged at the age of nine. Repressed sexuality, along with the experience of being "abandoned" by the mother for another, new man, has one consequence in Internet forums – misogynistic, hateful blogs. After large formerly Christian Yazidi territories were conquered in Iraq, social media openly discussed whether it would be *halal* (religiously permitted) to "enjoy" the "war booty" (see Schmidinger 2015,

174 Lost by the wayside – overstepping limits

81). Thus, a warrior could give himself free rein or be married to a young bride who admires him.

For girls, too, much turns on sexuality – in their case, romantic love for an idealized hero fighting the enemy infidel: this constitutes an idealization of the girl's own actions, a notably archaic form of the splitting into good and evil, termed the "paranoid-schizoid position" by Melanie Klein. Many young girls are courted in the Internet under selective "flirt-phishing"; however, with the IS offering a prospective groom, instead of his parents. The girl sees herself as a romantic rebel, demonstrating how selfless and sacrificing she is, rebelling against her dull parents in Austria. If her hero then falls in martyrdom, another prospective husband is supplied in his stead. A problematic life decision such as the separation from an Islamic husband can also be atoned for through engagement in the jihad. With girls, a pseudo-altruism dominates, the desire to help the "poor child warriors" who are being tortured by the brutal Assad regime.

Particularly surprising is the open glorification of violence and cruelty reminiscent of medieval methods of execution and torture (Benslama 2017). As in childhood fairy tales, beheadings and mutilations occur – this time not in films like *Bad Taste* (previously described) but in real life, similar to a reality TV show. Murderers are depicted as heroes; they post severed heads on Facebook, accompanied by a lapidary "Shaytanen (Teufel) slaughtered!" or an appeal to "fill the infidels with fear and horror" (Schmidinger 2015, 829). Indeed, Western states swollen with police and military defenses against terrorism fulfills the megalomaniacal fantasies of potential and actual perpetrators: after jihadist attacks, Brussels was shut down for days, and Paris descended into a vale of tears and rage. It has become clear that protection against the unscrupulous violence of a suicide attack is an extremely difficult enterprise. Seven young radicals can cause a whole city or nation to sink into fear and horror, as they project their own sense of powerlessness onto the populace and give free rein to their rage and destructive impulses. Death is glorified as martyrdom; sometimes, drugs are employed to repress the will to live.

Concrete stories of adolescents joining the jihad are quite various, but one common thread is a lack of connectedness, security, meaning and belonging in their life situations, things that are promised by the jihadists. Schmidinger cites six factors causing this condition:

- Familial problems within destroyed or authoritarian family structures, where affection and respect cannot be learned or experienced
- Problems at school, at vocational training or at work
- Problems with love or sexuality
- Problems related to the meaning of life or identity
- Experiences of discrimination
- Diagnosable psychic problems

When young people are in search of identity, religious enthusiasm and fanaticism offer an alternative to their feelings of insignificance, shame, failure and existential suffering. This enthusiasm allows the young person to experience a new identity, an osmosis into the common group that affords them the hope of total meaning. Thus, out of a difficult life situation becomes "a sedation of fear, a feeling of liberation and an application of total power" (Bernhama 2017, 45). The jihadist warrior becomes a new person, chooses a new name and assumes the behavior of his/her compatriots in battle, giving up his/her singularity and submitting in blind obedience. With many of those who return, psychological crisis, borderline syndrome or psychotic symptoms can be observed (Ibid, 44). "The jihadist . . . adopts an elaborate collective belief in the identity myth of Islam, nurtured by the reality of the war in which he is meant to play a heroic role, to be rewarded by material and sexual advantages as well as both real and imagined power. This fatal mixture of myth and historic reality is more dangerous than madness." (Ibid, 49.) We can speak here of a narcissistic madness through ideals.

I will here describe two of the case studies of radicalized Austrian adolescents from Schmindiger's book (Schmidinger 2015, 80ff).

Case study: Abdullah

Abdullah comes from a largely secularized Tunisian family and was one of the first adolescents from Austria to join the jihad and be killed in it. His father at first came to Austria alone and worked as a health care aide; his wife joined him five years later. Adbullah was their first son born in Austria, followed one year later by his younger brother.

Where they lived in Grossfeldsiedlung, Abdullah learned not only German but also Serbo-Croatian and Turkish (this in addition to Arabic, which the family spoke at home). His father prayed five times a day, his mother dressed in Western fashion, and they occasionally drank alcohol.

Abdullah only knew Tunisia from vacations spent there. At the age of 13 or 14, he had no interest in his Arabic roots. At high school he began to be interested in politics, joining other left-wing-tending students who were critical of the United States. Apparently, they "discovered" him as a token Muslim who could be radicalized in the struggle against the FPÖ (the Austrian far-right political party). Although he joined with them in their recreational activities, drinking beer, smoking marijuana and gathering sexual experience with girls, he never quite lost his exotic status in their eyes.

Only in 2005, when a Danish newspaper published caricatures of the prophet Mohammed, did he feel insulted in his Muslim identity. He took part in a demonstration against these caricatures, meeting members of the radical sub-group Hizb ut-Tahrir that propounds draconian punishments against "sodomy", incest, homosexuality and other divergences from Islam. At the end of 2013, one of his friends went to Syria to fight for the IS.

Abdullah's parents were already concerned in 2014 that their son was being radicalized. They consulted the police, who did not recognize the danger, simply advising them to send their son to Tunisia. They left the police station in disappointment.

176 Lost by the wayside – overstepping limits

One weekend in 2014, Abdullah entered Syria via Turkey. His parents only noticed that he was gone the next morning. However, he maintained contact to his mother via Facebook. He married a 17-year-old Austrian girl from a Bosnian family, and his wife informed Abdullah's parents in December that he had died a "martyr" in the battle for Kobane – killed in a US bombing that destroyed the building he was in; his body was never found.

Discussion

In his description of Abdullah, Schmidinger focuses mostly on the various Islamic splinter groups active in Austrian schools. Abdullah's family situation is hardly described. We only have one point for conjecture: his younger brother was born very soon after he was; thus, at the age of four or five months old he already had to share his mother with a sibling (albeit in his mother's uterus). However, if we read between the lines, we can infer that Abdullah's parents cannot have known much about their son, his problems and psychic situation; he seems to not have confided in either of them.

Case study: Petima

Petima was the oldest daughter of Chechenian parents who had come to Austria shortly before she began school. She learned German so quickly that she got into the academic high school after she finished elementary school. There, she got good marks and held to the strict patriarchal rules of her father, who was more influenced by Adat (the Chechenian custom) than Islam.

Petima's mother did not wear a head scarf and was a well-educated middle-class woman. For both parents, it went without saying that Petima should go on to higher education. At the same time, great importance was attached to her virginity. She was not allowed to go to discos or concerts with her friends, and she had to conceal her visits to a swimming pool from her father.

During a vacation job at a dentist's office, Petima fell in love with a young man with Tunisian roots, Muhammad. Several weeks later, he went to Syria and joined the IS. Petima was unhappy, since her first great love had now disappeared. She kept him a secret from her parents.

From the IS, Muhammad then made contact to Petima on Facebook, posting pictures of himself with a Kalashnikov, posing in front of severed heads and announcing that the IS would sell the prisoner Azidi women as slaves. Petima secretly made a plan to join Muhammad in Syria. With the help of a friend she had confided in, she fled her family's apartment and flew to Syria. A week later, she informed them via WhatsApp from Raqqa that she now wished to lead her life according to the rules of Islam. She sent a picture of her marriage certificate with Muhammad. In spite of her mother's massive attempts and those of her employer, Petima could not be convinced to return. She told of her first great love, of her heroic husband. She had no contact to her father.

Although her husband's parents lived in Vienna, they had no contact to Petima's parents, since her father was strictly against her marriage to a non-Chechenian. They made contact to the NSZ, omitting to mention that Petima was now pregnant. After Muhammad's "martyrdom" – his death – Petima's messages became less euphoric. She married another Chechenian but maintained only infrequent contact to her mother. She has shown no signs of wishing to return to Austria and continuing her studies.

Discussion

The sociological observation of this middle-class family that fled Chechenia for Austria shows what a difficult proposal it was for their daughter to integrate into Austrian society when her father prevented her from taking part in the social activities with her peer group. At first, she concealed her resistance against her anti-sexual education. Petima seemed to adapt, got good grades and apparently aspired towards social upward mobility through her education.

There is no sign in the description that Petima could confide in her parents or at least in her mother. Secretly, she wishes to escape the strictures and rigid norms set by her family. Her first great love, overshadowed by the holy war, exercised such an attraction on her that she left everything behind her to join Muhammad in Syria.

This case study shows how important preventive work in schools would be for countering recruitment efforts that succeed by employing false information. Behind a student's friendly, successful façade, a surprising amount of aggression and destructive wishes can lurk, waiting to be discharged in the "permitted" field of the IS and directed against all "infidels".

Summing up, we must emphasize how important it is with violent adolescents to recognize the psychic dynamic behind this obviously powerful violence: helplessness, powerlessness and rage, as well as the inability to conceive or influence a situation through thought, results in the situation being "acted" through behavior, i.e., acted out. For people working with violent and neglected adolescents, it is important to understand this dynamic – otherwise, the adult may feel humiliated or rejected. "Adults tend to misinterpret the enmity, silence, withdrawal and other reactions on abused children and adolescents as an answer to the current situation instead of seeing them as conditioned reactions to memories from the past," writes Annette Streeck-Fischer, editor of the important book *Adolescence – Connection – Destructivity* (2004, 27). My therapy patient Malcolm, who oscillated between great desire for closeness and massive provocation in his three-hour analysis, wished on the unconscious level to have me experience his helplessness and rage as a child. When I interpreted to him that he wanted to see if I would lose my patience and become so angry that I would give up, he answered: "You will never give up!" He was often astonished that I could recognize his vulnerability behind his pseudo-indifference. He, who had always been mocked, drew the word "HANDICAPPED" on the wall and mocked me, trying to spray me with

178 Lost by the wayside – overstepping limits

water. A play-acted pillow fight could have quickly become dangerous, and I had to set clear limits to it. For a time, I had to clear away his wooden blocks, since he was threatening to break the window with them. When he again broke his cars and demonstrated his broken inner world influenced by violent and unprotective adults, he was surprised to receive new Matchbox cars from me – as a reward for working through his problems according to my psychoanalytic method. He was often afraid of his own destructivity and protected his cars from himself by putting them in his drawer safely when he flew into a rage.

Neglected children's need to protect themselves from unexpectedly friendly and understanding adults through denial or apathy indicates the great psychic pain that arises when something longed for and unattainable now becomes possible. "Why are you talking to me, hit me instead, that's what I know," answers one adolescent in a stationary psychotherapeutic facility in Ursula Pav's book . . . *and when the thread breaks, I only want to strike again* (2010, 8). This unusual and valuable book can be recommended for teachers and supervisors. She draws a detailed picture of the work with heavily traumatized children and adolescents in the context of a project called "Prevention of Violence", with qualitative methods of participant observation and narrative interviews affording insight into the inner world of these adolescents. Particularly in the therapeutic and analytic work with this group of adolescents, collaboration with teachers and other pedagogues is of great significance. I believe that this "Prevention of Violence" project should not only allow flexibility to the adolescents, but above all enable insight into the mastery and techniques of transference – as Bion termed it, "work under fire" – where massive projections are often shot at the therapist like cannonballs, projections that can also reveal important preliminary information on the participating adolescents.

In conclusion, I wish to point out how important it is to offer problem families help at an early stage. In therapeutic work with parents and young children, emerging problems can be addressed and ameliorated at their roots if solutions are found together. Usually, problems extending over generations are underestimated, so that the parents in a parent-child therapy often are availing themselves of the possibility to talk about and work through their own traumatic experiences as children for the first time. "If abused adolescents were better cared for, supported and offered therapeutic help, long-term consequences could be considerably diminished" (Streeck-Fischer 2004, 35). Therapy in homes and orphanages, as well as for adoptive parents, constitutes another important focus.

6.2 The problems of teenage pregnancy

The phenomenon of early pregnancy during the teenager years may well be unplanned, but it is often the expression of an unconscious wish for a baby – and this wish may entail the desire to both give and receive affection. In particular, girls who did not grow up with their own mothers but instead with their grandparents

Lost by the wayside – overstepping limits   179

(or were adopted) tend to become pregnant at the same age as their own mothers, thus perpetuating the pattern under which they have also suffered. The way an adolescent experiences his body depends on his state of mind. As Freud has shown, the mental factor plays a central role in psychosexuality. Patterns of observing one's own body are conveyed through psychic experience. Repeating the (problematic) pattern of unplanned pregnancy in the second generation, the body plays the central role of "acting out". As already described, the earliest memories of our life live within us, determining our behavior, although both the baby-ego and adult components of an adolescent's personality are active. An adolescent girl can incorporate these various parts of her personality into being a mother, projecting her neediness, vulnerability and cared-for status onto her baby and employing her maternal "component" in caring for her baby. When caring for her baby, she is mothering not only her real baby but also herself – her "inner baby".

This constellation already points to an enormous inner pressure that must be mastered in addition to the actual, outer difficulties that render a young mother truly "needy". If teenagers have not yet finished their schooling, they must either manage both school and caring for their baby simultaneously, or risk the handicap to their future that dropping out of school would constitute. They must take responsibility for a small human being, something that is difficult even for an adult mother or father. Teenage relationships are often short-lived or turn on chance encounters: the young parents might have not yet truly gotten to know one another and built an emotional basis for their relationship. Economically, they cannot support themselves and their new family and thus require the shelter of their parents; paradoxically, this makes teenage parents temporarily not more but less independent at this stage of their lives.

The facts are dramatic and deserve a brief exposition: according to a report from UNICEF (2015), 15 million teenagers became unintentionally pregnant (in 2015) – in Austria 12 out of 1000 teenagers and in Germany 16 out of 1000. In Europe, British adolescents lead the statistic, with 22 out of every 1000, but the USA has 55 pregnancies per 1000 adolescents. The lowest number is found in Holland – only 4 pregnancies per 1000 adolescents. It is hard to comprehend these statistics in light of the facts that reliable birth control (in the form of the Pill) has existed for more than 60 years, that sex education is widely prevalent both in European and US schools, and that advice is available from gynecologists and consultation centers.

We can assume that there are strong unconscious motives for becoming unintentionally pregnant. Sexuality can serve various motives. Birksted-Breen writes that "Psychoanalytic developments also moved away from sexuality as that which needs to be uncovered, to sexuality as serving defensive purposes, used to avoid psychic pain and to deal with anxieties of a psychotic nature" Birksted-Breen 2016, 559).

In adolescence, sexuality and pregnancy are active on the unconscious level in many ways. This undoubtedly varies with each individual case, but typical

180 Lost by the wayside – overstepping limits

patterns incorporate widely divergent aspects – the adolescent's unfulfilled longings, rivalry with the mother, self-damaging impulses and fantasies of omnipotence. As described in the chapter about sexuality, earlier rivalries and envy of parents reawake in adolescence; the boy's wish to be an attractive partner for his mother and exclude the father as rival remains unconscious, just as is the girl's fantasy of taking her much-admired father away from her mother. Now, however, both the male and female adolescents have the physical power to render these fantasies reality. The longing to have the father's baby is projected onto a young man and often fulfilled through "carelessness". The unfulfilled longings of the young girl who was neglected in childhood, not sufficiently cared for and protected by her parents, are then shifted onto her impending baby.

The provocative behavior inherent in all relationships with adolescents – who stand to be the next sexually potent generation, thus relegating their parents' generation to the periphery – is rendered concrete through an actual pregnancy. An early pregnancy of a girl who has not yet finished her schooling also forces her parents to "mother" her, since they usually feel they must support her along with her new baby. Instead of attaining more autonomy, she usually intensifies her dependence on her parents. The destructive side of her behavior is self-directed: through her pregnancy, she is forced to radically alter her life, interrupt her education, or continue it with great effort alongside caring for her baby. Pregnancies often emerge out of a short relationship, "summer love" or the first sexual experience, meaning that the two incipient parents' relationship is still fragile; it is seldom possible for them to assume the great burden together and also develop their relationship.

It must be asked whether an unplanned pregnancy also is a symptom of insufficient family sex education, where parents rely on the purely cognitive sex education supplied at school. Parents might take interest in their daughter's first menstruation or son's first ejaculation as well as the question of birth control, in order to afford their child an emotional connection to this new area. Can they accompany their daughter to the gynecologist before she begins an intimate relationship? Can they explain the significance of menstruation and to the "realm of women"? Can the father point out the responsibility of birth control to his son?

Employing three case studies, I will now illuminate the various constellations of teenage pregnancy in the context of middle-class Austrian families. In her Master's thesis, Eva Pankratz discusses the background(s) of unwanted pregnancies in adolescence[2] (Pankratz: *Teenage Mothers: Backgrounds of Unwanted Pregnancy*, 1997).

Case study: Sarah[3]

At the age of 18, Sarah – a student at the academic high school – became pregnant. Both her parents worked for a living: her father was a trade salesman and her mother a salesperson in a shop.

Sexuality in Sarah's family

For Sarah's family, sex education was taboo: in her childhood, sexuality remained unmentioned, as if it did not even exist:

> I got my sex education from BRAVO – I really mean that – my parents never told me one thing, they kept it a complete secret from me . . . in biology it was that way too, but especially the feelings connected with sex. . . . I learned about them from BRAVO, unfortunately.
>
> (Pankratz 1997, 57)

When Sarah found a condom in her parents' suitcase, they were thoroughly embarrassed, but they did not discuss the matter. Only when her grandmother "caught" Sarah and a boy in bed did her mother bring Sarah to the gynecologist, remaining by her side during the examination and subsequent discussion with the gynecologist – even though Sarah was most discomfited by this.

Sarah's first menstruation found her unprepared: "Yes, that was terrible for me – since of course I told my mother, because I thought I had something awful. My mother only said that it's menstruation and she explained the hygienic things to me, but I was terribly embarrassed."

Sarah was also terribly embarrassed to get her sanitary napkins out of the cupboard in front of her father. It particularly shocked her to find out that her mother had told all of their relatives that Sarah was menstruating now – "That was a catastrophe for me".

Contraception and child fantasies

At her first visit to the gynecologist, she learned about contraception and got a prescription for the Pill.

> Then I took the pill, of course, just as you're supposed to, but I didn't have a good reaction at all since I was very, very prone to depression and psychically unstable back then. And quite soon, I stopped taking it . . . and I must say that I rather played with the idea that I might become pregnant. That's why when I did I didn't find it so bad – on the contrary.
>
> (Pankratz 1997, 59ff)

After this, Sarah and her boyfriend did not use any form of birth control. Since she continued to menstruate, she wondered if something might be the matter with her. She was terribly in love, and then "it worked after all". She is very proud to report that she is the only one in her class to have a baby.

Knowledge of pregnancy and birth

Sarah received practically no sex education or information from her mother. The short conversation she had with the gynecologist in her mother's presence

182 Lost by the wayside – overstepping limits

was also unhelpful. Although Sarah had considered dropping out of school even before she got pregnant, two of her teachers particularly supported her. Her gym teacher dedicated one hour of gym class to pregnancy and birth, showing the entire class the film *Gentle Birth* and referring Sarah to a preparatory pregnant mothers' group. She helped with "a lot of information" and made it clear to Sarah how important it is to "listen to your feelings". Sarah said that through this support from the (female) teacher, she got a "womanly feeling" she had never had before. She discovered "the woman in me" and could "incredibly quickly . . . mentally . . . in every possible way prepare myself for the baby". The "strong personal change" through her pregnancy and "a certain maturity" she had now acquired made it clear to her that "I would only like a 'gentle delivery'".

Sarah's life situation shortly before her pregnancy

Sarah describes her situation as unclear, diffuse. Shortly before she became pregnant, she had considered dropping out of school – partly because of her bad grades:

> Back then, I had terrible problems at school – actually, I had always wanted to drop out. My mother said she wouldn't mind – I would just have to start work somewhere.
>
> (Pankratz 1997, 51)

We can assume that Sarah's idea of dropping out of school was a cry for help to elicit her parents' support. But her mother did not react as expected, instead seeming to have no objection to Sarah's plan; Sarah characterized this as "somehow not moral support" – while smiling in order to not show (or feel) her disappointment and hurt. Paradoxically, her pregnancy and support from her school then enabled her to pass her final exam, in her fifth month of pregnancy. Her career plans were unclear at this point; she wanted to "go to the Film Academy or study something artistic", as she said. At the same point that she got failing grades in her courses, she learned that she was pregnant. "Somehow I was glad that I finally knew how things would develop," she said. In the interview, Sarah was no longer sure whether her first reaction to her pregnancy was to "throw everything overboard" or to carry on. She said the pregnancy lent an "amazing meaning to life". Her impending role as mother seemed to dissolve any uncertainty as to how her life would go on after the final exam. She did not yet have to decide between continuing her education or getting a job; she had a "time out" for taking care of the baby.

Discovery of the pregnancy

Sarah's mother was the first to suspect her daughter was pregnant. She seemed to be informed about her daughter's menstrual cycle and reminded her that her period was long overdue.

back then, I was pretty dreamy – or however you are at that age (she laughs) and it just made me – I don't know.

(Pankratz 1997, 54)

Only after Sarah's mother sent her to the gynecologist did she learn that she was expecting a baby. It is interesting that Sarah had not noticed any change in her body – or did not wish to. When she told her mother that she had tested "positive", her mother misunderstood this and believed she was *not* pregnant. "Thank God", she exclaimed. Sarah then had to explain that a positive test meant that she was in fact expecting a baby. Since Sarah and her partner had unequivocally decided to have the baby, her mother "completely kept out of it, after remarking that she had a totally different view of the matter". Sarah only later learned from her grandmother that her mother had cried when Sarah was picked up to deliver the baby. Sarah was surprised at this, since her mother otherwise did not show her feelings.

Her boyfriend also "accepted" the news of Sarah's pregnancy – "if it has to be – (she laughs) – that kind of thing." There never seems to have been any danger of his abandoning her. The teachers and other students ignored her condition and did not speak of it, although Sarah believes that at her final exam her teachers gave her some extra leeway due to her pregnant condition. Her gym teacher practiced autogenous training with the students and promoted body consciousness through massage. Sarah sees that as a major support. In conversation, Sarah expresses strong opposition to abortion.

Teenage life and pregnancy

Sarah said she had a "total inner bond" with her child, and that her pregnancy made clear to her what is "going on" with her, that she "will now have a responsibility in the future". Indeed, she immediately stopped smoking and altered her life "relatively quickly – towards more healthy food and so on." She took her body seriously and managed to treat it well, taking care of herself for her baby's sake.

Sarah suffered under stress at school as well as mood swings. In particular, her supervisory teacher (a math teacher) irritated her with how he dealt with her. She continued her teenager life, going to concerts and parties. "I didn't want to give up anything . . . back then I felt such a strong need to go out," she said. She attempted to carry on with her life as it had been before pregnancy. "Knitting socks like some other pregnant mothers, that was out of the question," she laughed. Even after the baby was born, she still "fulfilled my needs as a teenager even more . . . with parties, listening to loud music, dancing and so forth".

I think that was good, because if I had just stayed home, the ceiling would have just caved in on me – it was a good compromise. Now I'm different, and now I'd do it differently.

(Pankratz 1997, 56)

184   Lost by the wayside – overstepping limits

Her family and boyfriend were supportive, and her grandfather could provide the young couple with an apartment. They were also given organizational and financial support from both parents; their decision to move in together and have the baby was respected by both sets of grandparents.

Instead of going on the graduation trip with others in their class, Sarah took a trip alone with her boyfriend, where they could take time for each other, starting to "lead our own life"; Sarah regretted that she broke off relationships with the other students so "abruptly".

> They came to visit me, and a whole lot of people visited me in the hospital, but that came to a pretty fast end.
>
> (Pankratz 1997, 63)

At the beginning of her pregnancy, Sarah still fit in with the other students – they could relate to one another. Later, when her baby had been born, it stood between her and them. She had grown into the experience with the baby, and they felt excluded, then absenting themselves. Sarah initially preferred to be alone with the child and her boyfriend. Thus, the pregnancy put an abrupt end to her adolescence, and she developed a mature pair relationship, one that proved quite robust despite the narrow time frame (approximately a year). The child became the "absolute midpoint", and she would not have been capable of declaring, "I'm going my own way, I'm going to work and putting you in a crawlspace." Sarah's life situation was such that she was never bored. However, she professed understanding for single mothers who felt like the "roof caved in on them" when they spent the whole day alone at home with their child.

Discussion

Sarah's case shows the entanglement between destructive and constructive, loving, conciliatory aspects of a teenage pregnancy. At first, Sarah lags far back in her academics – with five failing grades in one semester so that she is considering dropping out of school. Presumably, this is due to an unconscious conflict or her provoking of her mother; but instead, the mother seemed to be indifferent. She is a salesperson and thus has no academic degree. One might ask whether there are unconscious envious feelings towards Sarah, who could outdo her in her education.

Sarah's becoming pregnant was made more probable through the taboo status of sexuality and the lack of sensitive sex education from the parents. Only after Sarah was discovered by her grandmother having sex does the mother accompany her to the gynecologist, but she does not allow Sarah a private talk with the gynecologist, instead remaining against Sarah's will, which indicates a fraught mother-daughter relationship. The mother then does not seek out further discussion with Sarah, tolerating her faulty birth control, so to speak. Sarah may have procrastinated on visiting the gynecologist in order to miss the deadline for a possible abortion.

However, Sarah is able to take up her gym teacher's offer of help and advice to visit a group for pregnant women. Parental figures such as teachers, relatives or family friends can strengthen the adolescent's inner parental images; we speak here of a "transference relationship" (Harris 2007, 248). The idea of an internalized parental couple or of parents and teachers who work together and constitute a vital couple indicates the establishment of an ethical inner system in the adolescent psyche. After all, this "inner family" with its masculine and feminine elements gives the adolescent orientation in her further life. At the same time, a less emotional relationship with an advisory person (such as Sarah's teachers) is very useful: they are able to offer advice that adolescents cannot accept from their own parents. At first, Sarah's pregnancy seems to magically solve all her problems. She manages to pass her final exam in her fifth month of pregnancy, in spite of her bad grades in the previous semester. Here we can observe the vitalizing, activating effect of pregnancy. Caring for more than her own self, Sarah now wishes to finish school before she gives birth. Her loving relationship to the impending baby lends her strength and energy, and she experiences none of the negative physical signs of pregnancy. If it is possible to have enough good in herself that a baby can grow there, then she can also have enough faith in her intelligence and strength to successfully pass her exam. Pregnancy often provides the impending parents with the strength to accomplish difficult tasks.

Sarah immediately has a "total" relationship to her baby, stopping smoking and beginning to eat a more healthy diet. This self-care for her baby's sake points to a good inner mother. In her inner world, Sarah carries the image of a loving, caring mother, from which she derives power and inner strength. Through her pregnancy, she experiences her "womanly" side – as if she were achieving a reconciliation with her own mother. She also manages to include her boyfriend (the baby's father) in the pregnancy, taking him to the preparations for the birth and to the ultrasound test.

Sarah's relationship to the baby's father withstands all turbulence. Together, they set up house in the grandfather's apartment: he moves into a nursing home for their benefit, thus making room for a young generation. Since Sarah's mother supports her financially and will take care of her baby, she can indeed free her daughter from many burdens. This constitutes a sign of respect for the young couple's decision to have the baby and reparations for an early lack of care and affection towards Sarah.

Case study: Babsi

At the age of 16, Babsi became pregnant as a junior in high school. Her father comes from a conservative Arab culture, is a veterinarian and often travels for work. Her mother is a housewife, and both her older brothers have already moved

186 Lost by the wayside – overstepping limits

out. She describes her upbringing as quite strict and very conservative, and says that she "really rebelled from the age of twelve, thirteen, fourteen".

Sexuality in Babsi's family

Sexuality seems to have hardly been discussed in Babsi's family, since she says: "Yes, well, I didn't hear so much at home, since nowadays you hear about it everywhere, I mean at school and so forth . . . so, sex education, I knew everything, I'm not stupid" (she laughs) (Pankratz 1997, 75). Babsi describes herself as on top of things, not stupid – yet she makes no connection between her lack of birth control and sex education.

Her first menstruation finds her unprepared: "I didn't know what that is, you know. My slip had a totally weird color and my mother said: 'Yes, now you're a woman' or something like that. Ooh, shit" (she laughs) (Pankratz 1997, 76).

Babsi was shocked at the blood in her slip; she calls her mother's reaction "relaxed", but the mother did not actually help Babsi to cope with this shocking situation. There was no discussion between mother and daughter, no embrace of Babsi in order to celebrate becoming a woman, as some other girls experience.

Contraception and child fantasies

> Well, the first time I went to a gynecologist . . . I wanted to get a prescription for the Pill . . . and then he wasn't there that day, he had to go to help with a birth, I didn't get the Pill, a month later I was back there pregnant – super!
>
> (Ibid)

Indeed, Babsi did not take responsibility for her pregnancy but held the doctor responsible. Her message is: if he had made enough time for her, she would not have become pregnant.

Her mainly negative attitude towards children is shown by her statements:

> I never wanted to have a child, I always said that putting a child in this shitty world is pure egoism, since you want a child for yourself. Because the poor child, I always thought, but now I've got one – and actually I would think the same thing now.
>
> (Ibid)

Babsi viewed her and the world's situation quite pessimistically. She was most discontented with the environment, speaking of the ozone hole and risk of skin cancer; she immediately went on to discuss marriage. "And I'm certainly not going to get married, I ain't stupid." She admits that although she earlier didn't want to have some man be a "weight around her neck", she became that very "chain" herself: "I totally loved him, somehow" and "didn't want to lose him". In place of the close relationship she wanted with Markus, the father of her baby, she now has her baby, who is completely helpless and dependent on her. Perhaps she wished to bind Markus more tightly to her through the baby.

> Well, with contraception and so forth that was pretty incompetent. We did get condoms, but when you're high and so on you don't think of something like that. And he always said it was a pleasure-killer, totally stupid really. He, who was older, he ought to really have taken a little bit of responsibility. That's how you're immature when you're sixteen. You know you can get pregnant, but you aren't really conscious of it, not really. . . . You think, I won't get pregnant after all, it won't happen to me, sort of like that. . . . Only when it happens do you think, what crap.
>
> (Pankratz 1997, 77)

Babsi contends that she didn't quite see the problems with contraception and pregnancy as relevant to her. Theoretically, she knew she could become pregnant, but could not put this knowledge into practice. In a kind of megalomania, she was convinced that it wouldn't happen to her, that she was somehow different. Her neglect of contraception was also fueled by Markus' rejection of condoms as "pleasure-killers", and a muddied consciousness due to alcohol and drugs. Here, her difficult life situation becomes evident.

Babsi's life situation shortly before pregnancy

Since her freshman year in high school, Babsi called attention to herself for provocative behavior. The teachers often sent her to the principal; after she was expelled from her first school, she also changed schools more than once. Babsi says she was a "Gruftie in the Scene for a long time – three or four years . . . and it's no secret that I was a drug addict." At school, she wore her hair

> in front of my face, I dressed in black, was pale and the teachers were always saying "for God's sake". And I drank a bottle of alcohol every morning and started acting pretty messed up already early in the day. Or I smoke grass in the morning and came to school totally stoned. Well, that wasn't even so bad then, but it got pretty terrible later toward the end. I took heroin – only for a month.
>
> (Pankratz 1997, 67)

In this interview excerpt, Babsi describes her provocative and self-damaging behavior in more detail. Using German slang for drugs, she stages a special situation vis-à-vis the interviewer: she becomes the expert, turning the tables so that the interviewer is meant to feel foolish and excluded. Babsi's increasing drift into the drug scene – to the dangerous point of a potential heroin overdose – shows how strong her inner need to extinguish her inner impulses, thoughts and fears is – something that became less and less possible as time

188   Lost by the wayside – overstepping limits

went on. She also mentions that she "saw friends die of drugs, too" and looks back on this period as "incredibly ugly" and "pretty shitty". Babsi also experienced a non-lethal overdose, and "I wanted out, but never really managed that". Very clearly, suicidal thoughts are behind her drug addiction, but there is also a good inner voice that draws her attention to the dangers, since she calls this time period "shitty".

> When I met him, I was completely pulled out of it, because he doesn't have any interest in that scene.
>
> (Pankratz 1997, 68)

Through Markus, her boyfriend, she managed to break away from the drug scene. Although he was a loner and "the guy who hates people", Babsi's parents were very glad about her new relationship with someone outside of the drug scene.

> My parents were definitely glad, because they saw that he was good for me. I went into the sun for the first time in three years. . . . I was totally brown, I looked good, I think, I gained weight again and so on.
>
> (Ibid)

She had been expelled from the school they both attended, where she was the black sheep and he was "the coolest kid in school". In the other school she had just completed the school year, approximately in her third month, and "just began to work" in order to later obtain her parental leave benefits.

Markus is not an easy man. "He had four girlfriends before, they all left him after one week, and he's been together with me for two years." Although Markus is several years older than Babsi, he is "extremely immature" due to his "unusual past".

> His father has smoked grass for the last 20 years and is already totally messed up. He (Markus) was pretty extreme, he gets up at 12 noon, sits in front of the computer all night – he only has a night life – that's how I lived too.
>
> (Ibid)

For Babsi, Markus was the man she had truly loved and trusted, the only one to really take a relationship seriously. However, she seemed to have a realistic image of Markus with his problems.

Babsi's discovery of her pregnancy and reactions from the environment

Between Babsi's first and second visit to the gynecologist – within one month – Babsi became pregnant. Previously, she had never wanted a child. For a week before Babsi told her mother, she made negative comments about media reports on abortion. Only then did Babsi tell her mother, who proceeded to tell Babsi's father. Although Babsi knew she had not used birth control, she described her pregnancy to her parents as an "accident".

> My father had a terrible time with it, he was brought up differently . . . well, my parents were totally cool, my mother was super, my father had half a heart attack (she laughs); my brother said I should on no account have the baby . . . that that would be bad for my future because I would ruin my youth. The men were all against it (she laughs), my mother was actually the only one who was loyal, I mean they all stood by me but really they were against it.
>
> (Pankratz 1997, 73)

Babsi's surprising revelation that she was pregnant seems to have gone off like a bomb – presumably this shock effect was part of her unconscious staging. In particular, her father was against her having the baby because he considered a virgin bride to be a precondition for marriage, and almost "had a heart attack". Babsi's relationship to her father was particularly close: she never felt herself as a girl, but instead a boy, and wanted to become a veterinarian like her father.

Her older brothers were also very much against her having the baby. Babsi explained that her oldest brother had a son with a woman who had renounced her rights and only saw the son once a month. The great tension and burden of Babsi's decision is evident. Then she spoke about the child's father, Markus:

> He didn't know what he should do. He never said no – he always said something like "I don't know". He didn't want to do that to me with abortion and so on. He kept out of it more or less.
>
> (Ibid, 74)

Markus didn't react much in her presence, wishing to leave the decision up to her; however, Babsi heard of stormy discussions between Markus and his parents. His mother wanted them to "get an abortion, are you crazy, I always told you you have to use birth control". His father said "you shouldn't have an abortion, he would help us." But in fact he did not help them. There were even physical fights between Markus and his father, "where blood flowed" when Markus' father asked him to choose between him and the new baby. Markus decided for Babsi and the baby, and moved out.

The experience of pregnancy and birth

> At the beginning of pregnancy, I always felt nauseated – but I liked the feeling of pregnancy, it's really great. . . . During the whole pregnancy . . . I ate a huge amount, tons of Black Forest cake and pickles . . . and cans of mushrooms with mayonnaise.
>
> (Ibid, 69)

190 Lost by the wayside – overstepping limits

With evident enjoyment, Babsi tells of her eating habits during pregnancy and that she used pregnancy "totally as an excuse". After she gave birth, she shed her weight increase of 30 or 35 pounds during pregnancy through diets and physical exercise.

Babsi noticed her own psychic changes: she was no longer concealed behind the mask of the "hard Babsi" who could protect herself from anything, but instead became extremely sensitive:

> The feeling is really great, but then you get totally strange, I mean as a feeling . . . I mean, sensitive; I cried all night because of something or other or something in the news, I teared up or because of every little thing. . . . I was also quite unhappy for a time in pregnancy.
>
> (Ibid)

Her expectations of Markus went unfulfilled – on the contrary, she had "a very difficult time with him". Her ideas and dream of a beautiful pregnancy were also unfulfilled. She would have liked to go with Markus to the preparations for birth, as an external signal of their bond to one another. For him, the pregnancy was a "shock" that he "couldn't fully wrap his head around". He was "also one of those hard types with tattoos, long hair and leather pants". When Babsi finished school and went out to work in order to get her maternity leave, she spent "lots of money on Markus, because he never had money". Since she lived at home, her parents were paying for her room and board. She changed, since "I can't live like this anymore . . . since I was pregnant and felt the baby, I mean, for God's sake, there's something alive there. I can't go on living like I was" (Ibid, 78).

From the outset, it was clear to Babsi that she wanted to keep the baby. She felt more feminine when she was pregnant, "just totally different."

Teenage life and pregnancy

Babsi stopped going to school in her third month of pregnancy and began to work. Since she was now gone from the "scene" due to Markus, she "actually didn't have any friends at all. . . . I'm sad about that, but it's coming back slowly."

The changes in her were major: before, she had enjoyed shocking people. Now, she spent most of her time with Markus.

> I was actually only with him and was pretty dependent on him. I was totally – I clung to him so, I have a fear of separation.
>
> (Ibid, 75)

Babsi mostly put Markus' interests first: she went to the sauna with him, played computer games or accompanied him to the Danube Island to watch him play volleyball. "So, I did have to sacrifice a lot, and we never went out at night." The time at home they spent listening to music and smoking pot, which did not please her parents. On the one hand, Babsi cared for her baby and did not attend a concert of her favorite band, but on the other hand, she continued to smoke pot, which was not good for the baby.

Babsi's attitude and relationship to the baby

Although the birth was not particularly easy, once the baby lay on her belly she felt "everything was right then, ooh, it was so small, sooo sweet, ooh, that was crazy how tiny it was. I never would have thought a child can be so small."

Babsi told of her great insecurity taking care of her newborn child: she was "incredibly frightened" that she would draw the baby's bathwater too hot, and had to get help from her mother. Her idea of a baby and taking care of it became more realistic:

> I always only thought about the great things with a child, but not getting up in the night and so. Or when somebody calls up and says, "You feel like coming out?", before, I would have said right away, come over and pick me up or I'll come myself. Now, uh oh, damn it, I can't – and those are the negative sides, but you have to accept them.
>
> (Pankratz 1997, 79)

Discussion

What drives Babsi – who comes from an "orderly family" – to drug addiction and other desperate, self-destructive behaviors? This intense mode of self-destruction, "no future", black "Gruftie" mourning apparel, and negative view of life point to an inner world full of guilt feelings and wishes for punishment. We know that adolescents, like young children, feel responsible not only for bad deeds they have committed but also for bad, envious or destructive fantasies – and believe they should be punished for these. Early rivalrous wishes for taking babies away from the mother, rendering her barren, occur in all children to a greater or lesser extent. With single children and youngest children like Babsi, there are no corrective experiences to confirm that these fantasies have not in fact destroyed the mother's fertility. In spite of great jealousy, it is extremely calming for the older child to experience that the father and mother can produce something new and creative in spite of this destructive fantasy of clearing out the mother's body. In adolescence, these repressed feelings are once again activated: the adolescent's inner world is then projected onto outer reality, the "shitty world" with its pollution, overpopulation and armaments. Babsi does not wish to have a baby in such a world – and thus accomplishes an act of punishment in her fantasy: she did not allow her parents another baby, and now she does not allow herself one. This behavior indicates a strict, cruel superego: she punishes herself and does not allow herself a baby because she finds herself and her evil fantasies and thoughts to be so despicable. She becomes a ghost, a "Gruftie", never goes in the sun and looks like death itself. She manages to comport herself at school in such a way that she is continually

192 Lost by the wayside – overstepping limits

excluded – an unconscious staging, a proof of how terrible she is. At the same time, there is also an urgent wish in her to be a baby herself and have a loving man at her side – as the father of her child. In fact she falls in love with Markus, the most attractive boy at school; he can pull her out of her swamp. I understand this to mean that there is in her an image of a loving mother who will allow her to have a loving, potent man. He can, in fact, "save" her. The idea of saving somebody originates from the Oedipal phase where the child is convinced her mother does not make the father truly happy and she, the daughter, would love him truly and save him. Or conversely, the son is his mother's savior – now, Markus is saving Babsi. Babsi manages to emerge from her inner vortices and choose Markus (who has enough of his own problems) as a substitute for her father. She also manages to make her parents support her emotionally and financially.

With Babsi, we also see how from two negative forces a mainly healing, constructive solution can come about; Freud speaks of the flexibility of psychosexuality. Pregnancy and the healthy baby Babsi brings into the world stand for her positive, inner forces. She is someone who has a healthy, good body, a body that nurtures not a sick but a healthy, strong baby – and her assumption that she is mainly bad is thus thoroughly disproven. Only slowly can her constructive component prevail; during her pregnancy she continues to wear only black, not cheerful pink – most likely out of a fear of an envious mother/bad fairy who could take the baby from her. We do not know whether Babsi's mother really wanted to have her (Babsi is considerably younger than her other siblings). Her older brothers had already moved out by the time Babsi was 12 and her problems began. Perhaps Babsi sensed her mother's ambivalence or secret refusal to deal with a baby at this late date, when the siblings were already older. The mother's behavior indicates a great emotional distance: she is unable to be glad when Babsi has her first menstruation. Did the mother feel forced into the role of the receding generation? Indeed, Babsi has made her mother into a grandmother. Her unintended/unconscious pregnancy is a partial solution that nevertheless creates new problems. Babsi has not yet finished her schooling and is more dependent on her parents than the other students. She has to go without many things other adolescents enjoy and take on an early responsibility. The chance that she can build a stable relationship with Markus is slight, as she indicates. Babsi would like to have gotten more attention and love from him during the pregnancy.

Her intense relationship to Markus, who is an outsider, enlivens Babsi's dependent and needy side; she hangs on him like a barnacle and is afraid to be separated from him. The pendulum swings in the other direction – from the wish for freedom to the longing for closeness. Presumably, her love for her baby also contains the wish to have somebody who is completely dependent on her, from whom she need never part. But Babsi's sense of reality is in any event strongly enough developed that she can perceive the needs of her actual baby, and in the main fulfill them. Her unconscious aggressive impulses are manifested in her worries: she is afraid to make the bath water too hot and burn her baby. At the same time, she

Lost by the wayside – overstepping limits **193**

can accept her mother's and father's help – not only financial aid but also support in caring for the baby. Babsi sleeps with her daughter in her former bedroom. On the one hand, she suffers from the family discussion of her, but on the other hand, it would be even more difficult for Babsi to go out without her mother as babysitter. Babsi's enthusiasm over her baby daughter's new abilities and characteristics, as well as the concerns she expresses at their visit to the pediatrician, point to a "good-enough" mother-child relationship.

The apartment promised by Markus' father never materialized. We can assume that Babsi's outer situation corresponds to her inner world: she still requires the protection of her parents, has dropped out of school and is preparing for the final exam at home. Her relationship to Markus is more difficult than not; presently they see each other only on weekends, since Markus has now taken a job. Babsi talks of a "relationship crisis", which leads one to doubt whether their relationship can bear these burdens. In the interview, she says how happy she is to be able to talk about all these concerns, since she has few friends.

Case study: Claudia[4]

Claudia is 17 and is in her eighth year at secondary school at the time of this interview. In May, she has her final exam there, and her daughter Moni is eight months old. Claudia's father is an engineer; her mother is a housewife and currently also a university student. Claudia has married 19-year-old Tom, the father of her child. The three of them are living in a small modern apartment. Tom is currently doing his military service and is also present during the interview.

Sexuality in Claudia's family

The topics of sexuality and sex education were not addressed in Claudia's family.

When she had Tom as a boyfriend, "My parents said, 'Yeah, well, you know'. I was, like, 'Yeah, yeah'. And they were, like, 'It won't be happening'" (Pankratz 1997, 102).

For Claudia's parents, this ended the conversation, and Claudia remained alone and unsure. Apparently, her parents were too inhibited to talk about sexuality but were then upset at her pregnancy. Claudia did not have the chance to learn the specifics of birth control.

Claudia's first menstruation

> It sort of announced itself before. I mean, I didn't menstruate all of a sudden. Before, I had a slight smear of blood . . . and my mother said, 'Watch out, it will be coming soon'. And it did. It was certainly annoying (she laughs).
>
> (Pankratz 1997, 102)

194 Lost by the wayside – overstepping limits

Claudia's mother did not adequately prepare her for the significance of menstruation, since she did not explain that she could now become pregnant.

Contraception and child fantasies

> Actually, I always wanted to have a child. I played with the thought of what it would be like if I had a child and so on. Back then I always was thinking I wouldn't be in my parents' way anymore, and in school I would also have certain advantages (she laughs). But my pregnancy was not intentional. When I found out, I was really blown away that I was truly pregnant.
>
> (Ibid, 103)

Tom and Claudia evaded answering direct questions as to birth control – because "until now, we actually haven't told anyone". Claudia only volunteered that "in any case, it wasn't 100 percent". Possibly, her wish for a child expressed itself in her inadequate birth control measures.

Claudia's life situation shortly before pregnancy

Claudia told of her difficulties at school, which "got on my nerves". In the subjects taught by their strict teacher responsible for supervising their class in general, she did not study or learn well. With her parents, she had "always fought, I mean intentionally" and had typical conflicts: "teenage things, tech things, going out, when you have to be home (she laughs)" and because of that she was "pretty exhausted".

Tom was the first person she could open up to and talk about herself, including all her stress at school and at home; he seemed like a safe harbor amidst her problems. He became her best friend, and soon they were "together", i.e., intimate.

When asked as to how long they had been together, Claudia consulted Tom. Laughing, they figured out that it had been half a year. "But with us, it wasn't that, it wasn't only half a year, it was somehow different. We knew from before that we would stay together." Tom adds: "After three or four weeks I already knew that we would stay together or something like that."

Perhaps having a baby together was meant to dispel any fears that their relationship would not last. Through the baby, Claudia and Tom are bound together for life. In fact, they are married at the time of the interview and live with the baby in a small apartment – in spite of somewhat excruciating circumstances. Claudia says:

> I mean, otherwise I never got outside of myself. I never had anyone to tell things to . . . and he was just everything for me, I told him everything . . . there was also never any doubt that we wouldn't stay together and that we would have children later or so forth.

Tom was Claudia's first love, her first intense experience of deep trust and security. They had already talked about a future together and had the wish to have children later. Claudia also never had any doubt that Tom would stand by her if she became pregnant, although her actual pregnancy was, as Tom remarked, "a shock".

Discovery of Claudia's pregnancy and reaction from the environment

With Claudia, discovering she was pregnant took a dramatic turn. She said:

> Ok. So it wasn't so good, that (she laughs) was bad (clears her throat), because I found out while Tom didn't happen to be here. He was in Greece with some friends, so, I was totally blown away . . . at first, I kept it to myself, which wasn't so . . . I don't know (she laughs) . . . good. Then I lost weight and just was kind of automatically . . . I wasn't doing so well, then I told it to my parents.
>
> (Pankratz 1997, 97)

Claudia's clearing her throat and laughing point to considerable inner tension; although she could tell of how terrible the situation was for her, the painful experiences from the onset of her pregnancy were once again activated. She spoke of these in detail:

> So, I got my pregnancy test from the drugstore and took it. At that time I had a summer job – I took the test quickly during a break and looked at it later. Ooh (she laughs) and then right away I told someone – we were three summer interns and the older one looked most trustworthy, so I told her.
>
> (Ibid, 98)

This woman then gave Claudia a gynecologist's address to make sure, since the test might also be inaccurate. The gynecologist confirmed the test result, which "didn't surprise me, since it would be strange if I weren't pregnant – I didn't eat much, lost weight until I was 40 kilos or something" (Ibid).

Claudia characterized her parents' reaction to her pregnancy as "terrible. They were totally crushed and . . . didn't know what they should do now (clears her throat), they wanted actually that I – since I was so young – that I get an abortion" (Ibid). The parents were at first against the pregnancy. Their main argument was that Claudia would ruin her entire life and herself.

For Tom, who learned by telephone in Greece that Claudia was pregnant, it was "certainly a shock". He didn't tell anyone else, "because first I needed to think about it myself – I didn't know what I would have said." In the two weeks that followed, he had "a lot of time to think about it. I thought about what we should do . . . yeah, because I knew that the parents would totally flip out" (Ibid).

196 Lost by the wayside – overstepping limits

Both Tom and Claudia had only telephone contact at a time when they had a strong need for one another; this was particularly difficult for Claudia. Tom told of what happened after his return to Austria:

> I had a discussion alone with Claudia's father, man to man. He absolutely wanted that. First he told me his standpoint, that they were advising us to get an abortion because we are so young. In the end, I could convince her parents that we did want the child." Tom said he convinced them by saying that "if you can fight for your child, so to speak, we also have the right to fight for our child. That's actually what convinced them and they acknowledged my argument, if that's what we really wanted and were prepared to do something about it.

> (Ibid, 99)

With this "man-to-man" discussion, Tom was accepted on an equal footing. He was successful in conveying their standpoint. This conversation showed Claudia's parents that Tom truly stood by her and that the two of them would master this challenge together – which certainly must have calmed the parents. Later, they "supported us fully the whole time . . . actually, they supplied us with the basis for what we have now". Tom and Claudia are able to demonstrate their thanks for the help given by Claudia's parents. Certainly, Claudia's earnest effort to study for her final exam along with caring for the baby shows how serious she and Tom are about the baby, and demonstrates that she is using her parents' help constructively.

At school, Claudia receives unexpected support. In the third week of school, she told her supervisory teacher – whom she "feared" – that she was pregnant. This teacher recognized and accepted that Claudia was in an extremely difficult situation and helped her to finish class. He also requested transparency, asking Claudia to tell the entire class that she was pregnant.

> Yes, that was painful. One day after I had told him – a week or so later – in physics in the physics room he called me in and said – because I wanted to tell my best friends first and then I thought the news would spread anyway. But he said . . . I should go out and tell the class myself.

> (Ibid, 100)

Claudia told everyone, they reacted with "ooh and ah (she laughs) – that was unpleasant, wow, that was disgusting". After this, she experienced reactions at school as "positive – they were all glad and supported both of us". Claudia particularly enjoyed her exceptional status, including exemptions from the requirements for finishing the school year. At school, "everything was super". She was able to study, and only when she was sick with an inflamed pelvis did it get "so hectic" with school and the hospital.

Claudia's experience of pregnancy and birth

Although Claudia suffered from serious illnesses during her pregnancy – a severe stomach flu which caused her to lose quite a bit of weight, and two inflammations of the pelvis, whereupon she had to go to the hospital – she described her pregnancy as "just normal, I mean, whatever can be normal". Due to intense back pain, she received "physiotherapy in the form of radiation and so on", and also took part in pregnancy gymnastics. Claudia was under quite some pressure, since she had to accomplish all of this in addition to school.

Emotionally, she felt less well since Tom was absent for two weeks and her parents were advising her to get an abortion. Her friends from school were also on vacation, and she felt very alone. Only when her parents accepted her wish to have the child and also supported her and Tom did she feel better.

At school, everything went "super", as Claudia remarked. She was able to study. Claudia explained that she was "fully aware that my life was going to change" when she had a child.

> I could imagine how it would be . . . I could put myself in that role. I thought: you can't go out anymore at night. In principle, I didn't mind, because I had already had that. . . . I took that into account . . . super, you have a child and you'll be staying at home.
>
> (Ibid, 100)

With Claudia, the child took "first place", with everything else relegated to the background. She seemed to have a realistic attitude. Tom suffered more than she did from the abrupt termination of his youth through her pregnancy. He said:

> She seemed to be able to get used to the idea better than I. I knew what was facing me, but in some form it just broke over me. I know it was very abrupt, before, I was just still at home with my parents . . . then I was together with Claudia, just stayed at home and played computer games.
>
> (Ibid, 101)

Before, Tom had gone out a lot with his friends, "playing soccer or attending soccer matches, I know . . . somewhere, going out for a drink, playing billiards or something." He regretted that now this was hardly possible. Recently, the two of them had started going out with friends again; they had the babysitter problem under control using friends. But Claudia always had "guilt feelings when I go out, since I don't see the baby much during the week anyway" and would rather stay at home with her, "but I can't always do that". She also attempts to take Tom's wish to go out into consideration. Both regret that they currently lack time to spend together. Tom recalls better times:

> Sometimes we were always together. We went to school together and we spent the holidays together in the garden, two months. That was super. But

198 Lost by the wayside – overstepping limits

now it's stupid, now we seldom see each other. And when we do, then Claudia's at home studying.

(Ibid, 101ff)

At the time of the interview, Tom is doing his military service and hence usually away during the week.

The birth was more strenuous than expected. But when Moni had been born, both Claudia and Tom were very happy.

Claudia: "The feeling was super, having a baby lie on your stomach." Tom is also elated: "The little hands and all that. I was always so happy when the baby came back, since I hadn't really seen her yet."

Claudia enthusiastically told of her first encounter with her baby, almost melancholic when she remembered "how she was still so little, she was just so sweet. (She laughs.) She's still sweet, but – she's already so big, she can already sit and do lots of things." Two weeks after the birth, Claudia had already written a paper for school; after a month, she attended classes again. She was, in fact, able to finish the seventh class and at the time of the interview was studying for her final exams.

Support and help

Tom and Claudia received major support from Claudia's parents, who gave them the "basis for everything we have now". They bought them an apartment, also paying maintenance and all the other costs. They also helped them take care of baby Moni so that Claudia could go to school. Tom spoke enthusiastically of Claudia's mother, who

did everything. She cleaned the whole apartment, cooked and really did everything . . . took care of Moni when we had to study . . . they let us stay there until Claudia had finished the seventh class and I had finished my final exams – as if it were just along with the rest.

(Ibid, 104)

The fact that Tom ironically characterizes preparing for his final exams – normally the overarching goal of academic high school and a major challenge – as "just along with the rest" shows the degree of burden he had assumed. His main task was taking care of the little family. Claudia also calls going to school her "free pleasure time", since her child took first priority.

Claudia managed this thanks to her organizational talent, her ambition and the support of Tom, her mother and the school. She breast-fed Moni exclusively and managed to finish the seventh class.

I was always pumping out my milk in school, then I would put it in the school icebox, took the milk home, freezing it till the next day so that my mother could feed Moni with it the day after while I was at school.

(Ibid, 108)

In his phase of preparing for the final exams, Tom also partially took on caring for Moni. In September, before he began his military service, he "did everything the whole month". Moni is "very cooperative". Since Moni's third month, "she actually slept through the night. Normally, that's normal, actually (he laughs), she's such a good baby that it doesn't seem normal at all."

Interpretation

Together, Claudia and Tom have accomplished an unbelievable feat. They were both certain that they wanted to remain together, and they managed not only to convince both Claudia's and Tom's parents of that, but to live in excellent cooperation with them. At first, Claudia fought her parents' wish that she marry Tom, but then she agreed.

The first phase of pregnancy, being alone without Tom and with the pressure her parents placed on her to have the abortion, was manifested in Claudia's illnesses: at first she had a stomach flu and then two pelvic inflammations which took her to the hospital. We assume that the great inner tension, uncertainty and challenge was manifested not only psychically but also physically, as described in McDougall's book *Theater of the Body* (1991). All illnesses were in the vicinity of her belly/uterus. During her severe flu she often vomited and had diarrhea, so that her weight decreased to 40 kilos. Like a reversal of the child fertility fantasy that babies enter a mother's stomach when she eats, Claudia experienced her pregnancy as if someone – a bad fairy, a witch, an envious mother, a vengeful woman – was threatening the baby within her, threatening to rob her of it. In fact, Claudia's parents wanted to destroy the baby, advising her or putting pressure on her to get an abortion. In every pregnancy, childhood fertility theories become revived and represented in fantasies or dreams. With her sick abdomen, Claudia was perhaps expressing that she had pushed herself into maternity too early – as if she has laid claim to the maternal position she has not earned – and then had to eject everything or have a painful pelvic inflammation. These psychological factors can lower the body's defenses; the stress could have been so great that Claudia became truly sick. The inner conflict is manifested somatically. Psychological and somatic factors are always present – actively, interactively (Engel 1962).

Conversely, the baby growing within Claudia undoubtedly supplied her with additional energy. She aimed to demonstrate that she could finish the seventh class at school while nurturing a baby within her body. The enormous support she received from her mother also presumably represents a kind of reconciliation. Perhaps Tom and Claudia's decisiveness in remaining together and having the baby has impressed the parents. At any rate, Claudia's physical problems stopped when her mother began to completely support them – as if the future grandparents now allowed the young people their baby.

Tom and Claudia are concerned about how well-behaved their daughter Moni is; they think that "it's not normal, how good she is". We assume that even very young babies have feelings and can recognize from their parents' vocal nuances, emphases and behavior whether they are a burden to their parents (in Claudia's case, arguably a significant burden). One possible reaction on the baby's part would be to be very well-behaved, sleeping a lot and being "easy" to care for, in order to unburden the mother. Claudia recognizes that she is often at the brink of her capacities. She often has guilt feelings, since she sees Moni so seldom and has to give her up to the care of various other people.

Claudia and Tom idealize their relationship – no doubt is allowed. One might ask how realistically they see one another. At the same time, they seem to have developed a close and trusting relationship to one another through the difficulties they have battled together. Claudia is very glad that Tom was present at the birth and supported her.

Claudia's school, and particularly her strict supervisory teacher, recognized the urgency of the problems, and he supported Claudia whole-heartedly. He asked her to talk about her pregnancy in front of the class, and the class' positive reaction and full readiness to help showed that his idea bore fruit. Instead of unstable rumor, Claudia could openly discuss her pregnancy and then accept the help offered by her fellow students, including visits to the hospital, babysitting, etc. In fact, Claudia became a better student than she had been before her pregnancy.

Closing remarks

In the families of teenage mothers – not only in these case studies, but worldwide – there is practically no discussion of birth control methods, because it embarrasses not only the parents but also the children (Crockett et al. 2003). Factual sex education extends the adolescent's knowledge but is not relevant for actual contraception.

The life chances of these adolescent girls and boys are more limited and risky than for their peers. Most teenage pregnancies occur in economically disadvantaged families. The chance of finishing school is only half that of other adolescents; teenage mothers have fewer chances for higher education and obtaining a job than other adolescents from the same social background (Miller et al. 2003). Their chances of marrying are less, and the probability of divorce considerably greater (Moore and Brook-Gunn 2002).

In an 18-year study (1966–84) conducted by Furstenberg et al. (1987) in the US, however, the results were more promising. After 18 years, the life situations of teenage mothers were surprisingly various: only one-quarter of the mothers were on welfare. Another quarter had achieved higher education and had successful job experiences. A majority of the mothers had finished secondary school; one-third had an academic education and had married.

In the three case studies I have described, all three teenage mothers aimed to pass their final exams at secondary school and planned to begin university study as soon as their child entered kindergarten.

Massive controversies with the parents centered on keeping the baby or having an abortion. It seemed that parental support had fostered a new kind of relationship between adolescents and their parents.

An overriding wish for security and tenderness constitutes a central motive in teenage pregnancy. Instead of completely renouncing their own wishes to be a baby, the pregnant adolescents project them onto their actual baby. These wishes are half-conscious when pregnant teenagers profess to "playing" with the thoughts of a baby. A pregnant teenager's fear and worry of whether she can cope with a baby are projected onto the future grandparents. They are meant to worry and oppose having the new child; this enables the young parents to avoid their inner conflicts, which nevertheless become manifest in major mood swings, vulnerability and conspicuous weight gains or losses.

Early pregnancies can be seen as an expression of separation conflict with the adolescents' parents – experienced on the conscious level as adulthood, although in fact the young parents are delayed in becoming autonomous. They become not only financially more dependent on their parents, but also in caring for the baby – often living together with the new baby in the child's former bedroom. In these heated, conflict-laden phases, adults such as teachers or family friends are of great significance. In all three case studies, teachers undertook to inform the future parents about pregnancy and natural childbearing, relaxation techniques and addresses of pregnancy groups. They used teenage pregnancy as an occasion for educating the other students about these themes.

The baby is seen as an expression of an intimate partnership: children are often conceived when parents are very much in love, but also during crises of the relationship. The baby is then seen unconsciously as a link between the mother and her romantic partner.

When unclear ideas of the future prevail, a pregnancy can supply a feeling of "amazing meaning to life", as Sarah describes it. The baby then constitutes a substitute for affection and recognition that is otherwise lacking. Throughout the pregnancy, the mother can experience an enhanced feeling of life and the meaning of life.

A pregnancy during the inner upheaval of puberty places the adolescent under double pressure. In every pregnancy, the inner world becomes restructured (Diem-Wille 2004), with early unconscious conflicts with parents and various fantasies from early childhood updated and newly ordered in the context of the maternal and paternal body. When the pregnant mother is an adolescent, these inner structures are turbulent enough, but also undergo yet another restructuring. On a very deep emotional level, having a baby represents great potency. In this case, adolescents have become persons who pass on life and create something new. These are not fantasies anymore, but are manifest in the real baby – which can be either terrifying or fulfilling, or both.

6.3 Psychic breakdown in adolescence

In this section, we examine serious psychic problems arising in puberty. Under the rubric of psychic breakdown, I will discuss psychic disturbances such as depression, psychotic episodes, mutism (the refusal to speak) and Asperger symptoms

202   Lost by the wayside – overstepping limits

(retreat into a private world). These phenomena signify psychic crises that can appear either gradually or suddenly. Laufer speaks of a "disruption in development" (Laufer 1995a) – disturbances in child development become visible that previously went unnoticed. The challenge of psychic crisis in puberty constitutes the last chance for help before a lifelong distortion of character sets in (Ibid). When evaluating an adolescent undergoing psychic breakdown, the following three areas should be investigated:

A: development that is dominated by *defensive functioning* (italics original)
B: *deadlock* in development that precipitates an acute crisis in functioning (italics original)
C: *foreclosure* in development, where there is a premature end to the developmental process (italics original)

(Laufer 1995a, 179)

Regarding A: Is only one specific area affected by the crisis, or is the patient's ability to work and form relationships affected? If several areas are affected, the danger of a total breakdown is imminent if the patient's psychic defenses collapse in the face of increasing fear. To what extent does the adolescent see his body as only an object to attack or neglect? Or does his actual body still possess the capacity for libidinous or narcissistic satisfaction?

Regarding B: Deadlock is the point where the patient's defenses, which until now could contain his fears, can no longer do so. Further development is stymied, with no possibility of reverting to an earlier stage of development. For instance, when an 18-year-old views the end of his first sexual relationship as confirming his latent conviction that his sexual body is meant to be rejected, he can no longer withdraw to a pre-pubescent attitude where he could obtain support from his parents. In such a deadlock, there is the serious risk of an acute psychotic episode, i.e., a temporary break with reality – in a manic, depressive or suicidal form.

Regarding C: Foreclosure means a developmental process that was prematurely ended and leads to the adolescent's acquiring a distorted body image where sexual satisfaction is reduced to a limited form without enabling new experiences (i.e., perverse forms of sexuality or satisfaction through addictive experiences).

Before this period of inner transformation, swift physical and psychic development and reorganization, the patient's defensive structures were still equal to her inner impulses, fears and challenges. Now, due to new challenges, they collapse. An interview can determine whether the crisis lies within the range of normal adolescent development or tends in the direction of a borderline or psychotic disturbance. Kernberg (1984) asks: "Do all adolescents present some degree of identity diffusion and hence are their symptoms and behavior indistinguishable from later borderline personality organization?" (quoted in Flynn 2004, 215).

The difficulty in evaluating such a crisis is that each of the possible symptoms also occurs in milder form during the normal transformations of adolescence: (only) one depressive or psychotic episode is experienced by approximately 30% of all adolescents. For the adolescents– and their parents – such a crisis certainly seems threatening. In addition, during this phase serious symptoms can become visible in an incipient form, calling for precise observation. Thus, it is important for parents, teachers and other persons in an adolescent's environment to remain open to both possibilities: symptoms as a sign of a serious illness or as a passing phenomenon.

Flynn (2004, 215) proposes three levels for distinguishing whether symptoms are pathological or normal:

1   *A capacity for reality testing*: in both normal and pathological adolescent functioning, primitive defensive operations such as splitting, denial and projective tendencies come into use, and there can be the lack of an integrated sense of self and a differentiated concept of others. It is the presence or absence of reality testing in a strict sense that permits diagnostic differentiation, especially with adolescents with the more severe types of narcissistic personality who may come for assessment.
2   *A capacity for recognition of the 'other'*: this is a central capacity that can help to differentiate normal adolescent turmoil when coming up against a combination of omnipotent control, grandiosity and devaluation with violent rebelliousness against the parents in the adolescent.
3   *A capacity for experiencing guilt and concern*: this is important in working in particular with adolescents who are suicidal or engage in severely destructive self-harming behaviour.

(Flynn 2004, 215)

Several elements from these three levels are important in starting a psychotherapy.

In the chapters on the body ego, emotional development and identity, I have described developmental crises in the "normal" context that nevertheless elicit fundamental insecurity and threaten adolescents. Parents also become uneasy when their child's character changes from a cheerful, trusting son to a lugubrious, withdrawn adolescent, causing them to feel rejected and devalued.

In two case studies, I will now show how such crises manifest themselves. In the first case study, the adolescent Mark managed to conceal his deep paranoia, hallucinations and desperation behind his withdrawal and refusing to speak. Only through his total refusal to speak in analysis did his deep disturbance become evident and addressable, and only when his behavior at school and in the family normalized did his parents recognize how ill he had previously been. Whereas Mark was in analysis for four years, the second patient, Chrisse (who was referred from a psychiatric ward), was treated in the framework of a brief crisis intervention for several months.

Case study: Mark

Mark was 13 years old when he was referred to me from Child Guidance with the diagnosis that he had "major problems with himself and others". I saw his parents,

204 Lost by the wayside – overstepping limits

who spoke about Mark's problems at school: he was an outsider, teased by his colleagues for being "gay", and even his former friend had recently changed sides and was now attacking him. His father presented Mark as a specially gifted boy who was bored at school because it was no challenge. Both parents negated his problems. The mother's brother, who had been psychoanalyzed as an adult, urgently advised the mother not to wait but to quickly organize help for Mark. I invited Mark to two interviews in order that I could speak with his parents on a possible course of therapy.

I will describe the first interview with Mark in detail, because it shows how quickly he established a relationship with me without using words. Here are notes from our first meeting:

Mark is a nice-looking boy of 13 with brown hair, who looks much younger than his years. He has his schoolbag on his shoulders and carries a half-full bottle with juice in his left hand. He looks at me as if to ask where to go, so I show him the way to the consulting room. He goes in and again looks at me, unsure what to do, and glances at the lamp. I tell him he can sit wherever he wants. He puts his schoolbag and his bottle down and sits down in one of the two chairs, sitting there rather stiffly, not leaning back, putting his elbows on the arms. I tell him about the arrangement with his parents: that I would see him a few times to find out whether he would like to work with me and also whether I thought he could use some help to sort things out. He could do whatever we wanted (talk, play, draw).

He looks at me as I talk, nods and says, "Hmm". As soon as I stop he starts to scrutinize the room as if he were touching everything with a paintbrush.

After a few minutes, I say: "You might not find it easy to be in a new room with a strange person so you want to take in what the room looks like." When I talk he looks at me, nods and seems to agree. I always get a reaction from him. While he continues looking around his fingers move constantly on the arms of the chair.

This is the pattern of the entire session. He looks around, sometimes he looks out of the window and watches the clouds, sometimes his eyes are fixed and his face has a sad expression, as if something is stirred up inside and he is preoccupied with it. I observe him and make several interpretations, for example, when he looks out of the window I connect it with his ambivalence about coming here, because he wishes to come, but partly his wish is to be somewhere else, far away. Later I comment on the different perspectives we both have, looking at the room from different angles. As he rarely looks at me, I point out that it seems easier for him to understand and concentrate on things, whereas people seem to be more complex and difficult to understand. After, I try to direct his attention to the toys in the box; he looks at the toys in a slightly curious way but does not move.

I say: "You use your eyes to take in the surroundings and you study them carefully. You seem to have ideas about how things work here." As I wonder aloud whether he thought I would talk to his parents about his sessions, I make it clear that everything that happens here is private and will be kept confidential. He seems to relax a bit but not much. So I take up the theme some time later by addressing

Lost by the wayside – overstepping limits   205

his doubts about whether he can really trust me. He smiles a bit, says, "Hmm", but after that he slowly leans back and seems more relaxed.

When his eyes rest on the white drawing paper on the table, I tell him that it is like the openness of our relationship and that he seems to be wondering how it might develop. I get an intense look of agreement. My countertransference is that sometimes I would like to press him to talk by asking him questions and later, that I would like to hold him like a baby.

I ask him whether he wants me to share with him what I imagine about what he is thinking. He seems delighted and nods. I then describe the whole session, the way he came in and his way of sitting silently that gives me the impression that he wants to be understood without words, like a baby. The expression on his face becomes filled with pain. He reminds me of an American Indian who sits still in order to control pain. I ask him whether it's possible that he thinks that what goes on inside is less painful if he holds still and whether he might also be uncertain that he can share it with me, that he can trust me.

We sit in silence.

As it is close to the end of the session, I try to find out whether he would like to come again. (His mother had told me he would never do anything he does not like.) His face is completely neutral, as if he were thinking. So I wait for a few minutes. Then I suggest that his thinking could partly mean that he would like to extend the session and partly that he would like to leave it to me to decide. I continue, "We should come to a decision. Even if I suggest meeting again next week, nobody but *you* can say whether you would like to come." His face seems to express his wish to come but also his wish to find out whether I want to see him again, so I ask whether he wants me to make a suggestion, and he looks at me and nods. Then he agrees to come. We say goodbye and arrange to meet next week at the same time, if he wanted me to share my observations and hypotheses of what he was thinking. He seems glad at this and nods.

Reflections on the first session

It was important to show Mark I accepted his silence – a silence that caught me unawares, since his parents had not mentioned it or his refusal to speak (mutism). The relationship he offered me was that I take the initiative in his therapy: apparently, his silence was meant for me to pose him questions. He showed me how difficult it was for him to establish contact to me and to other persons. I parsed his body movements for their possible significance; through Esther Bick's technique of Infant Observation, I had learned to observe and empathize with the slightest expressions of a baby's body and face. I posed hypotheses as to what his movements could mean. When I first spoke of his fear of being with an unfamiliar person in a strange room, he looked directly in my eyes. Could his quick eye contact with me mean that he was surprised I understood him? When I compared his reactions to my voice with a baby's, he twitched painfully; it was presumably a mistake to compare a 13-year-old to a baby. His direct reaction of (physical) withdrawal and stiffness was meant to demonstrate his irritation with me, since I had rendered him so young. I had the feeling of touching an open wound when he reacted so strongly and turned away from me; indeed, I found it difficult to finish my sentence. With his passivity, he presumably induced (or seduced) his mother to treat him like a baby and serve as his personal helper, getting all manner of things done for him. Because of this, it was important that I refuse his passive offer. He showed that he had grave problems and urgently required analysis in order to develop.

At this point, I was skeptical whether I could truly depend on my own feelings and countertransferential reactions. At the end of the first session I emphasized that only he could decide whether he wished to continue with me. Helping him would mean encouraging him to attend therapy, but also to allow him to determine the further details. I was very careful in discussing the possibility of his coming again, although I knew that if he stayed away this would drive him back into his fortress. His hesitation could signify that he was absolutely convinced nobody wanted to be with him and nobody would ever understand him.

It was important not to pose questions, but instead to attempt to understand his behavior as communication. I found it very helpful to discuss Mark with Betty Joseph in London, and whether my hypotheses about what his behavior meant were plausible. Betty Joseph (1986a) described the analytic process as a "total situation" that can be understood in the here-and-now as transference and counter-transference. In Vienna, my colleagues were skeptical as to whether I could come to understand his inner conflicts and difficult relationship to his parents without resorting to drawings, speech and games.

Hypotheses regarding Mark's communication through movement

Here is an example of how I tried to find out whether Mark was confirming or correcting my assumptions and attempts to decipher his movements.

He came to one session a few minutes early, after arriving too late for the previous session. He sat down, leaned back, putting both arms on the armrests and sitting in a more relaxed manner than the day before. After a short pause, I remarked that he must be noticing what a difference it made to come back already the subsequent day without having a gap of several days between sessions. He listened attentively, then looking at me and turning away, gazed out the window.

Mark reacted to my interpretation with two different behaviors. He listened attentively, looked at me and seemed to agree – but as soon as he took in my words, he turned away and looked out the window. Could his direct eye contact with me mean that he was expressing how glad he was to be with me again? Or when he then looked away, that he felt ashamed? And did his looking away signify that he had inimical feelings towards me because I showed him just how glad he was? When I later suggested that he might have many thoughts regarding whether he might bring his outside experiences to me in therapy, he seemed to soften and observe the room with interest.

Mark found it difficult to adjust to a four-hour analysis. At first he thought he could only come twice a week. Later, when he accepted that his serious problems required more frequent analysis, he shook his head when I suggested Monday and Tuesday, saying "We have afternoon classes at school". I then offered him Saturday in addition to Wednesday, Thursday and Friday, which he accepted. He must have known that I was making an exception for him: this session would have a special meaning. He seldom missed it, although it was unclear to me whether he came on his own or his mother brought him on Saturdays.

Only with difficulty did he find his place in analysis – just as he had had a difficult start as a baby: he had cried often, was hard to pacify and had difficulty going to sleep. His mother said they had wanted to have Mark, the pregnancy and birth were "normal", but he was a "terrible baby". During his first three years, he would wake up several times at night. Only when his mother told him (at three years old) that she was sleeping in the next room was he capable of calming himself and sleeping through the night. I presumed that his parents had not perceived his fears, and his mother could not contain his projections or understand his needs. Bion describes this type of mother when he discusses a patient who

> had experienced a mother who dutifully responded to the infant's emotional display. The dutiful response had in it an element of impatience. . . . From the infant's point of view she should have taken into her, and thus experienced, the fear that the child was dying. It was this fear, that the child could not contain.
>
> (Bion 1959, 104)

Bion's patient had a mother who could not perceive his intense feelings and denied them. In the case of Mark's mother, it turned out that at the time of his birth, she had had a serious crisis to master – as she related to me in subsequent parent conferences. Her father had left the family, saying that he had waited 18 years until she had grown up. After this, she refused to speak with him, so that he only saw Mark when Mark was ten years old. Mark's mother seems to have been over-challenged not only by her rage and grief, but also by her own mother's stress. She was also taking care of her handicapped brother, so that she had almost no inner psychic space to deal with little Mark. Mark's attempt as a baby to establish contact to his mother must have been increasingly massive and overwhelming – to the point of tortured screaming – which would have elicited even more fear from the mother. All of the mother's accounts of her difficult situation at Mark's birth came out during one parent conference where she had come to end Mark's analysis, although he had exhibited astonishing changes at school. I assumed that the mother envied her son for receiving so much attention when

208 Lost by the wayside – overstepping limits

she felt herself to be even needier than him. For this reason, I decided to dedicate this hour to her. As she told her story, she wept, using exactly four handkerchiefs (Mark had four hours a week of analysis) in expressing her pain. After this session, she thanked me, taking up my advice to go into therapy herself, and decided that Mark should continue analysis.

My countertransferential reactions were various – his passivity was meant to draw me close to him, make me more subject to his control; sometimes I had the impression that he did not reach me, and then I felt bombarded by feelings of panic, desperation and contempt.

Mark's father attended the parent conferences only twice; he was a successful computer specialist and did not like to talk. Either he let his wife speak or he finished her sentences. They spoke in an eccentric way, alternating as in an operatic duet, both looking at me and putting me under pressure to grant both of them attention.

Mark shared a room with two younger sisters and wanted a room of his own in order to have his private sphere; he attempted to draw a line of demarcation through the room, but his sisters ignored it.

Mark's first year in analysis

Only in Mark's first year in analysis did it become apparent how seriously disturbed he was. He conveyed how desperately he needed help. His appearance could alter surprisingly when he felt possessed and threatened by figures from his inner world. He wanted to have control. He often seemed to be caught up in daydreams where he was superior to everyone else. When he had problems with walking and moved like a robot, he looked fearfully in the left corner of the therapy room, apparently wishing to be pulled in that direction. Usually, he entered the therapy room so quickly that I had difficulty following him. When he was depressed, he walked very slowly. I often thought he was having hallucinations. Analysis seemed to alter his routine, which was both pleasant and disturbing to him. From the first session, he found it difficult to leave at the end, as if he had to tear himself away. When I said the session was over, he often tried unsuccessfully to get up, as if he were glued to his chair. Only after I stood up was he also able to do so.

His preferred mode of controlling me was to not come to the session, or to arrive 20, 30, 45 minutes too late – while simultaneously conveying to me how crucial the sessions were for him. After a session he had missed, his appearance was dramatically altered: he seemed absent and full of repressed aggression. Sometimes he moved lethargically, like a lifeless machine. He was always dressed casually but well, and well-groomed – normally an important measure of psychic health. Here is an excerpt from one session:

During the last week before Christmas, he suddenly said in an empty voice: "Today I have to leave at 2:50!" When I asked why, he answered with silence. I was confused and surprised, since he almost never spoke. Before I could comprehend the enormous significance of hearing a coherent sentence from Mark, I realized I would not let him off ten minutes early: if he wanted to, he should undertake this himself. Later I interpreted that he wanted to find out whether I would be glad like a teacher or student that the hour had been shortened; he wanted to see if I wanted to get rid of him early. This gave me goosebumps. When it was in fact 2:50, he looked at my clock and then at me. There was high tension in the air as we both remained seated. I returned his gaze without saying anything, and then he looked away. I said that he wanted to find out whether I truly wanted to have him here. Mark seemed to be deeply moved. He remained until the hour was finished and only got up after I had.

Mark showed me that he had ambivalent feelings: he wished to be understood and also not understood. On the one hand, he seemed to triumph through his ability to demonstrate his emotional distance. On the other hand, he showed me that he was deeply moved by my desire to keep him with me the entire hour and at my expressing his feelings and doubts. He kept attempting to force me to reject him. He was fearful and convinced that I would soon make him leave.

His failure to attend some sessions was frustrating and irritating for me. I often thought he would never come again, and that would be the end of his analysis. I asked myself why he was not coming. Did he feel claustrophobic and afraid he could not leave? I interpreted his absence in various ways to him, telling him that we both knew he could come but that he preferred to hit me over the head with his absence, punishing me in order to feel strong and powerful. Particularly before the first Christmas holidays, his attendance was inconsistent. One way to contact him was writing him a letter noting that he had failed to appear for his two last sessions and that I expected him at the next session. These letters had an effect – he came to the next session. In the course of four years, I wrote several such letters, and he managed things so that his parents never saw them.

Another difficult point was how to handle Mark's invasive mother while keeping his analytic space free for him, and also obtain her cooperation in bringing him to the sessions. She felt closely bound to Mark. When she came alone to the second parent conference and I described Mark as a sensitive child who had difficulties in expressing his feelings, she said: "Like me". When I continued that Mark was very intelligent but vulnerable, she said, "He's like me!" It was a refrain she repeated several times. It was difficult to deal with her; every transformation in Mark – including positive changes – seemed to threaten her. She was able to take up my suggestion to start therapy herself.

Before Easter, she came and reported that Mark's work at school had improved enormously, particularly his verbal expression. Earlier, when he had to write an essay, he would write only a few lines, but now he wrote two pages or more. He now had two good friends who also came to his house. He was very interested in computers and very good at them. But she could not link his improvement to our analysis.

In the first year, the extent of his disturbed concrete thinking became evident. When I said: "You are afraid I will throw you out", he seemed to hear "I will throw you out" as a concrete threat and fell into a panic. He often seemed to look into the left corner of the room in a particular way, as if he saw something concrete – a hallucination – and could not tear his eyes away. When he was so afraid, he began to rock with his whole body like a baby in a cradle in order to calm himself down.

He often only identified himself by name reluctantly on the intercom, as if he wished to come in quickly without any obstacles. Speaking seemed to cause him fear, as if he would have to recognize that we were two different persons and his fantasy world would collapse. His favorite books, which he read for hours at home, were by Stephen King; they completely enthralled him, as his mother remarked. Accordingly, I also read some books by Stephen King, in order to enter into Mark's magical thinking. His mutism in our friendly atmosphere could mean he was convinced that he and I were one person, bound together without words. At the end of the session, separation then constituted a shock. In other sessions, his silence could be a cruel form of torturing me, mistreating and controlling the situation. He triumphed by determining whether he attended our sessions, what he chose to show or hide of himself. His triumph over me was manifested in an arrogant mode of expression, which Bion sees as an expression of the death wish, when possible links to an analyst are attacked (Bion 1957b, 87). Analytic interpretation investigates the patient's inner world and is experienced by a seriously disturbed patient as a "penetrating component of a disaster", that must be massively defended against.

The first year moved from crisis to crisis, always threatened by Mark's breaking off therapy. After some months, his mother could admit how disturbed he was and how urgently he required help. She became more cooperative and tried to make him attend our sessions. She brought him more often to the session or telephoned with him to remind him to come. I asked myself how long I was willing to bear this painful and frustrating situation. Not attending therapy sessions is a common form of communication by adolescents to demonstrate their independence and resistance. Waiting for Mark elicited various feelings in me: I sometimes had the impulse to deny my interpretation of his absence and see it as a sign of his independence; sometimes I was worried I would lose him. Sometimes he was so confused that he rang my bell but did not come up. I discussed his case with Betty Joseph in London, and she encouraged me to tolerate his tardiness or absences as long as possible. I had announced I would tell his mother if he did not show up for more than two sessions in a row, which never became necessary. His mother then began to call me up to ask whether he had attended the session, to which I answered truthfully. Did Mark worry about a kind of claustrophobia – of getting stuck in therapy and not being able to end it? That could be the reason why he often showed up for a mere five minutes. Or did he wish to experience how relieved I was when he finally showed up? Or did he want to demonstrate he didn't care about the analysis, thus treating me so contemptuously that I experienced it as cruelty? Separation at the end of the session was always painful and difficult for him, and could enormously irritate him, which presumably increased his fear of coming back the next time.

In spite of this, there were changes in his outer world, and his parents supported the analysis. And yet he remained mute at our sessions – most information I obtained from his mother, whom I met twice every semester. When he once did not show up for three sessions, I confronted him with the possibility of ending the analysis. He groaned at the word "end". I described my function as custodian of the tiny portion in him that wanted to come to analysis and believed that life could also be friendly. As a reaction, I obtained a small, friendly smile. When I said how tiny this "portion" was, his smile grew, and I continued talking of this tiny, optimistic portion in him that was being cruelly shoved about, mocked and intimidated. But I also said that I did not know whether I could continue the analysis, and that this might be our last session if he continued his absences.

The first sentence his mother said to me in conversation the next day was: "I have a new child! Since yesterday, I have a new child! I am totally surprised!" Mark was now talking to her. He even offered to go buy milk. Usually he said "Mhm" when he was asked to do this, went back to his room and wouldn't go out. After this conversation, it was clear that Mark would come another year to analysis, since he had improved his performance at school substantially. Did he wish to show that analysis was helping him? For his parents, at least, it was an important argument for his continuing.

The following two years

After the first six-week summer pause, Mark neither showed up for therapy nor answered my letters. Then, he called me up, informing me that he did not wish to come anymore. When his mother called me up in an alarmed state, I said that we must accept his decision; I was sad, but also relieved. After four weeks, his mother called me up again, asking me if I would take Mark back. His performance at school had dramatically worsened, he hadn't done any homework at all and he did not participate in activities. I answered that I could take him back, but expected him to call me up to make an appointment. Mark called me reluctantly the same day, saying "I was supposed to call you." In scheduling his sessions, he would only accept the same times he had had before, taking refuge in a fib: he said he had afternoon school on Monday and Tuesday in order to get "his" Saturday session back.

In the following two years it became clear that he was even more ill than I had thought at the beginning; he had hallucinations, sometimes launched attacks on his relationship to me and others, and withdrew to an arrogant attitude where he could live out his fantasies of omnipotence. The first session he came back to me, he was completely withdrawn; the atmosphere was extremely chilly and tense. During the session, he relaxed somewhat, and his fearful facial expression became more gentle. He looked at me as if I were his life preserver. He seemed as if he could have a psychotic breakdown. I tried to understand how ill he was, in order to not be angry with him. Twice, he rang the buzzer without being able to come up. Did he enter the room so fearfully because the day before he had projected

212 Lost by the wayside – overstepping limits

such primitive fears? I tried to give him credit for coming in spite of these great problems.

Once again, I discussed these sessions with Betty Joseph in order to understand this patient, who was so difficult to reach (Joseph 1975). In difficult cases, it is very important to bear insecurity and doubt together and reflect on them together. There was also occasion to hope that he could further benefit from his analysis. As soon as he came back to analysis, he was able to actively participate in learning at school, to do his homework and achieve success. Mark also began to play with his two sisters. Once when the parents came home, they found Mark and his sisters playing a board game together for several hours. In school, he was no longer mocked as an outsider, but had two good friends. In the following year, he applied by himself successfully to a technical university and was accepted. He could even meet with a former friend from his old school, who earlier had turned against him. When the family moved to a bigger house, he got a room of his own.

A form of hallucination

I wish to describe why I made the assumption that Mark's looking into the corner of the room was a sign of hallucination. His gaze had a remarkable intensity, as if something in this corner were drawing him to it, enabling him to enter a secret world.

In the session, he was silent as always, but he showed me how he was drawn into his secret world. The therapy session stood for reality, which he was seeking to avoid.

Mark arrived 15 minutes too late, with a suntanned face; he sat down with his arms crossed, the soles of his shoes almost touching each other (about three-quarter inch apart).

A: (after a few minutes of silence, which I granted him in order to arrive emotionally) You're here again!

M: (looking very irritated, he raises his eyebrows and looks in the corner)

A: By not coming four times, you are showing me how irritated you are.

M: (seems to be more deeply drawn to the corner)

A: When I speak of how irritated you are with me, you look in this corner: you think you see something there that is eating up your session.

M: (becomes restless)

A: You feel attacked by me and run away from me as if I were a dangerous person.

M: (becomes calmer and sinks his gaze to the carpet at his feet)

A: And you want to know whether I see your panic and then you become calmer.

M: (relaxes; his eyelids close slowly; he opens them several times with effort)

A: With your feet, you are expressing your wish to be very close to me, but you keep a little distance between the soles, between us, in order to remain a separate person.

M: (pause, then he closes his eyes and falls asleep)

Lost by the wayside – overstepping limits 213

A: (after five minutes) You are withdrawing into sleep, because you don't want to know anything about the approaching summer pause.

M: (fast asleep)

A: (after several minutes) When you fall fast asleep, you can perhaps express your wish or fantasy to be inside me and make me watch over you.

M: (sleeps calmly)

A: (three minutes before end of the session) Now you are showing me your other side, that you want to stay here and not go away, and I have to be the cruel one when I tell you the session is over in two minutes.

M: (does not react, but instead sleeps so soundly that it appears nothing could awake him)

A: (stand up and raise my voice) Mark, the session is over!

M: (no reaction)

A: (take a pillow and touch his arm twice) Mark.

M: (opens his eyes and looks to see whether I have touched him, then notices that it was the pillow; he looks at the pillow, which I have put on the table, looks at me long and deeply, stands up, shakes my hand and leaves the room)

I believe this "anxiety corner" signifies a secret world to which Mark withdraws in order to cut himself off from reality – like a refuge, where something draws him in. His behavior reminds me of Bion's article "On Hallucination", where Bion writes that the patient uses "the hallucinatory activity as an attempt to deal with the dangerous parts of the personality" (Bion 1957c, 71). When I spoke of Mark's irritation, he split his feelings and withdrew into sleep, like a baby who flees into sleep from an unbearable situation. Although it was unclear what he saw in that corner, he apparently could not take his eyes from it. Perhaps he had projected the dangerous parts of his personality onto the analyst, who then became a dangerous object. I attempted to obtain a clearer reaction by later saying I thought he saw something in that corner, but he could not tell me what it was – a shadow, a figure, a movement. Towards the end of Mark's analysis, his mother told me that he sometimes felt heat waves or cold waves. Later, when I was talking about my vacation, he withdrew back into sleep, because he did not wish to think about the attendant separation.

Sometimes when he had arrived, he stormed into the therapy room and looked into the fear-corner as if somebody were waiting for him there, and then threw me a short, controlling glance, although he seemed absent. I interpreted that he thought these things were real and could truly pull him closer and closer; that he went into another world with the thought that he is powerful and has the entire world under control. He then relaxed, released his crossed arms and put one hand on the other in a protective gesture. I understood that as a reaction to my interpretation, telling him I thought there was another part of his personality that was quietly powerful and enabled him to come to therapy in order to conquer all his inner obstacles. After a pause, I said that he had felt himself understood and safe

214 Lost by the wayside – overstepping limits

for a moment and had put one hand on the other as protection, feeling himself touched and protected.

Although he reacted physically to my words, in this session he remained silent. He seemed determined not to give up. He said to his mother: "Will she never understand that I will never speak?" Has he instigated a type of relationship with his analyst that will make her suffer because that is the only type of relationship he knows? Is this a trusted, gratifying form of relationship for him? When he began to attend sessions more regularly, his mother said he was doing so in order to not disappoint her and also because she spoke well of me. How had she spoken earlier of me? Negatively? It seemed a lot had been accomplished. Mark's teachers were happy with his excellent successes at school, although they thought he could accomplish still more. His physical appearance had changed: he had grown and looked now like a 15-year-old, tall with broad shoulders. The fact that he had grown so fast could have increased his fear of losing control over his violence and anger. His sexual fears and their effects seemed to be bound to his paranoid fears of analysis.

The invisible Oedipal conflict

Mark's pattern of behavior pulled me through his silence into a powerful and extreme closeness. It seemed to me his wish was to make me so curious and attentive that we would no longer be two separate people. He wanted to control me and mistreated me because he trusted only such relationships. There was a conflict between his needy and his proud part, who did wish to know how important I was for him – something he found humiliating – and his needy part, for whom the analysis was of vital importance. When he felt he had control, he looked satisfied with himself. When I understood him, he was afraid that I could penetrate into his thoughts; then, he rubbed his eyes as if to wipe away my words. He would not tell me his sexual fantasies – in order to rob me of my success and satisfaction at my analytic activity, I felt.

Edna O'Shaughnessy's essay (1989), "The Invisible Oedipus Conflict", helped me to understand Mark's behavior as a manifestation of an early, reversed Oedipal conflict. Mark could have felt himself excluded from the Oedipal parental pair, as her patient did. She writes:

> (The Kleinian) approach, when the Oedipus complex is what I am calling "invisible", is that this is so, not because it is unimportant, but because it is so important and felt by the patient (from whatever causes) to be so unnegotiable that he employs psychic means to make and keep it invisible.
>
> (O'Shaughnessy 1989, 129)

As I saw it, Mark separated the link between his inner world and his analysis, and he wished to make me accept this separation along with his omnipotent fantasy that he was the big adult and I was the child waiting helplessly for him. When I interpreted that he wanted me to feel like a helpless child, he seemed glad and

Lost by the wayside – overstepping limits **215**

gave a cruel smile. When he rushed into the therapy room – and, by implication, into the analytic-maternal body – and remained there for an hour, he could sustain his fantasy that there was no change and no separation.

We can only interpret the particular way Oedipal conflict is expressed when an analyst feels under pressure from the patient to behave a certain way; patients' primitive inner objects come from the time before they could speak. I would like to demonstrate how I interpreted his wish to be inside me:

After two sessions he attended punctually – a rare occurrence – he came into the room as usual, without looking at me. He looked around and sat down, putting his jacket over his arm and thus hiding his arm under it.

A: When you are here, you don't think it necessary to speak, as if you feel safe in your jacket, in the room.

M: (moves one hand in his pants pocket)

A: You are showing me that you protect the space between the sessions.

M: (looks at me, pauses, whereupon I hear something rustling)

A: (seeing a piece of paper in his pocket) You would like to take something out of your pocket, but as soon as you try to, something holds you back, as if there would be a risk that the world collapses. You feel stuck in me.

M: (looks alarmed, then looks at the couch)

A: You are afraid of not being able to move when you get stuck. Maybe you would like to lie on the couch, but you're afraid not to be able to leave then.

M: (looks quickly out the window and then slowly takes a piece of paper out of this pocket, inch by inch so that it didn't rustle; at the end of the session he gave it to me)

Before, when he rang my bell, he assumed he could come directly into the therapy room and was irritated when I made him say his name over the intercom – as if I had made a barrier between him and me. What significance did the paper have? Something was hindering him from taking it out. His silence had the quality of a child's, who did not wish to speak because that would have demonstrated that it was separated from its parents. When he felt himself in me via the chair, the jacket and the room, he did not connect to me as a whole object (a person with good and bad qualities), but rather as a fetus in my belly. His mother told me that he was never in competition with his siblings, his father or the other students.

Since Mark's mother could not recollect anything unusual during his weaning – which represents an important inner pattern and model for separation – I was reduced to speculation. What was the link between his repressed aggression and the meaning of his difficulties at separation. His escape was to withdraw to his fantasy of being inside me. When he became aware of this desire, he became fearful, and I became for him a version of the unified Oedipal couple that had turned against him. Klein writes: "Sometimes the analyst appears simultaneously to represent both parents – in that case often in a hostile alliance against the patient, whereby the negative transference acquires great intensity" (Klein 1952, 54).

216 Lost by the wayside – overstepping limits

The beginning of the Oedipal conflict was so intolerable for Mark, when his mother suffered under the sudden departure of her father, that he presumably excluded his own and his parents' sexuality. Mark's experience of being excluded and his frustration must have been increased when his mother became pregnant with his sister, who took the space within his mother that he wanted to occupy. In addition to this, his sister was an attractive, easy baby who slept and ate well.

Presumably, Mark did not take in an image of the loving parental pair, one who thought about him, into his inner world – that is why he found it intolerable that his analyst thought about him. Instead, the analyst became a dangerous unified Oedipal pair, and he felt excluded. These images originated in an earlier phase of Mark where he could not speak. If the parents cannot be aware of their child's instinctive impulses and his projective identifications and are not firm within themselves, they cannot contain them. In Mark's case, his mother seemed to have been filled with hatred and resentment of her father's departure and the collapse of her nuclear family, and instead of being able to contain Mark's projective identifications, she rather projected her unresolved problems with her father into him. Selma Fraiberg (1980) calls this phenomenon of projected unresolved conflicts with the mother's parents onto the baby, thus distorting the new baby's perceptions, "ghosts in the nursery".

Feldman demonstrated that the image of an inner, creative pair in the child can only develop when the earliest relationship between mother and baby is adequately stable. Since Mark wishes to penetrate into me in order to be completely one with me, he does not speak. In this way, he puts pressure on me to be completely attentive, supporting his fantasy that it is not necessary to speak. In this way, the analyst embarks on a collusion – the understanding that she forms an intimate couple with the patient that excludes everyone else:

> This seems to be directly connected with the development of the patient's capacity to allow thoughts and ideas to interact in a kind of healthy intercourse. On the other hand, the phantasy that any connection forms a bizarre or predominately destructive couple seems to result in a damaged, perverse or severely inhibited form of thinking.
>
> (Feldman 1998, 106)

Negotiating the end of analysis

The end of Mark's analysis was as difficult as its beginning. Mark sent contradictory signals. In the outer world, he was successful: he passed the entrance exams to an excellent technical university. He had a friend with whom he went to discos, although his mother worried that this was too dangerous for a 16-year-old and that he could be lured into drug abuse. Mark managed a part-time job at a computer store, earning enough to buy himself a computer. His job consisted in explaining new computer systems to customers, and his supervisor was very satisfied with him. When his mother wanted him to give up the job, he made it clear to her that he wished to keep it: she had her work and he wanted his. Mark was now better able to fend for himself and had more self-confidence.

But in therapy, there was no development: he was trapped by a cruel part of himself that often did not allow him to attend a session or cooperate. Although I often seemed to constitute a crutch for him, something hindered him from using his analysis in order to understand or change something. Although his fear had diminished, it was clear that we could not continue in this way. I had to seize the initiative, try to help him find out what he wanted. It was important not to answer his expectations that I become irritated with him and dismiss him, but rather that he take the responsibility for leaving. It was also important to make him understand that he had reached a limit, and I had to allow him to become active. In the autumn of our final year, I began to address the subject of ending therapy.

In one session, when he had arrived five minutes late after skipping the previous three sessions altogether, I let two minutes go by and then confronted him with how I saw him threatening his analysis from various angles: he had not come the previous week, he kept the bill to himself for a protracted period, and he brought the insurance form too late. In this way, I continued, he was making me irritated and frustrated. He groaned, but quickly regained composure and adopted a stiff countenance. When he felt my words to be an attack on him, he became fearful. It was impossible not to respond to his provocative behavior. He elicited a reaction from me that corresponded to a massive projective identification. He compelled the external object (analyst) to behave like his inner object and thus created enormous pressure on the analyst (see Feldman 1999, 2000). Since he expected me to berate or attack him, I thought it important to grant him time with me before I said something, even when only five minutes of time remained. I wanted to allow him time to arrive emotionally. I also needed time to gain clarity regarding the feelings he elicited in me.

Sometimes he treated me as if I were a machine without feelings. Only when I described what he was doing with me could he notice this behavior. When he recognized that he had hurt me, he seemed to understand that I was a person, separate from him. His capacity for thought was stimulated by my reflections on his feelings; this had enabled him to develop from the childlike cognitive level to a differentiated level of thinking, as demonstrated in his essays for school. But he would not agree with me that he enjoyed analysis and that it vexed him that somebody (I) had become so important to him.

I had various ideas as to what this behavior might conceal. Was he unable to appreciate our sessions? Was he envious of the way I was able to help him? Or did he think if he spoke it would be humiliating, since he would then name his problems? Inevitably, he elicited more and more irritation and frustration in me by compelling me to wait for him.

When I told him I would have to take the initiative on thinking about ending the therapy and that it depended on him whether he could use the sessions profitably – in order to start speaking – he was shocked. He attempted to control me by calling me up and postponing the session because he had school earlier the next day. When I told him I didn't have any time, he never showed up at all. In a later session, when I said I could help him to find out whether he wanted to end analysis, he suddenly fell asleep (in order to flee my question, I thought). Before Christmas, he missed many sessions. I learned how significant the influence of my words had been when his mother told me: "For the last six weeks, Mark is a new child. He talks, shows good humor and offers to help at home. He is truly cooperative. He is really not any more our old Mark." She reported further that everything was going well at school. His main teacher had congratulated them on their son, something they had heard for the first time during his schooling.

Even after four years of work with Mark, I still hoped that he could change and would speak with me in the last few weeks. But in this I was disappointed. When he did not change his behavior, did not show up or showed up late, I suggested we make an appointment for the end of his analysis. He seemed sad, but also relieved. We agreed on the end of February. Mark's mother called me up, and I was surprised when I confirmed this appointment. She asked me if he had changed his behavior in analysis as much as he had at home. He was now eager to communicate, outgoing, spoke a lot – even small talk – as if he wished to make up for everything he had missed. He had even suggested going to the movies with his father. I answered her that Mark brought his problems to the sessions.

Mark was able to come to his last two sessions; he looked grown-up and stable, but was pensive and sad. After a period of silence together, I said that he found it important to show me without words that he appreciated being here and having a space and also that he had negative feelings about ending the analysis. Perhaps it was important for him to stick to his decision not to speak in analysis, and he wanted me to accept that. I understood that he wished to traverse one portion of his path together with me but also leave things as they stood now. As we shook hands in parting, he said "Auf Wiedersehen" and looked grateful.

Closing remarks

Mark left me with uncertainty as to his motives. It was clear that he had significantly improved in many dimensions. I heard from his mother's therapist that he had become very independent and had excellent successes in school. He had summer jobs in England and Denmark, had many interests and social contacts. But in the core of his personality he had a problem that he could not change, and he could not change his ill treatment of me. Although he could renovate his behavior toward his parents, siblings and teachers, he remained silent in therapy. It was clear that he heard my interpretations and made use of them. He had interesting questions at school, worked with others and was curious. He improved his verbal expression and was able to explain things well to customers at his job.

I remained alone with my various assumptions as to his behavior. His improvement took place only in the outer world. In analysis, he kept strictly to his mutism and seemed to me to be close to hallucination. John Steiner described the patient's fear of exposing herself when leaving her place of psychic retreat: "Emerging is felt to result in a loss of this protection and involves contact with anxieties associated with being exposed and unprotected" (Steiner 2002, 1). In Mark's case, I assumed that he also believed he could control anyone with his power games, just as his favorite author Stephen King describes. Pathology is sometimes idealized and reinterpreted as a magical power.

Precisely observing what Mark showed from moment to moment and projected onto me constituted an important approach towards developing hypotheses on his inner world.

Parental difficulties in understanding the psychic problems of their child

It was remarkable how long Mark's parents had not recognized his desperation and his loneliness, covered by arrogance and pseudo-independence. His father thought he was too intelligent and was bored at school, his mother thought he was an "intellectual", only interested in books and not in people. Only his teachers and his uncle helped to convince the mother of Mark's urgent need for therapy. With seriously disturbed children, it is often surprising how impenetrable (if unacknowledged) the parents' unwillingness is to see their child's problems.

In Magagna's book *The Silent Child* (2012), physically healthy children choose various life-threatening forms of retreat, usually surprising their parents. Some stop talking, while others hardly eat or move. In extreme cases, they must be treated in a hospital and force-fed, since they do not wish to live. This massive self-destructive behavior corresponds to a massive denial on the part of the parents of the problems between them and their children. "Milo was a normal baby" begins the shocking article Milo's mother wrote (Magagna 2012, 13ff). Although the parents had therapy for more than a year in order to change their attitude and behavior with Milo, they speak as if his sickness were merely somatic, the effects of the flu. There is almost no insight, no reflection or understanding, although they describe how their behavior with Milo changed radically. Milo's retreat began with strong stomachaches that could not be treated by medicine; speaking caused him physical pain. He wished neither to speak nor to walk (Magagna 2012, 13). He shielded his face with his hands. All examinations of his brain and body were negative; the doctors said he had a psychological problem. He was fed through a tube and remained in the hospital for more than a year. His mother viewed the doctors, friends and everyone else as difficult. Milo wanted to have one of his parents with him during his hospital stay. With his illness, he forced his parents in a dramatic fashion to finally, truly notice him. With the help of a therapist, they managed to make contact to Milo and talk about their feelings. They could in no way recognize Milo's jealousy towards his siblings. The mother asked herself:

220 Lost by the wayside – overstepping limits

"I still find myself wondering what on earth went wrong. Did something go wrong? Will we ever know?" (Magagna 2012, 28). The mother writes at the end of the article that Milo has now finished university. One can imagine how difficult it is – both for the child and the therapist – to gain emotional access to the parents through such a concrete wall of defenses in order to understand their sick, desperate but also very powerful child.

With psychotic episodes, it is impossible for parents to overlook their child's wholly disturbed behavior. Here is another case study.

Case study of an adolescent psychotic episode: Chrissie

The symptoms of a psychotic breakdown, such as hearing voices, hallucinations, withdrawal into a private world and refusal to participate in the outer world, cannot be overlooked. For parents, these symptoms are a shock, although parents report in the introductory session that their daughter was "always different".

Since the adolescent cannot distinguish clear borders between reality and fantasy, her fears and the persecuting quality of fantasy can become so threatening that death constitutes the only escape (see Bion 1957a). It is therefore very important to define clear areas of responsibility to be assumed by various institutions for these adolescents. These include juvenile psychiatry clinics, parents, school and the analyst. In the crisis situation embodied by the adolescent's testing of reality –her retreat into a fantasy world – the goal of analysis is to construct a bridge between madness and normal thought.

Referral

Chrisse's mother got my telephone number from a youth psychiatric ward, called me up and informed me that her 15-year-old daughter had stopped attending school, had taken to her bed and had thoughts of suicide. Chrisse herself then called me up and we arranged an appointment.

Our first session

Chrisse arrived with her mother, whom I then asked to pick her up in 50 minutes. Chrisse told me her medical history in a very distanced fashion. She wanted to make a birthday party, but her best friend, who wanted to take her own life, wanted to make a "farewell dinner". She then told of the argument with her friend and her retreat into her room, where she withdrew into fantasy while listening to loud music. She had always been an outsider, had no friends in elementary school, was always alone, and considered herself ugly and unloved.

Then Chrisse became much more animated and began to report on her fantasy world. Using a pendulum, she could induce a trance state in herself. In her world, there was a snow maiden that was occupied by a bad spirit. She could see this

Lost by the wayside – overstepping limits   221

spirit: he sank his head onto her shoulders, hurting her arms. She was persecuted by a black man. She sprang from the balcony into a propeller that propelled her far away. In the pond, she found a skeleton without arms and found out that this girl also had jumped down and that the propeller had severed her arms.

I asked her whether she was telling the story or was drawn into it.

Chrisse: Both, I can see the story from a bird's perspective and can see the figures in it from behind. Sometimes I have to laugh, too, when the maiden looks at herself in the mirror and thinks she's so beautiful. There is also a high--ranking warrior who is head over heels in love with her. But at some point I lose interest, then I only want to sleep and never wake up again.

I tried to discuss with her whether we could work together, whether she wanted to come to me and stay alive.

Discussion

Every detail in Chrisse's account points to a fragmentation of her thought: the snow maiden is occupied by a spirit, the head sinks into the shoulders and the arms are severed from the body, she jumps into a propeller that is turning quickly.

She displaces her suicidal thoughts onto her best friend, who wishes to give a farewell dinner doubling as Chrisse's birthday party. Intermittently, she describes her loneliness and desperation. As I explained earlier, in this case it should not be the analyst's main task to reveal her fragmented fantasy world or establish links between the fragments, but instead to actively support Chrisse's reconnection to reality. Does she recognize whether she wishes to come to me due to her grave illness? Can she recognize that she needs help?

Second preliminary session

In the meantime, Chrisse had been tested by a psychologist in the psychiatric ward and taken part in a family therapy session. Chrisse's mother accompanied her to my office; Chrisse was holding the letter with her diagnosis in her hands. In the waiting room, I discussed organizational matters with the mother, who informed me that her daughter would presumably be admitted for in-patient treatment at the clinic.

From my notes:

> Chrisse sat down in the consulting room. It was clear to me that I should not treat her as a mere object of her diagnosis, but should let her be the active one. Reading the diagnosis with difficulty, she passed it over to me. I would not take it from her, instead saying that I was interested in what the diagnosis meant to her.

Chrisse then began to tell of her first session of family therapy, where her mother's (previously untold) story had emerged: the mother's brother had committed suicide at the age of 15, and her mother's father was an alcoholic. As a young teenager, the mother had had a relationship and a baby she gave up for adoption and never saw again. Although this saddened her, according to Chrisse her mother had no feeling for the baby she gave away. Chrisse remarked that she could never go to school again; when the doctor had posed this as a possibility, "I fell down an inner abyss".

Death exerted an enormous attraction on her, just as in certain Japanese cartoons. In order to fantasize, she used a pendulum, in order to better enter her fantasy. She was afraid that people might now steal her ability to dream. In conclusion, we read her diagnosis together, and she inquired as to the meaning of all the terms she did not understand. In the "tree test", she drew a tree without roots. She added that she had not only seen a sunset and grey clouds (which she had also drawn), but "internally" a big, dangerous storm that could break out at any time.

Towards the end of the session, she said she would like to come again, remarking: "Now, the picture of the tree is changing: the tree is burning, but the fire has not yet spread to the thicker trunks".

Analyst: You are saying to me that you need help quickly, because your tree has already caught fire. I am not here next week, but I can see you Thursday and Friday the following week.

Chrisse: Now lightning has struck the tree.

A: Now you are warning me that it is dangerous to work with you when your tree, your thoughts, are already burning.

Chrisse: I would like to come if nothing comes up – not like going to school.

Since the session was over, Chrisse's mother rang the bell and came to pick her up. When the mother entered, I began to speak, then thought better of it and asked Chrisse to inform her mother about our arrangement. Chrisse moved very close to her mother and told her quietly of the two appointments we had made. I assigned her a session at 11:00 am Thursday and 10:00 am Friday. Chrisse saw that her mother had written down 11:00 for Friday, and corrected her. Now, the mother said she was going to bring Chrisse to work. When she asked me how she should behave with Chrisse, I referred her to the doctor at the hospital.

Discussion

Chrisse seemed to wish that I would accompany her into her private computer world and take interest in her fantasy figures. This was her psychic retreat (Steiner 1987), affording her a modicum of security, but she also feared it would be taken from her. I showed her that I tolerated this retreat. The Japanese "Mangas" are often chosen by schizophrenics to express their fragmented world.

Lost by the wayside – overstepping limits   223

In family therapy, Chrisse had learned about strictly kept family secrets and now told them to me, probably to share her sense of shock. The darkness in her fantasy world is connected to the "dark crime", her mother's giving away a baby. She attempts to master her threatening present and uncertain future through fantasy. She depicts a dark family situation with a mother who cannot empathize with her baby. I assumed that Chrisse's unconscious was communicating the great burden her mother had suffered under. What does a mother who gave away her first baby feel when she now held baby Chrisse in her arms, hungry for love and protection? Could she admit her guilt feelings at giving up her first baby? Could she mourn? We know that losses that are not "mourned" but instead suppressed take their place as "ghosts in the nursery" (Fraiberg 1980). It is as if this renounced child stands between Chrisse and her mother as a barrier. The mother's inability to adequately react to her daughter's needs, her lack of "reverie", seemed to me to be destructive, passive aggression. How can a baby recognize such complex links? Babies perceive other persons through their senses, including tactile qualities, the voice and skin contact. It is conceivable that Chrisse's mother was not able to pick her up with a confident, firm touch, which would convey security and a sense of the baby's own skin against the mother. Was Chrisse's mother able to speak baby talk with her, waiting for her to answer – or did thoughts of her first baby, the one she gave away, interfere? With psychoanalytic observation, we see quite clearly whether the mother and baby are in "harmony" (Stern 1985) or whether discordant tones arise as in an orchestra when one instrument plays a melody that does not fit, disturbing the harmony. If Chrisse's mother could not truly establish emotional contact to her as a baby, then this would have created a discordance that the baby then showed in her reactions, creating a "second skin" (Bick 1968) as substitute for being held by its mother or being held at all. Such a baby must attempt to hold itself and could escape into a pseudo-independence. How often did Chrisse attempt to establish eye contact with her mother and her mother was so deep in painful thoughts that she did not notice this? Could Chrisse experience the shine in her mother's eyes when she was glad of her baby's existence? All of these frustrations and disappointments can be stored in a baby, and if they are not compensated by enough loving and friendly experiences, can lead to a dangerous emotional storm or outbreak. (In a psychotic episode, the structure of consciousness collapses, so that it makes sense not to see the patient on two consecutive days, but at the beginning and end of a given week.) In later conversations with the parents, the mother told me that Chrisse was a "non-demanding baby", lay alone in bed for hours and amused herself. Only my interpretation that the mother might not have adequately comprehended Chrisse's need for attention made the mother reflect. She said that she had often hit her children, but then given up because it had been of no use. Chrisse was stubborn. The mother had the role of disciplinarian in the family.

Even in this acute crisis, the parents showed no comprehension of the degree of Chrisse's disturbance; the mother reacted with emotional flatness, as if she could not feel anything besides her own depression. Attempts to help the parents to see that their daughter might often feel herself to be a needy three-year-old in the body of a 15-year-old were not really heard.

It was important to clearly negotiate the institutional cooperation between the psychiatric hospital, Dr. E. and the parents (with Chrisse's participation) – with the proper emphasis on Chrisse's independence: I asked Chrisse to inform her mother as to our appointments. Dr. E. was responsible for the decisions as to whether and when Chrisse should come to me or could go home, since she was considered to be at strong risk of committing suicide. After our first sessions, I took up contact to Dr. E. in order to discuss what effect the sessions had had on Chrisse (as I also informed Chrisse). Dr. E. confirmed that Chrisse liked the sessions, she felt better after them and thus could spend weekends at home.

Regular psychotherapy

After a three-week Easter vacation, I saw Chrisse twice a week. She had changed considerably through her stay at the psychiatric hospital and strong medications: she had gained quite a bit of weight, seemed subdued and her words were unclear – something that improved over the course of the session, however. At the beginning she was very nervous and seemed confused. She brought a drawing portfolio with her, where she had collected her drawings from the past three weeks.

Analyst: A lot has happened since you were last here. You would like me to know what has happened with you without your telling me.

Chrisse shows me the Mandalas, very simply drawn as if she were three years old. Then we look together at her drawings; she has drawn beautiful faces. She said that she gained three kilos the first week and two kilos the second week. Now, she has a schedule with her advisor for sports, jogging and gymnastics. Coming to me caused her considerable stress, but it was very important to her because she wishes to become healthy again. In a tight voice, she sings the song texts she has written; their subjects are unhappy love, desperation and the abyss.

For Chrisse, therapy had become a space where she felt safe, and she came gladly. Sometimes she managed to distinguish between fantasy and reality. Yet she could not remember figures from her earlier fantasies, such as the snow maiden. Since she reacted well to therapy, Dr. E. had nothing against a two-hour-a-week plan. Through the medication, her daydreams had shed their torturing urgency, and she could once more read and listen to music. She still heard voices, and accordingly received stronger medications. Chrisse participated in activities at the hospital, playing soccer and scoring four goals to bring her team to victory, something she told me proudly.

For the next session, Chrisse's mother brought her a half an hour too early; I let them in only ten minutes before the session was to begin.

Chrisse was very nervous entering.

A: What did you think when I did not open the door for you right away?

Chrisse: I thought you were killed!! (greatly agitated) My parents were advised to be careful what they say to me, since I'm so sensitive. I always withdrew when I was hurt.

A: (addressing her wishful thinking) You would like me to solve everything by pushing a button.

Chrisse: Wouldn't be bad (laughs, pulling on her hair and casting a few strands to the floor).

A: You would like to leave something of yours here with me, your hair, that way you'd be sure you can come back on Monday.

Evidently, I opened a space where Chrisse could tell me about her situation at the hospital. I let her tell me about it. Every step in the direction of normality, such as participation in soccer games, other sports, drawing and singing, the hospital school, has a stabilizing influence. She has gained ten kilos by now – as if she wished to fill her inner emptiness with food, it seemed to me.

In the sessions, she often drew pictures and brought her portfolio with her. She would draw eyes or Satan, who could change gender at will. When drawing the collapsing world, she thematized her feelings: rage, contempt and the fear of collapse. She bought a key chain with a skull and wings. She was disappointed and frustrated that the other anorexic girls were already allowed to go home.

Chrisse felt persecuted by various compulsive thoughts – for instance, that she was pregnant although still a virgin. Usually she projected her fantasies and fears onto other girls in the psychiatric ward. Unsure of whether she had been raped, she was reassured only when she got her next period.

Once, she brought a dream:

> I am in a shopping center. There was a glass container in three parts there. In the first, there were harmless, peaceful animals. In the second, crocodiles and in the third a dangerous wildcat, a leopard monster who ate the crocodile. Then I notice that the three parts actually weren't separated by glass walls. I become afraid and run away. I get into an elevator that gets stuck. I wake up in a panic.

In her dream, she would like to separate the good animals from the dangerous ones, but does not succeed in this. Her impulses overwhelm her and threaten to demolish everything, expressing her confusion. Do the leopard and crocodile with its teeth represent her family? Are the crocodile's dangerous teeth those of her mother's with her humiliating, hurtful sentences? Chrisse's indistinct speech is not only a side effect of the medications, but expresses that her thoughts are "broken" in her head and then emerge in this fragmented nature from her mouth.

226 Lost by the wayside – overstepping limits

During my six-week summer vacation, Chrisse undertook a simple job in her mother's office; in autumn, she returned to me. She managed to turn up punctually and also travel to school in Vienna in order to remain in the same school yet sleep at home. She had confusing, burdensome dreams, which she related to me. During my summer vacation, she had been left completely alone with these threatening dreams.

From the first session after the vacation:

Chrisse arrived alone. She had gained weight, weighing approximately 80 kilos now, but wore more suitable clothing and looked more compact than before. She went to the bathroom and asked if she should close the door to the therapy room when she entered.

Chrisse: I don't know where I should begin.

A: It is difficult for you to begin after such a long time without therapy.

Chrisse: I was in the hospital and saw Dr. T. and told him about my dreams. He said, he wanted to see me alone after his vacation in order to talk about them.

A: You say to me that not only I but Dr. T. was on vacation and you were completely alone with your dangerous dreams.

Chrisse: I can tell you some of them. . . . I am alone in a canyon with rocks and sand, there are two layers. Children come who are running around and climbing on the rocks. I sexually abuse a girl.

A: How?

Chrisse: The girl is lying on a bed and I take the blanket away and lie down on her. It really wasn't nice. I'm ashamed, but I thought it was only a dream.

A: In the dream you are a perpetrator and victim, it is a confusing world you are caught in. You exploit that: you are victim and perpetrator, like an adult.

Chrisse: I had other dreams too, some I wrote down so that I wouldn't forget them: one of them was about Harry Potter. Do you know Harry Potter? In their bedrooms, they get three prizes for their academic successes – every year he gets better. Then the dream changes and I could fly – a few years ago I had a dream about flying but I couldn't do it. Now I can really fly, then the others are chasing me and I could find a hiding place.

A: In your dream you express that you want to be as good as Harry Potter, you want to improve your learning. You also want to find out what happened with your head when you had the breakdown. With my help, you want to find out the reasons for your breakdown and sort them out.

Chrisse: I can manage school. I get up at 4:30, take the bus at 5:20 to Vienna. The teachers are nice, my neighbor Marlies is very nice, I like her, but when she flips out, she gets on my nerves.

A: You are relieved that you manage to go to school, something that really is difficult over that distance. (Before the breakdown, she had been at boarding school.) You weren't sure and now it's possible. You sit next to a nice girl. Can you give me an example of what you mean by "flip out"?

Chrisse: For instance, she asks me if she can hit me.

A: Hit you?

Chrisse: Yes, hit me lightly on my arm with the ruler. First I didn't mind, but now it gets on my nerves.

A: You find it difficult then to say no, when it gets on your nerves. And how can you concentrate on the lectures then?

Chrisse: Only partially, then I concentrate on one point, and then I withdraw into my fantasy world.

A: Do you know the exact point in time when you go into your fantasy world?

Chrisse: In arithmetic, when he's talking and I can't follow him, then I go into my fantasy world.

A: When you're frustrated because you don't understand the teacher, you make up a story where you can determine the plot.

Chrisse: (taking a calendar out of her bag) I have a calendar where I write all my important appointments. (reading aloud) I went to the hospital, Tuesday I have to do English homework. I'm expecting a text message from a girl I met at the hospital, she wants to see me. On Friday, I'm coming to you. (shows me her school identity card) This is the first time I have an identity card.

A: You are showing me you are making a great effort to keep your things in order, as you want to make order again in your head. When it gets difficult, you make up a story.

Chrisse: Yes, my story goes like this: I invented a Manga girl, whose mother died. She was stillborn. (reflects) Or more like: her mother died before she was born, and she was cut out of her body. Her father had a wife who was sick, it was life-threatening. He took out her soul so that she would become healthy, but she died. With the girl's mother, I had only a one-night stand and didn't know she was pregnant. He took out her soul and she died. When he discovered that she was pregnant, he called excellent doctors to save the baby's life. But she was saved and came in an incubator where she can stay for a long time. Then she was put up for adoption. She comes to three adoptive families, all three die. It only goes well with the fourth family. There's a father, a mother, a sister and her. She later discovers that she is half spirit and half human. She has magical powers.

A: When you think of the story, you're thinking of a girl who hasn't gotten enough in life. She wasn't a full nine months in her mother's belly, she came into an incubator, her mother died and she can't find a secure place. In the story, you are expressing your feeling that you didn't get enough care and understanding. But there is hope, since the girl finds a fourth family, hope that your family can understand you and that I can carry your problems with you and understand them. You are describing a painful and difficult life.

Chrisse: (Thoughtful, then takes out a book, the second volume in a series. She seems rather absent.) This is the second volume of a vampire story. (She tells the story in detail.) I want to get the first volume, because I want to know how it began.

A: You are telling me of your wish to know how the vampire story began, but you are talking about your own story. You want to find out where the problems began in your life. Now at the moment you are going away from your description of how you're doing at school, you're looking for escape in your stories.

Chrisse: At school, I am half present and half absent. When it becomes too much, I concentrate on one point where the stories come out. Later I wake up and don't know what the teacher was talking about.

A: When you tell me about the girl that is half human and half spirit, you are also talking about yourself and your fear of what you would find out about your dark side.

Chrisse: I want to tell you two more things. I am fast. My teacher said something that sounds funny: I am done right away. That has two meanings.

A: Yes, that you're "done" in the sense that you can't stand it anymore and maybe also that you think that I am "done" when you burden me with all these stories. And you say that the time is so short and you would like to tell me much more.

Discussion

When she entered the therapy room, Chrisse asked whether she should close the door. It is a good sign that she did not leave it open, but instead wanted to construct a border and close the room. She varied her accounts of the great lengths she went to in order to master reality, getting up exceedingly early in order to stay at the same school. When she felt overly challenged, she went into her fantasy world. In her dreams, her real problems were rendered visible.

Although Chrisse knew that her dreams were dreams, she felt threatened by them. She sensed that flying expressed her wish for omnipotence and embodied the compulsive images she feared. She spoke of her wish to become healthy once again. When she was afraid – for instance, afraid of the session ending – she changes the subject as in a dream, but also in the session. She partly idealized her madness, yet could still return to therapy. All her insane figures were on her side – the vampire, the werewolf. She had one friend who was normal and another who found Chrisse's dark side attractive. In transference, she also tried to draw me into her crazy world: I was meant to see the werewolf as a benevolent mythological figure and disregard his craziness, violence and the injuring of borders. She was absolutely convinced that nobody could like her. The story of the Manga girl that was born too early showed her deep conviction that she had been deprived and that she had been not accepted emotionally. But she had hopes (as in her dream) of finding a fourth family where she could stay – this must be an indication of her hope to find a place here in therapy where she (as she said) feels accepted. When I took this into transference and said: "You think that nobody likes you, not even I!", she said: "I haven't thought about that yet." She indicated that she needed more time in therapy by saying at the end of the session that she had still more to tell. When I proposed a third session per week, she understood this as a proof that I could tolerate her, as crazy and terrible as she was. She wanted to use this chance to get to know herself. Due to organizational reasons and to her parents' failure to support her, there was no third session, which would have greatly helped her. Chrisse was able to accept clearly my interpretations and showed that she felt understood. Verbalizing the link between her dreams and feelings made conscious her massive unconscious reproaches against her parents and her feeling of being abandoned and lonely, thus diminishing her fear and inner pressure. She was able to speak with her parents of this directly afterwards in family therapy in the psychiatric ward.

Further development of therapy

Chrisse could now participate once again in school, and her medication was reduced. The psychiatrist said her development was very positive: earlier she could not articulate, but now she addressed problems with other family members directly. In our sessions, it was important to realize whether she wished to pacify me with her "normality" and secretly plan suicide. The sessions constituted an unburdening for her: she brought her burdens to me, and could thus fulfill her tasks in her outside life. I did not always succeed in taking in her worries and fear with the requisite seriousness. It helped when I could put into words how great her confusion and fear of a new relapse were.

She could recognize that she was different from other girls. The demands of school constituted great stress for her. Her fear of being put back into the psychiatric ward could be understood in a second sense: it constituted a retreat, a place where it was not unusual to have such problems. Between the two poles of hospital and school, therapy represented a compromise. Here, she could be herself and show her symptoms, coming to understand them with me. She could listen to my offer of a third session without taking this as a sign of relapse or a demand for hard work – more like an oasis. She began the next session by saying: "Thank God, here's someone I can talk about my hallucinations to!" (And someone who did not provoke fear in her, I would add.) This was a relief for her. She could also discuss how hard it was to fulfill the demands of her strict teachers, in particular her French teacher. She still idealized death – as an escape, an alternative to winning the difficult struggle for normality. This made it all the more important and relieving to have access to analysis. Her constructive, hopeful side became stronger.

From a Monday session at the end of September:

She arrived ten minutes too early, and I requested her to wait in the waiting room. She went to the toilet.

Chrisse: I just took my medication. I forgot to take them at school, now it was two hours too late. (looks at her watch)

A: When you were waiting, which was difficult for you, you remembered to take your medication.

230 Lost by the wayside – overstepping limits

Chrisse: I looked at the white wall and saw bloodstains there from my hand. Then I looked again and knew it was a fantasy. Those are disturbances in my perception.

A: When I let you wait – and already since Friday, this time – you are disappointed and irritated – then you see bloodstains from your hand on the white wall. When you look again and know that I will be with you right away, you recognize that it was a fantasy and you can take your medication. Does this happen often?

Chrisse: Today at school, I looked at my thumbs and saw a burn. (she shows me the spot) When I look more closely, I don't see anything. When you were talking last time about a third session, I was afraid of having a relapse.

A: You are afraid you are crazy when you express your feelings through pictures. It is painful to talk about your symptoms with me.

Chrisse: On Friday, we're going to Dr. T (youth psychiatrist in the General Hospital), and I am curious what he will say about my dreams after the holidays.

A: You think it is so long since you saw Dr. T., but also so long since our last session before the weekend, and then I wasn't available. And then you were confused as to what my offer of a third session meant. Is it an indication that you might have a relapse? That is a real possibility.

Chrisse: There are times I'd like to have a relapse. I think sometimes it's all too much for me – school – over, over, over. No school anymore. I had a test in bookkeeping and I was one point under passing. I have a makeup test on Tuesday. Claudia, the girl I don't like, got eleven out of eleven points and looked at us with triumph. Marlies had two points under. I almost wanted to make a joke out of it: "two points" – worse than me, but I didn't say it.

A: You're saying to me that you stand all this pressure just barely, even though it's very difficult. Then you gave up the idea. When did you exactly get the idea of going back to the hospital?

Chrisse: After the fight with my mother on the weekend, when she was upset that I was sitting at the computer so much playing games, she yelled at me again. I wanted to get away, in the hospital or just away.

A: The psychiatric ward is a kind of retreat, then, but "just away" means completely away, away from life.

Chrisse: I don't think so, but for a moment I thought that "end" would be an escape.

A: You are afraid that something fatal in you could seduce you to end your life.

Chrisse: Claudia asked me if I only draw swords, only am interested in swords.

A: You understood Claudia's question to ask whether you are normal or crazy, different from the others. And you presumably understood my remark the same way.

Chrisse: My French teacher was tactless. She asked me what grade I got last year in French. I answered that I hadn't gotten a grade, and she asked what grades I got for the semester. I said I failed. Then she asked me why I hadn't gotten a report card. I told her about my long absence, two to three months. She then said in an irritated way: "Was it two or three?" I said: "I don't know!" She asked if I wanted to talk about it and I shook my head. Then she understood.

A: You are talking about the tactless French teacher and are glad that I treat you differently.

Chrisse: Yes. I am more normal-crazy, I don't yell. I'd like to yell: "You die!" I drew something at school: a sword, a dagger, a knife. A song text that fits here too: blood running down.

A: You show me pictures and tell me what thoughts occupy you. But you are also excited by these threatening objects, they fascinate you.

Chrisse: Yes, I like reading books about vampires. I often sing the song "I am bleeding, do you forget me?" as I read.

A: Now at the end of the session, you think of this song and also the question of whether I will forget you when you leave.

Discussion

Chrisse showed how glad she was to be able to speak about all of her threatening and fascinating fantasies. Here, she could speak about her fascination with the attraction of death, blood and pain without my becoming tactless or yelling as her mother did. It calmed her when I understood her fear and concern over this dark side in her. Indeed, she basically managed the physical effort of commuting to school and scholastic demands, which constituted a major satisfaction to her. She was reasonable enough to recognize that she was different from other people. The French teacher had a rough side, as presumably did Chrisse's mother – the side that prevented her from empathizing with Chrisse's burdens and confusion. At therapy, she was not compelled to present herself as normal. Then, her constructive side also became visible, the side that wanted to become healthy again. A third session per week would enable more closeness between her and her analyst, something she wanted but also did not want, since it would demonstrate her neediness. In countertransference, I sometimes reacted with fatigue at the sessions and found Chrisse's stories very burdensome. I tried to be internally open as to whether she was becoming more stable and her situation improving, or whether she only wanted to pacify me and secretly was considering suicide. When she was reading, she was also able to make me tired as a countertransferential reaction, in order that I not feel her horror.

Two weeks later, Chrisse's mother phoned me and said she thought two sessions per week were too many. On the one hand, I thought she seemed jealous that Chrisse entrusted me with thoughts that she did not entrust to her mother. Actually, she could not recognize the seriousness of her daughter's problem. If she put herself into her daughter's shoes, she would like to run away. She acted as if the therapy was the problem, as if it created problems, and denied the link between Chrisse's improvement and the therapeutic work. She wanted to run away, just as she had tried to push aside her problems and not grieve for her first baby she had given up.

232 Lost by the wayside – overstepping limits

Excerpt from a session:

> Chrisse entered without her schoolbag and told me she was coming from Marlies' house, since school had ended three hours earlier and she could stay there.

Chrisse: After this session, I'm going over to her house again and staying until 6, then we're going to watch movies together. On Monday I'm going to the hospital again for a checkup. I had a dream:

> I am with a friend and we have a bow and arrow and we are walking through the woods. We come to a cliff with a steep drop, but in front of it is a mediumhigh stone wall. When I look down, I see a big turquoise lake – a forest on its shores would be even better. A little dinosaur comes towards us. I span my bow – I don't know if I shot the arrow, but the dinosaur falls down. We walk onwards, I don't know if it's a male or female friend. We get into the river with a strong current. With our last strength, we manage to save ourselves from the river. Then a figure comes up, like the black prince I told you about. He was my brother – but only as camouflage, so that nobody would recognize that he represents my dark side.

Once recently I had the idea that my soul could separate from me.

A: That makes you afraid, when you have such thoughts.

Chrisse: Afraid, no. I don't have any kind of feeling – and in the dream I also didn't have any feeling. I also didn't know whether I was active. I only spanned the bow. Otherwise I am always dreaming that something happens to me, that I'm the victim and I can't do anything.

A: In the dream, you manage to save yourselves with your last strength out of the water. You are telling me also how desperately you need help in order to get you out. You noticed that you weren't at all afraid in the dream, as if it were happening to another person. You are also showing me how threatening it is to spend the weekend without a session.

Chrisse: I could speak twice with my mother about my dreams and my worries whether I would really manage at school.

A: When I am not there, you can speak with your mother. You want to see if I can recognize how dangerous your situation is, being almost on the edge of a cliff with an attractive turquoise lake beneath.

Chrisse: Anyone who was so close to death and has cut herself will never forget it.

Discussion

Interestingly, Chrisse's feelings in the dream were completely polarized. She did not feel fear. Her dream and the way in which she recounted it show her psychotic structure. Although the dream resembled her fantasy stories, another factor was also present: she is afraid of becoming insane again. Indeed, the very fact that she was not disturbed by her dream was disturbing. Its form shows a splitting between the content of the story and her feelings. Chrisse seems to have a minimal insight that she cuts off her feelings. Her insight that she might drown in this powerful river signifies the possibility of a relapse and new breakdown. She showed me that she knew she could fall into the dangerous river again, and she needed me to pull her out. For her, death has become impersonal. Chrisse's dialogue with her chronically depressed mother was difficult: the mother suffered under her own illness and did not want to support Chrisse coming regularly to therapy. She often cancelled her daughter's sessions or kept her at home during school vacations.

End of therapy

Chrisse and her parents ended her therapy in November, after I had cancelled one session due to my week-long vacation. Particularly with child or adolescent therapy, success and continuity are dependent on parental support. This means cooperation between therapist and parents. In Chrisse's case, the father was very withdrawn and found it difficult to attend more than one parental meeting in Vienna from his apartment outside the city. The mother found it difficult to see how much Chrisse received from me, how important analysis was in her life, although the mother unconsciously felt herself to be much needier than Chrisse. Her life philosophy was to suppress all problems and pain and act as if there were no problem, although she was depressed, moody, irritable and a complainer, experiencing the world as inimical.

From the last two sessions:

Chrisse: (looks absentminded when entering) I saw a movie: it was about a form of life that was in the deep-freeze for 100 years, and that's why they could fly and do other things people can't.

A: You come and tell me not about your life, but about the movie.

Chrisse: These movies are my life.

A: You are telling me that these films replace your life since your life is a nightmare.

Chrisse: I had a dream. It was about a vampire who almost dies because he didn't get any new blood. Then he found a mixture of old and fresh blood.

Dr. T., to whom I also told my dream about the girl, the girl who was raped and abused, he said that he believes in reincarnation. That I dreamed things that happened to my mother. I asked my mother, she said yes, it did happen, but she can't remember – it's like a big black hole.

A: It must be confusing when you don't know whose problems you are dreaming. But after the session you missed, you're telling me about a hungry vampire – like a baby who hasn't gotten enough to eat from me and almost starved. Then there is only a black hole, as your mother says, full of terrible things . . .

Discussion

Chrisse reacted very strongly to interruptions and missed sessions. In the image of the hungry vampire (supplemented by her description of it as an eternally unsatisfied, hungry baby that could not establish contact to its mother), she transferred her own problem to the vampire. He did not receive fresh blood and almost starved before he received a mixture of old and new blood. Does this express the "old" feelings of Chrisse's mother connected to giving away her baby and Chrisse's "fresh" feelings towards her mother? Presumably, Chrisse must have launched stronger and stronger attempts to penetrate her mother's emotional armor (unconscious guilt feelings), until she perceived herself as aggressive and became convinced that she would kill her mother with her urgent wishes – as in the image of the vampire who sucks out its victim until the victim dies, in order to itself survive. So to speak, only one of them can survive. In this difficult situation, it would be too much for Chrisse to depict her dark side as a hungry baby; it is enough to understand the hungry and desperate vampire. The black hole presumably signifies various things; it can attract other matter – Chrisse herself, her confusion. It could also be the black hole of the mother – a highly powerful negative energy capable of swallowing every kind of matter.

In Chrisse's dream of flying, she creates bizarre creatures who are missing a gene – the reason they can do so many things, including fly. She identifies with them and flies herself, simply taking off. At the same time, she expresses her fear of a genetic defect that she holds responsible for her breakdown. She became manic, professing that she had no problems, instead elevating herself above all else, in particular her analyst. She did not wish to be vulnerable, instead flying and fleeing. These various moods shifted quickly within her, within the session.

The psychiatrist T. did not behave respectfully towards me, did not assume contact to me, unlike Dr. E. His interpretation of reincarnation – if in fact he made it – was still more confusing for Chrisse.

Final session

Chrisse: (she arrived punctually) On the weekend I can't stay at my friend's house, because her uncle is coming and I was told I shouldn't come.

A: You are disappointed because you can't go to your friend's and also because you can't come to me next week since I'm away.

Chrisse: (irritated) I have my own life! You don't give me any suggestions, we only talk. I was in an exhibit about the Renaissance with my father. He didn't know the names of the painters, but I did: Rafael, Michelangelo and Pintorello.

A: You are hurt because your friend and I can't be with you, then you close off these feelings and talk about what you're good at.

Chrisse: (touches her finger and says in a gentle voice) Today at school I hurt my finger when I was trying to sharpen my fountain pen. This is exactly the same place where I hurt myself rope-climbing in gym class.

A: You are showing me how hurt you are when you show me your finger, and you feel hurt by me.

Chrisse: I feel good, everything's ok. (As she speaks, she pulls her scarf around her neck until she is half-strangled.)

A: You are showing me two things at the same time: you say how good you feel and at the same time how you can't get any air, when you pull your scarf so tight, how strongly you are under pressure. Your parents want to end your sessions.

Chrisse: That's a habit of mine, I always do that when I'm wearing a scarf. It's ok. (She turns to the plants and strokes them.)

A: You are stroking the plants and thoughts are going through your head.

Chrisse: What do you think, what will happen when my parents die?

A: You are telling me it is like death when you won't have any sessions anymore. Then you think what will happen when your parents die. Even if we can't continue therapy now, you could come back later.

It was a painful parting not only for Chrisse but also for me, who understood how urgently Chrisse needed more sessions. The parents quoted her psychiatrist, who had taken Chrisse off medication, contending that she was doing much better. Chrisse was not strong enough to make her own decisions. I thought she was still very fragile, and her thinking required outer help and stabilization. The parents thanked me for the good collaboration and were appreciative of how much therapy had helped Chrisse. I thought Chrisse's conviction that she could heal herself constituted a form of megalomania that was supported by the parents. In a letter, I offered that she could turn to me again.

Case study of liberation from the maternal web: Vinzenz

I will now describe the development of Vinzenz from the perspective of his mother's analysis. At the beginning of his mother's analysis, Vinzenz was in a psychiatric ward, since he had poured alcohol over his mother and spat on her. She called the police to have him committed. She knew that she was too intimately bound to her son and urgently sought help, not knowing what she should do.

Family background

Vinzenz is the second son in his family; he has one brother two years older than him and another four years younger. Both parents work for a living. From the age of three, he was conspicuously difficult. The family had various kinds of therapy, but nothing really helped. Vinzenz became quite obese, he weighed approximately 100 kilos, did not finish school and is now 18 years old. His older brother has already moved out and is a university student; the younger brother is in the fifth class of middle school. At the age of 14, Vinzenz was first committed to a psychiatric ward because he became violent with his younger brother, beating him

236 Lost by the wayside – overstepping limits

until he drew blood and threatening to kill him, whereupon the younger brother locked himself in the bathroom and called their mother on his mobile phone.

Initial interviews

During the initial interviews the mother was already in tears, reproaching herself that Vinzenz would have become another person with another mother. He was at the center of her narrative: her second son, who had been diagnosed as a schizophrenic, had continually threatened suicide, and imparted to her the feeling she had failed.

The mother's family history was as follows: she was the second of three sisters – one two years older, the other 14 months younger. She never felt understood by her parents; her grandmother and great-grandmother lived with them; she felt nurtured by the grandmother. Three months after her birth, the mother went back to work in the legal profession.

She decided to have psychotherapy with two sessions per week.

Escalation

In the third session, she brought a dream that took place in a foreign country where everyone was killed by an old-fashioned gun. To my interpretation that she was full of murderous hate towards Vinzenz, she added: "and towards my mother. She is always saying she was able to bring up her three daughters well, why can't I do that with my three sons?"

Discussion

The old-fashioned guns indicate early feelings from her childhood: the murderous rage in her that she herself calls dangerous. She is both victim of parental violence – it is still unclear in what form – and perpetrator (presumably in fantasy). The patient projects her neediness onto Vinzenz, but actually shows that she would have needed and still needs a mother.

She called me before her seventh session quite upset, because Vinzenz had just been brought to the psychiatric ward in an ambulance by the police. Since he gambles and drinks, he demanded more money from her; she refused him, whereupon he blocked her way and pushed her aside. The father hurried to help, but Vinzenz caught him in a stranglehold, causing the mother to call the police. When they arrived, Vinzenz let himself be committed. The plan was to have Vinzenz do an intensive six- to eight-week therapy after spending one week in the hospital. His mother was worried about him. Indeed, he broke off this intensive therapy after two days and came home.

When I addressed her rage and aggression towards him, she could say that she sometimes thought: "then just kill yourself, then I'll finally have peace from you." When I interpreted that her great fear of her own aggression and destruction impeded her from embarking on a four-session-per-week analysis, she became thoughtful.

The patient succeeded in acting out her conviction of being unloved, sent away and having no place in the world in analysis, i.e., she actually experienced it. After the escalation with Vinzenz, she agreed to a four-times-a-week analysis. Already in the first week she arrived at her Wednesday 11:00 session at 9:50 and asked if she could use the bathroom. When I informed her that I expected her at 11:00, she left and returned an hour later. She was furious at being sent away. She linked this experience to her childhood where her older and younger sisters were given preferential treatment – there was never space for her. I was able to keep to a temporal structure, which although it made her furious, also relieved her. Spitefully, she added that she was proud of her chaos; order was bourgeois and ridiculous.

In the following weeks, she forgot her hairband, in order to leave something by me. She could show her great unconscious wishes for security and closeness only through small mistakes or Freudian slips. She was, however, able to accept my interpretation and felt herself understood.

She could not exhibit joy regarding her husband and children and could not express praise for them. But after she felt very strong joy that I expected her four times a week, it occurred to her how seldom she showed joy to her husband. The day after this session, she managed to say, while shopping for a new kitchen with her husband, that she liked it and was glad. She kept forgetting her hairband before the weekend and was ashamed of thus expressing her urgent wish to stay with me. She had the feeling of being bound to Vinzenz "with a chain".

At the beginning of the new year, Vinzenz moved to a supervised apartment where he was visited once a week by a social worker. During the day, he attended vocational training. The mother had found it difficult to let Vinzenz move away. She was able to recognize my interpretation of her worry: that she wished Vinzenz could *not* manage without her. She wept when I understood how happy she was to finally find her place with me. She wavered between her conviction that Vinzenz would return within two days and the understanding that she didn't actually want to give him up and let him become independent. Vinzenz was now regularly attending behavioral therapy – without her management.

After three months, when spring had come, she could recognize that she had always been dissatisfied. She talked of her suicidal impulses, of driving a car and wanting to run it into a tree so that everything would be over. Once, she wanted to jump out of a window in her house, but she was unhappy with the idea of "slinking away".

In one Wednesday session, the relation between her experiences with Vinzenz and her own wishes as a baby became clear. After Vinzenz began to do well in his supervised apartment, her youngest son Justin began to develop problems at school.

Wednesday session

At first, she made sure she put her hairband where she would not forget it (it was the last session before a ten-day vacation).

Patient: I asked my friend why she thinks her children developed well. She is also psychologically educated and said, "They are securely attached." That made

238   Lost by the wayside – overstepping limits

me so furious. I helped her back in school when she was new there, and now it's reversed, she does everything better.

Analyst: You experience your friend as finding herself superior to you. She does things right and you do things wrong. Perhaps you think that I am also like your friend. You are wondering whether I have children who are doing well.

Patient: Here we go again. I'm not thinking about that at all. And if I were to ask you, you wouldn't answer. I already thought whether I displace my feelings to Justin. For me, it would be the worst thing, to get left back in school. But maybe it's not so bad for him. But in the night when I think about Justin, it's so awful. I am so afraid that everything will be like it was with Vinzenz.

A: You can't even say openly what this could mean, what happened with Vinzenz.

Patient: That he could be put in a psychiatric ward. The situation then where they sent me away and he had to stay there alone.

A: And behind this separation there is an earlier one, when they separated you from Vinzenz.

Patient: Yes, when he was a baby and was put in the hospital since he was breathing with such difficulty.

A: You haven't told me yet how that happened, how you noticed his breathing problems.

Patient: I went to a birthday party with both children. My husband couldn't come with us. It was very strenuous and a big challenge. I shouldn't have gone to it just four weeks after giving birth. When we were going home, I noticed that Vinzenz was breathing so badly that he was retracting his throat (she demonstrates). I went straight to the hospital.

A: And today, in the last session before our long separation, the point is not your separation from Vinzenz, and you bring your hairband to show me how much you'd like to stay here.

Patient: We've already talked about that, how I'd like to stay. And then I think of some thoughts I had as a child. (pause)

A: You are remembering thoughts, but you can't say them.

Patient: (begins to weep) Yes. I have them in my head, but something's missing. I feel myself only up to there (she points to her chest) and the head – and in between something is missing.

A: Something was interrupted and is missing. You are pointing to the same place you pointed to when you said that Vinzenz retracted his throat, like a great burden. Presumably Vinzenz was not only bearing his own burden but also yours and showing the burden with his body.

Patient: (sobbing) And – I – can't – say – it!

A: (after several minutes) Maybe you also want to see if I really want to know it or am just like your mother, who thinks it is completely normal to go back to work after four weeks and wean the child, and there is no difference between a mother and a grandmother.

Patient: I – say – that – she – should – not – go – away!

A: What words did you use?

Patient: (sobbing violently) Stay – here! Don't – leave!

A: When you say the exact words, you are completely connected to your feelings. You wanted to say it to your mother and didn't have the confidence and now you're saying it to me, to your analytic mother, and hope that I understand it. When you leave your hairband here, you are here in your fantasy and I won't leave.

Patient: I said it but my mother just left. It was like when my oldest son went to kindergarten. The teacher said to the mothers, they should go . . . But I kept standing there and waited until he stopped crying . . . now my neck is free again.

A: And here too I send you away and I don't want to hear you anymore when you are in the middle of telling me such important things.

Patient: (stands up, says goodbye and leaves. By the door, she turns around, looks at the couch, takes her hairband, looks at me and smiles.)

Discussion

This session moved me deeply. We both experienced how thin indeed defenses can be. When she did not feel "contained", she projected her needs onto her children. She did not wish to be a bad mother, but she had had a mother who left her with the grandmother in good conscience, not knowing what she was doing to her baby. In this moment, the patient felt herself understood in her own estimation as an inadequate mother for Vinzenz. I recognized how she acknowledged her suffering under not being with her longed-for mother but with her grandmother. When she felt understood, she could internalize this experience. She felt relieved and could take her hairband with her. Her smile when she turned around showed that she could well recognize her wish to remain with me.

The patient began this session with themes related to her second or youngest son. Vinzenz could live alone in the supervised apartment, absolving his training and apprenticeship in protected workshops or in accompaniment in actual workplaces. In her dreams, violent scenes occurred: a playground slide that had a knife built into it, cutting the children's bottoms when they slid down. Her associations led to her infant experience of neediness and greed. She had experienced separation from her mother, along with an early and abrupt weaning, as crippling. In her fantasy, she had severed her mother's breasts. The separations from me at the end of the week were also very painful, like a wound. She projected her neediness onto Vinzenz and was worried about him. At the same time, she and he were so furious that both had thoughts of suicide. She remembered that she once came into his room and saw an open window. He had hid himself to scare her, and she was indeed convinced that he had jumped out the window; already once before, he had stepped out onto the windowsill and threatened to jump. She did not dare to look out the window in dread of viewing his mutilated body.

240 Lost by the wayside – overstepping limits

Now she told of Vinzenz's positive development: he had lost weight, had a girl-friend and went on boating trips with her family. In a sort of waking dream, she had imagined that he was on the boat with the girlfriend, whose father pushed Vinzenz into the water, whereupon he drowned. She was terribly worried about him.

To my interpretation that behind her worries lay her suppressed aggressive impulses, she answered: "I myself was wondering why I can't be glad that Vinzenz now has a girlfriend. Can I bear it, that another woman is taking my place? Really, that's what I wanted – and now it totally bothers me."

Her deep bitterness against her parents could now be addressed: she had never felt accepted by them, was never as smart as her two sisters, had to stick to exacting rules. She wanted to be different with her own children: they ought to be allowed to live out her rebellion and her contrary notions. In old photographs, she could see that Vinzenz was completely naked through the age of five. It had impressed her that he was so "animal" and attractive. She was not able to set him limits. Through age three, Vinzenz had been a particularly capable child. Only during her third pregnancy (with Justin) had he become so difficult that she was hardly able to give attention to her other two children. She took Vinzenz from test to test, from doctor to doctor, and embarked on systemic family therapy. Everyone said she was too closely bound to Vinzenz, but she knew better: he just needed her, that was all. At first, he was diagnosed with a perceptual-sensory defect. But then he refused to go to school – she "had to" put his shoes and socks on him, which she continued until he was 17, although it made her feel like his slave.

Gradually, it became evident how strongly she identified with Vinzenz. She had been five months old when her mother had become pregnant with the youngest sister. In the session, she was not able to figure out how old she had been – as if she had a mental block or was simply stupid. She was never allowed to exhibit her jealousy of her sister – and thus Vinzenz was meant to assert his "animal" instincts and will without limits, something she had never dared. Emotionally, my patient was stuck at the age of three, although she was very successful in her career and able to care for her family.

As could be expected, after the problems with Vinzenz had lessened, her main symptom was redirected to another family member. Immediately, Justin (her youngest son) began to cause problems, locking himself in his room and sitting in front of the computer. He didn't see his friends, got bad grades in school and had not done any homework since March. Now the patient had a new theme she could speak about at length. It was important to establish a connection between her and her life to the transferential situation to me in our sessions, in order to enable her to have vital experiences. Here is an excerpt from one session:

Thursday session in June

She paid the bill and noticed that she had not brought enough money.

P: I thought I would have enough money, but I gave my husband some money for the gas. I know, money has a great symbolic meaning. I appreciate the work

Lost by the wayside – overstepping limits   241

we do here in analysis and I know that a lot has changed in my life. But I'm coming four times a week! Couldn't I aim for a faster result? I want to find out more about my feelings.

A: You have mixed feelings about paying and also about continuing analysis.

P: Yesterday I thought some more about Justin, it's so difficult for me not to annoy him with reproachful questions. Yesterday he was on an excursion and when he came home I asked him where they had been. He said he didn't know. I pressed him and said you must know where you were. I can't hold myself back. He didn't say anything more then. I talked on and after a while he said: "Mother, you're getting on my nerves!" I don't know his exact words anymore. I asked him then: "How?" He answered: "In every way" – and shut himself in his room.

A: It is so painful when he is older (15) and doesn't want to be so close to you anymore.

P: (becomes very sad) Justin was the only child who liked to cuddle with me so, more than the two others. And now he doesn't want to touch me anymore, when I stroke his hair, he turns away. That hurts so much!

A: The two others live by themselves, he is the only child still at home.

P: Now that I have more time, I would like to spend more time with him. I feel guilty too, since I neglected him so when I took Vinzenz from doctor to doctor . . .

A: You are longing so for closeness and physical contact. Here, you are sometimes touched by my words, but that doesn't seem to be enough. You want to feel it quite concretely.

P: I said to my husband: "Please, hold me tight, touch me! I need that!" Now, he can do it.

A: Now that the session is over, it's hard for you to go.

P: Yes. But I'm coming back tomorrow.

In this phase, where her second son is becoming more independent, she feels flooded by her own infantile neediness, which she previously projected onto her other sons – although in reality, she needs Justin much more than he needs her. Now, she has gradually come to feel her neediness, instead of hiding it behind her nagging and her conviction that she was missing out on something. Her husband was then able to respond to her neediness. In analysis, she wanted to be a good patient and make exemplary progress. In transference, I was like Justin who did not need her, spending my weekend and vacation with my family, not with her. Although she felt the desire to stroke Justin's hair, she actually wished to be stroked and cared for like a baby; she wanted to sit on my lap, since her rejecting mother could never satisfy these wishes. After long discussion, she now had the confidence to fulfill her wishes to travel. Since her husband received no vacation this year, she traveled with a friend and was able to enjoy their trip.

Gradually, feelings such as the longing for closeness and security emerged in her alongside the familiar, dark feelings of accusation, bitterness, reproach and desperation. Could life also be friendly and pleasant in addition to all her painful

242 Lost by the wayside – overstepping limits

experiences? Would she be allowed to fulfill her own wishes? Her birthday became a crystallizing point for these questions. Could she fulfill her great wish to have a party where she would be the central focus, where she could invite friends from various areas of her life? Could she stand in the center and give a speech? Did she have the confidence for this? Would her three sons want to celebrate her? Could she present her own family to all her friends, her sisters and parents? Would I accept her having such a beautiful party and even support her emotionally, or instead criticize her for it?

Her experiences in analysis had a reconciliatory aspect. She had a sensual experience on the couch that satisfied her longing, like a baby who finally experienced the body contact that had been withheld from her. While relating her problems with Justin, she realized she had brusquely demanded he go to school in spite of his fear. She was just as unable to be friendly to him as to herself. She reproached herself. She had the impression of bringing her mistakes and failures as a mother to analysis, yet I did not – as she expected – accuse and judge her like a prosecutor. She seemed to experience a new repertoire of behavior, reacting lovingly and with understanding. Sometimes, she could then also offer her sons help instead of criticism. In the sessions, I heard and acknowledged her inner, unrelentingly critical voice. Her criticism of herself and her sons gradually gave way to a more understanding attitude. Buoyed by her own goodwill and in spite of her fears, she was organizing a large birthday party for herself – carefully planning it with the support of her husband and a friend.

The party was a great success, although she had been pessimistic about its outcome. All the friends she invited came, and the food was well-prepared, with only minor mishaps. She had prepared a speech. For the first time, she was able to publicly acknowledge her parents' accomplishments without leaving the difficult areas unmentioned, but also without reproaching them. She also discussed her difficulties and actions on Vinzenz's behalf, thanking her husband for bearing the responsibility with her.

> My husband then made a beautiful speech where he said how much he loved me, which greatly moved me. Then, to my great surprise, all three sons sang a song together with my husband using the refrain "applause, applause!" along with a new text written for me. I was overcome when all four men hugged me tight and kissed me. I was so proud! Then, my parents were asked which experience was the best they had had with me: my mother said it was my wedding, and my father – usually so strict and aloof – said in tears: this party. When we embraced, all three of us were moved to tears.

Since she pressed my buzzer so lightly that it didn't ring, I interpreted that she perhaps wished to punish herself because the party had been such a success and she would not grant herself such a success. The patient said how grateful she was since she could only have given such a party after her work in analysis.

Discussion

To the extent that she can allow Vinzenz to extricate himself from their bond – now that she has found a safe place in analysis – the patient can also tend to her own needs in a caring way. Instead of reproaching her parents and life, criticizing and expecting catastrophe, she could reflect on what she wants. She pointed out that all her friends at the party talked about how much better Vinzenz was doing and how glad they were about this. She also said that he behaved quite normally with the guests. However, she complained that although now Vinzenz was doing better, nobody was praising *her* for his progress, whereas while he was doing badly, everyone thought this was due to their overly close relationship. She only felt recognized and appreciated by her analyst. A month after the party, she told me with surprise that she no longer needed to fight her impulse for calling Vinzenz up several times a day – since he now called her regularly.

Vinzenz's mother began to observe herself in her interactions with Vinzenz and Justin. She noticed that in subtle ways, she had tried to hinder their independence and emotional development, even though she had ostensibly welcomed this development on the conscious level. Justin, who had earlier spent all his time in his room before the computer – she was afraid that he had become addicted to it – now wished to travel one week to Germany to visit four online chat friends, one of whose parents had invited him. But she began to find problems in his plan: were they respectable parents? Could he travel there alone? Although all four friends liked to play soccer, she was afraid that they would only sit in their room. She then suggested that Justin sleep in a hotel with her, and only spend the days with them. Justin then said: "Forget it, Mom. I know you don't want me to go."

Through our discussion, it became clear that she envied Justin his courage in travelling alone to Germany. At his age, she had to travel to France to family friends, but had almost died of homesickness. Unconsciously, she wanted to prevent him from being able to do what she had not even dared to dream of.

She observed a similar pattern of behavior in her interaction with Vinzenz. When his attendance at training became irregular one week, and his social worker consequently scheduled a conference with him, she tried to assert influence – calling up the central housing office and managing to obtain information about Vinzenz, even though this was prohibited. When he then came for dinner that weekend, she not only posed a barrage of questions as to whether he had gone to training that week, but would not believe his answers, asking "Really? Every day? What did you do there?" When Vinzenz told her he had taken up his handball training again (something she had earlier pushed him to do against his resistance), she now discouraged him, saying, "Isn't that too strenuous?" But he said with conviction, "No, on the contrary. Then I'm more fit the next day!" It became clear how difficult it was for her to accept that her sons were becoming independent. Her feeling of emptiness here was palpable.

Three months after his mother had started analysis, Vinzenz stopped taking his medication against "borderline disorder": his therapist said that the diagnosis

244   Lost by the wayside – overstepping limits

no longer applied. One year later, the institution responsible for Vinzenz's case has asked for a new diagnosis, since his behavior is in no way remarkable; he lives in the supervised apartment, has a relationship and regularly attends therapy. Vinzenz has begun a project-based vocational education and hopes to complete it in good time. He doubtless will require a long trajectory in attaining the "capability to love and work", as Freud defined it.

Only after the dissolution of this entanglement with her sons can the patient tend to her own life, instead of deflecting her problems onto them.

I meant this case study to demonstrate how important it is to reflect on the child and baby *within* the mother, instead of assigning her guilt or perhaps describing her as an "icebox mother" (Laing 1964).

6.4 Thoughts of suicide – suicide attempts

In this chapter, I discuss fantasies, thoughts and attempts at suicide from a psychoanalytic perspective, in order to understand not only what is transpiring in adolescents contemplating suicide, but also the situation of people attempting to help them.

> I do not stir,
> The frost makes a flower,
> The dew makes a star,
> The dead bell,
> The dead bell,
> Somebody's done for.
> —Sylvia Plath

Sylvia Plath already heard death chimes in her adolescent years – perhaps even since the painful loss of her father when she was seven. She made her first suicide attempt – a serious one – when she was 16. In her half-autobiographical novel *The Bell Jar* (2013), she describes secretly hoarding sleeping pills and then leaving a note in her room explaining away her absence so that her mother would not look for her. She hid in a crawl space in their basement behind a woodpile. Then she swallowed 50 sleeping pills and only survived by a miracle, discovered by chance three days later. In her poems, we see the inner struggle between her longing for death as an expression of desperation and depression and the will to live. This will to live can be seen in many suicide attempts through the method they are carried out – unconsciously designed so that the attempter will be saved. This need not function as (unconsciously) intended: as Al Alvarez writes in his book about Plath, *The Savage God*: "In her last attempt, she seemed to be taking care not to succeed. But this time everything conspired to destroy her" (Alvarez 1971, 50).

Sylvia Plath went at 6:00 am to her children's bedroom, placing bread and butter as well as two glasses of milk by their beds so that they would have something to eat before the au pair girl arrived. Then she returned to the kitchen, sealed the doors and window as well as she could with towels, opened the oven, put her head inside and turned on the gas. Although the au pair girl arrived punctually at 9:00 am and rang the doorbell, nobody let her in. Since the inhabitant of the apartment under Plath had also been induced into deep sleep by the gas, he also heard nothing. Thus, the door was only forced open at 11:00 am. Plath's body was still warm. She had left a note behind: "Please call Dr. N." – the therapist she planned to visit – with his telephone number. But it was too late (Alvarez 1971, 51ff).

As with Sylvia Plath, thoughts of suicide often go back to very early traumatizing experiences or are an expression of emotional conflicts. In adolescence, thoughts of death play a particular role – where it is often unclear how serious a threat this constitutes.

Adolescence is a time of stormy physical and psychic development, and the restructuring of the adolescent's inner world is so dramatic that he often cannot reflect calmly on this. The newly developed adolescent physique, sexual maturity and the development of physical strength as well as the possibilities society now affords would make it possible for the adolescent to realize his fantasies and unconscious wishes. The young child who fantasizes sexual contact or having a baby with the parent of the opposite sex knows somehow that this is not realistic – that the boy does not really have such a big penis as his father, that the father cannot really make a baby with the girl, that the wish to vanquish or kill the paternal rival cannot be carried out. But now, these things are physically possible and cause great fear – a fear entailed in all the physical changes over which the adolescent has no control; even if she wishes to stop or reverse them, she is helpless. The great insecurity, along with the question of "Who am I?", can then lead to the question: "Do I want to live as I am now?" The adolescent is also now capable of killing himself. I will discuss this particular constellation. The questions of "Who am I? What am I living for?" are real questions with real challenges. On the unconscious level, they can be an expression of guilt feelings evoked through an unconscious wish for punishment (see Anderson 2009). Before we now examine these inner dynamics more closely, we should remind ourselves that as with small children, adolescents (and adults, for that matter) hold themselves culpable not only for their bad deeds, but also for those they committed in their fantasies. This is related to the residue of magical thinking operative in the young child – for example, one so angry at her mother that she wishes she were dead, consequently feeling guilty when the mother dies or harms herself in an accident.

Suicide and suicide attempts as a social problem

According to the 2014 WHO report, "Preventing Suicide", 800,000 people between the ages of 12 and 19 commit suicide each year. In Austria, 1,319 people committed suicide in 2012 – if we do not consider ambiguous cases where death is caused by risky driving or sports influenced by unconscious suicidal wishes. Particularly regrettable are adolescent suicides, where the perpetrator's life lies before him or her. It is thus especially important to consider the types of inner

246 Lost by the wayside – overstepping limits

conflict whose "solution" leads to such a violent end. The member states of the WHO agreed upon a plan of action with the goal of reducing suicides by 10% by 2020 (WHO report 2014).

Suicide is the second most frequent cause of death for this age group. After a suicide attempt, not only the adolescent's family but also members of her school become deeply shaken. One senior graduating from academic high school described her reaction to a suicide attempt:

> Another pupil told me one day that a good friend of hers had tried to kill herself. Without warning, she jumped out a fourth-floor window of her classroom. Nobody had had any idea, and all the students were totally thrown. She was seriously injured and was brought to the hospital. Only afterwards did I learn that the girl had already made a similar attempt before. She had stood by the window in order to jump, but her neighbors saw her and immediately called the police, who were able to deter her. Neither my friend nor I knew what the cause was for these two attempts. My friend told me later that this girl's mother was an alcoholic and that she lived with her father, who was seldom at home and had financial problems.
>
> I wondered whether there are signs beforehand when someone is thinking of suicide or is concretely planning it. What are the reasons for somebody wanting to die so young – a thought I that is completely unimaginable to me. If somebody understands the reasons and sees the signs or can recognize them, the family or friends could help this person to master this psychic crisis.
>
> (Hadaya 2015, 3)

This shocking story led Samira Hadaya to the theme of "Adolescent Suicide" for her final paper in secondary school, in order to better understand these problems.

Particularly for adolescents, suicide is an extremely effective "weapon" to deeply shake family, friends and teachers and elicit guilt feelings. Questions and self-blame arise: could I have seen the signs earlier? Did I neglect concerning myself with this girl/boy adequately? Suicide attempts elicit a range of intense feelings, shock and trauma as well as fascination – along with the phenomenon of other adolescents in the same social context also attempting suicide (Liu 2006).

Robin Anderson points out that not only suicides, but also suicide attempts deserve to be taken with special seriousness, since those who attempt suicide are part of a particularly endangered group (Anderson 2009, 220).

Tomadl writes:

> the ratio of suicides to suicide attempts lies somewhere between 1:5 to 1:10. (For every ten attempts, one is saved.) There are many more suicide attempts than people who actually die from suicide.
>
> (Hadaya 2015, 5)

The death of these young people constitutes a tragic loss not only for society, but also for their families and friends. As Anderson points out, this trauma is disastrous for other family members, who often suffer for years on end. Siblings can be greatly disadvantaged in their development through suicide and even become at risk themselves. Suicides are greatly upsetting to the surrounding society, especially in schools and universities, where they can set off waves of attempted or achieved suicides (Anderson 2009, 219ff).

An overview of the extent of suicide worldwide is shown in Figure 6.6.

In this graph, we see a dramatic increase in the age group 15 to 30, above all in countries with low and middle incomes, with a figure of 600,000 deaths for adolescents, and in the high-income countries almost 200,000 suicides.

There is a clear gender-specific difference. Male adolescents between ages 15 and 24 manage to commit suicide much more frequently than do girls in this age group – by a ratio of 3:1. "Hard" methods such as shooting (when firearms are easy to come by) and hanging, which quickly lead to death, are preferred with little chance of being saved when found. Girls most often choose an overdose of some medication, so that they can be saved when discovered.

Nevertheless, the rate of suicide *attempts* is considerably higher – in fact, four times as high – for girls than for boys (Arnett and Hughes 2012, 477). In the last 20 years, focus has been given in the pedagogical and social areas on preventing suicide and suicide attempts. The number of adolescent suicides has fallen – in the UK, by 38% for the age group 10 to 19 between 1997 and 2003. After a crisis intervention center was established in Austria, the suicide rate fell from 28.3 per 100,000 of the population – one of the highest in the world – to 15.6 per 100,000 in 2006; this means a 45% drop (in Vienna, 61%). Presently the suicide rate is 11.8 per 100,000. Taking suicidal thoughts seriously has led to helping potential suicide attempters to get professional help in time (Sonneck et al. 2008, 66).

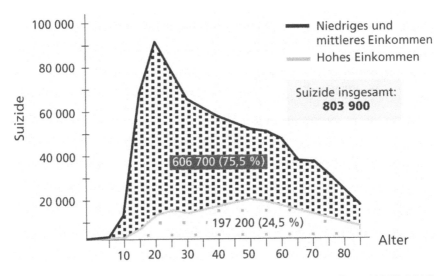

Figure 6.6 Worldwide suicides in relation to age and income (from WHO 2014)

248   Lost by the wayside – overstepping limits

Hughes describes the shock he felt at age 13 when a classmate took his life:

> I remember (MH) a boy at my school, Martin, who hanged himself early one Saturday morning. I think we were about 13. The story going around school first thing on Monday morning was that he had been caught shoplifting and that the police were going to call round to talk to his mother. He had ridden his bike to the Duke's Drive (part of our school cross-country running route). . . . He threw a rope over a branch of one of the trees that lined the drive, leaned his bike against the tree, balanced on the cross bar and saddle then kicked the bike away. There was a hushed and shocked reverence to the whispered conversations in the playground and on our way into school assembly; the head teacher John Scott, took the opportunity for a moving tribute, a minute of silence and a warning that there was no problem that couldn't be faced up to. By the end of the day some boys were re-enacting what we thought had happened right from the shoplifting through the final awful seconds for Martin, alone and miserable in a cold dawn. Perhaps those play actors were coming to terms in some way with the enormity of what had now become a personal experience for us all. Even now, when I meet old school friends from 50-plus years ago we still talk about Martin and why he "did it". What effect did it have on us?
>
> (Arnett and Hughes 2012, 477)

The children managed to work through this shock by replaying the terrible hours between the shoplifting and Martin's suicide. In play, they identified with Martin, attempting to make the incomprehensible comprehensible. Children spontaneously develop healing powers through their games, then employing these to master their experiences. A shock can be better mentally "processed" through identification. None of the students attempted suicide. This terrible experience was instructive for the others – an experience that the principal used to give the students confidence that every problem can be solved when one deals with it.

One important point made in the WHO study "Preventing Suicide" could be applied to Martin's case. For him, the pressure he felt after his mother informed the police became unbearable, and he took his own life as a way of escaping this situation. Accordingly, WHO recommends any punitive measures *immediately* after an adolescent misdeed; this minimizes his lurking fear of the consequences and the attendant pressure towards suicide.

Psychoanalytical understanding of psychic motives for suicide

Peter Turrini has attempted to show the contradictory inner forces for and against suicide:

> *A suicide*
> *Is something remarkable.*
> *One plunges*

Into one's own meat
But feels
Nothing.
No blood sprays.
One sees
A long cut
And thinks:
I don't want
To die.

(Peter Turrini, "In the Name of Love" (2005), *Poems*, 91.
Copyright Suhrkamp Verlag, translation McQuade)

How can the question of why a healthy young human being intentionally ends her life be answered from a psychoanalytic point of view? As opposed to a sociological perspective, which attempts to establish societal and economic reasons for suicide, psychoanalysis turns its attention to conflicts within the adolescent's inner world. What is occurring in the adolescent's psyche that can evoke thoughts of suicide, following him like a compulsion and finally causing him to make concrete plans? What occurs on the emotional level between the planning and the carrying out of a suicide? Will the suicide attempt be carried out "unsuccessfully", in order for somebody to save the attempter? Which inner forces are competing with each other?

Freud addressed the question of why adolescents so often submit to the death wish just at the time when they are undergoing a reawakening of drives, sexual curiosity and massive desires to satisfy the (opposite) life force. In his examination of melancholy and sadism, Freud discerned a struggle between two opposite drives. A strong inner force, a destructive component of the superego, "often enough succeeds in driving the ego into death, if the latter does not fend off its tyrant in time by the change round into mania" (Freud 1932, 53). How does this cruel superego "work"? Freud speaks of a sadistic, extremely rigid superego that expresses itself as guilt feelings – or more often as criticism – and "extraordinary harshness and severity" (Ibid).

Melanie Klein (1928) detected a connection between this archaic superego and the early stages of the Oedipus complex, where the child experiences its parents not as two separate people, but as a single dangerous, threatening "monster".

Freud understood the competition between life and death wishes as taking place in suicidal fantasies. Here is an example of a male adolescent, Donnie, 16 years old:

When Sandy told me she wanted to break up, I thought there was no point in going on. I loved her so much. I wanted to spend the rest of my life with her. So I started thinking about killing myself. I imagined how I could do it and what kind of note I'd leave my parents. Then I started thinking about my parents and my little sister, and I thought of them at the funeral crying and being so sad, and I knew I couldn't go through with it. I realized I didn't really want to die; I just wanted everything to be okay again.

(quoted in Bell 1998, 176)

Discussion

After separating from his girlfriend, Donnie at first thinks he cannot live without her. The first romantic love is a reminder of the first loving pair – mother and baby – which unconsciously activates early memories of being stroked and loved: memories of (in psychoanalytical terms) the good, ideal breast that carries everything good in it and secures the baby's survival, or of the absent breast – the unavailable mother; this polarization is operative as long as the baby has not internalized a whole object, i.e., a mother with her good and bad aspects. Since the unconscious is incapable of negation, the absent mother is experienced as a bad mother who leaves the baby alone and refuses to fulfill its momentary needs. Donnie also idealizes his girlfriend, with whom he wanted to spend the "rest of his life". Here, there is no realistic image of Sandy, but probably only an idealized image. The transformation of love into hate and murderous rage is completely blocked. In his essay "Mourning and Melancholia" (Freud 1915, SE XIV), Freud showed how the ego splits itself after losing a love object – just as the baby did. Donnie's hatred towards the loved person who left him is redirected towards this part of himself who is identified with the loved/hated person. Only when the person observes a part of himself as an object can he split it off and want to kill it. How close the first love is to the mother is shown by Donnie's thoughts, who writes a farewell to his parents – and not to Sandy. He first enjoys the thought of how his parents and little sister will weep and grieve at his burial. Many conscious and unconscious insults and impositions from childhood are presumably revitalized in this fantasy; Donnie wants to punish his parents by taking the dearest thing to them, namely his own life. Then, however, he recalls affectionate memories of his parents and sister, and his life forces gain the upper hand: he wishes to live, wants everything to be "ok" again. In Donnie's fantasy of his own burial, we see a separation between body and the bodiless ego. The reality of death's finality is denied, resulting in a "good surviving ego" plus an evil body – derived according to Campell (1999, 77) from the idea of a union with the evil, archaic mother.

Suicidal behavior is often hidden behind so-called tests of courage that actually are games with death. Here, Heuves describes a test of courage as a kind of Russian roulette:

> David is thirteen years old. He is under treatment due to episodes of depression. In one session, he confesses to a game he has been playing with himself for a few weeks. He makes an appointment with himself for a certain day and time. Then, he goes to a four-lane, busy road near his school, counts to thirteen with his eyes closed, and then crosses the street without looking. He calls this exercise "the mastering of fear". He has done it three times, and the third time, a car was barely able to swerve around him with its brakes screeching. To his own surprise and with horror, he realized he had never thought that the exercise could really have a fatal outcome.
>
> (Heuves 2010, 122)

Only in the session with his therapist does David realize that he was risking his life; it is as if he had split off his capacity for taking care of himself. The therapist is meant to take care of him and assume the fear for his survival. Although these covert suicidal attempts were not consciously planned by David, the risk of their succeeding was no less substantial.

Death from "accidents", particularly automobile accidents, is the most common cause of death for adolescents. In the USA, 45% of adolescents who die between ages 15 and 24 do so from accidents, 16% from acts of violence and 12% through suicide (Balk 2014, 64). How many of these accidents were actually covert suicides cannot be determined.

The particular susceptibility adolescents have for suicidal thoughts and suicide attempts has come to be considered a serious problem by pedagogues and parents in the last 20 years. It is now common knowledge how important it is to take adolescents' remarks concerning death seriously. Anderson cites a series of risk factors that point to the planning of a suicide.

The following is a list of risk factors which can be borne in mind:

1   Preoccupation with themes of death expressed in talking or writing
2   Expressing suicidal thoughts or threats
3   Actual suicidal threats or gestures, even in the distant past
4   Prolonged periods of depression, such as change in sleeping patterns, too much or too little sleep or sudden extreme changes in weight or eating
5   Withdrawal and isolation from family and friends
6   A history of prolonged family conflicts and instability
7   Deteriorating academic performance reflected in lower grades, dropping lectures and tutorials, and dropping out of school or college activities
8   Pending disciplinary issues in school or college
9   A history of severe or prolonged bullying
10 A history of family suicides
11 Persistent abuse of drugs or alcohol
12 Major personality and behavioral changes indicated by excessive anxiety, or nervousness, angry outbursts, apathy, or lack of interest in personal appearance or the opposite sex
13 Recent loss of close relationship through death or suicide, or a suicide within school or college
14 Making final arrangements, leaving a 'goodbye' note, drawing up a will, or giving away prized possessions
15 Telling someone of their state and intentions

(Anderson 2009, 232ff)

Close observation of the adolescent's behavior by family members and friends can help assess – or reduce – the risk of suicide. The mere fact that close friends and family members are paying attention can send a signal to the suicidal adolescent that it matters whether or not she lives.

Struggle between the life and death wish

Hanna Segal discusses how the life wish can automatically determine the behavior even of a suicidal adolescent during a suicide attempt, allowing them to remain alive. In her essay "On the Clinical Usefulness of the Concept of Death Instinct" (1993), Segal contends that it is not death which causes pain, but rather the wish to live. She begins with a quote from *Martin Eden*, a novel by Jack London:

> Martin commits suicide by drowning. As he sinks he automatically tries to swim. "It was the automatic instinct to live. He ceased swimming, but the moment he felt water rising above his mouth his hands struck out sharply with a lifting movement. 'This is the will to live', he thought, and the thought was accompanied by a sneer."
>
> (London 1909, quoted in Segal 1993, 55)

In this description, Jack London reveals the hate and distaste Martin feels for the part of him that wants to live.

> "The will to live," he thought disdainfully. . . . "The hurt was not death" was the thought that oscillated through his reeling consciousness. It was life – the pangs of life – this awful suffocating feeling. It was the last blow life could deal him.
>
> (London 1909, Ibid)

London shows Martin's derision for his own wish to live on. The pain of life – this awful, pressing feeling that Martin Eden feels at the end of his life. Hanna Segal interprets the conflict between the life and death wish by contending that all pain comes from life and vitality. In *Beyond the Pleasure Principle* (1920), Freud describes the death instinct as a biological drive to return to the inorganic. He also mentions the Nirvana principle as a formula for forgetting everything – an important motive in suicidal thoughts. The life instinct aims towards life and reproduction (thus including sexuality). The death wish aims towards destruction, dissolution and death. Freud developed the concept of the death instinct in explaining the phenomenon of repetition compulsion, masochism and the murderous superego of a melancholic person.

The destructive and traumatizing influence a suicidal parent can have on a child is revealed in many case studies spanning two or more generations. A child who has to live for years with the suicidal threats of a mother or father is placed under enormous pressure. The parent is conveying to the child that he is not a sufficient reason for supplying life with meaning, which can be taken as an erasure of the child's right to exist. Here is an example of one suicidal adolescent who turned to the adolescent department at the Tavistock Clinic, followed by reflections of John Cleese (of *Monty Python's Flying Circus*) on the traumatizing experiences connected with thoughts of his mother.

Anne was 16 when she turned to the Tavistock Clinic after numerous suicide attempts. She had fainted after inhaling noxious substances, had taken an overdose of sleeping pills and cut herself substantially. These attempts were of varying seriousness – some were more symbolic gestures, whereas others led to protracted treatment in intensive care. When she entered a state of fear, she escaped by numbing herself with drugs or gas from a heating unit in order to forget her fear. Her social worker knew neither Anne's nor her family's name and felt burdened by her case, which she felt was a full-time job.

> Anne, a young woman of 16, was referred to us following multiple suicide attempts. These ranged from using lighter fuel and making herself unconscious, to overdoses, to cutting herself. These attempts were of varying severity – some seemed merely gestures while others, really put her life in danger requiring treatment in intensive care units. When any level of anxiety seemed to be mobilised in her, she would become agitated and want to run away to seek oblivion, either partially with drugs or gas, or to cross the line towards clear suicide attempts. She was an 'anonymous' girl, no-one knew her real name or had contact with her family and she was taken on as the responsibility of social services. Her social worker found her a tremendous burden, almost a full time job.
>
> Anne said she had run away from a family in which she had been sexually abused by her father who had threatened to kill himself if it ever came out. Anne was also sabotaging every kind of help she was offered and at this time, had been though our care, three or four social services homes, an adolescent unit and several foster placements. She seemed to find good experiences as disturbing as bad ones, for example, she was placed for a time with a foster mother who she said she really liked but still ran away suggesting that for her to be having loving feelings towards helpful figures stirred up emotions that she could not stand.
>
> (Anderson 1998, 76ff)

Discussion

Anne's behavior communicates her deep desperation, in that she elicits the same desperation in her therapists who wish to help her. By running away, she shows she has despaired of finding a fitting place on earth, a place where she could find peace or warmth. She could only stand intense feelings where they fell at the border between life and death. She could not ask for help or establish contact to her family: she was convinced that her father would kill himself if she told the therapists his name.

As Anderson remarks:

> It was as though her loving feelings about her family and her sense of needing to be cared for were so mixed up with her hatred, her sense that this was a

254   Lost by the wayside – overstepping limits

terrible place where terrible things had been done to her were quite mixed up with her sense that this was *her* family and included even her father, and this confusion was experienced with anyone else who behaved in a parental way towards her. She did not know whether to love or hate, to stay or go.

(Anderson 1998, 68)

In addition, the intensity of the concern she elicited in therapists through her high-risk behavior seems to have been her only form of a close emotional relationship – where Anne staged the same confusion experienced by an abused child. Sexual abuse does not only damage corporal integrity, but also causes grave mental confusion when the foundations of security are hurt and perverted by parents. It was hardly possible to create a therapeutic space between Anne's life-and-death themes, where her mixed feelings, ideas and fantasies concerning sexual abuse could be investigated and worked through.

Anne could not directly ask for help:

Anne could not seek help straightforwardly. As soon as she found something good that might put her in touch with the family that she had lost, she became persecuted and had to escape though escape was usually to a false haven. Often it was a group of friends who would share her wish for oblivion and they would sniff gas together, as she had done with her brother, as though this group of young people in trouble like herself were turned to in preference to the adult world which had let her down so badly. What particularly struck me about Anne was that unlike so many young people in London, she really had been offered good help; she had not been treated with disdain by the hospital which had admitted her unconscious from the local train station, she had been assigned a social worker who had worked tirelessly with her, she had been offered a whole range of help but somehow, all this seemed either to make no difference or to make her worse.

(Ibid, 68ff)

This sadistic approach to offers of help, which elicited a corresponding reaction on the helpers' part, is important in understanding the dynamic of Anne's inner world.

This process often has a sadistic overtone; there is gratification as well as punishment in the self-destructive activity and this sense of revenge and triumph that also accompanies much suicidal behavior is another reason why we find it so disturbing to become involved.

(Ibid, 70)

This particularly affected the social worker actively engaged in Anne's case. Anne kept coming back to her. We can assume that Anne was trying to establish the same cruel emotional relationship with her that she had experienced with her father. Instead of facing the psychic pain of what it means to have a father who abused her and simultaneously threatened her with suicide, she becomes her father. She has identified with the father and treats the social worker as her father treated her, bringing the social worker into the role of the fearful, guilty child. Instead of being able to separate herself emotionally from her father, she remains intimately connected to him; she is he. This connection between the self and others is a surprising permutation suicidal adolescents turn to in order to not renounce their loved and hated object.

In a loving and caring relationship to parents, the destructivity native to all of us is compensated for by love. If either the maternal function of lovingly holding her baby (holding function) or the baby's aggression looms too large, then integration with the idealized image of the mother and the self-image as good and bad becomes impossible. In Anne's case, presumably the evil, cruel aspects of her father (we know little of her relationship to her mother) were not integrated into her personality and threaten her stability.

Now on to an example of how a child found a robust manner of dealing with his mother's permanent suicide threats. In his autobiography, John Cleese describes a situation when he cannot stand her constant complaints and her wish to die. He remembers on one occasion when he was listening to her as she methodically itemized all the reasons why she didn't want to go on living, while he experienced his powerlessness to help. He remembers saying:

> "Mother, I have an idea." She said: "Oh? What's that?" And he continued: "I know a little man who lives in Fulham, and if you're still feeling this way next week, I could have a word with him if you like – but only if you like – and he can come down to Weston and kill you." There was silence and then his mother said: "Oh God, I've gone too far." And then she cackled with laughter. "I don't think I ever loved her as much as I did at that moment."
>
> (Cleese 2014, 13ff)

Discussion

What exactly is happening between the mother and the seven-year-old son? Undoubtedly, John perceived these thoughts of suicide as a massive aggression against him. He, her son, does not constitute a sufficient reason for his mother to remain alive. His murderous rage is camouflaged as an "offer of help" – finding a murderer who accomplishes what she wishes, thus almost fulfilling her wish. He twice emphasizes he will do this only if his mother wants it. After a long silence, the tension is dissolved in a laugh where mother and son presumably share the same tension and resolution. *So, Anyway* – in the full range of its connotations – is also the title of Cleese's autobiography.

Why could little John deal in this way with the fatal threat he was so often exposed to? Was it his robust nature? His resilience? John had a very good relationship to his sensitive but rather passive father, whom he very much admired. Cleese also

256   Lost by the wayside – overstepping limits

experienced moments of bonding with his depressed mother that enabled him to bear the burden of her continual thoughts of suicide and find a humorous approach. This form of black, off-beat humor found its place in the Monty Python brand.

In conclusion, I will describe the political, social, psychological and therapeutic measures that have considerably reduced suicide rates. The WHO has set a goal of sinking the worldwide suicide rate 10% by 2020 (WHO 2014, 2).

Measures that help to reduce suicide

1   Hindering access (through legislation) to the means of suicide, including: firearms, medications, drugs and other addictive substances. The affective suicide impulse can abate when the pistol or sleeping pills are not immediately accessible and the suicide attempter calms himself, for instance by sleeping on his decision.
2   Precise documentation regarding the age, gender and method of suicide or suicide attempt.
3   Increased attention by government agencies, including Ministries of Health and all social agencies.
4   Involving the media in reporting responsibly on suicide. In Austria, there exists a voluntary declaration on the part of print media and public radio and television that they will not report on suicides, including spectacular cases. This has helped considerably to drastically sink the number of suicides.
5   Educating social workers in matters pertaining to suicide, and planning the psychological care of people who have attempted suicide. This includes above all direct psychological help in the hospital after a suicide attempt.
6   Increased attention to the problem of suicide and discouraging the stigmatization and persecution of suicide attempters (until 1961, attempting suicide was a criminal act in the UK).
7   Increased sensitivity on the part of teachers, educators, parents and adolescents. The most helpful discussions take place between suicidal adolescents and schoolteachers.

In most European cities, there are crisis intervention centers for anyone undergoing a psychic crisis. When someone talks of or announces suicide, friends or acquaintances should recommend she get psychotherapeutic help. Here is a statement by Tomandl:

> 50% of the people who come to us for treatment have thoughts of suicide. But we lose very few of them to suicide, because these people have turned to us in time and want to get help from us. Naturally, it is easier to consider further steps with people who are willing to be helped, and to actually help them.
>
> (Hadaya 2015, 24)

It is very important that people know that there exist such crisis intervention centers to which friends or family members can be directed. A suicidal crisis can also constitute a turning point in life and open new possibilities.

> There, we attempt to give support where possible, in other words, we have very close contact to these people who come to us. Thoughts of suicide do not necessarily mean that the person is truly in danger of committing suicide. It is often a cry for help and a cry outwards, in order for something to change in life. These are often very important changes that are germinated, so to speak – which is also confirmed by the study on the Golden Gate Bridge, that those are short isolated events and often life can become very positive, so to speak. . . . One can say that the crisis is a low point and also a turning point and often, many things can be changed in a positive direction.
>
> (Ibid, 24)

Tomandl makes clear that a large percentage of adolescents can learn from their crisis and their mastering it. A crisis is a low point where one can part with old things and new things can be born. We learn something eminently new about ourselves, something we probably have never yet experienced.

Every adult who talks with an adolescent about his suicidal crisis can greatly help him. Nobody should be afraid to speak openly with the adolescent and make him understand that his life is still in front of him and he has the possibility to change things, whereas suicide constitutes a definitive end.

Help from friends

Samira Hadaya asked Tomandl what an adolescent can do in order to help a friend in crisis. Here, his answer:

> The most important thing is to give the friend attention, be interested, actively ask him questions such as "Hey, you just said you don't want to live anymore? Tell me what has happened in your life?" Suicidal thoughts do not fall from the sky without any reason, but always have some origin or catalyst, a reason somebody has the feeling their life cannot continue further. One can offer conversation and motivate the person, or consider who else could be a trusted conversational partner for him. If there are too few people, for example as with the client I previously mentioned, one can also motivate her, as in "Hey, I will accompany you to the counseling center for children and adolescents, for instance this one. I will go with you, I'll show my interest and not let you down." I think that's the most important message that we want to hear from our friends when we are in a crisis, that someone is there who is not indifferent to how we are doing. . . . And often, it's enough for one or

two people to be involved for the person in crisis. It could be love problems, it could be a work problem etc. . . . But the most important thing is a heart-to-heart talk with the person in crisis, where you show your interest."

(Hadaya 2015, 25)

It is indeed important to emotionally engage the suicide-endangered adolescent, in order to show her that she is important to others. Sometimes it is necessary to accompany her to a counseling center. The message should be: "I will stay with you, no matter what happens, and stand with you." This is also the best way of ameliorating one's worries about a suicidal person.

Notes

1 I provide a thorough case study of Malcolm in my book *The Young Child and Their Parents* (Diem-Wille 2009/2012).
2 This was a qualitative investigation, with data being gathered through narrative interviews.
3 The story given here of Sarah's case mostly follows the descriptions of Pankratz (1997, 50–65).
4 Description of this case study as described by Pankratz (1997, 94–109), interpretation by the author.

Epilogue

This book has described the stormy transition from childhood to adulthood, a transition set into motion by hormonal development. Every reader must have experienced these turbulences to a lesser or greater extent; some adults are still captive to their adolescent attitude, and some aspects of our personality remain "adolescent", rebellious or non-conformist. These emotional, impulsive elements arise from the revival of early Oedipal desires containing a sexual and aggressive component – but now in a sexually mature body. I would like my book to encourage its readers towards reflection, to afford them moments of recognition, surprise or explanations for their own earlier behavior.

The overarching question is whether an adolescent son or daughter's "crazy" behavior constitutes a necessary component of this developmental spurt or is instead an indication of a massive disturbance or pathology. Steps in adolescent development that lead to greater independence demand a difficult balancing act from parents: they must "let go" without breaking their ties to the adolescent. In my book I have described this "normal drama" with its extreme emotional vacillations – a "normality in crisis" – both theoretically and with examples of "normal" adolescents as they develop in feeling and thinking. Our goal should not be to suppress or conceal the manifestations of adolescence, the psychic working through of biological maturation processes. On the contrary: an adolescent who exhibits no characteristics of this stormy developmental phase would worry psychoanalysts, and indicates deep disturbances or inhibitions.

The great fear we have of ending a phase of life is often unconscious, because it actualizes earlier experiences of separation. Isca Salzberger-Wittenberg (2013, 12) writes:

> The dread evoked by even ordinary endings comes understandable if we realize that they stir up fears of the loss of security, of being abandoned, left to die.
>
> These powerful feelings stem from earliest infancy, the time when our life of being carried within the womb comes to an end, and the cord that connected us to mother is cut. Equally our excitement and anxieties at beginnings has its roots in the experience of the new-born opening his eyes to a whole

260 Epilogue

new world, one that as well as being terrifyingly unfamiliar, is full of wonder and beauty.

In my book, I have illuminated the massive impact on the inner world of parents by their children's projections and the mastering of this transitional phase, as well as parents' unconscious envy of their children's budding sexuality. By describing everyday scenes, diary entries and statements of adolescents, I attempted to render comprehensible the wide range of behavior in puberty and construct a link to theory. The goal of my theoretical explications was to achieve a better understanding and reduce the fear elicited by the surprising transformations of adolescents – but also to encourage attention on dangerous symptoms of withdrawal or self-harm. This double strategy also corresponds to the double strategy required for parents, teachers and educators of adolescents: to be open to new adolescent behaviors, but also to observe adolescents carefully and accompany them emotionally – a difficult balancing act.

Another goal was to introduce a new perspective by showing hidden dimensions behind manifest behavior, using a psychoanalytic perspective. Adolescents' attribution and displacement of their problems onto parents or educators – "my parents are starting to get on my nerves" – can irritate parents who care for their children (or, when they have access to the psychoanalytical perspective, perhaps amuse them). It is helpful when parents can exchange their impressions with one another. Single parents are particularly dependent for their assessments of their adolescent child's behavior on a support system of friends, so as not to be defenseless against their child's massive projections.

An important means of mastering the turbulences of adolescence is adolescent humor, particularly within her peer group, which allows her to not take her problems over-seriously.

Transition to young adulthood is marked by relinquishing dependency on other people (parents, teachers), instead reconstructing them as stable images in the inner world, where they become a source of encouragement towards independence and autonomous development of the personality. This process is, as I have shown, only possible after a phase of mourning for what has been given up. In a slow process – as with putting together a puzzle – parts can be integrated into the personality piece for piece, after intense conflicts and altercations. Only then can the capacity for closeness and sexuality in a stable relationship be developed. Finding one's own position in the world, a "mind of one's own", and one's own position in the world depends on the capability for experiencing and mastering love and separations.

> For the task of becoming oneself, now and always, involves relinquishing the denigrated and idealized version of the self, of other people and of relationships, in favor of the real. It involves renegotiating dreams, choices and hopes, whether self-generated or imposed from without. It involves tolerating opportunities lost, and roads not taken. . . . These sorts of losses test the

capacity to mourn, to feel remorse, to take responsibility, to experience guilt and also gratitude.

(Waddell 2002, 177)

Thus, becoming an adult is no easy goal, but remains a lifelong task, a continual aspiration that can never be fully attained. The restructuring of the psyche and inner world in adolescence also constitutes a new chance for adolescents, psychotherapists and parents. Massive symptoms can no longer be so easily ignored and suppressed and thus often serve as an impetus for the adolescent to get therapeutic help.

The stormy period of travelling from childhood into adulthood has been compared with the journey from a relinquished motherland to a new country (Grinberg and Grinberg 1989). The goal is often indistinct where the emigrant will land and how quickly she will feel at home there. The new territory in adult life is genital sexuality. Which sexual identity will I discover in myself? The core of sexual orientation is already set at the age of one-and-a-half to two years old, but the time of its discovery is open – something that cannot be consciously and reasonably controlled, but instead explored and accepted. The adolescent attitude of fearful avoidance often remains in place for decades, until somebody has the confidence at the age of 30 or 40 to acknowledge her homosexuality, to "come out". Sometimes, the impulse of a man to be together with another man sexually is only given free rein in old age – perhaps only in an exceptional situation. But within the heterosexual group, sexual desires can go unspoken and only experienced with prostitutes in a "strict chamber". The force of sexuality, intensive pleasure and the drive towards satisfaction can be repressed for an entire life. The fear of closeness is often even more threatening because it reveals wishes for dependency and neediness: a 70-year-old man about to embark on a new, intense relationship can almost collide with a streetcar – presumably wishing unconsciously to punish himself or to see whether the woman walking beside him pulls him away and saves his life. Sometimes it is only possible in old age – within hailing distance of death – to fulfill the wish for emotional and sexual intimacy. All of these themes have their origins in adolescence, but they can be avoided for an entire life or be satisfied only very late (or never, for that matter).

In his book *Rites of Passage* (1980), for which he received the Nobel Prize, William Golding tells the story of Reverend Colley from the perspective of Talbot, a young aristocrat, who investigates Colley's case during a six-month trip to Australia. After the sailors had gotten Colley drunk and involved him in homosexual acts, he died from shame over the homosexual lust he experienced during an orgiastic party. Talbort attempts to reconstruct these events from Colley's diaries. When the sailors mention the participation of an officer, the investigation is broken off by the captain since homosexual acts ("buggery") are punishable by death. Colley receives a burial with full honors on the ship, and the case is closed. The search for sexual identity, often fraught with shame and guilt, is thus not always finished in puberty, but remains a challenge for

262 Epilogue

one's entire life. Golding employs the symbolism of a ship journey and coming-of-age rituals in his book.

As with emigration, which affords the enriching possibility of becoming a citizen of two cultures, the transition from childhood into the adult world can also be enriching when the person manages to be an adult and also remain a child. Retaining the child's openness, playfulness, emotional intensity and joy in experimentation and understanding one's "inner child" can be one result of a psychoanalytic investigation and working through of one's own life story. An adult must accept the difference between his desired and actual place in society, which minimizes a child's fantasies of omnipotence, so that a playful investigation of outer and inner reality enables innovation and creativity.

In the second part of my book, I described the problems that arise when the border to antisocial and destructive behavior is crossed. Adolescents often do not know where the borders to extreme and abusive behavior lie. I described the problem areas of violence, teenage pregnancy, and thoughts of and attempts at suicide and discussed possible causes and solutions using case studies. These case studies should afford insight into the occasionally amorphous character of these problems, sometimes quickly addressed by professionals, sometimes only with progress over several years. However, if the chance is not exploited, addressing such problems can take much longer later (or too late), when an adolescent commits drastic acts or even takes her own life. Numerous pessimistic reports about outsiders and violence can be relativized when we look closely at the results of psychotherapeutic work with these adolescents. We then see that behind an apparent coldness and readiness to violence is hidden a great vulnerability and longing, manifested either in violence and self-harm or in the acceptance of emotional help. Therapists must nevertheless be prepared first to be employed as transferential objects and second to be confronted with all the attendant disappointments, reproaches and rage over experienced humiliations and deprivations – all of which they must tolerate and contain. The therapist's interpretation of psychotic hallucinations and images can also be a relief for the patient; it helps to recognize the childlike mode of perception an adolescent resorts to in the face of threatening inner forces.

A question often posed is why children from the same family develop so differently: why does one child become alcoholic, violent or schizophrenic, while his siblings have a good development? There are three dimensions of this divergent development: 1) the divergent temperaments of various babies, 2) the divergent positions of siblings and 3) family circumstances, as well as the factor of "resilience".

Psychoanalysts presume that babies have various temperaments from birth on: approximately one-quarter of babies are particularly robust, patient and resilient, approximately one-half have an average temperament and one-quarter are delicate, easily irritated, difficult to calm and impatient. Parents require a special approach to create appropriate conditions for their sensitive baby – for instance, only presenting it with one stimulus when it is easily distracted. It might be necessary to begin breast-feeding in a quiet, dark room, for instance. It is important that parents recognize the particular personality of their baby. How well parents cope with their baby's temperament depends on their own personalities.

Case studies show how divergent the development of children from the same parents can be. Sometimes, the same burdensome family situation causes one child to become a dropout from society, another to become a criminal, and another to become a good citizen. Every child takes up consciously and unconsciously different aspects from the same family, as one famous analyst (an expert on schizophrenia) described her own family (Parker 1972a, 1972b). She describes herself as a problem child who grew up in a problem family and "by slow and painful steps, became a woman, a doctor, a psychiatrist and a psychoanalyst" (Parker 1987, IX). Of three children, one of them became a schizophrenic and killed himself, her sister fell into depression and became an alcoholic, and the author went to medical school and studied psychoanalysis. She turned her attention to her beloved brother's illness. In her book *My Language is Me* (Parker 1975), she describes the analysis of a schizophrenic adolescent who developed his own language that enabled him to withdraw into his private, psychotic world in the face of upsetting and deracinating feelings and events. She describes the special kind of communicative dysfunction in families where one family member exhibits schizophrenic reactions.

In the last 30 years, psychiatrists have systematically addressed the problem of why different people master the same traumatic experiences, disadvantageous family constellations, deprivation and psychic and sexual abuse. Under the rubric "resilience", researchers have attempted to find out why some people deal with protracted stress, poverty and duress better than other people who are exposed to the same disadvantages. Resilience is understood as an "interactive phenomenon", with factors both of nurture and risk examined for how they affect this capacity. "The most powerful influence on our capacity to manage life's hurdles is the quality of care we received in childhood, especially the earliest years," writes Kraemer (1999, 273). This entails the capability of reacting flexibly and elastically to difficulties, with the courage and self-confidence to master them. The greatest risk is posed by early neglect and physical or psychic attacks, marital problems and permanent conflicts between parents. In academic studies, risk factors have been closely examined as to whether children of divorced parents or adopted children have less resilience than other children. Burdensome familiar conflicts are often handed down through the generations, as described by Fraiberg as "ghosts in the nursery" or by Byng-Hall (1995) as "family scripts" that can only be revised with difficulty. The unconscious handing down of these fraught modes of behavior often subverts a parent's conscious wish to do things differently with his/her own children. The experiences children have in mastering minor difficulties, learning to deal with frustration and short separations, are seen as positive factors towards developing resilience. One example from research is that children who regularly have experienced happy separations from their parents – sleeping over at their grandparents' or friends' – can later master far better complicated experiences of separation when in the hospital (Stacey et al. 1970). Resilience does not mean toughness, but rather flexibility. In general, boys are less resilient and flexible than girls: even before birth, miscarriages are more common with boys than with girls, as well as the probability of birth defects. Male babies are generally fussier, with a greater incidence of dyslexia, autism, hyperactivity and delayed development. In adolescence, they are more likely to come into conflict with the law, and suicide rates are higher for boys than for girls (Kraemer 1999, 276). Attractive looks and above-average intelligence also are favorable conditions for resilience.

People who enjoy good development in spite of difficult socio-economic or family circumstances, in spite of neglect and abuse by parents, often had the luck of having some trusted person within their extended family or perhaps a teacher. Experiencing some affectionate relationship during the first months of life is often enough to provide some measure of immunity against later suffering and unhappiness (Kraemer 1999, 276). Irritation and contrariness, rebellion and resistance can function as protection. Fanny Kemble describes her cruel childhood, where her parents forced her at the age of four to don a dunce cap and stand in the street. She was meant to be humiliated and mocked, but she danced through the front door and encouraged passersby to admire her. "I never cried, I never sulked, I never resented, lamented or repented either my ill doings or their consequences, but accepted them, alike with a philosophical buoyancy of spirit which was the despair of my poor bewildered trainers" (Kemble 1879, quoted in Kraemer 1999, 274). Instead of drilling and demanding absolute obedience, parents should provide affection and empathy, as well as a readiness to stand by their children during the mastering of small frustrations. The goal is helping the child to accept his own body and capabilities and develop his own independent opinion. Only a child who has felt understood can later understand other people.

Bibliography

Aichhorn, A. (1925). *Verwahrloste Jugend. Die Psychoanalyse in der Fürsorgeerziehung.* Stuttgart, Wien: Hans Huber Verlag, p. 9, 1977 ed.

Albert, M., Hurrelmann, K., Quenzel, G., and Schneekloth, U. (eds.) (2010). *Jugend 2010: Die 16. Shell Jugendstudie.* Hamburg: Fischer TB Verlag.

Alvarez, A. (1971). *The Savage God. A Study of Suicide.* London: Penguin Books.

Alvarez, A., and Reid, S. (eds.) (1999). *Autism and Personality: Findings from the Tavistock Workshop.* London and New York: Routledge.

Ammerer, H. (2006). *Krafft-Ebing, Freud und die Erfindung der Perversion (Versuch einer Einkreisung).* Marburg: Tectum.

Anderson, R. (1998). "Suicidal Behaviour and its Meaning in Adolescence", in *Facing it Out. Clinical Perspectives on Adolescent Disturbance.* London and New York: Karnac Books, pp. 65–78.

Anderson, R. (2000). "Assessing the Risk of Self-Harm in Adolescents: A Psychoanalytic Perspective", *Psychoanalytic Psychotherapy, 14(1):* 9–21.

Anderson, R. (2009). "Adolescence and the Body Ego: The Reencountering of Primitive Mental Functioning in Adolescent Development", unpublished paper presented in Vienna.

Anderson, R., and Dartington, A. (eds.) (1998). "Introduction", in *Facing it Out. Clinical Perspectives on Adolescent Disturbance.* London and New York: Karnac Books, pp. 1–6.

Archer, J. (2006). "Testosterone and Human Aggression: An Evaluation of the Challenge Hypothesis", *Neuroscience Biobehavioral Review, 30(3):* 319–345.

Arnett, J.J., and Hughes, M. (2012). *Adolescence and Emerging Adulthood. A Cultural Approach.* London and New York: Pearson.

Balk, D.E. (2014). *Dealing with Dying, Death and Grief During Adolescence.* New York: Routledge.

Bell, R. (1998). *Changing Bodies, Changing Lives* (3rd ed.). New York: Times Books.

Benslama, F. (2017). *Der Übermuslim. Was junge Menschen zur Radikalisierung treibt.* Berlin: Matthes & Seitz.

Bettelheim, Bruno (1962). *Symbolic Wounds: Puberty Rites and the Envious Male.* New York: Collier Books, 1st edition 1954.

Bick, E. (1964). "Notes on Infant Observation in Psychoanalytic Training". *International Journal of Psycho-Analysis, 45:* 558–566.

Bick, E. (1968). "The Experience of the Skin in Early Object Relations", *International Journal of Psycho-Analysis, 49:* 484–489.

266 Bibliography

Bion, W. (1956). "Development of Schizophrenic Thought", *International Journal of Psycho-Analysis, 37, part 4–5*, Vol. 37, reprinted in: *Second Thoughts. Second Thoughts on Psycho-Analysis*. London: Marsfield Library, 1967, pp. 36–42.

Bion, W. (1957a). "Differentiation of the Psychotic from the Non-psychotic Personalities", in *Second Thoughts*. London: Heinemann, 1967, pp. 43–64.

Bion, W. (1957b). "On Arrogance", in *Second Thoughts. Selected Papers on Psycho-Analysis*. London: Marsfield Library, 1967, pp. 86–82.

Bion, W. (1957c). "On Hallucination", in *Second Thoughts. Selected Papers on Psych-Analysis*. London: Marsfield Library, 1967, pp. 65–85.

Bion, W. (1959). "Attacks on Linking", in *Second Thoughts*. London: Karnac Books, 1976, pp. 93–109.

Bion, W. (1962). *Learning from Eperience*. London; Heimann Medical Books.

Bion, W. (1979). "Making the Best of a Bad Job", in *Clinical Seminars and Four Papers*. London: Karnac Books (reprinted 1994).

Bion, W. (2005). *The Tavistock Seminar* (Francesca Bion, ed.). London and New York: Karnac Books.

Birksted-Breen, D. (2016). "Editorial", *International Journal of Psycho-Analysis, 97(3)*: 559–561.

Bléandonu, G. (1990). *Wilfried Bion, His Life and Works 1897–1979*. London: Free Association Books.

Blos, P. (1962). *Adoleszenez. Eine psychoanalytische Interpretation*. Stuttgart: Klett-Cotta, 1995.

Bohleber, W. (2004). "Adoleszenz, Identität und Trauma", in Streeck-Fischer, Annette (Hrsg), *Adoleszenz – Bindung-Destuktivität*. Stuttgart: Klett-Cotta, pp. 229–242.

Britton, R. (1998). "The Missing Link: Parental Sexuality in the Oedipus Complex", in Britton, R., Feldman, M., and O'Shaughnessy, E. (eds.), *The Oedipus Complex Today. Clinical Implications*. London: Karnac Books, pp. 83–102.

Britton, R. (2014). "Die Ödipussituation: normale Entwicklung oder unterbrochene Beziehung?", in *Psychoanalyse in Europa*. Barcelona: Bulletin der EPF, pp. 59–64.

Brizendine, L. (2006). *The Female Brain*. New York: Morgan Road Book.

Brizendine, L. (2010). *The Male Brain*. New York: Random House (Harmony Books).

Bürgin, D. (2004). "Psychodynamik und Destruktivität", in Streeck-Fischer, Annette (ed.), *Adoleszenz – Binding Destruktivität*. Stuttgart: Klett-Cotta, pp. 243–266.

Busch, W. (1865). "Max und Moritz, eine Bubengeschichte in 7 Streichen", in *Das grosse Wilhelm Busch Album*. München: Bassermann.

Busch, W. (1902). *Max and Maurice. A Juvenile History in Seven Tricks* (C.T. Brooks, Transl.). Boston: Little Brown.

Byng-Hall, J. (1995). *Rewriting Family Scripts*. New York: Guilford Press.

Campell, D. (1999). "The Role of the Father in a Pre-suicidal State", in Perelberg, R.L. (ed.), *Psychoanalytic Understanding of Violence and Suicide*. London: Routledge.

Cavell, S. (2010). *Little Did I Know. Excerpts from Memory*. Stanford, CA: Stanford University Press.

Chasseguet-Smirgel, J. (1974). "Die weiblichen Schuldgefühle", in Chasseguet-Smirgel, J. (ed.), *Psychoanalyse der weiblichen Sexualität*. Frankfurt: Edition Suhrkamp, pp. 134–191.

Cleese, J. (2014). *So, Anyway . . .* London: Random House.

Coudenhove-Kalergi, B. (2013). *Zuhause ist überall. Erinnerungen*. Wien: Paul Zsolnay Verlag.

Bibliography 267

Crockett, L.J., Rafaelli, M., and Moilanen, K.L. (2003). "Adolecent Sexuality: Behaviour and Meaning", in Adams, G., and Berzonsky, M. (eds.), *Blackwell Handbook of Adolescence*. Malden, MA: Blackwell, pp. 371–392.

Diem-Wille, G. (2004). "Using the Concept of the Total Situation' in the Analysis of a Borderline Adolescent", *Journal for Child Psychotherapy, 30*: 8–329.

Diem-Wille, G. (2011). *The Early Years of Life: Psychoanalytical Development Theory According to Freud, Klein and Bion*. London: Karnac Books.

Diem-Wille, G. (2014). *Young Children and their Parents. Perspectives from Psychoanalytic Infant Observation*. London: Karnac Books.

Diem-Wille, G. (2018). *Latency: The Golden Age of Childhood*. London: Karnac Books.

Diem-Wille, G., and Turner, A. (eds.) (2012). *Die Methode der psychoanalytischen Beobachtung. Über die Bedeutung von Containment, Identifikation, Abwehr und anderen Phänomenen in der psychoanalytischen Beobachtung*. Wien: Fakultas Verlag.

Dolto, R. und Dolto-Tolitch, C. (1992). *Von den Schwierigkeiten, erwachsen zu werden*. Stuttgart: Klett-Cotta.

Duthie, J.K., Nippold, M.A., Billow, J.L., and Mansfield, T.C. (2008). "Mental Imagery of Concrete Proverbs: A Developmental Study of Children, Adolescents and Adults", *Applied Psycholinguistics, 29(1)*: 151–173.

Eisner, M. (2002). "Crime, Problem Drinking, and Drug Use: Patterns of Problem Behaviour in Cross-National Perspective", *Annals of the American Academy of Political and Social Science, 580*: 201–225.

Engel, G.L. (1962). *Psychological Development in Health and Disease*. New York: Saunders.

Erhard, J. (1998). "Liebes Tagebuch! Dir kann ich mich anvertrauen", Diplomarbeit, Universität Wien.

Erikson, E. (1950). *Childhood and Society*. New York: W.W. Norton. info

Feldman, M. (1998). "The Oedipus Complex: Manifestations in the Inner World and the Therapeutic Situation", in Britton, R., Feldman, M., and O'Shaughnessy, E. (eds.), *The Oedipus Complex Today. Clinical Implications*. London: Karnac Books.

Feldman, M. (1999). "Projektive Identifizierung: Die Einbeziehung des Analytikers", *Psyche, 8(19)*: 991–1014.

Flammer, A., and Alsaker, F.D. (2011). *Entwicklungspsychologie der Adoleszenz. Die Erschliessung innerer und äusserer Welten im Jugendalter*. Bern, Göttingen, Toronto and Seattle: Huber Verlag.

Flasar, Milena Michiko (2014). *Ich nannte ihn Krawatte*. München: Random House.

Fleck, L. (1977) *Weiblicher Orgasmus. Die sexuelle Entwicklung der Frau – psychoanalytisch gesehen*. München: Kindler Verlag.

Flynn, D. (2004). *Severe Emotional Disturbances in Children and Adolescents. Psychotherapy in Applied Contexts*. Hove and New York: Brunner-Routledge.

Fraiberg, S. (1980). "Ghosts in the Nursery: A Psychoanalytic Approach to the Problem of Impaired Mother-infant Relationship", in *Clinical Studies in Infant Mental Health. The First Year of Life*. London and New York: Tavistock Publications.

Freud, S. (1900) "The Interpretation of Dreams". S.E. V.

Freud, S. (1905). "Three Essays on the Theory of Sexuality", S.E. VII.

Freud, S. (1908a). "Creative Writers and Daydreaming", S.E. IX.

Freud, S. (1908b). "Hysterical Phantasies and their Relation to Bisexuality", S.E. IX, 157.

Freud, S. (1911). "Formulations on the Two Principles of Mental Functioning", S.E. XII. Formulierungen über die zwei Prinzipien des psychischen Geschehens, S.F. *Studienausgabe, Bd. III, Frankfurt 175*, 13–24.

268 Bibliography

Freud, S. (1912). "The Dynamics of Transference", S.E. XII, 99.

Freud, S. (1915). "Mourning and Melancholia", S.E. XIV.

Freud, S. (1917). "A Childhood Recollection from *Dichtung und Wahrheit*", S.E. XVII.

Freud, S. (1919). "A Child is Being Beaten", S.E. XVII, 177.

Freud, S. (1920). *Beyond the Pleasure Principle*. S.E. XVIII. London.

Freud, S. (1923). *The Ego and the Id*. S.E. XIX.

Freud, S. (1932). "Neuen Folge der Vorlesungen zur Einführung in die Psychoanalyse", *GW*, XV.

Freud, S. (1939). *Moses and Monotheism*. S.E. XXIII.

Freud, A. (1958). *Adolescence. Psychoanalytic Study of the Child*. New York: International University Press, Inc.

Freud, A. (1992). *The Ego and the Mechanisms of Defence*. London: Karnac Books.

Furstenberg, E.F., Brooks-Grunn, Morgan, S.P. et al. (1987). *Adolescent Mother in Later Life*. New York: Cambridge University Press.

Gavalda, A. (2004). *Ensemble, c'est tout*. Paris: Le Dilettante.

Goethe, J.W. (2003). *The Autobiography: Truth and Poetry: From My Own Life*. Honolulu: University Press of the Pacific.

Goethe, J.W. (2004). *The Sorrows of Young Werther*. Edited and Translated by Appelbaum, S. Mineola: Dover Publication (first publisher in 1774).

Golding, William (1980). *Rites of Passage*. London: Faber and Faber (reprinted 2001).

Gone With the Wind, Film, Metro-Goldwyn-Mayer, 1939.

Gottfredson, M., and Hirschi, T. (1990). *A General Theory of Crime*. Stanford, CA: Stanford University Press.

Green, A. (1993). *On Private Madness*. Madison, CT: Int. Universities Press.

Grillparzer, F. (1847). "Libussa", in Bachmaier, H. (ed.), *Franz Grillparzer. Werke in sechs Bänden*. Frankfurt: Deutsche Klassiker Verlag, 1979.

Grinberg, L., and Grinberg, R. (1989). *Psychoanalytic Perspectives on Migration and Exile*. New Haven and London: Yale University Press.

Hadaya, S. (2015). "Selbstmord bei Jugendlichen. Welche psychischen Probleme sind ausschlaggebend für einen Selbstmordversuch bei adoleszenten Mädchen?" Vorwissenschaftliche Arbeit, Wien.

Hall, S.G. (1904). *Adolescence: Its Psychology and its Relation to Physiology, Anthropology, Sociology, Sex, Crime, Religion, and Education* (Vol. 1 & 2). Englewood Cliffs, NJ: Prentice-Hall.

Halpern, C.T., Udry, J.R. et al. (1998). "Monthly Measures of Salivary Testosterone Predict Sexual Activity in Adolescent Males", *Arch Sex Behaviour, 27(5)*: 445–465.

Harris, M. (2007). *Your Teenager. Thinking about Your Child During the Secondary School Years* (M.H. Williams, ed.) London: Karnac Books.

Heuves, W. (2010). *Pubertät, Entwicklung und Probleme, Hilfen für Erwachsene*. Frankfurt am Main: Brandes & Apsel Verlag GmbH.

Inhelder, B., and Piaget, J. (1974). *The Growth of Logical Thinking from Childhood to Adolescence*, New York: Basic Books.

Jaeger, H. (1885). *Frau Kristiania-Bohemen*. München: belleville (reprinted 2006).

Jahnn, H.H. (1974). "Selbstversuche", in *Werke und Tagebücher*. Hamburg: Hoffmann und Campe, pp. 5–17.

Joseph, B. (1975). "The Patient Who is Difficult to Reach", in Feldman, Michael and Spillius, Elizabeth Bott (eds.), *Psychic Equilibrium and Psychic Change*. London and New York: Routledge, 1993.

Joseph, B. (1986a). "Transference: The Total Situation", in Feldman, Michael and Spillius, Elizabeth Bott (eds.), *Psychic Equilibrium and Psychic Change*. London and New York: Routledge, 1993, pp. 153–167.

Joseph, B. (1986b). "Envy in Everyday Life", in Feldman, Michael and Spillius, Elizabeth Bott (eds.), *Psychic Equilibrium and Psychic Change*. London and New York: Routledge, 1993, pp. 181–191.

Kafka, F. (1915). *Die Verwandlung*. Köln: Anconda, 2005.

Kaplan, L.J. (1991). *Female Perversions*, excerpted in *International Journal of Child and Family Welfare*, 3: 273–287.

Kernberg, O. (1984). *Severe Personality Disorders: Psychotherapeutic Strategies*. New York: Yale University Press.

Klein, M. (1922). "Inhibitions and Difficulties at Puberty", in *The Freud-Klein Controversies 1941–45*. London: Routledge, 1999, pp. 54–58.

Klein, M. (1928). "Early Stages of the Oedipus Conflict", in *The Freud-Klein Controversies 1941–45*. London: Routledge, 1999, pp. 186–198.

Klein, M. (1934). "On Criminality", in *Love, Guilt and Reparation and Other Works, 1921–1945*. London: Vintage, 1998.

Klein, M. (1940). "Mourning and its Relation to Manic-Depressive States", in *The Freud-Klein Controversies 1941–45*. London: Routledge, 1999, pp. 344–369.

Klein, M. (1944). "The Emotional Life and Ego-development of the Infant with Special Reference to the Depressive Position", in *The Freud-Klein Controversies 1941–45*. London: Routledge, 1999, pp. 752–797.

Klein, M. (1945). "The Oedipus Complex in the Light of Early Anxieties", *International Journal of Psycho-Analysis*, 26: 11–33.

Klein, M. (1952). "The Origins of Transference", *International Journal of Psycho-Analysis*, 33: 433–438.

Kraemer, S. (1999). "Promoting Resilience: Changing Concepts of Parenting and Child Care", *International Journal of Child and Family Welfare*, 3: 273–287.

Kraus, K. (1926). *Presse*, June 4.

Kuhn, Thomas (1957). *The Copernican Revolution*. Cambridge: Harvard University Press.

Laing, Ronald D. (1964). *Sanity, Madness and the Family*. Abingdon (Oxfordshire): Routledge.

Laplanche, J., and Pontalis, J.B. (1988). *The Language of Psychoanalysis*. London: Karnac Books.

Larson, R., Csikszentmihalyi, M., and Graef, R. (1982). "Time Alone in Daily Experience: Loneliness or Renewal", in Peplau, L.A., and Perlman, D. (eds.), *Loneliness: A Sourcebook of Theory, Research, and Therapy*. New York: Wiley, pp. 40–53.

Larson, R., and Richards, M. (1994). *Divergent Realities. The Emotional Lives of Mothers, Fathers, and Adolescents*. New York: Basic Books. Quoted in Arnett, J., and Hughes, M. (2012). *Adolescence and Emerging Adulthood. A Cultural Approach*. London and New York: Pearson.

Laufer, M. (1995a). "Psychological Development in Adolescence: 'Danger Signs'", in Laufer, M. (ed.), *The Suicidal Adolescent*. London: Karnac Books, pp. 3–20.

Laufer, M. (ed.) (1995b). *The Suicidal Adolescent*. London: Karnac Books.

Laufer, M., and Laufer, E. (1997). *Adolescence and Developmental Breakdown. A Psychoanalytic View*. Adolescence and Developmental Breakdown. London: Karna Books.

Lebovici, S. (1983). *Le nourisse, la mere et le psychoanalyse*, Paris: Editoins du Centurion.

Lebovici, S. (2003). *Der Säugling, die Mutter und der Psychoanalytiker. Die frühen Formen der Kommunikation*. Stuttgart: Klett-Cotta.

270 Bibliography

Liu, R. (2006). "Vulnerability to Friends' Suicide Influence: The Moderating Effects of Gender and Adolescent Depression", *R.X. J Youth Adolescence*, *35*: 454.

London, Jack (1909). *Martin Eden*. New York: Macmillan.

Magagna, J. (ed.) (2012). *The Silent Child. Communication Without Words*. London: Karnac Books.

McDougall, J. (1991). *Theatres of the Body*. London: Free Associated Books.

Melzer, D. (1988). "The Aesthetic Conflict", in *The Apprehension of Beauty*. Strath Tay: Clunie Press.

Miles, B. (2005). *Hippies*. Collection Rolf Heyne, München.

Miller, B.C., Bayley, B.K., Christensen, M., Laevitt, S.C., and Coyl, D.D. (2003). "Adolescent Pregnancy and Childbearing", in Adams, R.G., and Berzonsky, D.M. (eds.), *Blackwell Handbook of Adolescence*. Malden, MA: Blackwell, pp. 415–449.

Miller, L., Rustin, M., Rustin, M., and Shutteleworth, J. (1989). *Closely Observed Infants*. London: Duckworth.

Moffit, T.E. (2003). "Life-course-persistent and Adolescence-limited Antisocial Behaviour", in Lahey, B-B., and Moffit, T.E. (eds.), *Causes of Conduct Disorder and Juvenile Delinquency*. New York: Guilford Press, pp. 49–75.

Moffitt, T.E. (2007). "A Review of Research on the Taxonomy of Life-course Persistent versus Adolescence-limited Antisocial Behaviour", in Flannery, D.J., Vazonyi, A.T., and Waldman, I.D. (eds.), *The Cambridge Handbook of Violent Behaviour and Aggression*. New York: Cambridge University Press.

Moore, M., Brook-Gunn, J. (2002). "Adolescent Parenthood", in Bonrstein, M.H. (ed.), *Handbook of Parenting. Vol. 3: Being and Becoming a Parent* (2nd ed.). Mahwah, NJ: Erlbaum, pp. 173–214.

Musil, Robert (1990). "Political Confessions of a Young Man: A Fragment", in Pike, Burton, and Luft, David S. (eds. and transl.), *Precision and Soul: Essays and Addresses*, Chicago and London: University of Chicago Press.

Niztschke, B. (1976). "Die Bedeutung der Sexualität im Werk Sigmund Freuds", in Ecke, D. (ed.), *Psychologie des 20. Jahrhunderts, Bd. I: Sigmund Freud – Leben und Werk*. Weinheim und Basel: Beltz.

Norman, J. (2004). "Der Psychoanalytiker und der Säugling. Eine neue Sicht der Arbeit mit Babys", *Analytische Kinder-und Jugendpsychotherapie, H. 122(35)*: 245–275.

Nunberg, H. (1932). *Allgemeine Neurosenlehre auf psychoanalytischer Grundlage*. Bern: Huber Verlag, 1959.

O'Shaughnessy, E. (1989). "The Invisible Oedipus Complex", in Britton, R., Feldman, M., and O'Shaughnessy, E. (eds.), *The Oedipus Complex Today, Clinical Implications*. London: Karnac Books, pp. 129–150.

Pankratz, E. (1997). "Teenagermütter. Entstehungsbedingungen ungeplanter Schwangerschaften im Jugendalter. Mißlungene Prävention/ Kontrazeption oder geheimer Kinderwunsch?" Diplomarbeit, University of Vienna.

Parker, B. (1975). *My Language is Me: Psychotherapy with a Disturbed Adolescent*. London: Random House.

Parker, B. (1987). *The Evolution of a Psychiatrist. Memoirs of a Woman Doctor*. New Haven: Yale University Press.

Pav, U. (2010). *"Ich selbst hätte ja überhaupt kein Problem . . ." VerHALTENsraster als Instrument im Umgang mit Verleugnung, Projektion and Spaltung. Strukturiertes Feedback im sozial-pädagogischen Alltag*. Saarbrücken: VDM.

Person, E.S. (1988). *Dreams of Love and Fateful Encounters. The Power of Romantic Passion*. New York: W.W. Norton.

Person, E.S. (1997). *On Freud's "A Child Is Being Beaten". Turning Points and Critical Issues.* London and New York: Int. Psychoanalytic Association.

Piaget, J. (1970). *Meine Theorie der geistigen Entwicklung* (R. Fatke, ed.). Weinheim und Basel: Beltz Verlag.

Piaget, J. (1972a). *Theorien und Methoden der modernen Erziehung.* Wien, München and Zürich: Molden Verlag.

Piaget, J. (1972b). "Intellectual Evolution from Adolescence to Adulthood", *Human Development* (Geneva 2008), *51*: 40–47, www.karger.com/hde

Plath, Sylvia (2013). *The Bell Jar.* London: Heinemann.

Quinodoz, J. (2008). *Listening to Hanna Segal. Her Contribution to Psychoanalysis* (D. Alcott, transl.). London: Routledge.

Radiguet, R. (1968). *The Devil in the Flesh* (A.M. Sheridan Smith, transl.). London: Calder and Boyars (first published in 1923).

Rousseau, J.J. (1953). *Confessions* (A. Scholar, transl.). Oxford: Oxford University Press (first published 1782).

Rustin, M., and Bradley, B. (2008). *Work Discussion. Learning from a Reflective Practice in Work with Children and Families.* London: Karnac Books.

Rutter, Michael (2013). "Annual Research Review: Resilience – Clinical Implications", *Journal of Child Psychology and Psychiatry, 54*: 4, 474–487.

Sacher-Masoch, L. (2000). *Venus in Furs.* London: Penguin Classics (first published in 1870).

Salzberger-Wittenberg, I. (2013). *Experiencing Endings and Beginnings.* London: Karnac Books.

Schmidinger, T. (2015). *Jihadismus. Ideologie, Präventio und Deradikalisierung.* Wien: Mandelbaum Verlag.

Segal, H. (1952). "A Psycho-analytic Approach to Aesthetics", reprinted in *The Work of Hanna Segal.* New York and London: Jason Aronson, pp. 185–206.

Segal, H. (1991). *Dream, Phantasy and Art.* New York: Routledge.

Segal, H. (1993). "On the Clinical Usefulness of the Concept of Death Instinct", *International Journal of Psycho-Analysis, 74*: 55–61.

Seiffge-Krenke, I. (1985). "Die Funktion des Tagebuchs bei der Bewältigung alterstypischer Probleme in der Adoleszenz", in Oerter, R. (ed.), *Lebensbewältigung in Jugendalter.* Weinheim: VCH-Verlagsgesellschaft, pp. 131–159.

Sherfey, M.J. (1966/1972). *Die Potenz der Frau. Wesen und Evolution der weiblichen Sexualität.* Köln: Kiepenheuer und Witsch.

Sonneck, G., Goll, H., Kapitany, Th., Stein, C., and Strunz, V. (2008). *Krisenintervention. Von den Anfängen der Suizidprävention bis zur Gegenwart.* Wien: Verlag Bibliothek der Provinz.

Stacey, M., Dearden, R., Pill, R., and Robinson, D. (1970). *Hospitals, Children and Their Families: The Report of a Pilot Study.* London: Routledge & Kegan Paul Ldt.

Staudner-Moser, A. (1997). "Sozialpädagogik im Jugendstrafvollzug. Das Wiener Modell des Anti-Aggressionstrainings", Diplomarbeit, University of Vienna.

Steiner, J. (1987). "The Interplay between Pathological Organizations and the Paranoid-schizoid and Depressive Positions", in Spillius, E.B. (ed.), *Melanie Klein Today.* London and New York, 1988, pp. 324–342.

Steiner, J. (2002). "The Dread of Exposure to Humiliation and Ridicule". Unpublished paper, Westlodge Conference, London, March.

Stern, D. (1985). *The Interpersonal World of the Infant. A View from Psychoanalysis and Developmental Psychology.* New York: Basic Books.

272 Bibliography

Stern, D. (2001). "Handeln und Erinnern in der Übertragungsliebe", in *Über Freud's "Bemerkungen über die Übertragungsliebe"*. Freud heute: Wendepunkte und Streitfragen Bd. 3, Stuttgart, pp. 213–230 xx eng

Streeck-Fischer, A. (2004). "Selbst-und fremddestruktives Verhalten in der Adoleszenz – Folgen von Traumatisierung in der Entwicklung", in Streeck-Fischer, A. (ed.), *Adoleszenz – Binding-Destruktivität*. Stuttgart: Klett-Cotta, 2004, pp. 9–43.

Sutterlüty, F. (2001). "Kreisläufe der Gewalt und der Mißachtung. Die familiären Wurzeln jugendlicher Gewaltkarrieren", in *Mitteilung des Instituts für Sozialforschung*. Frankfurt: H. 12, pp. 119–156.

Titze, M. (1995). *Die heilende Kraft des Lachens. Mit therapeutischen Humor frühere Beschämung heilen*. München: Kösel.

Turrini, P. (2005). *Im Namen der Liebe. Gedichte (In the Name of Love)*. Frankfurt: Suhrkamp.

Twain, M. (2015). *Quotes and Facts* (B. Kirov, ed.). New York: CreateSpace.

UNICEF (2015). "Preventing Suicide Report", https://www.who.int/mental_health/resources/preventingsuicide

Vogt, W. (2013). *Mein Arztroman. Ein Lebensbericht*. Wien: Edition Steinbauer.

Waddell, M. (1994). *Understand Your 12–14 Year Old*. London: Rosedale Press.

Waddell, M. (2002). *Inside Lives. Psychoanalysis and the Growth of the Personality*. London: Karnac Books (first published in 1998).

Waddell, M. (2005). " Erstgespräche mit Adoleszenten. Auf der Suche nach einem Raum zum Denken", in Rustin, M., and Quagliata, E. (eds.), *Der Anfang. Klinische Erstkontakte mit Kindern und Jugendlichen*. Tübingen: edition diskord, pp. 199–218.

Waddell, M. (2018). *On Adolescence*. London: Karnac Books.

Walser, M. (2015). "Die Verteidigung der Kindheit" (*The Defense of Childhood*), in Scharpe, M. (ed.), *Die lieben Eltern. Mütter und Väter in der Literatur*. Stuttgart: Radius Verlag, pp. 53–55.

Weiss, H. (2014). "Vertiefende Konzeptualisierungen des Unbewussten", in Luzinger-Bohleber, M., and Weiss, H. (eds.), *Psychoanalyse. Die Lehre vom Unbewussten. Geschichte, Klinik und Praxis*. Stuttgart: Kohlhammer Verlag, pp. 121–156.

Werner, W. (1972). *Vom Waisenhaus ins Zuchthaus. Mit einem Nachwort vom Martin Walser*. Frankfurt: Suhrkamp.

Winnicott, D.W. (1960). "Ego Distortion in Terms of True and False Self", in *The Maturation Processes and the Facilitating Environment*. London: International Psycho-Analytic Library.

Winnicott, D.W. (1963). *The Capacity to be Alone*. London: Hogarth Press and Institute of Psycho-Analysis.

Winnicott, D.W. (1967). "Die Spiegelfunktion von Mutter und Familie in der kindlichen Entwicklung", in Winnicott, D.W. (ed.), *Vom Spiel zur Kreativität*. Stuttgart: Klett-Cotta, 1971, pp. 128–136.

Winnicott, D.W. (1969). "Übergangsobjekte und Übergangsphänomene. Eine Studie über den ersten, nicht zum Selbst gehörenden Besitz", *Psyche, 23*.

Winnicott, D.W. (1984). *Aggression, Versagen der Umwelt und antisoziale Tendenzen*. Stuttgart: Klett-Cotta.

World Health Organization. (2014). *Preventing Suicide. A Global Imperative*. Geneva: WHO.

Yeats, W.B. (1989). "Sailing to Byzantium", in Finneran, R. (ed.), *The Poems of W.B. Years*. New York: Macmillan (first published in 1933).

Zimbardo, P., and Gerrig, R. (2004). *Psychologie*. München, Boston, and San Francisco: Pearson Studium, p. 16.

Index

Abdullah, case study 175–176
abstract thinking 118, 120, 123, 124–126
"accommodation" 121–122
adolescence: concept of 2–3; development of feeling 85–117; development of thinking 118–128; impact on parental psyche 111–117; psychic breakdown in 201–244
Adolescence – Connection – Destructivity (Streeck-Fischer) 177
adolescent B: background 152; case study 152–159; discussion 153–155; dynamics of inner world 155–159
Adolescent Diary and its Function in the Mastering of Typical Adolescent Problems, The (Erhard) 105
adolescent R: "anti-aggression training" 160–162, 165; background 159–161; "balloon trip" 168–169; case study 159–175; drawing 166–168; dynamics of inner world 162–163, 171–172; puzzle pieces 169; role-playing 163–166
adolescents: adolescent logic 126–128; concept of 2; psychic breakdown 201–244; relationship between parents and 92–111; suicide 244–258; teenage pregnancy 178–201; in therapy 53–84; violent 147–178
"Adolescent Suicide" (Hadaya) 246
aggression: in adolescent therapy 54, 68, 74–78, 82, 87, 149–150, 192, 208, 215, 223, 234, 236, 240; "anti-aggression training" 151–152, 155, 160–162, 165, 171–172; in baby experience 46, 52; baby experience 255; eye contact in 26; male body development and 14; masturbation fantasies 41; meanings of 150; Oedipal desires in 38–39, 259

"All You Need is Love" (The Beatles) 19
"alpha elements" 23
Alvarez, Al 244
"ambivalence of feelings" 20, 21–22, 51, 55, 117, 167, 172, 192, 204
Anderson, Robin 5, 34–35, 55, 87, 111, 246–247, 251, 253–254
androgen 21
. . . and when the thread breaks, I only want to strike again (Pav) 178
"anti-aggression training" 151–152, 155, 160–162, 165, 171–172
antisocial behavior 145–146, 148
Anzengruber, Ludwig 45
"Arrogance, On" (Bion) 28–29
artistic expression 77–78
Asperger symptoms 201
"assimilation" 121–122
autism 8, 26, 29, 264
autism spectrum disorder (ASD) 151

Babsi: attitude and relationship to the baby 191; case study 185–193; child fantasies 186–187; contraception 186–187; discovery of pregnancy 188–189; discussion 191–193; experience of pregnancy and birth 189–190; life situation before pregnancy 187–188; reactions from the environment 189; sexuality in family 186; teenage life and pregnancy 190–191
"baby talk" 27
Bad Taste (Jackson) 51–53, 174
"balloon trip" 168–169
beating fantasy 43
Beatles, The 19
Bell Jar, The (Plath) 244

274 Index

Bernstein, Leonard 144
"beta elements" 22–23
Bettelheim, Bruno 146
Betty, case study 91
Beyond the Pleasure Principle (Freud) 44, 252
Bick, Esther 70
Bieber, Justin 59
Bion, Wilfred R.: "On Arrogance" 28–29; "bizarre objects" 53; container-contained model 23, 46, 170; "Hallucination, On" (Bion) 213; identity 86; knowledge 118–119; meaning of aggression 150; projections 90–91, 178
birth 181–182
bisexuality 20, 21, 32, 138
"bizarre objects" 53, 76
Bloch, Ernst 129
body: contact 25–26; female body development 6–13; male body development 13–17; as medium of protest 17–19; as medium of provocation 17–19; as object of observation 6–17
body contact 26, 36, 74, 242
bonding 29
Brent Adolescent Center 29, 45
Britton, Ron 35
Brizendine, Louann 14
Busch, Wilhelm 147–148
Byng-Hall, John 263

case studies: Abdullah 175–176; adolescent B 152–159; adolescent R 159–175; Babsi 185–193; Betty 91; Chrisse 220–235; Christine 91–92; Claudia 193–200; Dorothy 87–88; Elfi 53, 56–70; Ian 112; James Frost 53, 70–84; Katharina 91; Lucy 99–104, 115; Mark 29; Petima 176–177; Rosalin 87–88; Sarah 180–185; Sebastian 93–98; Vinzenz 235–244
"castration anxiety" 31
Cavell, Stanley 114–115
character development 131–132
Chasseguet-Smirgel, Janine 98
child fantasies 181, 186–187, 194
"Childhood Recollection from *Dichtung und Wahrheit*, A" (Freud) 49
"Child is Being Beaten, A" (Freud) 43
Chrisse: case study 220–235; discussion 221, 222–224, 228–229, 231, 232–233,

234; end of therapy 233; final session 234–235; first session 220–221; further development of therapy 229–231; referral 220; regular psychotherapy 224–228; second preliminary session 221–222; session excerpt 232
Christine, case study 91–92
Claudia: case study 193–200; Mark 203–219; sexuality in family 193
Claudia, case study: child fantasies 194; contraception 194; discovery of pregnancy 195; experience of pregnancy and birth 197–198; first menstruation 193–194; interpretation 199–200; life situation before pregnancy 194–195; reactions from the environment 195–196; support and help 198–199
Cleese, John 109–111, 252, 255–256
"Clinical Usefulness of the Concept of Death Instinct, On the" (Segal) 252
Cocteau, Jean 51
cognitive development 34, 122–123
complex thinking 126–128
concrete operations 123
Confessions (Rousseau) 44
container-contained model 23, 46, 170
contraception 181, 186–187, 194
Coudenhove-Kalergi, Barbara 129–130
countertransference 55, 58, 59, 62, 64, 66, 70, 112, 205–206, 231
"Creative Writers and Day-Dreaming" (Freud) 45–46
criminal groups 143–144

dancing 74
daydreams 37–41, 43–44, 45, 120
deadlock in development 202
"dead mother" concept 7
death instinct 44, 150, 171, 252
"Dedication to My Wife, A" (Eliot) 126
defensive functioning in development 202
defensive operations 15, 29, 87, 98–99, 120, 154, 203
denial 19, 53, 68, 95, 178, 203, 219
Denzin, Norman K 171
depression 7, 27, 48, 69, 88, 110, 113, 132, 142, 159, 181, 201, 223, 244, 250–251, 263
"depressive position" 86
Deutsch, Helene 138
Devil in the Flesh, The (Radiguet) 46, 50–51

Index 275

diaries 105–109, 134–142
Die Verteidigung der Kindheit (*The Defense of Childhood*) (Walser) 42
divergent development 262–263
Dorothy, case study 87–88
drawing skills 127
Dunedin study 151
"Dynamics of Transference, The" (Freud) 21

ejaculation 14, 180
Elfi: adulation for pop stars 59–60, 117; analysis during adolescence 58–59; case study 53, 56–70, 117; discussion 60–70; family background 56–58; sexual fantasy 64; summer holidays 60
Eliot, T.S. 126
Eliot, Valerie 126
emotional development 7–9
"Ensemble, c'est tout" (Gavalda) 25
envy 112–113, 130
"Envy in Everyday Life" (Joseph) 112–113
Erhard, Janette 105
Erikson, Erik 28
erogenous zones 5–6, 23, 25
Eros (life instinct) 150
estrogen 7
exhibitionistic behavior 21
expulsion 86
eye contact 7–8, 26–27, 163

feeling: adolescent perspectives 92–111; development of 85–117; guilt feelings 31–32, 41–45, 88, 106, 108, 130–131, 134, 143, 154, 191, 197, 200, 203, 223, 245–246, 249, 261; impact on parental psyche 111–117; problems for parents 89–92
Feldman, Michael 34, 216
female body 6–13, 87
femininity 10, 14, 21, 32, 190
"femininity phase" 32
Fethi, Benslama 172
Fifty Shades of Grey (James) 43
first dance 103–104
Flasar, Milena Michiko 130
Fliess, Wilhelm 21
foreclosure in development, 202
formal operations 123–124, 128
"Formulations Regarding the Two Principles in Mental Functioning" (Freud) 8–9

Fraiberg, Selma 216, 263
Fra Kristiania-Bohemen (Jaeger) 105
Fra-Kristiania-Bohemian Society 105
Freud, Anna 2, 99, 120
Freud, Sigmund: on artistic expression 77; *Beyond the Pleasure Principle* 44, 252; body ego 4, 19; "Childhood Recollection from *Dichtung und Wahrheit*, A" 49; "A Child is Being Beaten", Freud (1919) 43; concept of sexuality 20–21, 56; "Creative Writers and Day-Dreaming" 45–46; "Dynamics of Transference, The" 21; on eye contact 26; "Formulations Regarding the Two Principles in Mental Functioning" 8–9; *Interpretation of Dreams* 39; "Introductory Lectures on Psycho-Analysis" 20; on love 36–37; meaning of aggression 150; "Moses and Monotheism" 31; "Mourning and Melancholia" 250; on puberty 5–6; *Three Essays on the Theory of Sexuality* 5, 132; *Totem and Taboo* 53; unconscious mechanism of repetitive compulsion 171
Frost, James: as adolescent 73–74; case study 53, 70–84; discussion 71–72, 74–84; family and school background 71; psychoanalytic- pedagogical aid for 72–73
Furstenberg, Frank F., Jr. 200

games: childhood 38, 40, 45, 58, 124, 248; computer 145, 190, 197, 230; love relationship 32; power 206, 219; Remscheider group of 168; sports 15, 76, 225; suicidal behavior 250
gang groups 98, 143–144
Gavalda, Anna 25
Goethe, Johann Wolfgang von: letter to Eckermann 125; *my Life, From* 49; *Sorrows of Young Werther, The* 46, 47–50
Golding, William 261–262
Gone With the Wind (movie) 37
"good enough mother" 8, 104
grandparents 72, 77, 98, 178–179, 184, 199, 201, 263
Green, André 7
guilt feelings 31–32, 41–45, 88, 98, 106, 108, 130–131, 134, 143, 154, 191, 197, 200, 203, 223, 245–246, 249, 261

276 Index

Hadaya, Samira 246
Hall, G. Stanley 2
hallucination 212–214, 262
"Hallucination, On" (Bion) 213
Halpern, Carolyn T 14
H (Hate) 150
"hikikomori" 39
hippie movement 19
homosexuality 21, 138–140, 175, 261

Ian, case study 112
identity: body ego and 4; character
    development 131–132; "collection
    of identities" 86; crisis 34–35, 87,
    130, 203; diffusion 202; gang groups
    143–144; Muslim 175; peer groups 98,
    101, 140–142; search for 51, 129–133,
    172–175; sexual identity 20–21, 33,
    139, 261–262; superego 134–138
inferiority 134
Inhelder, Bärbel E. 123
initiation rites 17, 26
"intellectualization in puberty" 120
Interpretation of Dreams (Freud) 39
"Introductory Lectures on Psycho-
    Analysis" (Freud) 20
"Invisible Oedipus Conflict, The"
    (O'Shaughnessy) 214
Islamic State (IS) 173–174

Jackson, Peter 51–53
Jaeger, Hans 105
Jahnn, Han Henny 44–45
Jan (diary entries) 105–109
jihad: Abdullah case study 175–176;
    fascination of jihad 172–175; Petima,
    case study 176–177
Joseph, Betty 112–113, 206, 212

K- 118
Kafka, Franz 35
Katharina, case study 91
Kemble, Fanny 264
King, Stephen 219
kissing 23–24, 38, 50–51, 93–94, 99,
    106–109
K (Knowledge) 118–119, 150
Klein, Melanie 20, 31, 32, 33, 46, 54, 77,
    85–86, 94, 148, 150, 174
knowledge 118, 150
Kplus 118
Kraemer, Sebastian 263
Krafft-Ebing, Richard von 44

language 27–30
Lari (diary entries) 105–109, 135–142
Larson, Reed 101
latency phase 34–35, 120
Laufer, Eglé 45
Laufer, Moses 29, 45, 139
laughter 78
life and death wish 249, 252–254
L (Love) 150
London, Jack 252
loneliness 51, 57–59, 66, 83, 89, 103, 132,
    137, 146, 155, 158, 169–170, 219, 221
love-hate relationships 105
love object 7–8, 11, 20, 22, 31–33,
    35–37, 42, 98, 109, 115, 133, 250
Lucy, case study 99–104, 115

MAD (magazine) 126
Madonna 59, 117
Magagna, Jeanne 219–220
male body 13–17, 86–87
Mark: background 203–205; case study
    29, 203–219; end of analysis 216–219;
    first session 204–206; first year in
    analysis 208–211; following two years
    in analysis 211–212; hallucination 212;
    hypotheses regarding communication
    through movement 206–208; Oedipal
    conflict 214–216
Martin Eden (London) 252
masculinity 21, 33, 146, 173, 185
masochism 37, 41, 43–44, 252
masturbation 37, 41–46, 52–53
maturation 121–122
Max and Maurice (Busch) 147–148
Mead, Margaret 2
menstruation: first 1, 4, 10–11, 14,
    16–17, 32, 58, 64, 180–181, 186,
    192, 193–194; masculine rituals lies
    imitating 146
Metamorphoses (Kafka) 35
mirror-gazing 6, 7–9, 101
"mood management" 101
"Moses and Monotheism" (Freud) 31
mother-baby couple: baby experience
    7–8, 46, 170; body contact 25–26;
    eye contact 7–8, 26–27, 163; infant
    emotional development 7–9; as model
    for romantic love 22–30
"Mourning and Melancholia" (Freud) 250
Munch, Edvard 105
music 36–37, 101
Musil, Robert 119, 129

mutism 201, 205, 210, 219
My Language is Me (Parker) 263
my Life, From (Goethe) 46

narcissistic personalities 28–29
Nazi Hitler Youth 18
"negative Oedipus" 32
Netzwerke Sozialer Zusammenhalt (NSZ; Networks of Social Solidarity) 173
Nine Bohemian Commandments 105
Nirvana principle 252

Oedipal desires: aggression in 259; daydreams with 37–41; development of Oedipal fantasy 31–32; flaming up of 30–37; longing for union with love object 7–8, 11, 20, 22, 31–33, 35, 36–37, 42, 98, 109, 115, 133, 250; Mark case study 214–216; psychotic illness and 29–30; resolution of Oedipus conflict 33–34
omnipotence fantasies 22, 30–31, 34, 87, 148, 180, 211, 228, 262
opprobrium 19
oral gratification 5–6, 23–24
orgasm 39, 43
O'Shaughnessy, Edna 214

"paranoid- schizoid position" 86, 94
parents: adolescent perspectives 92–111; comparison of adolescence with children 92, 112–113; divergent development of children 262–263; impact of adolescence on parental psyche 111–117; as love object 7–8, 22, 31–33, 35–36, 42, 98, 115; mother-baby couple 7–9, 25–27, 46; Oedipal desires 30–41; problems for 85–92; relationship between children and 92–111; sexuality 42, 90, 111, 180, 260; values 34–35
Pav, Ursula 178
peer groups 98, 101, 140–142
"pendulum problem" 123
personality: affects of psychosexual reformation on 20, 28, 30, 34–35, 44, 98–99, 179; depressive 57; development 29–30, 136, 259–261, 263; development of character 131–132; development of thinking and 118, 120; formation of 3, 7–8, 70, 85–89; gang/criminal group influence 143–144; impact of physical changes

on 4–5; narcissistic 203; peer group influence 140–142; psychotic 53, 202, 213, 218; restructuring of 129; suicidal factors and 251; violence and 149
Petima, case study 176–177
Pfadfinder youth movement 18
physical appearance 4–5
Piaget, Jean: capacity for abstract thinking according to 121–128; "pendulum problem" 123; stages of cognitive development 122–123
Plath, Sylvia 244–245
"Political Confessions of a Young Man" (Musil) 129
pop stars 59–60, 117
pregnancy 178–201
Presley, Elvis 19
"Preventing Suicide" (WHO study) 248
"Prevention of Violence" project 178
primal trust/mistrust phase 28
projective identification 52, 87, 90–91, 178, 203, 217
provocative behaviors 13, 17–19, 21, 80–82, 92, 180, 187, 217
"pseudo-adulthood" defense 99
psyche 30, 44, 46, 53, 77, 86, 111–117, 119, 131, 170, 185, 249, 261
psychic breakdown: in adolescence 201–244; background 201–203; Chrisse case study 220–235; evaluating an adolescent undergoing 202; levels for distinguishing symptoms as pathological/normal 203; Mark case study 203–220; Oedipal desires and 35; search for identity and 130; sexual fear and 111; Vinzenz case study 235–244
psychosexual development: adolescents in therapy 53–84; masturbation fantasies 41–45; mother-baby couple 22–30, 46; Oedipal desires 30–41; significance of 20–22; themes in art 45–53
psychotic episodes 201, 220–235
psychotic illness 29–30
"psychotic self" 28
puberty: changes in female body 6–13; changes in male body 13–17; concept of 1–2; physical changes 4–17
pubic hair 14

Radiguet, Raymond 50–51
rape 38–39
repetitive compulsion 171
resilience 263–264

278 Index

Richards, Maryse, H. 101
Rites of Passage (Golding) 261–262
role-playing 163–165
romantic love: jihad and 174; language of
27–30; mother-baby couple 22–30
Romeo and Juliet (Shakespeare) 39
Rosalin, case study 88–89
Rousseau, Jean-Jacques 44

Sacher-Masoch, Leopold 44
sadism 37, 42–44, 53, 120, 147, 171, 249,
254
sadomasochism 43–44, 171
"Sailing to Byzantium" (Yeats) 113–114
Salzberger-Wittenberg, Isca 259–260
Sarah: case study 180–185; child fantasies
181; contraception 181; discovery
of pregnancy 182–183; discussion
184–185; knowledge of pregnancy and
birth 181–182; life situation before
pregnancy 182; sexuality in family 181;
teenage life and pregnancy 183–184
Savage God, The (Alvarez) 244
Sebastian, case study 93–98
Segal, Hanna 33, 46, 77, 252
self-aggression 45
self-destructive behavior 35, 54, 88, 130,
145, 155, 158, 191, 219, 254
"Self-Experiments" (Jahnn) 44–45
"self-explanation" 134
self-image 7, 32, 42, 54, 69, 85–86, 114,
118, 119, 133, 162, 165, 169, 255
self-injury 17, 171
self-reflection 33, 55, 101, 109, 121, 135,
170, 172
sexual fantasy 64
sexual fear 29, 39, 57, 109–110, 214
sexual identity 20–21, 33, 139, 261–262
sexuality: in Babsi's family 186;
bisexuality 20, 21, 32, 138; in Claudia's
family 193; concept of 20–21, 56;
as dangerous 39–40; depiction of
adolescent sexuality in art 47–53;
development of adolescent 5; double-
sided nature of 132; healthy 59–60,
64, 66, 114, 261; homosexuality 21,
138–140, 175, 261; initiation rites
17; jihad and 173–174; masturbation
fantasies 44; menstruation 17; of parents
42, 90, 111, 180, 260; pregnancy and
179–180; psychic breakdown and
201–244; in Sarah's family 181, 184

sexual union 12, 24, 31, 38–39, 109, 150
Shakespeare, William 39, 85
Silent Child, The (Magagna) 219–220
Simpsons, The (TV show) 126
Social Pedagogy in Prison (Staudner-
Most) 151
solitude 93, 101
Sonia Shankman Orthogenetic School 17
Sorrows of Young Werther, The (Goethe)
47–50
splitting 51, 86, 87, 94, 99, 108, 154, 174,
203, 233
Staudner-Most, Andrea 151
"storm and stress" (the German *Sturm und
Drang*) period 2–3
Streeck-Fischer, Annette 177
suicide: attacks 174; attempts 55,
244–248; committing 28, 222, 224;
life and death wish 252–254; loss
of hope and 28; measures that help
to reduce 256–258; as medium of
communication 172; Oedipal desires
and 35; psychoanalytical understanding
of psychic motives for 248–251;
secretly planning 229; as social problem
245–248; *Sorrows of Young Werther,
The* (Goethe) 47, 49; thoughts of 80,
105, 159, 220, 231, 239; threatened 71,
72, 236
superego 134–138
"swinging 50s" 18–19
Symbolic Wounds (Bettelheim) 146

Tavistock Clinic 252–253
teenage pregnancy: Babsi case study
185–193; Claudia case study 193–200;
problems of 178–201; Sarah case study
180–185
testicles 1, 14
testosterone 13–14
Thanatos (death instinct) 150
thinking: abstract thinking 118, 120, 123,
124–126; capacity for abstract thinking
according to Piaget 121–128; complex
thinking 126–128; development of
118–121; formal operations 123–124,
128
Three Essays on the Theory of Sexuality
(Freud) 5, 132
Totem and Taboo (Freud) 53
transference 59, 64, 68, 70, 112, 178, 185,
206, 215, 228, 241

triadic relationships 33–36
"turning point experience" 171
Twain, Mark 104

Urphantasie (primal fantasy) 31

Valentin, Karl 89
Venus in Furs (Sacher-Masoch) 44
Vinzenz: case study 235–244; discussion
    236–237, 239–240, 243–244;
    escalation 236; family background
    235–336; initial interviews 236;
    Thursday session 240–242; Wednesday
    session 237–239
violence: Abdullah case study 175–176;
    adolescent B case study 152–159;
    adolescent R case study 159–172; as
    fascination and denial 147–178; jihad
    172–177; laughter and 78; meaning

of aggression 150; Petima, case study
    176–177; psychic dynamic behind
    177–178; sociological data 150–152

Waddell, Margot 2, 54–55
Walser, Martin 42
Wandervogel youth movement 18
Weininger, Oskar 21
West Side Story (musical) 144
"wet dream" 17
Winnicott, Donald W. 8, 25, 101, 104,
    163, 170
withdrawal 172
"womb and vagina envy" 32
Woodstock Festival 19
World Health Organisation (WHO) 2,
    248, 256

Yeats, William Butler 113–114